PRAISE FOR

the conquest of cool

"An invaluable argument for anyone who has ever scoffed at hand-me-down counterculture from the '60s. . . . A spirited and exhaustive analysis of the era's advertising. . . . *Conquest* not only puts a cork in graying ex-hippies who like to recall their VW-bus trips as transgressive, but further serves to inoculate audiences to the hip capitalism that's everywhere—including these pages—today."
—**Brad Wieners,** *Wired Magazine*

"Seeking the origins of the countercultural critique, Frank finds them not on the campus or in the commune but in the business management books and ad agency creative departments of the 1950s. . . . Indeed, by Frank's own account, the book's title is a bit of a misnomer. Business didn't conquer the counterculture. It invented it."
—**Debra Goldman,** *Los Angeles Times Book Review*

"Tom Frank is perhaps the most unfashionable man ever to appear in *Details*. He's not only old-fashioned, he's anti-fashion, with a place in his heart for that ultimate social faux pas, leftist politics."
—**Roger Trilling,** *Details*

"Frank is a leading Gen-X cynic. His favorite target: how corporate America forces conformity on the masses."
—**Newsweek, "100 Americans for the Next Century"**

"[Thomas Frank is] perhaps the most provocative young cultural critic of the moment. . . . After reading Frank, in fact, you'll have a hard time using words like 'revolution' or 'rebel' ever again, at least without quotation marks."
—**Gerald Marzorati,** *New York Times Book Review*

"Frank makes an ironclad case not only that the advertising industry cunningly turned the countercultural rhetoric of revolution into a rallying cry to buy more stuff, but that the process itself actually predated any actual counterculture to exploit."
—Geoff Pevere, *Toronto Globe and Mail*

"This is a powerful and important argument. Unlike many practitioners of cultural studies, whose celebrations of consumer sovereignty merely mimic advertising mythology, Frank acknowledges the centrality of corporate strategies in shaping our dominant values. . . . *The Conquest of Cool* helps us understand why, throughout the last third of the twentieth century, Americans have increasingly confused gentility with conformity, irony with protest, and an extended middle finger with a populist manifesto. Frank deftly shows the myriad ways that advertising has redefined radicalism by conflating it with in-your-face consumerism. . . . His voice is an exciting addition to the soporific public discourse of the late twentieth century."
—T. J. Jackson Lears, *In These Times*

"In accessible, muscular prose, Frank traces agencies' revolt against inflated '50s jargon and creation of aggressively hip spots that simultaneously mocked consumer culture's empty promises and sold consumption-as-rebellion. . . . This book is frequently brilliant, an indispensable survival guide for any modern consumer."
—*Publishers Weekly*, starred review

"A wide-ranging, and often hilarious, overview of ads that attempted to adopt the language, pose or style of the youth and counterculture movements."
—Michiko Kakutani, *International Herald Tribune*

"A lucid history of how long-haired, bell-bottomed admen replaced rule-laden repetition and simple selling propositions with clever, unpredictable approaches."
—Abe Peck, *Chicago Tribune*

"Frank argues persuasively that the 'counterculture' has been co-opted by business forces, who use putatively countercultural ideas and images to sell their products and accelerate consumption."
—Scott Stossel, *Boston Phoenix Literary Supplement*

"Frank's study of 1960s advertising is first-rate."
—Philip Gold, *Washington Times*

"The marriage of counterculture and capitalism is hardly a new subject, but Frank does provide a refreshingly unsentimental look at it. . . . *The Conquest of Cool* is blessedly free of academic throat-clearing and professional jargon. There isn't a dull page in the book."
—Alexander Star, *Slate*

"An indispensable book that is so retro it's the closest thing our culture has seen lately to hip. . . . With *The Conquest of Cool*, Frank—brilliant, excoriating and wickedly funny—assumes the mantle of the preeminent cultural critic of his generation. Not bad, considering he's only . . . what? Thirty-something."
—Tom Grimes, *Houston Chronicle Books*

"A refreshingly spirited book. . . . After reading *The Conquest of Cool*, it's hard not to conclude that the folks who brought you Mr. Clean and the Marlboro Man helped bring the Cultural Revolution too."
—Brain Murray, *Weekly Standard*

"Brilliant, polemically charged. . . . By eschewing the bogus populism of business elites to focus on their moral and symbolic power, Frank makes an important contribution to the cultural history of the 1960s. He also provides a needed (if not altogether original) corrective to 'cultural studies' mavens who see 'subversion' in every market-researched *épater* of the *bourgeoisie*."
—Eugene McCarraher, *Commonweal*

"An important, highly readable and provocative examination of 1960s advertising trends, that reveals more about how mass marketing shaped North American society than any other book in recent memory."
—Ron Foley MacDonald, *Daily News*

"Thomas Frank argues convincingly in *The Conquest of Cool*, the advertising community was a willing, even eager co-conspirator in the eruption of hip consumerism. . . . The bohemian cultural style started as the native language of the alienated and became the dominant force in mass society. This book explains how that happened, and why."
—Stuart Levitan, *ISTHMUS*

"Chicago's favorite wonky killjoy is Tom Frank, the curmudgeonly editor of *The Baffler*. He's great in his self-appointed role as cultural iconoclast."
—*Chicago Magazine*, "Best Chicago"

"Thomas Frank's *The Conquest of Cool* is a forceful and convincing demonstration of the cunning of commercialism. Advertisers knew what was hip before hippie entrepreneurs, and this story, told here with verve and lucidity, is well worth the attention of all serious readers."
—Todd Gitlin, author of *The Twilight of Common Dreams*

"Thomas Frank has written a history of advertising in the last half of the twentieth century so accurate and insightful that it can even illuminate events for the people who participated in them. *The Conquest of Cool* is the remarkable debut of a cultural critic whose work can look forward to reading for many years to come."
—Earl Shorris, author of *A Nation of Salesmen*

the conquest of cool

the conquest

the university of chicago press

thomas frank

of cool

BUSINESS CULTURE,

COUNTERCULTURE,

AND THE RISE OF

HIP CONSUMERISM

chicago and london

The University of Chicago Press, Chicago 60637
The University of Chicago Press, Ltd., London
© 1997 by The University of Chicago
All rights reserved. Published 1997
Paperback edition 1998
Printed in the United States of America

06 05 04 03 02 01 00 99 98   2 3 4 5

ISBN 0-226-25991-9 (cloth)
ISBN 0-226-26012-7 (paperback)

Library of Congress Cataloging-in-Publication Data

Frank, Thomas C.
    The Conquest of cool: business culture, counterculture, and the
rise of hip consumerism / Thomas Frank.
        p.   cm.
    Includes bibliographical references and index.
    ISBN 0-226-25991-9 (alk. paper)
    1. Marketing—United States—History—20th century.
    2. Advertising—United States—History—20th century.
    3. Advertising and youth—United States—History—20th century.
    4. Nineteen sixties.   5. Consumer behavior—United States—
History—20th century.   6. United States—Social
conditions—1960–1980.   7. United States—Social conditions—1980–   .
    I. Title.
    HF5415.1.F72   1997
    381.3'0973'0904—dc21   97-17556
                                                                              CIP

This book is printed on acid-free paper.

For Wendy

This is an old story in art, of course,
genius vs. the organization. But the [car]
customizers don't think of corporate
bureaucracy quite the way your
conventional artist does, whether he be
William Gropper or Larry Rivers, namely,
as a lot of small-minded Babbitts, venal
enemies of culture, etc. They just think
of the big companies as part of the vast
mass of adult *America, sclerotic from*
years of just being too old, whose rules and
ideas weigh down upon Youth like a vast,
bloated sac.

— TOM WOLFE, "THE KANDY-KOLORED
    TANGERINE-FLAKE STREAMLINE BABY,"
    1963

We're young too.
And we're on your side.
We know it's a tough race.
And we want you to win.

— ADVERTISEMENT FOR LOVE
    COSMETICS, WELLS, RICH, GREENE
    AGENCY, 1969

contents

Acknowledgments   ix

one   A Cultural Perpetual Motion
Machine: Management Theory and
Consumer Revolution in the 1960s   1

two   Buttoned Down: High Modernism
on Madison Avenue   34

three   Advertising as Cultural Criticism: Bill
Bernbach versus the Mass Society   52

four   Three Rebels: Advertising Narratives of
the Sixties   74

five   "How Do We Break These
Conformists of Their Conformity?":
Creativity Conquers All   88

six   Think Young: Youth Culture
and Creativity   104

seven   The Varieties of Hip: Advertisements of
            the 1960s   132

eight   Carnival and Cola: Hip versus Square
            in the Cola Wars   168

nine   Fashion and Flexibility   184

ten   Hip and Obsolescence   206

eleven   Hip as Official Capitalist Style   224

            Appendix   237

            Notes   245

            Index   273

            Photos following page 86

acknowledgments

Even though I am too young to remember much about the 1960s, in writing this book I found it impossible to escape the feeling that I was writing about my temporal homeland. By this I mean more than that Led Zeppelin and the Rolling Stones remained almost hegemonic radio fixtures in my hometown well into the 1980s. For me and, I assume, for others my age, the sixties are the beginning of the present, the birthplace of the styles and tastes and values that define our world. Music, movies, ads, clothes, and writing from before that era sometimes seem to us like artifacts an incomprehensibly naive age.

This feeling was driven home for me by the astonishing changes that went on in American culture while I was writing *The Conquest of Cool*. When I started on this project back in 1990, the enthusiasm of corporations for youth culture in the sixties seemed like a curious and slightly obscure topic. But as I worked, the subject became less and less distant. Beginning in 1991–92 (when *Nevermind* ascended the *Billboard* charts and Tom Peters's *Liberation Management* appeared), American popular culture and corporate culture veered off together on a spree of radical-sounding bluster that mirrored events of the 1960s so closely as to make them seem almost unremarkable in retrospect. Caught up in what appeared to be an unprecedented prosperity driven by the "revolutionary" forces of globalization and cyber-culture, the nation again became obsessed with (of all things) youth culture and the march of generations. It was as though we were following the cultural stage directions of a script written thirty years before. People in advertising began referring to and even swiping from the great ads of the creative revolution. In business literature, dreams of chaos and ceaseless undulation routed the 1980s dreams of order and "excellence." "Theory Y" made a triumphant comeback, decked out in any number of new vocabularies of transgression derived from sources like Zen and the historical left. Even the publications devoted to the menswear industry showed signs of a renaissance: after embracing the commodification of deviance with such enthusiasm as to put readers clearly in mind of the trajectory of GQ in the late 1960s, *Details* magazine won the plaudits of media observers and saw its editor promoted in 1994 to head Condé Nast.

While my subject is arguably one of considerable current interest, my approach will seem antiquated to many. *The Conquest of Cool* is a study of cultural production rather than reception, of power rather than resistance; it does not address the subject of consumer evasiveness except as it is discussed by advertising executives and menswear manufacturers; it has little to say about the effectiveness of particular modes of popular resistance to mass culture, how this or that symbol was negotiated, detourned, or subverted. While cultural reception is a fascinating subject, I hope the reader will forgive me for leaving it to others. Not only has it been overdone, but our concentration on it, it seems to me, has led us to overlook and even minimize the equally-fascinating doings of the creators of mass culture, a group as playful and even as subversive in their own way as the heroic consumers who are the focus of so much of cultural studies today.

Strangely enough, the works of these lively capitalists were nearly as difficult to track down and quantify as the subjective impressions of TV viewers must be. Television advertising in particular proved difficult to research, since old commercials are only cataloged, indexed, and made available at a very limited number of institutions, and the few archives of broadcast advertising that do exist are, for the most part, made up of the exceptionally successful commercials which sponsors and agencies want the public to see. To gather a sampling of more representative commercials is a formidable task, and one in which I was not entirely successful. Fortunately, the Center for Advertising History at the National Museum of American History in Washington, DC, has made a monumental effort in this regard, compiling reel upon reel of commercials for Pepsi, Alka Seltzer, Marlboro, and Federal Express, and conducting lengthy taped interviews with just about everyone ever associated with the production of these companies' advertising. I am also grateful to the Museum of Broadcasting in New York and the Museum of Broadcast Communications in Chicago for allowing me to clock so many hours on their premises staring at reels of television commercials from the fifties and sixties.

More valuable still were the recollections and comments of a number of people with firsthand knowledge of the industries in question. For their time and assistance, I wish to thank Jerry Fishman, John Furr, George Lois, Quinn Meyer, and Charlie Moss. A number of advertising agencies, including DDB-Needham, Young & Rubicam, J. Walter Thompson—Chicago, and Wells, Rich, Greene/BDDP (to whom I am particularly indebted), kindly permitted me to rummage through their files of clippings and to screen old commercials.

A handful of libraries have amassed impressive advertising collections. The J. Walter Thompson archives at the William R. Perkins library of Duke University are remarkably thorough, and the Fairfax Cone papers at the Regenstein Library of the University of Chicago were also useful. Of course, no study of this kind can be completed without several weeks in the New York Public Library, and to their unbelievably dedicated staff as well as that of the Miller Nichols Library at the University of Missouri—Kansas City I wish to express my appreciation. I must also acknowledge the crucial assistance of Bridget Cain and Nathan Frank in the early stages of my research on the menswear industry.

In the sixties, television was only beginning to surpass magazines as the advertising showplace of note, and to get a feel for the consumer dreams of the decade, there was no substitute for simply slogging through old mass-circulation publications like *Life* and *Ladies' Home Journal* issue by issue. For help in that project and in transforming what I found there into the "Hip/Square" study that makes up this book's appendix, I am immensely obliged to my wife Wendy Edelberg.

The Conquest of Cool is substantially derived from a dissertation I wrote at the University of Chicago in 1994, and I wish to thank Leora Auslander, Michael Geyer, and especially Neil Harris for their patience with the strange enthusiasms of my graduate-student days and their assistance in transforming what was a slow and plodding idea into one with zip and impact. Doug Mitchell, my editor at the University of Chicago Press, has provided the encouragement and direction without which this project would never have been completed. Readers of my criticism of contemporary culture in the *Baffler*, the *Chicago Reader*, the *Nation*, and *In These Times* will be familiar with many of the ideas I apply here to the culture of the 1950s and 1960s. The many opportunities I have had to discuss these themes publicly have only strengthened and sharpened

acknowledgments

them, so I must thank my colleagues at the *Baffler*, Steve Duncombe, Greg Lane, Dave Mulcahey, Matt Weiland, Keith White, and Tom Vanderbilt, whose criticism and suggestions shaped everything in these pages. For myself I claim any and all errors of fact, theory, or interpretation that lurk herein.

chapter one

A CULTURAL

PERPETUAL MOTION

MACHINE:

MANAGEMENT THEORY

AND CONSUMER

REVOLUTION IN THE

1960s

Why do this kind of advertising if not to incite people to riot?

— NIKE COPYWRITER, 1996

of commerce and counterculture

For as long as America is torn by culture wars, the 1960s will remain the historical terrain of conflict. Although popular memories of that era are increasingly vague and generalized—the stuff of classic rock radio and commemorative television replayings of the 1968 Chicago riot footage—we understand "the sixties" almost instinctively as the decade of the big change, the birthplace of our own culture, the homeland of hip, an era of which the tastes and discoveries and passions, however obscure their origins, have somehow determined the world in which we are condemned to live.

For many, the world with which "the sixties" left us is a distinctly unhappy one. While acknowledging the successes of the civil rights and antiwar movements, scholarly accounts of the decade, bearing titles like *Coming Apart* (1971) and *The Unraveling of America* (1984), generally depict the sixties as a ten-year fall from grace, the loss of a golden age of consensus, the end of an edenic epoch of shared values and safe centrism. This vision of social decline, though, is positively rosy compared with the fire-breathing historical accusations of more recent years. For Allan Bloom, recounting with still-raw bitterness in his best-selling *The Closing of the American Mind* the student uprising and the faculty capitulation at Cornell in 1969, the misdeeds of the campus New Left were an intellectual catastrophe comparable only with the experiences of German professors under the Nazis. "So far as universities are concerned," he writes in his chapter entitled, "The Sixties," "I know of nothing positive coming from that period; it was an unmitigated disaster for them." Lines like "Whether it be Nuremberg or Woodstock, the principle is the same," and Bloom's characterization of Cornell's then-president as "of the moral stamp of those who were angry with Poland for resisting Hitler because this precipitated the war," constituted for several years the high watermark of anti-sixties bluster.[1] But later texts topped even this.

By 1996 it had become fashionable to extend sixties' guilt from mere academic developments to portentous-sounding things like the demise of "civility" and, taking off from there, for virtually everything that could be said to be wrong about America generally. For Robert Bork, "the sixties" accomplished nothing less than sending America *Slouching Towards Gomorrah*: thanks to the decade's "revolutionary nihilism" and the craven "Establishment's surrender," cultural radicals "and their ideology are all around us now" (a fantasy of defeat which, although Bork doesn't seem to realize it, rephrases Jerry Rubin's 1971 fantasy of revolution, *We Are Everywhere*).[2] Political figures on the right, waxing triumphal in the aftermath of the 1994 elections, also identify "the sixties," a term which they use interchangeably with "the counterculture," as the source of every imaginable species of the social blight from which they have undertaken to rescue the nation. Republican speechwriter Peggy Noonan puts the fall from grace directly, exhorting readers of a recent volume of conservative writing to "remember your boomer childhood in the towns and suburbs" when "you were safe" and "the cities were better," back before "society strained and cracked," in the storms of sixties selfishness.[3] Former history professor Newt Gingrich is the most assiduous and prominent antagonist of "the sixties," imagining it as a time of "countercultural McGoverniks," whom he holds responsible not only for the demise of traditional values and the various deeds of the New Left, but (illogically and anachronistically) for the hated policies of the Great Society as well. Journalist Fred Barnes outlines a "theory of American history" related to him by Gingrich

in which the 1960s represent a crucial break, "a discontinuity." From 1607 down till 1965, "there is a core pattern to American history. Here's how we did it until the Great Society messed everything up: don't work, don't eat; your salvation is spiritual; the government by definition can't save you; governments are into maintenance and all good reforms are into transformation." Then, "from 1965 to 1994, we did strange and weird things as a country. Now we're done with that and we have to recover. The counterculture is a momentary aberration in American history that will be looked back upon as a quaint period of Bohemianism brought to the national elite."[4]

The conservatives' version of "the sixties" is not without interest, particularly when it is an account of a given person's revulsion from the culture of an era. Their usefulness as history, however, is undermined by their insistence on understanding "the sixties" as a causal force in and of itself and their curious blurring of the lines between various historical actors: counterculture equals Great Society equals New Left equals "the sixties generation," all of them driven by some mysterious impulse to tear down Western Civilization. Bork is particularly given to such slipshod historiography, imagining at one point that the sixties won't even stay put in the 1960s. "It was a malignant decade," he writes, "that, after a fifteen-year remission, returned in the 1980s to metastasize more devastatingly throughout our culture than it had in the Sixties, not with tumult but quietly, in the moral and political assumptions of those who now control and guide our major cultural institutions."[5] The closest Bork, Bloom, Gingrich, and their colleagues will come to explanations is to revive one of several creaking devices: the sixties as a moral drama of millennialist utopians attempting to work their starry-eyed will in the real world, the sixties as a time of excessive affluence, the sixties as a time of imbalance in the eternal war between the generations, or the sixties as the fault of Dr. Spock, who persuaded American parents in the lost fifties to pamper their children excessively.

Despite its shortcomings, the conservatives' vision of sixties-as-catastrophe has achieved a certain popular success. Both Bloom's and Bork's books were best-sellers. And a mere mention of hippies or "the sixties" is capable of arousing in some quarters an astonishing amount of rage against what many still imagine to have been an era of cultural treason. In the white suburban Midwest, one happens so frequently across declarations of sixties- and hippie-hatred that the posture begins to seem a sort of historiographical prerequisite to being middle class and of a certain age; in the nation's politics, sixties- and hippie-bashing remains a trump card only slightly less effective than red-baiting was in earlier times. One bit of political ephemera that darkened a 1996 congressional race in south Chicago managed to appeal to both hatreds at once, tarring a Democratic candidate as the nephew of a bona fide communist *and* the choice of the still-hated California hippies, representatives of whom (including one photograph of Ken Kesey's famous bus, "Furthur") are pic-

chapter one

tured protesting, tripping, dancing, and carrying signs for the Democrat in question.[6]

In mass culture, dark images of the treason and excess of the 1960s are not difficult to find. The fable of the doubly-victimized soldiers in Vietnam, betrayed first by liberals and doves in government and then spat upon by members of the indistinguishable New Left/Counterculture has been elevated to cultural archetype by the Rambo movies and has since become such a routine trope that its invocation—and the resulting out-rage—requires only the mouthing of a few standard references.[7] The ex-ceedingly successful 1994 movie *Forrest Gump* transformed into arche-type the rest of the conservatives' understanding of the decade, depicting youth movements of the sixties in a particularly malevolent light and their leaders (a demagogue modeled on Abbie Hoffman, a sinister group of Black Panthers, and an SDS commissar who is attired, after Bloom's interpretation, in a Nazi tunic) as diabolical charlatans, architects of a national madness from which the movie's characters only recover under the benevolent presidency of Ronald Reagan.

But stay tuned for just a moment longer and a different myth of the counterculture and its meaning crosses the screen. Regardless of the tastes of Republican leaders, rebel youth culture remains the cultural mode of the corporate moment, used to promote not only specific products but the general idea of life in the cyber-revolution. Commercial fantasies of rebellion, liberation, and outright "revolution" against the stultifying demands of mass society are commonplace almost to the point of invisi-bility in advertising, movies, and television programming. For some, Ken Kesey's parti-colored bus may be a hideous reminder of national unravel-ing, but for Coca-Cola it seemed a perfect promotional instrument for its "Fruitopia" line, and the company has proceeded to send replicas of the bus around the country to generate interest in the counterculturally themed beverage. Nike shoes are sold to the accompaniment of words delivered by William S. Burroughs and songs by The Beatles, Iggy Pop, and Gil Scott Heron ("the revolution will not be televised"); peace sym-bols decorate a line of cigarettes manufactured by R. J. Reynolds and the walls and windows of Starbucks coffee shops nationwide; the products of Apple, IBM, and Microsoft are touted as devices of liberation; and adver-tising across the product-category sprectrum calls upon consumers to break rules and find themselves.[8] The music industry continues to reju-venate itself with the periodic discovery of new and evermore subversive youth movements and our televisual marketplace is a 24-hour carnival, a showplace of transgression and inversion of values, of humiliated patriarchs and shocked puritans, of screaming guitars and concupiscent youth, of fashions that are uniformly defiant, of cars that violate convention and shoes that let us be us. A host of self-designated "corporate revolutionaries," outlining the accelerated new capitalist order in magazines like *Wired* and *Fast Company*, gravitate naturally to the imagery of rebel youth culture to dramatize their own insurgent vision. This version of the countercultural myth is so pervasive that it appears even in the very places where the historical counterculture is being maligned. Just as Newt Gingrich hails an individualistic "revolution" while tirading against the counterculture, *Forrest Gump* features a soundtrack of rock 'n' roll music, John Lennon and Elvis Presley appearing in their usual roles as folk heroes, and two carnivalesque episodes in which Gump meets heads of state, avails himself grotesquely of their official generosity (consuming fifteen bottles of White House soda in one scene), and confides to them the tribulations of his nether regions. He even bares his ass to Lyndon Johnson, perhaps the ultimate countercultural gesture.

However the conservatives may froth, this second myth comes much closer to what academics and responsible writers accept as the standard account of the decade. Mainstream culture was tepid, mechanical, and uniform; the revolt of the young against it was a joyous and even a glorious cultural flowering, though it quickly became mainstream itself. Rick Perlstein has summarized this standard version of what went on in the sixties as the "declension hypothesis," a tale in which, "As the Fifties grayly droned on, springs of contrarian sentiment began bubbling into the best minds of a generation raised in unprecedented prosperity but well versed in the existential subversions of the Beats and *Mad* magazine."[9] The story ends with the noble idealism of the New Left in ruins and the counterculture sold out to Hollywood and the television networks.

So natural has this standard version of the countercultural myth come to seem that it required little explanation when, on the twenty-fifth anniversary of the historical counterculture's greatest triumph, a group of cultural speculators and commercial backers (Pepsi-Cola prominent among them) joined forces to put on a second Woodstock. But this time the commercial overtones were just a little too pronounced, and journalists rained down abuse on the venture—not because it threatened "traditional values" but because it defiled the memory of the apotheosized original. Woodstock II was said to be a simple act of exploitation, a degraded carnival of corporate logos, endorsements, and product-placement while the 1969 festival was sentimentally recalled as an event of youthful innocence and idealistic glory.

Conflicting though they may seem, the two stories of sixties culture agree on a number of basic points. Both assume quite naturally that the counterculture was what it said it was; that is, a fundamental opponent of the capitalist order. Both foes and partisans assume, further, that the counterculture is the appropriate symbol—if not the actual historical cause—for the big cultural shifts that transformed the United States and that permanently rearranged Americans' cultural priorities. They also agree that these changes constituted a radical break or rupture with existing American mores, that they were just as transgressive and as menacing and as revolutionary as countercultural participants believed them to be. More crucial for our purposes here, all sixties narratives place at their center the stories of the groups that are believed to have been so transgressive and revolutionary; American business culture is thought to have been peripheral, if it's mentioned at all. Other than the occasional purveyor of stereotype and conspiracy theory, virtually nobody has shown much interest in telling the story of the executives or suburbanites who awoke one day to find their authority challenged and paradigms problematized.[10] And whether the narrators of the sixties story are conservatives or radicals, they tend to assume that business represented a static, unchanging body of faiths, goals, and practices, a background of muted, uniform gray against which the counterculture went through its colorful chapters.

But the actual story is quite a bit messier. The cultural changes that would become identified as "counterculture" began well before 1960, with roots deep in bohemian and romantic thought, and the era of upheaval persisted long after 1970 rolled around. And while nearly every account of the decade's youth culture describes it as a reaction to the stultifying economic and cultural environment of the postwar years, almost none have noted how that context—the world of business and of middle-class mores—was itself changing during the 1960s. The 1960s was the era of Vietnam, but it was also the high watermark of American prosperity and a time of fantastic ferment in managerial thought and corporate practice. Postwar American capitalism was hardly the unchanging and soulless machine imagined by countercultural leaders; it was as dynamic a force in its own way as the revolutionary youth movements of the period, undertaking dramatic transformations of both the way it operated and the way it imagined itself.

But business history has been largely ignored in accounts of the cultural upheaval of the 1960s. This is unfortunate, because at the heart of every interpretation of the counterculture is a very particular—and very questionable—understanding of corporate ideology and of business practice. According to the standard story, business was the monolithic bad guy who had caused America to become a place of puritanical conformity and empty consumerism; business was the great symbolic foil against which the young rebels defined themselves; business was the force of irredeemable evil lurking behind the orderly lawns of suburbia and the nefarious deeds of the Pentagon. Although there are a few accounts of the sixties in which the two are thought to be synchronized in a cosmic sense (Jerry Rubin often wrote about the joys of watching television and expressed an interest in making commercials; Tom Wolfe believes that Ken Kesey's countercultural aesthetic derived from the consumer boom of the fifties), for the vast majority of countercultural sympathizers, the only relationship between the two was one of hostility.

And from its very beginnings down to the present, business dogged the counterculture with a fake counterculture, a commercial replica that seemed to ape its every move for the titillation of the TV-watching millions and the nation's corporate sponsors. Every rock band with a substantial following was immediately honored with a host of imitators; the 1967 "summer of love" was as much a product of lascivious television specials and *Life* magazine stories as it was an expression of youthful disaffection; Hearst launched a psychedelic magazine in 1968; and even hostility to co-optation had a desperately "authentic" shadow, documented by a famous 1968 print ad for Columbia Records titled "But The Man Can't Bust Our Music." So oppressive was the climate of national voyeurism that, as early as the fall of 1967, the San Francisco Diggers had held a funeral for "Hippie, devoted son of mass media."[11]

This book is a study of co-optation rather than counterculture, an analysis of the forces and logic that made rebel youth cultures so attractive to corporate decision-makers rather than a study of those cultures themselves. In doing so, it risks running afoul of what I will call the co-optation theory: faith in the revolutionary potential of "authentic" counterculture combined with the notion that business mimics and mass-produces fake counterculture in order to cash in on a particular demographic and to subvert the great threat that "real" counterculture represents. *Who Built America?*, the textbook produced by the American Social History project, includes a reproduction of the now-infamous "Man Can't Bust Our Music" ad and this caption summary of co-optation theory: "If you can't beat 'em, absorb 'em." The text below ex-

chapter one

plains the phenomenon as a question of demographics and savvy marketing, as a marker of the moment when "Record companies, clothing manufacturers, and other purveyors of consumer goods quickly recognized a new market." The ill-fated ad is also reproduced as an object of mockery in underground journalist Abe Peck's book on the decade and mentioned in countless other sixties narratives.[12] Unfortunately, though, the weaknesses of this historical faith are many and critical, and the argument made in these pages tends more to stress these inadequacies than to uphold the myths of authenticity and co-optation. Apart from certain obvious exceptions at either end of the spectrum of commodification (represented, say, by the MC-5 at one end and the Monkees at the other) it was and remains difficult to distinguish precisely between authentic counterculture and fake: by almost every account, the counterculture, as a mass movement distinct from the bohemias that preceded it, was triggered at least as much by developments in mass culture (particularly the arrival of The Beatles in 1964) as changes at the grass roots. Its heroes were rock stars and rebel celebrities, millionaire performers and employees of the culture industry; its greatest moments occurred on television, on the radio, at rock concerts, and in movies. From a distance of thirty years, its language and music seem anything but the authentic populist culture they yearned so desperately to be: from contrived cursing to saintly communalism to the embarrassingly faked Woody Guthrie accents of Bob Dylan and to the astoundingly pretentious works of groups like Iron Butterfly and The Doors, the relics of the counterculture reek of affectation and phoniness, the leisure-dreams of white suburban children like those who made up so much of the Grateful Dead's audience throughout the 1970s and 1980s.

This is a study of business thought, but in its consequences it is necessarily a study of cultural dissent as well: its promise, its meaning, its possibilities, and, most important, its limitations. And it is, above all, the story of the bohemian cultural style's trajectory from adversarial to hegemonic; the story of hip's mutation from native language of the alienated to that of advertising.

It is more than a little odd that, in this age of nuance and negotiated readings, we lack a serious history of co-optation, one that understands corporate thought as something other than a cartoon. Co-optation remains something we vilify almost automatically; the historical particulars which permit or discourage co-optation—or even the obvious fact that some things are co-opted while others are not—are simply not addressed. Regardless of whether the co-opters deserve our vilification or not, the process by which they make rebel subcultures their own is clearly an important element of contemporary life. And while the ways in which business anticipated and reacted to the youth culture of the 1960s may not reveal much about the individual experiences of countercultural participants, examining their maneuvers closely does allow a more critical perspective on the phenomenon of co-optation, as well as on the value of certain strategies of cultural confrontation, and, ultimately, on the historical meaning of the counterculture.

To begin to take co-optation seriously is instantly to discard one of the basic shibboleths of sixties historiography. As it turns out, many in American business, particularly in the two industries studied here, imagined the counterculture not as an enemy to be undermined or a threat to consumer culture but as a hopeful sign, a symbolic ally in their own struggles against the mountains of dead-weight procedure and hierarchy that had accumulated over the years. In the late 1950s and early 1960s, leaders of the advertising and menswear businesses developed a critique of their own industries, of over-organization and creative dullness, that had much in common with the critique of mass society which gave rise to the counterculture. Like the young insurgents, people in more advanced reaches of the American corporate world deplored conformity, distrusted routine, and encouraged resistance to established power. They welcomed the youth-led cultural revolution not because they were secretly planning to subvert it or even because they believed it would allow them to tap a gigantic youth market (although this was, of course, a factor), but because they perceived in it a comrade in their own struggles to revitalize American business and the consumer order generally. If American capitalism can be said to have spent the 1950s dealing in conformity and consumer fakery, during the decade that followed, it would offer the public authenticity, individuality, difference, and rebellion.

If we really want to understand American culture in the sixties, we must acknowledge at least the possibility that the co-opters had it right, that Madison Avenue's vision of the counterculture was in some ways correct.

look at all the lonely people

The standard story of the counterculture begins with an account of the social order against which it rebelled, a social order that was known to just about everyone by 1960 as the "mass society." The tale of postwar

chapter one

malaise and youthful liveliness is a familiar one; it is told and retold with the frequency and certainty of historical orthodoxy. Author after author warned in the 1950s that long-standing American traditions of individualism were vanishing and being buried beneath the empires of the great corporations, the sprawl of prefabricated towns, and the reorientation of culture around the imperative of consuming homogenized, mass-produced goods. Although the poverty and deprivation of earlier times had been largely overcome, in the "affluent society" that had succeeded those difficult decades the descendants of the pioneers were in danger of being reduced to faceless cogs in a great machine, automatons in an increasingly rationalized and computerized system of production that mindlessly churned out cars, TVs, bomber jets, and consciousness all for the sake of the ever-accelerating American way of life.

By the end of the 1950s, there could have been very few literate Americans indeed who were not familiar with the term with which these problems were summarized: "conformity." It was said to be a time of intolerance for difference, of look-alike commuters clad in gray flannel and of identical prefabricated ranch houses in planned suburban Levittowns, all stretching moderately and reasonably to the horizon. Conformity was not supposed to be merely a transitory problem of the moment, an intolerance which would fade eventually like the red scares of the past. According to its more sociologically and historically oriented observers, conformity was forever, a symptom of vast economic and social shifts, part of a permanent cultural sea-change that accompanied the ongoing transformation of the American economy. Sociologist David Riesman asserted in 1950 that the advanced prosperity of the United States had brought with it a new dominant "characterological" type: the "other-directed" man who, unlike his "inner-directed" predecessors, looked for guidance not to abstract, unchanging ideals, but to the behavior and beliefs of those around him.[13] In 1956, business writer William H. Whyte, Jr., tagged this new American with what would be his most durable moniker: "Organization Man." Whether employed by a gigantic private corporation or by the government, he was the well-adjusted product of ever-increasing bureaucracy and collectivism. For this new figure the Protestant ethic and the traditional American ideology of individualism were obsolete; the honor once perceived in entrepreneurialism and the lonely upward struggle had evaporated. In their place Organization Man elaborated a "Social Ethic" to better explain his new situation, a belief in the transcendent value of the Organization and in the power of "science" to solve any problems.[14]

Today, with the hierarchy that once allowed easy distinctions between "high" and "low" culture having been long demolished, it is a commonplace of academic cultural writing to dismiss the mass culture theory of the 1950s as "elitist," that most retrograde and loathsome of intellectual qualities. Whatever its particular, immediate qualities, we now find in the scornful criticism of television, movies, and popular music leveled by everyone from Irving Howe to Theodor Adorno simple and unforgivable snobbery. Historian Andrew Ross strikes a typical note when he writes, in *No Respect: Intellectuals and Popular Culture*, that Dwight MacDonald's excoriation of what he called "midcult" served largely "to guarantee and preserve the channels of power through which intellectual authority is exercised."[15] But the historical effects of mass culture theory are not so easily brushed off. The tumult of the 1960s is impossible to understand apart from the central fact that the mass culture critique was, if not populist, enormously popular. *The Lonely Crowd* and *Partisan Review*, which dissected the mass culture threat in a famous 1952 symposium, may have been accessible to highbrow audiences only, but both *Organization Man* and John K. Galbraith's *The Affluent Society* were read by large portions of the general public. By the middle of the 1950s, talk of conformity, of consumerism, and of the banality of mass-produced culture were routine elements of middle-class American life.[16] The mass society refrain was familiar to millions: the failings of capitalism were not so much exploitation and deprivation as they were materialism, wastefulness, and soul-deadening conformity; sins summoned easily and effectively even in the pages of *Life* magazine and by the sayings of characters in the cartoon *Peanuts*. One could read the building moral panic in the vast suburban exodus, in the ecstatic baroquerie of the ever-ascending tailfins on cars—both phenomena that, before they became symbols of conformity themselves, had originally promised somehow to put us back in touch with primal vigor and jet-age excitement. In the last few years of the decade, journalist Vance Packard penned a series of extraordinarily popular analyses of the various aspects of the mass society malaise: *The Hidden Persuaders* (1957) discussed the perfidy of the advertising industry; *The Waste Makers* (1960) dissected the sinister strategies of planned obsolescence; *The Pyramid Climbers* (1962) pronounced the futility of the junior executive's long struggle for power. Meanwhile, social critic John Keats hammered both the suburban way of life (*The Crack in the Picture Window*, 1957) and the culture of the automobile (*The Insolent Chariots*, 1958). When articles decrying conformity had finally appeared in no less august a periodical than *Reader's Digest*, Daniel Bell wrote that

chapter one

no one in the United States defends conformity. Everyone is against it, and probably everyone always was. Thirty-five years ago, you could easily rattle any middle-class American by charging him with being a "Babbitt." Today you can do so by accusing him of conformity. The problem is to know who is accusing whom.[17]

The most important contribution to the mass society literature was made by Norman Mailer, who wrote in 1957 not just another rendering of suburban anomie but an actual solution for the problem of the age, a blueprint for the cultural eruption by which the civilization of conformity would be overturned. The answer to conformity was hip, he announced in his essay, "The White Negro," thereby founding one of the great public myths of our times, the earliest and most compelling statement of the scheme by which the over-organized postwar world would be resisted. "The only life-giving answer" to the deathly drag of American civilization, Mailer wrote, was to tear oneself from the security of physical and spiritual certainty, to live for immediate pleasures rather than the postponement of gratification associated with the "work ethic," "to divorce oneself from society, to exist without roots, to set out on that uncharted journey with the rebellious imperatives of the self." The antithesis to the man in the gray flannel suit was a figure Mailer called the Hipster, an "American existentialist" whose tastes for jazz, sex, drugs, and the slang and mores of black society constituted the best means of resisting the encroachments of Cold War oppression. The choice was clear for Mailer, as it would be for the rebels of the 1960s and the admen of the 1990s: "one is Hip or one is Square . . . , one is a rebel or one conforms, . . . trapped in the totalitarian tissues of American society, doomed willy-nilly to conform if one is to succeed." Unlike the "over-civilized man" with his diligent piling of the accoutrements of respectability, the hipster lives with a "burning consciousness of the present," exists for ever-more-intense sensation, for immediate gratification, for "an orgasm more apocalyptic than the one which preceded it."[18]

None of this was entirely new in the 1950s. Since its earliest manifestations, aesthetic modernism has been defined by its discovery that the fundamental moral and religious values of Western civilization lack credibility and meaning; that traditional culture serves more to stifle and constrict the individual than to bring him closer to God. As Jackson Lears has noted, this sense of the "unreality of modern existence," of alienation from the nation's "official culture"—the bland, optimistic credos of progress and success that Lears labels "evasive banality"— was a standard element of late nineteenth-century religious and aesthetic movements.[19]

In the 1910s and 1920s, this spirit of disaffection would inspire cultural revolt against the meaninglessness of received ways and the banality of the provincial Babbitry, would make of "art" a lifestyle credo, and would cause the founding of bohemias in Greenwich Village and numerous lesser enclaves across the country, places where one could experiment openly with the forbidden pleasures of sex and drugs. But Mailer's invocation of the old bohemian idea, of the quest for authentic experience, marked a drastic change: this was the democratization of the modernist impulse, the extension of highbrow disaffection with over-civilization (reflected in the common countercultural disdain for such tasteless travesties of the mass society as white bread, suburbs, tailfins, and "plastic") and elite concerns with individual fulfillment to the widest possible audience.[20] By the end of the 1950s, the culture of "unreality" had been elaborately analyzed in popular books and magazines and its shortcomings made familiar to millions of Americans. During the decade that followed, bohemia itself would be democratized, the mass society critique adopted by millions of Organization Men, and the eternal conflict of artist and bourgeoisie expanded into a cultural civil war.

The meaning of "the sixties" cannot be considered apart from the enthusiasm of ordinary, suburban Americans for cultural revolution. And yet that enthusiasm is perhaps the most problematic and the least-studied aspect of the decade. Between the denunciations of conservatives and the fond nostalgia of 1960s partisans, we have forgotten the cosmic optimism with which so many organs of official American culture greeted the youth rebellion. It was this sudden mass defection of Americans from square to hip that distinguished the culture of the 1960s—everything from its rock music to its movies to its generational fantasies to its intoxicants—and yet the vast popularity of dissidence is the aspect of the sixties that the contemporary historical myths have trouble taking into account. The fact is that the bearers of the liberal cultural order were strangely infatuated with the counterculture (especially after 1967), hailing the Beatles with breathless reverence and finding hope and profundity in different aspects of the insurgent youth culture.[21]

This was phase two of the critique elaborated during the 1950s by Riesman, Whyte, and the Frankfurt School: the youth movement showing up everywhere now was to be the bona fide solution to the ills of mass society. In *Life* magazine it appeared in an April, 1967, series of articles entitled, "Modern Society's Growing Challenge: The Struggle to Be an Individual." The first installment ("Challenge for Free Men in a Mass Society") consisted of rather predictable art photographs (pictures of commuters, aerial views of freeway interchanges, new suburban developments) supposed to "evoke . . . the modern mood of uniformity under pressure, of distorted scale and distorted values, that can lead to a sense of emptiness and anonymity." The second proposed the solution: "The Search for Purpose: Among the Youth of America, a Fresh New Sense of Commitment." The obligatory article on Esalen and the psychic healing to be found there followed in July of 1968.[22]

But all that was a sideshow. The most influential contemporary accounts of the cultural revolution focused almost exclusively on the young and emphasized their purity of intent, exaggerated the contrast between them and a larger, oppressive culture, and were prone to flights of ecstasy over the millennial promise of the movement. *The Making of a Counter Culture*, written in 1968 and 1969 by Theodore Roszak, a professor of history, and *The Greening of America*, a 1970 best-seller by Yale law professor Charles A. Reich, both found in the counterculture the solution to the meaninglessness, alienation, and absurdity familiar to 1950s readers of *Life* and *Reader's Digest*. The counterculture, Roszak wrote, "looks to me like all we have to hold against the final consolidation of a technocratic totalitarianism in which we shall find ourselves ingeniously adapted to an existence wholly estranged from everything that has ever made the life of man an interesting adventure."[23] Charles Reich was even more sanguine. The counterculture had given rise to no less than a new "Consciousness," a way of envisioning the world that was utterly at odds with the prevailing mores of the over-organized society. Under the "corporate state," Americans had been trained in the ways of what Reich calls "Consciousness II": they became automatons, thinking of themselves in terms of their duties as workers and consumers. They endured "a robot life, in which man is deprived of his own being, and he becomes instead a mere role, occupation, or function." But unlike their parents, the young of the 1960s retained a "capacity for outrage," a sense of "betrayal" of the "promises" made by the postwar society of abundance, the vast gulf between the official talk of "freedom" and "liberty" and the dreary, conformist lives of their parents. The youth counterculture was thus the historical bearer of "Consciousness III," which encourages people to pursue their own liberation from the imposed values of the "corporate state," to choose liberation and self-direction over the conformity and other-direction of the mainstream.[24]

Although the millennial ecstasies of these books are now more than a little embarrassing, their binary understanding of the counterculture as the life-affirming opponent of mass society—hip as mortal foe of

square—has continued to characterize scholarly writing on the 1960s.
Serious works, such as Morris Dickstein's 1977 literary study, *The Gates of Eden*, although more balanced and enlightening than the popular tracts of the early 1970s, still insist on this binary structure, recapitulating the oppressions of mass society and casting the counterculture as its historical negation. The titles that follow this trajectory seem to multiply by some logic of their own year after year: academic histories run again over the usual roster of bright antecedents (the Beats, *Mad* magazine, C. Wright Mills) and down the familiar list of confrontations and media events (Human Be-in, Chicago, Woodstock); these are supplemented with countercultural memoirs and nostalgic looks back at the golden age of rock or muscle cars or television sitcoms.[25] Even writing on the culture of the fifties itself is now sometimes done with the binary historiography of the counterculture in mind: W. T. Lhamon goes out of his way to remind the readers of his book *Deliberate Speed* that the cultural rebellion of the sixties had its roots in those very years cursed with a "5" as their third digit.[26]

What might be called the standard binary narrative goes something like this: spearheaded by a dynamic youth uprising, the cultural sensibility of the 1960s made a decisive break with the dominant forces and social feeling of the postwar era. Rebellion replaced machinelike restraint as the motif of the age. Conformity and consumerism were challenged by a new ethos that found an enemy in the "Establishment," celebrated difference and diversity, and sought to maximize the freedom and "self-realization" of the individual. The "rationality" that had fueled a Cold War and subordinated people to the necessities of industrial efficiency was discredited in favor of more subjective, spontaneous, less mediated ways of knowing. The long-standing cultural and social monopoly of white males was broken, with the values of formerly subaltern groups rising suddenly to the fore. So familiar has the historical equation become (conformist fifties, rebellious sixties) that it now functions like the "historical boundary" used by Henry May to describe the way his generation remembered the teens and twenties: on one side is a stilted, repressed, black-and-white "then"; on our own is a liberated, full-color "now."[27]

Most important of all, the counterculture is said to have worked a revolution through lifestyle rather than politics, a genuine subversion of the status quo through pleasure rather than power: "When the mode of the music changes, the walls of the city will shake," as the saying had it.[28] Despite its apparent enthusiasm, goes the standard binary narrative, the Establishment was deeply threatened and in mortal conflict with a counterculture that aimed to undermine its cherished ethics of hard work and conformity. *Easy Rider* concludes with its hip heroes murdered by white Southerners; the hero of *Zabriskie Point* and those of *Bonnie and Clyde* are shot as well; the hero of *Hair* disrupts a society dinner party, is arrested, and then is killed in Vietnam; and in *Shampoo*, a free-spirited hairdresser is bested by a loathsome financier. "This society fears its young people deeply and desperately and does all that it can to train those it can control in its own image," wrote Ralph Gleason, one of the founding editors of *Rolling Stone*, in January, 1969.[29] Theodore Roszak compared the counterculture's battle against the dominant forms of social organization to an "Invasion of the Centaurs" of Greek mythology. So strange were the ideas of the young, so hostile to prevailing mores, "so radically disaffiliated from the mainstream assumptions of our society that it scarcely looks to many as a culture at all, but takes on the alarming appearance of a barbaric intrusion." The young were demanding an "epochal transformation"; the conflict was Manichean, and the war was to be a total one.[30]

But of course it wasn't. Enter the theory of co-optation. According to the standard binary narrative, the cascade of pseudo-hip culture-products that inundated the marketplace in the sixties were indicators not of the counterculture's consumer-friendly nature but evidence of the "corporate state's" hostility. They were tools with which the Establishment hoped to buy off and absorb its opposition, emblems of dissent that were quickly translated into harmless consumer commodities, emptied of content, and sold to their very originators as substitutes for the real thing. The co-optation theory has been an inescapable corollary of the hip-as-resistance thesis since its inception: Norman Mailer even discussed it in an essay on the redemptive power of hip back in 1959.[31] Toward the end of the 1960s, when both talk of the counterculture's redemptive power and mass-cult knockoffs were at their zenith, co-optation was the subject on everybody's lips. In December, 1968, Ralph Gleason ran down the list: an automaker proselytized for the "Dodge Rebellion," AT&T used the slogan, "The Times, They Are A-Changin'," and Columbia Records ran ads featuring the line "If you won't listen to your parents, The Man, or the Establishment, why should you listen to us."[32] According to Theodore Roszak, the counterculture was in danger of being "swamped with cynical or self-deceived opportunists," media and fashion figures who market themselves as the bearers of "'the philosophy of today's rebellious youth'" and imperil the counterculture with "exploitation as an amusing side show of the swinging society" (the attention of academics like himself was presumably benign). But however the technocracy may imitate, the essence

of the counterculture remained unco-optable: "there is, despite the
fraudulence and folly that collects around its edges, a significant new culture a-borning among our youth. . . ."[33]

hip as hegemon

Contemporary academic readings of youth culture are considerably more sophisticated than those of the 1960s and 1970s, but they continue to echo a recognizable version of the Mailer thesis—that hip constitutes some kind of fundamental adversary to a joyless, conformist consumer capitalism. Recent cultural studies are much more willing than the standard sixties authorities to admit the power of marketing over the ingenuous revolutionary potential of the young, but still the battle lines are clearly drawn. Taking for granted that youth signifiers are appropriated, produced, and even invented by the entertainment industry, recent writers argue that resistance arises from the ways in which these signifiers are *consumed* by the young, used in ways that are divergent or contradictory to their manufacturers' oppressive intent. Whatever form prefabricated youth cultures are given by their mass-culture originators ultimately doesn't matter: they are quickly taken apart and reassembled by alienated young people in startlingly novel subcultures. As with the counterculture, it is *transgression* itself, the never-ending race to violate norms, that is the key to resistance.

John Fiske, for example, argues that mass-produced culture is both a site of oppression and rebellion: even as it is calculated to exploit consumers, it unintentionally provides various groups and individuals with the implements of empowerment. The results are "popular culture," which Fiske affirms with enthusiasm: window-shopping consumes space and air conditioning without anything being purchased and is hence an "oppositional cultural practice"; actual shopping, if it's done by women, is liberating, "an oppositional, competitive act, and as such . . . a source of achievement, self-esteem, and power." Similar readings by others are commonplace almost to the point of self-parody: Madonna subverts gender norms; dancing subverts religious order; the Rolling Stones subvert musical hierarchies.[34] And all without the culture industries that have produced these things catching on. Again the narrative is predictable: what Fiske calls the "power-bloc" intends that the public be conformist, complacent consumers while the "people" rebel through a million ineluctable, unfinalizable, individualistic devices:

The opposition can . . . be thought of as one between *homogeneity*, as the power-bloc attempts to control, structure, and minimize social differences so that they serve its interests, and *heterogeneity*, as the formations of the people intransigently maintain their sense of social difference that is also a difference of interest.

In order for mass culture to be "popular," it must make concessions to this impulse toward "heterogeneity," it must contain elements of such facets of "liberation" as "the carnivalesque," "evasion," and "*jouissance*"; it must allow for rebellion against the "patriarchy;" it must make gestures toward an "inversion" of values. And when these various things appear in mass culture, Fiske hails them as instruments of subaltern empowerment.[35] The values of consumer society are still those attacked by the mass society theorists: by its nature, capitalism requires rigid conformity and patriarchy in order to function. The transgressive practices of the hipster are innately modes of resistance, and mass culture only makes concessions to them from necessity.

From both the anti-sixties bombast of Newt Gingrich and from cultural studies' celebration of difference, transgression, and the carnivalesque, a curious consensus emerges: business and hip are irreconcilable enemies, the two antithetical poles of American mass culture. Whether it is the crude rendering of Jerry Rubin and Charles Reich or the complex analysis of later academics, the historical meaning of hip seems to be fixed: it is a set of liberating practices fundamentally at odds with the dominant impulses of postwar American society. As in the standard binary narrative of the sixties, cultural studies tends to overlook the trends, changes, and intricacies of corporate culture, regarding it as a monolithic, unchanging system with unchanging values. Described variously as the "technocracy," "the power bloc," "hegemony," or "everyday life," its cultural requirements are assumed to be static, hierarchical, patriarchal, and conformist, having changed very little since the 1950s. Despite its ever-changing surface and curious excesses, management theory is, generally speaking, not a popular subject of cultural studies, and few cultural theorists bother with the various histories of American business that have appeared in recent years.[36]

Yet the subject couldn't be more compelling. Today corporate ideologues routinely declare that business has supplanted the state, the church, and all independent culture in our national life. Curiously enough, at the same time many scholars have decided it is folly to study business. For all of cultural studies' subtle readings and forceful advocacy, its practitioners often tend to limit their inquiries so rigorously to the consumption of culture-products that the equally important process of cultural production is virtually ignored. While the most fanciful of motives may be safely attributed to rock stars and culture consumers, efforts to study the doings of the culture industry are widely regarded with a sort of suspicious disdain, as tantamount to accepting the snobbish contempt for popular culture once expressed by the now-discredited theorists of mass society. Worse, to analyze the machinations of advertising or record company executives suggests that one believes the public to be mere "cultural dopes," pawns of a malevolent and conspiratorial culture industry.

These oversights have more serious consequences for scholarship than they might seem at first: as analysts from Marx to the editors of *Wired* have noted, capitalism is dynamic stuff, an order of endless flux and change. Both the way businesspeople think and the way corporations are organized have shifted dramatically over the last forty years; by glibly passing over these changes when describing the culture of capitalism—even were one to grant that only cultural reception matters—one seriously miscontextualizes American daily life. Ultimately, though, something much greater than simple academic error is at stake: recent cultural studies are concerned with the nature and practice of dissent itself; and to identify capitalism, its culture-products, and its opponents according to an inflexible scheme of square and hip—"homogeneity" versus "heterogeneity," the "power bloc" versus "the people," conformity versus individualism—is to make a strategic blunder of enormous proportions.

It is also to contradict rather directly some of the basic findings of recent American cultural history. Despite the homogeneity, repression, and conformity critique favored by so many avatars of cultural studies, historians like Warren Susman, William Leach, and Jackson Lears have pointed out that the prosperity of a consumer society depends not on a rigid control of people's leisure-time behavior, but exactly its opposite: unrestraint in spending, the willingness to enjoy formerly forbidden pleasures, an abandonment of the values of thrift and the suspicion of leisure that characterized an earlier variety of capitalism. Susman placed the battle between these two philosophies, a "culture that envisioned a world of scarcity . . . , hard work, self-denial . . . , sacrifice, and character" and a new order emphasizing "pleasure, self-fulfillment, and play" at the center of his understanding of twentieth-century America.[37] Leach points out that early ideologues of consumerism described the new regime not as one of repressive adherence to tradition or patriarchy but as a valorization of constant change, of individuality, and of the eternal new. Consumer capitalism, he notes, has taught a "concept of humanity" according to which "what is most 'human' about people is their quest after the new, their willingness to violate boundaries, their hatred of the old and the habitual . . . , and their need to incorporate 'more and more'—goods, money, experience, everything." Consumer capitalism did not demand conformity or homogeneity; rather, it thrived on the doctrine of liberation and continual transgression that is still familiar today: for one department store chief whom Leach studies, "modern capitalism was positively liberating; by its very nature, it rejected all traditions and embraced desire." [38]

American business was undergoing a revolution in its own right during the 1960s, a revolution in marketing practice, management thinking, and ideas about creativity. It was a revolution as far-reaching in its own way as the revolutions in manners, music, art, and taste taking place elsewhere, and it shared with those revolutions a common hostility for hierarchy, for inherited wisdom, and for technocratic ideas of efficiency. The strange relationship of corporations and counterculture becomes considerably less strange when examined from the perspective of management literature. During the 1950s and 1960s, management thinkers went through their own version of the mass society critique, first deploring the demise of entrepreneurship under the stultifying regime of technocratic efficiency (*The Organization Man*), then embracing all manner of individualism-promoting, bureaucracy-smashing, and antihierarchical schemes (*The Human Side of Enterprise, Up the Organization*). Infatuation with youthful cultural insurgency came almost as naturally for them as it did for Charles Reich and Theodore Roszak: it seemed to be a lively cultural fermentation dedicated to many of the same principles as were the leaders of the business revolution.

The only episode in the development of management literature to have attracted much attention outside of business schools is the scheme of time-and-motion studies performed by Frederick Winslow Taylor and the body of theory which arose in their wake. Applied to the shop floor, Taylor's theories brought about the meaningless, alienating labor lampooned by Charlie Chaplin in *Modern Times*; applied to office work, they gave rise to the hyperorganized world of the pre-1960s corporation, to the values of conformity and hierarchy that still form such an enormous part of the popular vision of capitalist life. The Taylorist impulse dominated business thinking well into the 1950s, with efficiency, hierarchy, and organization long thought to be the keys to productivity. Business historian Art Kleiner calls it a time of "the numbers," an era in which rigid order-

liness took on a certain metaphysical value: "At General Electric,
AT&T, Procter & Gamble, and nearly every other large company, ency-
clopedic manuals . . . dictated every aspect of workplace practice, from
the layout of stamping machines to the format of quarterly reports to the
placement of pencils on a secretary's desk."[39] This, of course, is the familiar world of mass society and its good citizen, Organization Man, easily
summoned up to this day by photos of look-alike executives in narrow
ties, gray suits, and horn-rimmed glasses.[40] Its classic text, Alfred Sloan's
My Years With General Motors, is a terrifyingly boring tale of committees
and calculation and flow charts and layer upon layer of organization.[41]

But even in the most complacent management literature of the fifties
one finds harbingers of dissidence and upheaval. The February 1951 edition of *Fortune*, for example, was a special issue devoted to laying out a
manifesto for American world dominance and conducting a snarling de-
fense of the middle-class consensus against all who doubted it. But, as
the issue's cubist illustrations and title (borrowed openly from Trotsky—
"U.S.A. The Permanent Revolution") make clear, all was not perfect in
the corporation, that "organization of vast powers, which exacts of its
managers purely impersonal decisions," and the eternal rebellion of the
individual which the magazine celebrated would continue in unpredictable ways in the future.[42] *Fortune* also featured a number of prominent
intellectuals on its editorial staff: Dwight MacDonald, Reuel Denney, and
Daniel Bell all wrote for Henry Luce's business publication, as did James
Agee and Archibald MacLeish. However absurd management literature
would eventually become, during this period (a time when *Fortune* also
printed serious labor journalism, something virtually unknown today) it
was capable of something close to real social criticism. And within a few
years, the proto-dissidence that glimmers in "The Permanent Revolution" would be in full outcry against the dangers of conformity. Before
long, management texts would be counseling against hierarchy, sneering
at the old Taylorist management theories, celebrating human qualities,
and downplaying the abilities of computers.

It is somehow appropriate that the book through which the culture
of the American 1950s will always be remembered was written by an
editor of *Fortune*. *The Organization Man* may have been astute social criticism, and it may have been one of the first sparks in the cultural uprising
that would later become the counterculture, but it was also a management book, a sweeping study of American business and its problems. For
Whyte, apparently unconcerned with the propaganda requirements of

the Cold War or with imagining America as a place of finely tuned balance, the triumph of "group-mindedness" had serious negative consequences for the conduct of business as well as for American life. The most deleterious effect of the "social ethic," he warned, was that it inhibited creativity. Only individuals were capable of offering "the bold new plan," but "it is the nature of a new idea to confound current consensus." Indeed, certain large corporations were taking active measures to weed creative people out of the white-collar workforce.[43]

Business concern over the creativity crisis roughly paralleled the larger culture's worries about conformity. As the 1960s began, an array of management texts appeared addressing the problems of the 1950s and suggesting, as one book's rather direct title put it, *How to Be a More Creative Executive*.[44] In 1960, Douglas McGregor published *The Human Side of Enterprise*, one of the most popular business texts of the era, codifying Whyte's analysis of corporate life into one of the elaborate metatheories to which management literature has always been partial. All American corporations subscribed to one of two grand schemes of human organization, McGregor insisted: "Theory X," the Taylorist "traditional view," according to which workers must be "coerced," supervised, and "directed" by a hierarchy of power; and "Theory Y," a more sophisticated approach according to which workers' ingenuity is recognized, and they are motivated by progress toward an objective rather than fear of punishment. "Theory Y" promised, through participative strategies, to "link improvement in managerial competence with the satisfaction of higher-level ego and self-actualization needs," to open the way for "developments . . . with respect to the human side of enterprise comparable to those that have occurred in technology."[45] Just as Mailer's "White Negro" suggested a solution to conformity, *The Human Side of Enterprise* set out the alternative to the creativity-stifling "social ethic." It was an enormously influential book, spawning dozens of spinoffs and winning disciples across the corporate spectrum. Today, with popular business writers vying constantly to come up with an evermore transgressive strategy for disrupting corporate hierarchy, the bloated corpus of recent management literature seems like one long tribute to McGregor's thought, an interminable string of corollaries to "Theory Y." Yet neither McGregor nor his book are mentioned in any of the standard academic accounts of the 1960s.[46]

Nonetheless, the 1960s were a time of radical change in business theory, what Kleiner calls an "age of heretics." In the wake of *The Human Side of Enterprise* and with hierarchy discredited, conformity under attack,

and "creativity" and "leadership" back in the fore, the old Taylorist
"Theory X" principles were headed toward theoretical extinction. The
characteristic business text of 1970—published at just about the same
time that Timothy Leary was denouncing corporate America as a "hu-
manoid robot whose every Federal Bureaucratic impulse is soulless, heart-
less, lifeless, loveless"—was a diatribe against hierarchy, entitled *Up the
Organization: How to Stop the Corporation from Stifling People and Stran-
gling Profits*, written by Robert Townsend, an executive at a company
(Avis Rent-a-Car, whose rule-breaking ads were made by Doyle Dane
Bernbach) that had grown dramatically over the decade by aggressively
defying the conventions of marketing and advertising.[47] A pugnacious
champion of "Theory Y," Townsend declares himself for those corporate "subversives" who have "a talent for spotting the idiocies now
built into the system" and roundly denounces "monster corporations"
where, "trapped in the pigeonholes of organization charts, [employees
and executives have] been made slaves to the rules of private and public
hierarchies that run mindlessly on and on because nobody can change
them." *Up the Organization* is composed of terse declarations of revolutionary ardor: "True leadership must be for the benefit of the followers,
not the enrichment of the leaders"; "Don't hire Harvard Business School
graduates"; "We've become a nation of office boys." And in a savage rebuke to Alfred Sloan, whose book boasts of his massive contributions to
the various war efforts of the twentieth century, Townsend holds up none
other than Ho Chi Minh as exemplary of Theory Y, which explains his
"unbelievable twenty-five year survival against the mighty blasts of Theory X monsters of three nations."[48]

Ho Chi Minh indeed. The shift in American business writing during
those high-water years of prosperity was also accompanied by a revolution
in industrial organization of the most tangible sort. The 1960s saw the
maturation of the economic regime that theorists of marketing call
"market segmentation," the discovery of demographics and the now-
commonplace insight that targeting slightly different products to specific
groups of consumers is significantly more effective than manufacturing
one uniform product for everyone. Business historian Richard S. Tedlow
describes market segmentation as a stage of development in which demographics and "psychographics" are used "to create divisions in markets
that [marketers] can exploit with competitive advantages." Physical characteristics of products are no longer as important as before: under market
segmentation, competitive battle is joined over issues like brand image
and consumer identity, with advertising taking an ever-more prominent

part in business development.[49] The epic battle of Coca-Cola and Pepsi is the best-known illustration of the change in which uniformity quite literally gave way to diversity. Over the first half of this century, Coke built an unrivaled dominance of the once-localized soft-drink marketplace: it offered a single product that was supposed to be consumable by people in every walk of life—rich and poor, old and young, men and women—and in every part of the country. It was the "brand beyond competition," with a single, zealously guarded formula and a single container size that was supposed to be adequate for everyone. Pepsi's rise during the 1960s, more than any other single event, signaled the arrival of the segmented market. By appealing to youthfulness and the young as a philosophy and a people apart from the values associated with Coca-Cola, Pepsi transformed itself quickly into a competitor to be reckoned with. The ensuing "Cola Wars" have had much less to do with the rival companies' actual products than with the "psychic benefit" promised by each, with the war of symbolism in which both have invested so much.[50]

At its most advanced stages, according to business writers, this new species of marketing is concerned with nothing other than the construction of consumer subjectivity, as manufacturers and advertisers attempt to call group identities into existence where before there had been nothing but inchoate feelings and common responses to pollsters' questions. About this rather startling point Tedlow is completely candid. "Segmentation based not on logistics or on some genuine product characteristics but on demographic and psychographic groupings carved out of the general population is an invention of late twentieth-century American marketing," he writes.

> The old fragmentation was based on realities [primarily geographic], but this new segmentation springs wholly from the imagination of the marketer. Pepsi and other such companies have been more interested in the term segment as a verb than as a noun. They have segmented markets, rather than merely responded to a market segment that already existed. There was no such thing as the Pepsi Generation until Pepsi created it.[51]

It is significant that the market element utilized in (or invented by) Pepsi's ur-segmentation was youth. Before the 1960s, young people had always been an established part of marketing and a staple image in advertising art, largely because of their still unformed tastes and their position as trend leaders. This was especially true in the 1920s. But during the 1960s, this standard approach changed. No longer was youth merely a "natural" demographic group to which appeals could be pitched: sud- denly youth became a consuming position to which all could aspire. "Pepsi not only recognized the existence of a demographic segment," observed marketing historians Stanley Hollander and Richard Germain, "but also in essence manufactured a segment of those who wanted to feel youthful."[52] The conceptual position of *youthfulness* became as great an element of the marketing picture as youth itself.

Writers who are critical of capitalism identify these changes in management theory and marketing practice as part of a larger ideological realignment spanning the postwar era. David Harvey, for example, attributes the shift from centralized "Fordism" of the 1950s and before to the mobile, segmented economy of "flexible accumulation" as the rise of a sort of hyperconsumerism in which the production of image, consumer and corporate identity, and publicity strategies have taken precedence over the actual production of goods. As culture increasingly became the battleground of business competition, the frenzied obsolescence of fashion was introduced into all manner of cultural endeavors, providing "a means to accelerate the pace of consumption not only in clothing, ornament, and decoration but also across a wide swathe of life-styles and recreational activities (leisure and sporting habits, pop music styles, video and children's games, and the like)."[53]

The 1960s were a time of revolution in American business, as they were in so many aspects of American life, an era that saw both the rise of market segmentation and a shift from a management culture that revered hierarchy and efficiency to one that emphasized individualism and creativity. Readers of the mass society texts and partisans of the counterculture, it seems, were not alone in their suspicions of the conformist powers of the great corporations. No one knew the horrors of the social ethic better than Organization Man himself. Not that too many of the vast corporations were persuaded by books like McGregor's to restructure themselves utterly, of course: the change was largely a matter of ideology and of marketing, of the symbols and referents by which business understood itself and by which it addressed the public. But what's important about these facts is that American business culture was not the flat gray monotone that most accounts of the sixties imagine it to have been. Changing the cultural background of the standard binary sixties story, though, has serious implications for the theory of co-optation, implications that become even more pronounced when corporate responses to the counterculture are examined closely. Far from opposing the larger cultural revolution of those years, the business revolution paralleled—

chapter one

and in some cases actually anticipated—the impulses and new values associated with the counterculture. Art Kleiner, who worked as an editor of the *Whole Earth Catalog* before taking up business history, is explicit about the connection between management theory and the counterculture. He depicts the 1960s as a long struggle to recover what he calls "vernacular" human relationships amid the hyper-rationalism of the technocracy, an effort that "could only have existed against the backdrop of the counterculture." "As the influence of the counterculture spread," he writes, "a few managers began to question the prevailing assumptions of the corporations they worked for."[54]

The curious enthusiasm of American business for the symbols, music, and slang of the counterculture marked a fascination that was much more complex than the theory of co-optation would suggest. In fields like fashion and advertising that were most conspicuously involved with the new phase of image-centered capitalism, business leaders were not concerned merely with simulating countercultural signifiers in order to sell the young demographic (or stave off revolution, for that matter) but because they approved of the new values and anti-establishment sensibility being developed by the youthful revolutionaries. They were drawn to the counterculture because it made sense to them, because they saw a reflection of the new values of consuming and managing to which they had been ministering for several years.

Hip capitalism wasn't something on the fringes of enterprise, an occasional hippie entrepreneur selling posters or drug paraphernalia. Nor was it a purely demographic maneuver, just a different spin to sell products to a different group. What happened in the sixties is that hip became central to the way American capitalism understood itself and explained itself to the public.

hip consumerism

Advertising and menswear, the two industries with which this book are directly concerned, were deeply caught up in both the corporate and cultural changes that defined the sixties. The story in men's clothing is simple enough and is often cited as an indicator of changing times along with movies, novels, and popular music: the fifties are remembered, rather stereotypically, as a time of gray flannel dullness, while the sixties were an era of sartorial gaudiness. The change in the nation's advertising is less frequently remembered as one of the important turning points between the fifties and sixties, but the changes here were, if anything, even more remarkable, more significant, and took place slightly earlier than those in music and youth culture. Both industries were on the cutting edge of the shifts in corporate practice in the 1960s, and both were also conspicuous users of countercultural symbolism—they were, if you will, the leading lights of co-optation.

But both industries' reaction to youth culture during the sixties was more complex than that envisioned by the co-optation theory. Both menswear and advertising were paralyzed by similar problems in the 1950s: they suffered from a species of creative doldrums, an inability to move beyond the conventions they had invented for themselves and to tap into that wellspring of American economic dynamism that *Fortune* called "the permanent revolution." Both industries underwent "revolutions" in their own right during the 1960s, with vast changes in corporate practice, in productive flexibility, and especially in that intangible phenomenon known as "creativity"—and in both cases well before the counterculture appeared on the mass-media scene. In the decade that followed, both industries found a similar solution to their problems: a commercial version of the mass society theory that made of alienation a motor for fashion. Seeking a single metaphor by which to characterize the accelerated obsolescence and enhanced consumer friendliness to change which were their goals, leaders in both fields had already settled on "youth" and "youthfulness" several years before saturation TV and print coverage of the "Summer of Love" introduced middle America to the fabulous new lifestyles of the young generation.

Then, in 1967 and 1968, advertising and menswear executives seized upon the counterculture as the preeminent symbol of the revolution in which they were engaged, embellishing both their trade literature and their products with images of rebellious, individualistic youth. While leaders of both industries appreciated the demographic bonanza that the baby boom represented, their concentration on the symbols of first youth and then culture-rebel owed more to new understandings of consumption and business culture than to a desire to sell the kids. The counterculture served corporate revolutionaries as a projection of the new ideology of business, a living embodiment of attitudes that reflected their own. In its hostility to established tastes, the counterculture seemed to be preparing young people to rebel against whatever they had patronized before and to view the cycles of the new without the suspicion of earlier eras. Its simultaneous craving for authenticity and suspicion of tradition seemed to make the counterculture an ideal vehicle for a vast sea-change in American consuming habits. Through its symbols and myths, leaders of the menswear and advertising industries imagined a consumerism markedly different from its 1950s permutation, a hip consumerism driven by disgust with mass society itself.

Capitalism was entering the space age in the sixties, and Organization Man was a drag not only as a parent, but as an executive. The old values of caution, deference, and hierarchy drowned creativity and denied flexibility; they enervated not only the human spirit but the consuming spirit and the entrepreneurial spirit as well. And when business leaders cast their gaze onto the youth culture bubbling around them, they saw both a reflection of their own struggle against the stifling bureaucracy of the past and an affirmation of a dynamic new consuming order that would replace the old. For these business thinkers, the cultural revolution that has come to be symbolized by the counterculture seemed an affirmation of their own revolutionary faiths, a reflection of their own struggles to call their corporate colleagues into step with the chaotic and frenetically changing economic universe.

The revolutions in menswear and advertising—as well as the larger revolution in corporate thought—ran out of steam when the great postwar prosperity collapsed in the early 1970s. In a larger sense, though, the corporate revolution of the 1960s never ended. In the early 1990s, while the nation was awakening to the realities of the hyperaccelerated global information economy, the language of the business revolution of the sixties (and even some of the individuals who led it) made a triumphant return. Although on the surface menswear seemed to have settled back into placidity, the reputation of the designers and creative rebels who made their first appearance during the decade of revolt were at their zenith in the 1990s; men's clothes were again being presented to the public as emblems of nonconformity; and the magazines which most prominently equated style with rebellion (*Details* and *GQ*, the latter of which had been founded at the opening of the earlier revolution in 1957) were enjoying great success. The hottest advertising agencies of the late 1980s and early 1990s were, again, the small creative firms; a new company of creative rebels came to dominate the profession; and advertising that offered to help consumers overcome their alienation, to facilitate their nonconformity, and which celebrated rule-breaking and insurrection became virtually ubiquitous. Most important, the corporate theory of the 1990s makes explicit references to sixties management theory and the experiences of the counterculture.[55] Like the laid-back executives who personify it, the ideology of information capitalism is a child of the 1960s; the intervening years of the 1970s and 1980s may have delayed the revolution, but they hardly defused its urgency.

Placing the culture of the 1960s in this corporate context does little to support any of the standard countercultural myths, nor does it affirm the consensual notion of the 1960s as a time of fundamental cultural confrontation. It suggests instead that the counterculture may be more accurately understood as a stage in the development of the values of the American middle class, a colorful installment in the twentieth century drama of consumer subjectivity. This is not, of course, a novel interpretation: in the 1960s and 1970s it was a frequent plaint among writers who insisted that the counterculture was apolitical and self-indulgent, or, when it did spill over into obviously political manifestations, confused and anarchistic.[56] This critique of cultural liberation even extends back to the late 1950s, when Delmore Schwartz reacted to the rise of the Beats by pointing out that the attack of the "San Francisco Howlers" on "the conformism of the organization man, the advertising executive, the man in the grey flannel suit, or the man in the Brooks Brothers suit" was

a form of shadow boxing because the Man in the Brooks Brothers suit is himself, in his own home, very often what [Bertrand] Russell has called an upper Bohemian. His conformism is limited to the office day and business hours: in private life—and at heart—he is as Bohemian as anyone else.[57]

Michael Harrington described the counterculture in 1972 as a massification of the bohemia in which he had spent his youth, an assumption of the values of Greenwich Village by the decidedly nonrevolutionary middle class. "I wonder if the mass counterculture may not be a reflection of the very hyped and video-taped world it professes to despise," he wrote.

Bohemia could not survive the passing of its polar opposite and precondition, middle-class morality. Free love and all-night drinking and art for art's sake were consequences of a single stern imperative: thou shalt not be bourgeois. But once the bourgeoisie itself became decadent—once businessmen started hanging nonobjective art in the boardroom—Bohemia was deprived of the stifling atmosphere without which it could not breathe.[58]

Others understood the counterculture explicitly in terms of accelerating consumer culture and the crisis in corporate thought. "Having professed their disdain for middle-class values," wrote novelist and adman Earl Shorris in 1967, "the hippies indulge in them without guilt." Shorris envisioned the counterculture not as a movement promising fundamental transformation but as an expression of a solidly middle-class dream:

> The preponderance of hippies come from the middle class, because it is there even among adults that the illusion of the hippies' joy, free love, purity and drug excitement is strongest. A man grown weary of singing company songs at I.B.M. picnics, feeling guilty about the profits he has made on defense stocks, who hasn't really loved his wife for 10 years, must admire, envy and wish for a life of love and contemplation, a simple life leading to a beatific peace. He soothes his despair with the possibility that the hippies have found the answers to problems he does not dare to face.[59]

In a famously cynical essay that appeared in *Ramparts* in 1967, Warren Hinckle pointed out that, for all the rhetoric of alienation, the inhabitants of the Haight-Ashbury were "brand name conscious" and "frantic consumers."

> In this commercial sense, the hippies have not only accepted assimilation . . . , they have swallowed it whole. The hippie culture is in many ways a prototype of the most ephemeral aspects of the larger American society; if the people looking in from the suburbs want change, clothes, fun, and some lightheadedness from the new gypsies, the hippies are delivering—and some of them are becoming rich hippies because of it.

Looking back in 1974, Marshall Berman directly equated "cultural liberation" in the sixties sense with dynamic economic growth.[60] Andrew Ross pointed out in 1989 that this curiously ambivalent relationship with consumerism has always been the defining characteristic of hip: an "essentially agnostic cult of style worship," hip is concerned more with "advanced knowledge about the illegitimate," and staying one step ahead of the consuming crowd than with any "ideology of good community faith."[61] Nor did those who were the counterculture's putative enemies feel that it posed much of a threat to the core values of consumer capitalism. On the contrary, they found that it affirmed those values in certain crucial ways, providing American business with a system of easy symbols with which they could express their own needs and solve the intractable cultural problems they had encountered during the 1950s.

The counterculture has long since outlived the enthusiasm of its 31
original participants and become a more or less permanent part of the
American scene, a symbolic and musical language for the endless cycles
of rebellion and transgression that make up so much of our mass culture.
With leisure-time activities of consuming redefined as "rebellion," two of
late capitalism's great problems could easily be met: obsolescence found a
new and more convincing language, and citizens could symbolically resolve the contradiction between their role as consumers and their role as
producers.[62] The countercultural style has become a permanent fixture
on the American scene, impervious to the angriest assaults of cultural and
political conservatives, because it so conveniently and efficiently trans-
forms the myriad petty tyrannies of economic life—all the complaints
about conformity, oppression, bureaucracy, meaninglessness, and the dis-
appearance of individualism that became virtually a national obsession
during the 1950s—into rationales for consuming. No longer would
Americans buy to fit in or impress the Joneses, but to demonstrate that
they were wise to the game, to express their revulsion with the artifice
and conformity of consumerism. The enthusiastic discovery of the counterculture by the branches of American business studied here marked the
consolidation of a new species of hip consumerism, a cultural perpetual
motion machine in which disgust with the falseness, shoddiness, and everyday oppressions of consumer society could be enlisted to drive the
ever-accelerating wheels of consumption.

Both of the industries studied here are often written about in quasi-
conspiratorial terms. Many Americans apparently believe advertising
works because it contains magic "subliminals"; others sneer at fashion
as an insidious plot orchestrated by a Paris-New York cabal. Both ideas
are interesting popular variations on the mass society/consumerism-as-
conformity critique. But this book makes no attempt to resolve the perennial question of exactly how much the garment industries control fashion trends. Obviously the Fairchild company is unable to trick the public
into buying whatever look it chooses to launch in one of the myriad
magazines it owns, but it is hardly conspiracy-mongering to study the
company's attempts to do so. Nor does this book seek to settle the debate
over whether advertising causes cultural change or reflects it: obviously it
does a great deal of both. Business leaders are not dictators scheming to
defraud the nation, but neither are they the mystic diviners of the public
will that they claim (and that free-market theory holds them) to be. Fur-

chapter one

thermore, the thoughts and worries and ecstasies of business leaders are worth studying regardless of the exact quantity of power they exert over the public mind. Whether the cultural revolution of the 1960s was the product of conspiracy, popular will, or the movement of market or dialectic, the thinking of corporate America is essential in judging its historical meaning.

This study is not concerned with the counterculture as a historical phenomenon as much as it is concerned with the genesis of counterculture as an enduring commercial myth, the titanic symbolic clash of hip and square that recurs throughout post-sixties culture. On occasion, the myth is phrased in the overt language of the historical counterculture (Woodstock II, for example); but for the most part the subject here is the rise of a general corporate style, phrased in terms of whatever the youth culture of the day happens to be, that celebrates both a kind of less-structured, faster-moving corporation and that also promotes consumer resistance to the by-now well-known horrors of conformist consumerism. Today hip is ubiquitous as a commercial style, a staple of advertising that promises to deliver the consumer from the dreary nightmare of square consumerism. Hip is also the vernacular of the much-hyped economic revolution of the 1990s, an economic shift whose heroes are written up by none other than the *New York Times Magazine* as maximum revolutionaries: artists rather than commanders, wearers of ponytails and dreamers of cowboy fantasies who proudly proclaim their ignorance of "rep ties."[63]

The questions that surround the counterculture are enormous ones, and loaded as they are with such mythical importance to both countercultural participants and their foes, they are often difficult to consider dispassionately.[64] Furthermore, the critique of mass society embraced by the counterculture still holds a profound appeal: young people during the 1960s were confronting the same problems that each of us continues to confront every day, and they did so with a language and style that still rings true for many. This study is, in some ways, as much a product of countercultural suspicion of consumerism as are the ads and fashions it evaluates. The story of the counterculture—and of insurgent youth culture generally—now resides somewhere near the center of our national self-understanding, both as the focus of endless new generations of collective youth-liberation fantasies and as the sort of cultural treason imagined by various reactionaries. And even though countercultural sympathizers are willing to recognize that co-optation is an essential aspect of youth culture, they remain reluctant to systematically evaluate business thinking on the subject, to ask how this most anticommercial youth movement of them all became the symbol for the accelerated capitalism of the sixties and the nineties, or to hold the beloved counterculture to the harsh light of historical and economic scrutiny. It is an intellectual task whose time has come.

chapter one

chapter two

BUTTONED DOWN:

HIGH MODERNISM ON

MADISON AVENUE

The Old Man looked amused. "Only a singer you say, Mr. Norman. Well, I want you to know that the Beautee Soap Company thinks singers are mighty important. And I'll tell you why, Mr. Norman."

He opened the drawer of the table and triumphantly held aloft a bar of Beautee Soap.

"Because singers can sell soap, Mr. Norman. Right, Kimberly?"

"RIGHT," said Kimberly.

"That is, if they're the right kind of singers, eh, Kimberly?"

"Right on the barrelhead," Kim said.

And then Vic noticed still another thing. The Old Man had consistently called him Mr. Norman, and Kim he had consistently addressed as Kimberly.

Was that good or bad? Good for which one? Bad for which one?

— FREDERIC WAKEMAN, *THE HUCKSTERS,* 1946

Advertising agencies, according to the media images common in the 1990s, are exceedingly hip places. Advertising people are deeply immersed in the tastes, the music, and the slang of young people, obsessed with the rapid movement of youth culture. And, being an industry that burns out creative talents in an extraordinarily short time, it is a world populated largely by actual young people.

But in the 1940s (when outside media first became interested in the advertising business), 1950s, and 1960s, popular American ideas of the advertising industry were very different. Madison Avenue was "Ulcer Gulch," the preserve of the famous "Man in the Gray Flannel Suit"; it was the archetypal destination for look-alike commuters from Westchester; it was slow-moving, WASPy, and serious; it was populated by other-directed organization men. It was a shrine of "Theory X" conformity, the seat of all that was wrong with American culture. Admen[1] were hopeless yes-men, dedicated to affirming their clients' every whim. They suffered from an excess of three-martini lunches at "21." An agency's most important employee was the high-powered account man, a figure like that played by Rock Hudson in the 1961 movie *Lover Come Back,* whose job was simply to entertain clients with stiff drinks and a smooth line—advertisements themselves (the stuff that idealistic Doris Day thanklessly produced) were secondary. Industry observers warned that the business was floundering in tedium. The culture-products churned out were monotonous, repetitive, and dull, defined strictly by well-established precedents: advertising present mimicked advertising that had been acceptable in the past. The making of striking and effective ads had given way to the all-stifling fear of rocking the boat, presenting a client with something unfamiliar or risque. Losing a client was the worst possible result of a campaign; the sales of his products were another matter.

Frederic Wakeman's 1946 novel *The Hucksters* established the image of the advertising industry that would become so powerful in the 1950s and 1960s. Following the brief career of Victor Norman, who returns from World War II and takes over the high-paying but thankless account of a difficult client for a large agency, the book anticipated many of the issues that would turn the industry on its head in the 1960s. Vic, as he is called, is a Hemingwayesque figure: quiet, masculine (he even bears the Hemingway code hero's two male names), and extremely competent at what he does—radio production. He is also irredeemably cynical about the advertising business: he is disgusted by mass culture, by the behavior of live studio audiences, and by the tiresomely repetitive and sophomoric campaign he himself has devised ("Love That Soap!"), even as he recognizes its usefulness in building sales. At one point he mocks an executive board's unwillingness to use vulgar approaches in terms that anticipate contemporary contempt for the elitism of high culture:

> "You guys talk like a medical society," Vic next said. "All this professional crap about highclass business versus lowclass business. Christ, we ought to face it. We're hustlers. We don't steal, probably because it's bad for business, but we sure as hell do everything else for our clients. And I say if a radio show helps us get business who are we to stick up our noses?"

Vic's point is not that high culture is indistinguishable from low but that all such distinctions are irrelevant in the cultural marketplace. To further emphasize the utter meaningless of conventional standards in the world he inhabits, Vic speaks sarcastically throughout the novel of "sincerity," buys a "sincere" tie, and asks for "sincere" opinions.

Traditional aesthetics matter for naught in the relativist world of Madison Avenue: the subjective whims of the client are what rule here, and the adman who defies them—as does *The Hucksters'* hard-boiled hero—is destroyed. Victor Norman is a "rugged individualist" (as his boss calls him), an "inner-directed" person in a world of "cringing sycophants." He will not abide by corporate custom, arriving late to work and

for meetings, and does not recognize the authority of the dollar. At one
point he even throws a handful of money, Yippie-like, out an office window, astonishing an audience of underlings and nonchalantly repeating a
favorite remark, "It's only money." But in despotic soap magnate Evan
Llewelyn Evans, a figure patterned after the famous president of American Tobacco, George Washington Hill (the man responsible for Lucky
Strike ads), Vic encounters the ultimate corporate threat to his indepen-
dence. The conflict between the two men becomes the focus of the book:
a Theory X tyrant of the first water, Evans has long since transformed
everyone around him into hapless yes-men, and only Vic dares to defy
him. During meetings, Evans announces his assessment of campaigns and
the various radio shows he sponsors (his judgment is usually poor), shouts
"Check!," and everyone present echoes him, "like a whipcrack." No one
will stand up to him for a good idea or attempt to dissuade him from a
bad one. Even the agency president is reduced to calling home or office
every two hours, regardless of what he is doing, so that he may be ever-
available to receive his client's blustering wrath. The book's denouement
directly foreshadows the warnings of the management literature of the
1960s. When Evans finally breaks Vic's resistance, finally succeeds in im-
planting "the Fear" and in forcing him to shout "Right!" to his platitudes
about "Organization," Vic realizes he must leave advertising or surrender
his individuality.[2]

Troubled and inner-directed, Wakeman's hero carries all of the signifiers of the "creative genius" that would soon be a commonplace type
on Madison Avenue, although in 1946 the word "creative" had not yet
entered the business vocabulary. Victor Norman violates taboos; he invents slogans and campaigns spontaneously; and he is "mad," as one par-
amour calls him, prone to occasional bursts of enigmatic eccentricity.
There was no place for such a figure in the advertising world of the 1940s
and 1950s. On Madison Avenue, as in the popular sociology of the day,
the organization reigned triumphant; the creative nonconformist either
learned his (subordinate) place or failed. Real-life admen disliked The
Hucksters for obvious reasons: Wakeman's vision of big agency practices
was regarded, in the best of Cold War spirits, as a denunciation of advertising in general. They also derided the process by which Victor
Norman invents the "Love That Soap" campaign—sheer spontaneous
inspiration—as wildly unrealistic: all admen knew that advertising campaigns were careful, scientific programs, arising from years of research and
precedent and polling.[3] Twenty years later, though, the cynical, client-
defying, rule-breaking Victor Norman reappeared throughout New York

as a new generation of creative admen (recounting their antics in memoirs that read like much racier versions of *The Hucksters*) who conquered the industry and confronted the clients that had so humbled Wakeman's hero.

In Wakeman's eyes, the large agency system was dysfunctional, even dehumanizing. But the advertising literature of the fifties, like the books analyzed by William Whyte in *Organization Man*, cast the organization as a site of self-actualization, its challenges as a normal and even healthy aspect of daily life. Sloan Wilson's 1955 novel *The Man in the Gray Flannel Suit* is a quintessential text of Organization society, with its title and commuter settings quickly becoming synonyms for conformity. But for all the praise it has received, the book conspicuously lacks the critical perspective of *The Hucksters*. Its hero, PR man Tom Rath, seems rooted so firmly in suburbia that he can imagine no alternative to the corporation and the commute. Tom's co-workers at the United Broadcasting Corporation are annoying and sycophantic organization men, Tom's salary is insufficient, but there is certainly no *other* way for things to be done. Disgusted they may be, but Wilson's characters don't question and don't worry about what the Organization is doing to their souls; they muddle heroically through and are rewarded, in updated Alger style, for their perseverance. To be sure, there are some sticky patrimonial entanglements left over from the existentialist days of the war; but Tom quickly solves these with the help of an understanding lawyer. He and his family may have serious financial problems, but they will continue to live a happy suburban existence; better still, Tom will win the ear of a hard but just boss, get a raise, and inherit a large estate. Wilson's hero is fundamentally contented with the order of the 1950s: he and his wife solve their financial problems by becoming suburban developers and even Tom's job at U. B. C. is concerned with further delimiting the boundaries of normality—he writes speeches that help the company president to construct himself as a leader of the crusade against "mental illness." The novel actually concludes with Tom Rath quoting Browning approvingly: "God's in his heaven, all's right with the world."[4]

science, reason, order

In his authoritative 1994 history of American advertising, *Fables of Abundance*, Jackson Lears argues that the symbolism of advertising derives from two largely antithetical cultural poles: the riotous, irrational carnivalesque and the "managerial values" of "personal efficiency" and "pseu-doscientism." During the twentieth century, he notes, while an aesthetic of "bureaucratic rationality" was applied in ads to "the iconography of the body," the "managerial" side of the business, buttressed by the theories of Frederick Winslow Taylor and his followers and speaking always in the language of science, slowly subsumed the carnivalesque. But the carnivalesque was never fully extirpated, Lears points out: it "kept resurfacing in the workaday life of the agencies," especially in the frenzied doings of agency art directors and copywriters. Creativity, the mysterious processes by which the ads were actually made, always posed problems for the "managerial ideology," even amounting for some to "an antidote to smooth professionalism and an alternative to bureaucratic notions of expertise." By the time Lears takes his leave of Madison Avenue—in the 1950s—the battle lines were clearly drawn: the "Theory X" values of science, efficiency, and management were at their zenith, and those of creativity and carnival noticeably in eclipse.[5]

But by the end of that decade, the limitations of the Taylorist style of advertising had become apparent to most in the industry: the ads of the period lacked drama and meaning. Their idealized vision of consuming life had little to do with the actual experience of American consumers. They were trite, repetitive, and literally unbelievable. And during the 1960s they would be swept away along with the bureaucratic agency structures that had created them in a "creative revolution" that celebrated the mystical carnivalesque properties of creativity and that actually embraced the critique of mass society that the ads of the fifties had done so much to inspire. As in the menswear industry, the slow-moving and hierarchical organizations of Madison Avenue would yield to a more flexible new capitalism that imagined consuming not in terms of conformity and orderly progress but in those of the glorious chaos of hip.

In the fifties, the central principle of the advertising industry was "science": ads were to be created according to established and proven principles, after thorough research on public attitudes had been conducted. Advertising men were professionals, and the effectiveness of their works could be proven scientifically, with batteries of studies and laboratory tests. One of the most popular advertising books of the decade was *Scientific Advertising*, a tract that had been written by the famous Lord & Thomas copywriter Claude Hopkins in 1923 and reissued to great acclaim (and with an introduction by David Ogilvy) in the fifties. The book opens with this astounding statement of order and absolute business certainty:

chapter two

The time has come when advertising has in some hands reached the status of a science. It is based on fixed principles and is reasonably exact. The causes and effects have been analyzed until they are well understood. The correct methods of procedure have been proved and established. We know what is most effective, and we act on basic laws.[6]

Curiously, most of Hopkins's actual "methods of procedure"—his principles of mail order and psychology, his techniques for laying out print ads—were long obsolete in the decade of television and motivational research. It was his general biases that fired the imagination of Organization Man, his insistence on understanding advertising as an application of unchanging, scientifically verifiable principles, his caustic portrayal of the hapless romantic art director and whimsical copywriter. Another work that caught the temper of the times was the 1955 anthology edited by Edward L. Bernays, *The Engineering of Consent*. Like Hopkins's tract, it was a fantasy of order and public manipulation. In these modern times, public relations "activities are planned and executed by trained practitioners in accordance with scientific principles, based on the findings of social scientists," Bernays wrote in the book's introduction. "Their dispassionate approach and methods may be likened to those of the engineering professions which stem from the physical sciences."[7] Public relations and advertising were, like all other great works of civilization, merely an application of science to the problems of humanity.

Others found the implications of scientific advertising deeply alarming. Vance Packard's 1957 book, *The Hidden Persuaders*, ignited a national outrage over ad agencies's sinister use of scientific techniques. The first and one of the most thoughtful efforts to understand consumer society as a gigantic fraud, a conspiracy to manipulate the public and sell people items they did not need, *The Hidden Persuaders* followed the doings of a legion of "Co-operative scientists" who provided advertising with "awesome tools," scary-sounding strategies like "Motivational Research" with which they "are systematically feeling out our hidden weaknesses and frailties in the hope that they can more efficiently influence our behavior." The ultimate danger of advertising's dalliance with science, Packard hinted, was something considerably worse than the national spirit of conformity then being analyzed by writers like William Whyte and David Riesman: "The Packaged Soul."[8] Most irritating of all to Packard's democratic sensibilities, though, was the unbelievably high-handed treatment of the public that accompanied the advertising industry's scientism. Repeatedly quoting the marketers' and social scientists'

unbelievably candid expressions of contempt for the intelligence of the
masses, Packard drove home a deeply disturbing point: *They think we're dopes!*

Typically they see us as bundles of daydreams, misty hidden yearnings, guilt complexes, irrational emotional blockages. We are image lovers given to impulsive and compulsive acts. We annoy them with our seemingly senseless quirks, but we please them with our growing docility in responding to their manipulation of symbols that stir us to action. They have found the supporting evidence for this view persuasive enough to encourage them to turn to depth channels on a large scale in their efforts to influence our behavior.

It would be difficult to overstate the influence of Packard's book. A bestseller, the book inspired a still-thriving faith in high-tech advertising trickery and, more important, it crystallized future criticism of Madison Avenue around an understanding of the industry peculiar to the way it was organized in the 1950s. The problem with advertising, *The Hidden Persuaders* taught, was that it was overly manipulative, that it opposed and even subverted "man in his long struggle to become a rational and self-guiding being," that it sought to transform us into a nation of robot consumers like "Pavlov's conditioned dog" or laboratory animals with electrodes implanted in their brains. Today, of course, many of the wickedly subconscious campaigns which alarmed Packard sound innocent or comical (the Maidenform bra ads are particularly amusing), and the advertising of the fifties which he found so perfidious is recalled, if it's recalled at all, as the whimsy of an impossibly naive society. But the most curious consequence of the book's success was its impact on advertising itself: during the sixties, Madison Avenue itself would adopt a version of Packard's critique and cast products as solutions to the problems of mass society he had done so much to publicize.[9]

Even so, at the time of its publication, *The Hidden Persuaders* incited in the advertising industry only measured, reasonable-sounding defenses. The most important rebuttal to Packard was journalist Martin Mayer's 1958 book, *Madison Avenue, U.S.A.*, perhaps the classic statement of the ad world's postwar sense of scientifically sanctioned corporate normalcy. Here the advertising industry is a rational, smoothly functioning machine typified by the vast J. Walter Thompson company, then the nation's largest ad firm. Mayer takes pains to minimize the use of psychological techniques by admen, but otherwise the industry's infatuation with what it believes to be "science" is quite clear. Creativity, for example, with its implications of the intuitive, the nonrational, and the eccentric, had no place in Mayer's vision of advertising reason and is almost entirely ignored. Hopkins had criticized creative workers for their impracticality; Mayer points to them as a source of unfounded unrest, having "persuaded the public to share their concern about the alleged crassness and unscrupulousness of the advertising industry." In *Madison Avenue, U.S.A.*, logocentrism and Theory X reign supreme: art directors are universally subordinate to copywriters in the advertising world, Mayer notes, and in very few cases are either allowed to meet directly with a client.[10]

In the place of creativity, which would obsess advertising writers of the 1960s and after, Mayer emphasizes process: the organization of agencies, the execution of a given idea, media placement, and, above all, research—the collection of statistics, polling, studies to determine how well certain appeals have worked. Rules guide each step. The head of J. Walter Thompson, Mayer notes, is producing "a series of monographs, thirty-four in all, submitting the techniques of the trade to rigorous logical analysis." The Kenyon & Eckhardt agency "has a thick book of such prescriptions for advertisements (known inside the office as 'the Bible'), and ads will not even go out for testing if they break K & E's established rules."[11] Mayer also details the habits of admen themselves elaborately, which are remarkable both for the way they bear out the "gray-flannel" stereotype and for their divergence from later patterns. Admen, Mayer informs the reader, are a group about which it is safe to generalize. They ordinarily work extremely hard, live in Westchester suburbs, and commute to Grand Central, which is a short walk from their offices on Madison Avenue. They do indeed drink martinis, especially during client lunches at "21." And, although they no longer wear gray flannel now that that fabric has developed an unflattering reputation, "the advertising man's habitual avoidance of clothing that might seem flamboyant denies him the role of a leader of fashion." This judgment in particular would be wildly incorrect only ten years later. But in *Madison Avenue, U.S.A.* there are no suggestions of the kind of panic or intimidation or skullduggery which Wakeman suggested were commonplace in the industry, nor are there any hints of the chaos that would reign supreme in just a few years.[12] *Madison Avenue, U.S.A.*, as elsewhere in the American 1950s, was a place of order, stability, and reason; a necessary and normal component of the civilization of consensus.

Mayer's attention to the J. Walter Thompson Company indicates the esteem with which that largest of agencies was held in the period before the Creative Revolution. And if its operations were typical of the Orga-

nization age, so were its attitudes toward the creative individual and his 43
role in the making of advertising. In 1947, *Fortune* magazine printed a
study of J. Walter Thompson that was apparently one of the first in the
popular press to discuss the creation of ads. The article's chief point of
emphasis was the priority of corporate procedure and scientific study over
individual creativity at Thompson. Company president Stanley Resor, it
maintained,

> has an abiding mistrust of the word "brilliant" or of any individual or process that
> can be so described. So Thompson men are not approvedly brilliant. Thompson
> copy does not consciously sparkle. Neither Thompson layouts nor the artwork that
> goes into them draw low whistles of admiration from competitive connoisseurs. . . .
> Thompson wants to sell its clients' products, not make splashes with individual ads.

The key word for this company's operations, *Fortune* noted, was "thor-
oughness," the compiling of study upon study, the diligent sifting of data,
the "market research" and "field interviews" and "Product Research studies" Thompson was always undertaking. "We think *endlessly* about the
total problems of our clients," one Thompson employee said. "We think
so damn long and so damn hard that the final business of writing the copy
and making the layout becomes, in one sense, almost subsidiary."[13]

If J. Walter Thompson is the corporate symbol for the advertising
paradigm of the 1940s and 1950s, Rosser Reeves, chairman of the Ted
Bates agency, was its greatest theorist and archetypal practitioner. He directed the first-ever television ads for a presidential candidate (those for
Eisenhower in 1952), he wrote the most widely read advertising treatise
of the era, and he was the individual most responsible for the stereotypical advertising style of the day, the so-called hard sell, whose "main idea,"
as David Halberstam has put it, "was to hit people over the head with the
product as bluntly as possible."[14] Reeves's 1960 statement of principles,
Reality in Advertising, is a remarkable mixture of pseudoscience and barely
concealed contempt for public intelligence. The Ted Bates Company,
Reeves announces, had discovered a "scientific" means of quantifying the
effectiveness of a given advertising campaign and had happened upon the
fundamental formula for concocting a successful sales message. The secret, according to Reeves, was not "deep Freudian techniques" but good
old repetition, continuity (never abandoning a successful campaign), and
adherence to a single simple message that the viewer could easily absorb.
In a revealing metaphor, Reeves asserted that there was "no more room
in the box" of the public mind. Competition between adversaries was

fierce for consumers' attention, and any success for one brand necessarily meant decline for its competitors. Once an advertiser had penetrated that "box," there was only one reliable method of convincing the consumer to buy: offer him or her a "unique selling proposition" (USP), a quality by which the product in question was demonstrably different from all others. In many cases, of course, competing brands were so similar that this demonstrable difference had to be a feature common to all, but which none had bothered to claim.[15] As an example, Reeves directed Martin Mayer to one of his company's favorite inventions, the claim of Colgate toothpaste that it

"cleans your breath while it cleans your teeth." Now, every dentifrice cleans your breath while it cleans your teeth—but *nobody had ever put a breath claim on a toothpaste before*. That USP is eighteen years old now. Using it, Colgate has had as much as fifty per cent of the whole toothpaste market.[16]

These methods, Reeves insists, represent the first application of rational experimentation and observation to advertising. The Ted Bates Company, he proudly notes, has devised a "Copy Lab," which essays various approaches with a group of typical consumers and produces clean, bar-graph illustrations of exactly how effectively each sales text has communicated. Charts showing how well various ads are remembered, which USP's delivered what percentage of sales, and what percentage of the public remember a given ad are scattered throughout *Reality in Advertising*.

Reeves's rules made for assertive, insistent advertisements that, like Reeves's theories, tended to refer to the sanction of "science." Years later, *Advertising Age* summarized the cliche-heavy Reeves style by recalling

ads for such accounts as Anacin ("Fast! Fast! Fast relief!); Palmolive soap ("You can have a lovelier complexion in 14 days with Palmolive soap, doctors prove!"); and Viceroy cigarettes ("Only Viceroy gives you 20,000 filter traps in every filter tip to filter—filter—filter your smoke while the rich—rich flavor comes through.")

Bates ads often referred to laboratory studies and doctors' endorsements as a way of establishing a USP.[17] Bates television commercials from the 1950s occasionally used graphs with no notation along the X or Y axes; forceful demonstrations like the notorious animated hammer inside a head for Anacin; and profusions of scientific-sounding product advantages: the "five extra laundratives" found in Fab detergent; Preparation

H's "biodyne, the wonder substance"; Colgate toothpaste's "Gardol," which promised to clean the consumer in three distinct ways; the "Seven-way stretch" of Playtex girdles; and, of course, Wonder Bread, which "helps build strong bodies twelve ways." One Bates commercial for Colgate Rapid Shave must constitute some kind of high watermark of Lears's "managerial values": a man is shown shaving in the desert, duly monitored by an assortment of official-looking men in lab coats, apparently measuring the product's effectiveness in this most arid and noncarnivalesque environment. Reeves's admaking theory remained unchanged into the mid-1960s. He told *Advertising Age* in 1965 that a copywriter must "subordinate his own creative impulses to this overall objective: Does this advertisement move an idea from the inside of my head to the inside of the public's head? The most people at the lowest possible cost."[18]

Commercials produced according to the Reeves system all seem to combine a reverence for learning with an assumption that viewers know nothing about the content of that learning. Reeves's book heaped scorn on the assertions of Vance Packard, but largely because Packard had mistaken the species of science to which advertising was beholden (Reeves wanted "duplicable" results from his science, not psychological speculation): Otherwise, Reeves might well have been a model for Packard's manipulative adman who regards his audience as laboratory animals. Reeves's repetitive, attacking style clearly assumed a hypothetical consumer who was little better than a fool. Martin Mayer's book even has Reeves repeating a favorite anecdote in which the attention of a stubborn mule is drawn with a blow on the head from a sledgehammer.[19]

David Ogilvy was a close runner-up to Rosser Reeves as the decade's leading proponent of managerial rationality in advertising. Reeves was a copywriter, but Ogilvy entered the business after working on polling at the Gallup Company, giving him an aura of scientific expertise to which he refers frequently in his various memoirs and articles. His visual and symbolic style also was very different from Reeves's. The campaigns his firm, Ogilvy & Mather, devised in the 1950s for Hathaway shirts and Schweppes soda are textbook examples of the power of brand-image advertising, and they swept him and his fledgling agency to rapid prominence. But despite the creative talent that was required to invent as peculiar an icon as the eyepatch-wearing Hathaway man, the advertising theories Ogilvy proposed were even more constricting and invasive than those of his competitors at Ted Bates. The title of every chapter of Ogilvy's 1963 *Confessions of an Advertising Man* begins with the words

"How To . . . ," and each is packed with long lists of guidelines for every step of the advertising process. It is in fact a book of rules, including: a "list of thirty-nine rules for making good layouts"; "ten criteria" for new accounts; and "eleven commandments which you must obey if you work at my agency." Ogilvy's lists sometimes descend into astonishing detail, from the ten hints for writing headlines and nine for writing body copy in chapter 6, to the fourteen more on how to arrange the words on the page that he offers in chapter 7.[20]

Nor were these mere bits of friendly advice. In one 1959 art director's publication, Ogilvy actually judged advertisements by his minute standards, deducting points from the works submitted for each infringement of a list of twenty criteria and concluding that the ads praised by other art directors were in fact substandard. Among his criteria were these:

> If the layout looks more like an advertisement than an editorial page, deduct 7 points. . . .
> If a drawing is used instead of a photograph, deduct 6 points. . . .
> If the body copy is set in reverse, or on a tint, deduct 4 points. . . .
> If the illustration is defaced in any way, e.g., by having the headline run into it, deduct 2 points. . . .
> If the body copy is set in a sans serif face, deduct 2 points.[21]

Thanks to such rules, Ogilvy's own ads from that era are easily recognizable: a large but simple photograph on the upper two-thirds of the page, a headline beneath, and three columns of sedate (serif) type on white below, absolutely packed with facts.[22]

Ogilvy explained his passion for rule-making and his abhorrence of disorder by asserting, like Rosser Reeves, that the mysteries of advertising success had been penetrated by science. The artistic talents of creative workers was nice when kept in its place, but Ogilvy had been trained as a pollster, and he referred frequently to his knowledge of statistics to buttress his opinions. When judging the 1959 advertising layouts, for example, he notes that his fellow jurors were "art directors, equipped to judge the *esthetics* of advertisements—from a subjective point of view." But Ogilvy himself was a man of science. And while his rigid requirements for ad illustrations and layout may have been antithetical to the teachings of art schools, he argued—as had both Reeves and Claude Hopkins—that their frivolous ways had no place in the deadly-serious business of advertising:

Most of the art schools which train unsuspecting students for careers in advertising still subscribe to the mystique of the Bauhaus. They hold that the success of an advertisement depends on such things as "balance," "movement," and "design." But can they *prove* it?

My research suggests that these aesthetic intangibles do not increase sales, and I cannot conceal my hostility to the old school of art directors who take such preachments seriously.[23]

The copywriters and art directors who so irritated David Ogilvy were often considered problem employees on Madison Avenue in the 1950s. Attuned to the old advertising carnivalesque, the irrational talents of the creatives naturally conflicted with the managerial orderliness of the day. As Jackson Lears points out, the battle between the two visions extended back to the beginnings of the profession. But in the 1950s and the 1960s, when the creatives would momentarily gain the upper hand, the conflict was intense. Ogilvy complained about "art-directoritis, the disease which reduces advertising campaigns to impotence."[24] Rosser Reeves was even more unyielding in his efforts to press down upon the fancy of the artistically inclined the rationality of the marketplace. "No longer can the copywriter, like Tennyson's Lady of Shalott, view life through his own magic mirror," Reeves insisted. "He must make his imagination function under the strict discipline of attaining a commercial goal."[25] Both men denounced the annual contests in which art directors and copywriters chose their favorite ads.[26] The only place for artists on Madison Avenue in the 1950s, they felt, was under the responsible direction of a scientific manager of the Theory X persuasion.

"nonconformists, dissenters, and rebels"

To flip through any copy of *Life* or *Look* from the fifties, though, is to understand almost instantly that the ads produced by the industry that Reeves and Ogilvy dominated were perhaps the worst, given their social and cultural context, that Madison Avenue has ever created. To this day, nothing more effectively summons the ills of the technocratic and overorganized society better than the advertising it produced during the 1950s. Here one will look in vain for anything that deviates even slightly from the Cold War orthodoxy of prosperity, progress, and consumer satisfaction. From its radiant tots, rosy-cheeked and grasping for frozen dinners, to its jolly workers, visibly joyous over the technological advances that their benevolent boss has made possible, the advertising of the period was fatuous in the extreme and transparently so to much of the audience it aimed to persuade. The accuracy of Michael Schudson's famous comparison of advertising to Soviet socialist realism is driven home forcefully by 1950s advertisers' frequent use of Cold War terminology and descriptions borrowed from the jet-age military: here a car is posed next to a fighter plane; there a chemical company uses renderings of military hardware to solicit public goodwill.[27] Never has advertising been so unwilling to acknowledge the myriad petty frustrations, the anger, the fear that make up so much of daily existence, consuming and otherwise. Never has it insisted so dogmatically on such an abstractly glowing vision of American life. And never has it been so vulnerable to mockery.

In no industry was the 1950s critique of mass society and its business corollary, the dead-end of Taylorism, more applicable than in advertising. "Organization Men" staffed the orderly offices of the great agencies, and in an industry that once redounded with colorful personalities, there seemed to be little place for individualists or dissenters. Standard 1950s images—of commuters in fedoras crowding suburban platforms, ranks of conservatively dressed executives entering office buildings through revolving doors—all seemed particularly descriptive of the men who worked in advertising. John Furr of J. Walter Thompson's Chicago office recalls the postwar "management era" in familiar terms:

The management of the office were all in their late fifties, maybe early sixties. It did not look, smell, or feel like an advertising agency. It was like a country club. And all the management went home at 4:30 in the afternoon, they all lived in Lake Forest, most of them had divorced their first wives and married their secretaries, and they drank on the bar car.[28]

If capitalism as a whole was slowed by the initiative- and individual-suppressing climate of managerial rationality, the advertising business, where imaginative thinking had traditionally been even more critical than elsewhere, was particularly affected.

For William H. Whyte, Jr., later the author of *The Organization Man*, the advertising industry's problems—in particular its fondness for cliche and its reliance upon formulaic and unpersuasive speech—were direct results of the overorganizational malaise afflicting the rest of the business world. Two things in particular, Whyte argued in a 1952 article in *For-*

tune, were responsible for making advertising so bad: the idea of "the Mass Audience," a "great anonymous dope" to whom cliches were believed to appeal; and the familiar problem of "groupthought." Advertising agencies, like so many other large enterprises, Whyte argued, had become places in which layer upon layer of bureaucracy and the preservation of "group harmony" effectively stifled the business of communicating convincingly. "It's not that we don't know better," one copywriter told him.

We do. But when the chips are down, if we're the layout man or the copywriter, we don't dream of going by our own convictions. What we're after is an ad that will appeal to all the top people. It's a sort of guessing game—and you win by playing the right clichés. You write for other advertising people, not the public. You write ads that look like ads.

Although he strongly hinted that, in their rush to deliver safe and nondisruptive copy, advertising agencies were not serving their clients well, Whyte concluded on a hopeful note. The continuing triumph of "groupthought," he asserted, will ultimately open such an enormous and profitable opportunity to those willing to be truly creative that, according to the logic of the market, some agency must come forward that is willing to defy them all. "Thanks to the language of advertising, the potential shock value of ordinary English usage has probably never been greater," he wrote. "Manufacturers who will use it will have an advertising dollar of more heft, those who compose the ads infinitely more satisfaction from the task; the consumers will find ads they will read; and last but not least, MORE goods will be sold!"[29] Whyte was describing, nearly ten years in advance, the creative revolution that would turn the placid world of Madison Avenue, U.S.A., on its ear.

The primary cultural function of advertising is, as *Fortune* magazine put it in 1947, "the creation of new and daring, but fulfillable, consumer demands; demands that would not occur if advertising did not deliberately incite them."[30] But for all of its studies and surveys, its rules and white lab coats, the advertising of the 1950s was ill-attuned to the carnivalesque spirit that undergirds American consumerism. Order and stability also meant stagnation and stasis, the direct opposites of the "new and daring" that have long animated American affluence. Rosser Reeves, the great champion of research, even carried the decade's hostility to the unreason of aesthetics so far that he denounced "difference" itself.[31] Over the next decade, advertising would abandon its self-imposed restrictions and leap headlong into rebellion; transform itself from a showplace of managerial certainty to an ongoing corporate celebration of carnival-esque difference.

Strangely enough, David Ogilvy was one of the first to recognize what was wrong with the science-bound advertising world of the 1950s. "The creative process requires more than reason," he noted.

> Most original thinking isn't even verbal. It requires "a groping experimentation with ideas, governed by intuitive hunches and inspired by the unconscious." The major-ity of business men are incapable of original thinking, because they are unable to escape from the tyranny of reason. Their imaginations are blocked.

Clearly the hyper-rational management theory descended from Taylor-ism had served the advertising business poorly. "The sad truth is that despite the sophisticated apparatus of the modern agency, advertising isn't getting the results it used to get in the crude days of Lasker and Hopkins," Ogilvy wrote. "Our business needs massive transfusions of *talent*. And talent, I believe, is most likely to be found among nonconformists, dis-senters, and rebels." [32]

chapter three

ADVERTISING AS

CULTURAL CRITICISM:

BILL BERNBACH VERSUS

THE MASS SOCIETY

tripping from theatre to theatre
living in volkswagen buses
tortured by self doubt
tormented by anxiety
fleeing in exile from the supermarkets the mortuaries and their
  factories with seventy high rising smokestacks their bugles
  their suffocations their immolations of souls who arrive in
  parking lot turn the key slam the door and surrender hope
  all who enter here

—JULIAN BECK, 1979

Looking back across forty years, the hyper-rational, science-dazzled Madison Avenue of the 1950s, with its ponderous bureaucracy and its armies of suburban commuters, seems to have been more a bizarre aberration than the advanced and enlightened place of wise consensus its apologists believed it to be. Admen today, although historical judgment is hardly their forte, look back at the rule-bound preachments of Reeves and Ogilvy with a kind of horror: if they study those pronouncements at all, it is to remind them of what they must *never* do. In other eras, the values and symbols of the industry have usually been the reverse of what they were during the 1940s and 1950s; the business's heroes a series of brazen rule-breakers in touch with the anarchic power of the carnivalesque, its villains the dead-weight yes-men. Tales of workplace madness have been particularly prominent in industry lore in recent years: a full-page newspaper ad placed in 1995 by the employees of the ultracreative Chiat/Day agency remembers Jay Chiat as a man who would "cut off a client's tie if he thinks it's ugly" and who "taught us to squash conventionality like ripe fruit"; Randall Rothenberg's 1995 account of ultracreative Wieden & Kennedy, makers of Nike advertising, details their office basketball playing, their officially sanctioned eccentricity, and at one point has agency principle Dan Wieden instructing his employees that the agency works like "a slime mold. . . . we don't do things with what appears to be order."[1] Raymond Rubicam, founder of Young & Rubicam, obtained his first job in advertising by exploding angrily at a rude, pompous boss. The manic 1930s adman J. Sterling Getchell was notorious for his accelerated pace of living, his reckless personal behavior, and his defiance of clients. He mistrusted "science" and, according to one employee, "composure was against the rule" at his agency.[2] Admen have long served symbolically as über-entrepreneurs, eulogists of capitalism's endless cycles of change, its celebration of success, its scorn for failure. Their industry, as nearly every account of it not written during the 1950s agrees, tends to celebrate difference and encourage discontent, not to squelch them.[3] After all, the slogan of Young & Rubicam has always been "Resist the Usual."

But during the 1950s, advertising was marked by what Jackson Lears calls "containment of carnival," a powerful effort to suppress the industry's impulse toward difference under a stifling vision of managerial order. In the 1960s, this vision was turned on its head. Advertising narratives suddenly idealized not the repressed account man in gray flannel, but the manic, unrestrained creative person in offbeat clothing. The world of advertising was no longer bureaucratic and placid with scientism; but artistic and dysfunctional, a place of wild passions, broken careers, fear, drunkenness, and occasional violence.

The ads produced by the anarchic figures who led what came to be called the "creative revolution" broke decisively with the stilted, idealized, cliche-ridden style of the 1950s. A clean minimalism replaced complex layouts cluttered with different product claims. Humor, wit, and stylistic elegance returned from the advertising oblivion to which they had been exiled by deadly-serious USP scientism. But the ads of the creative revolution not only differed from those of the gray flannel past: they were openly at war with their predecessors. What distinguished the advertising of the 1960s was its acknowledgment of and even sympathy with the mass society critique. It mocked the empty phrases and meaningless neologisms that characterized the style of the 1950s. It deftly punctured advertising's too-rosy picture of American life and openly admitted that consuming was not the wonder-world it was cracked up to be. It sympathized with people's fears about conformity and their revulsion from artificiality and packaged pleasure. It pandered to public distrust of advertising and dislike of admen. Comparing one brand to another and finding it lacking was and is a routine advertising technique; in the sixties, advertising actively compared a new, hip consumerism to an older capitalist ideology and left the latter permanently discredited.

It is a curious quirk of sixties historiography that, when running through the list of seismic shifts (in music, literature, movies, youth cul-

ture) that gave the decade its character, annalists never include advertising. And yet, given advertising's immense presence in American public
space, the big change in the attitude and language of advertising must be
counted as one of the primary features distinguishing the cultural climate
of the sixties from that of the fifties. Read as a whole, the best advertising
of the sixties constitutes a kind of mass-culture critique in its own right,
a statement of alienation and disgust, of longing for authenticity and for
selfhood that ranks with books like *Growing Up Absurd* and movies like
The Graduate. The difference between the advertising critique and the
others, though, is the crucial point: for the new Madison Avenue, the
solution to the problems of consumer society was—more consuming.

how to do it different

The towering figure of the advertising world of the 1960s—and a man of
immense cultural significance generally—was Bill Bernbach, the guiding
spirit of the Doyle Dane Bernbach agency (DDB). DDB altered the look,
language, and tone of American advertising with its long-running campaign for Volkswagen and dozens of other brands; it altered the managerial style of Madison Avenue when its competitors, stunned by the power
of DDB's ads, rushed to replicate its less ordered corporate structure and
its roster of creative talent. Advertising writer Larry Dobrow does not
exaggerate when he insists that "among advertising professionals then
and now, there is unanimous—often reverent—belief that the Doyle
Dane Bernbach agency was the unchallenged leader of the creative revolution of the sixties."[4] Nor does Randall Rothenberg when, discussing the
agency's landmark campaign for Volkswagen, he writes simply that it
"changed the culture of advertising."[5] Bernbach was at once a hard-
headed adman and one of postwar consumerism's most trenchant critics,
Madison Avenue's answer to Vance Packard. The ads his agency produced had an uncanny ability to cut through the overblown advertising
rhetoric of the 1950s, to speak to readers' and viewers' skepticism of advertising, to replace obvious puffery with what appeared to be straight
talk. Bernbach was the first adman to embrace the mass society critique,
to appeal directly to the powerful but unmentionable public fears of
conformity, of manipulation, of fraud, and of powerlessness, and to sell
products by so doing. He invented what we might call anti-advertising: a
style which harnessed public mistrust of consumerism—perhaps the most
powerful cultural tendency of the age—to consumerism itself.

Doyle Dane Bernbach, the agency which he founded in the decidedly unrevolutionary year of 1949, was dedicated to what proved to be a unique but sound advertising principle. As the industry's preeminent leaders and theorists were amassing mountains of research and formulating scientific rules for effective advertising, Bernbach was declaring that rules were to be scrupulously ignored. The advertising business was fundamentally a matter of creating convincing advertisements, he believed, and no amount of formulas could replace the talented creative individual who performed this function. Bernbach's impulses ran in direct contradiction to the larger trends of the fifties. While writers from Norman Mailer to Theodore Roszak assumed (as many still assume) that the business "establishment" required a rigid, repressive system of order, Bernbach's philosophy of advertising, which would reign triumphant in the 1960s amid a seemingly endless series of successful and celebrated DDB campaigns, was exactly the opposite—a hostility to rules of any kind; a sort of commercial antinomianism.[6]

Bill Bernbach was an enemy of technocracy long before the counterculture raised its own voice in protest of conformity and the Organization Man. In 1947, he wrote a letter to the owners of the Grey agency, where he was then employed, which spelled out his opposition to the features of business organization that the mass society theorists would soon identify and attack. "I'm worried that we're going to fall into the trap of bigness," he wrote, "that we're going to worship techniques instead of substance. . . ." The crucial problem, Bernbach insisted, was the dominance of rules and science, the priority of statistics and routines, the methods that would soon be heralded by Reeves and others as the hallmarks of an era of certainty.

There are a lot of great technicians in advertising. And unfortunately they talk the best game. They know all the rules. They can tell you that [pictures of] people in an ad will get you greater readership. They can tell you that a sentence should be this short or that long. They can tell you that body copy should be broken up for easier and more inviting reading. They can give you fact after fact after fact. They are the scientists of advertising. But there's one little rub. Advertising is fundamentally persuasion and persuasion happens to be not a science, but an art.[7]

Bernbach was an ideologue of disorder, an untiring propagandist for the business value of the principles of modern art. He repeated his mantra in a variety of forms for years: advertising was an art; art could not be produced by a rigid scientific system. A booklet of his memorable sayings compiled by DDB begins with this aphorism: "Rules are what the artist breaks; the memorable never emerged from a formula." "Imitation can be commercial suicide," runs another. "Research inevitably leads to conformity," he announced in 1967. "For creative people rules can be prisons," he said elsewhere.[8] Not only were rules deleterious to the creation of good advertising, but the very idea of established techniques had to be resisted. "Even among the scientists, men who are regarded as worshippers of facts," he wrote in a pamphlet called "Facts Are Not Enough," intuition is critical to discovery: "the real giants have always been poets, men who jumped from facts into the realm of imagination and ideas."[9] Sometimes Bernbach's hostility to rules even took on a Consciousness III sort of aversion to reason generally. "Logic and overanalysis can immobilize and sterilize an idea," he said. "It's like love—the more you analyze it the faster it disappears."[10]

In his 1957 account of *Madison Avenue, U.S.A.*, Martin Mayer treats DDB as a peculiar anomaly among the large agencies he studies since it "deliberately rejects most of the tenets of modern agency operation," including research along with rules.[11] Instead, Bernbach maximized the freedom of creative workers and eliminated much of the hierarchy and bureaucracy that was customary at large agencies in the 1950s, aiming several years before the publication of Douglas McGregor's book on Theory X and Theory Y to create a less inhibited environment where creative inspiration could be translated more directly into finished advertising. Pointing out in a 1969 interview that excessive supervision was "part and parcel of the big agency curse," DDB copywriter Bob Levenson noted that the agency "isn't highly disciplined, supervised, committed, raked over, mulled over."[12] Bernbach's second great organizational innovation was to rationalize the creative operation. Artist and writer would work together on a project rather than somewhere down a chain from top executives. DDB represented a shift in management style that would have vast consequences for the way ads were made, for the way ads appeared, and, ultimately, for the way American capitalism understood itself: Theory X hierarchy came to an end here, and Theory Y management arrived with great financial success.[13] So great was the contrast between the organizational style of corporate agencies and that of DDB that, in her early days at the agency, star copywriter Phyllis Robinson told a Japanese publication that "we just felt very free, as if we had broken our shackles, had gotten out of jail, and were free to work the way we wanted to work."[14] In 1968, Robinson recalled how DDB's less hierarchical organization proceeded to revolutionize the industry:

In the early days of DDB, everybody on the outside was very hot to know how it was on the inside. How did we do it? So we told them. Bill told them. And told them. And told them.

So then they knew. And what happened? Whole agencies introduced their copywriters to their art directors. They'd never met before. The way I understand it, the writers used to put the copy in those pneumatic tubes they used to use in department stores, and it would scoot over to the art director to be "laid out." So—the agencies introduced them, and left them Alone Together. And they gave them Freedom. They said, make, do, create! Break rules! And you know what? A lot of very fine stuff started to come out. Some not so fine. But a lot that was.[15]

For Bernbach's anti-organization to work, though, he had to dramatically alter the traditional relationship between agency and clients in order to convince those who paid for advertising that, even though art had dethroned science in the offices of DDB, his assortment of scribblers was every bit as expert as the "scientists" of Rosser Reeves, and their opinions must be respected. Admen—even of the creative sort—were advertising specialists, he argued. DDB would produce no campaigns like Wakeman's repetitive "Love That Soap" because it refused to accede to clients' tastes, however strong-willed they were. As Bernbach told Martin Mayer, "I feel that if the agency makes an ad and the client doesn't like it, the client ought to run it anyway." "Factual error and a violation of corporate policy are the only reasons we'll accept for correction," added DDB account executive Joe Daly.[16] Charlie Moss, who began his advertising career at DDB before moving on to Wells, Rich, Greene, one of the era's "hottest" and most successful creative agencies (he ultimately became WRG's president), tells this story about the seriousness of Bernbach's attitude toward a client:

Doyle Dane had a major client, a big advertiser. They had been used to having their own way of advertising for years and years, very specialized product category. They had a brand from this client, and they had been trying to come up with a campaign the client would accept for months and months and months, and they kept getting rejected. Every time they'd go to the client, marketing people, advertising people, they'd say, "no, we don't like that, we want to do it this way, and this and that." And Doyle Dane, the people were outraged, because this was not the normal for Doyle Dane, they were normally used to getting their way. So they went to Bill Bernbach, and they said, "Look, you've got to come to this next meeting, we're going to have it with the chairman of the client company, . . . you've got to convince the chairman to tell his people to let us have our way, we know what we're doing." So . . . they all went, they're sitting across the table in this big board room. Bernbach says to this guy, "you know, we're working with your people for six months now, we can't get anything through, you have to tell them that we are advertising experts, we know what we're doing, and we demand some respect in this area." And the chairman says to Bernbach, "Well, I'm sorry, Mr. Bernbach, but we've been selling our products for years and years and years, and we've been extremely successful as you know, we think we know something about how to market them. And I'm sorry, but our people will have to have final say over what the advertising's going to be." At which point Bernbach, who was prepared for this, turned to him and said, "well, then in that case, Doyle Dane Bernbach will have to resign your business." And the chairman of the client company looked at his marketing director and said, "Are they allowed to do that?" [17]

Even as it was overturning the pseudo-science of Reeves and Ogilvy in favor of the intangibles of aesthetic inspiration, the Creative Revolution greatly advanced those men's efforts to professionalize advertising. In Wakeman's day, admen had been glorified "hucksters," cringing yes-men without independent will or access to any knowledge at all that might contradict the client's authority, but in the age of Bernbach they were to be creative geniuses, in touch with a spirit of commerce that resided beyond the mundane world of hierarchy and order. The limitations Bernbach placed on his clients' authority also led directly to the rapidly escalating willingness to violate the conventions of commercial speech that characterized his agency's—and the coming decade's—advertising. A number of DDB's most famous campaigns, like the Volkswagen ads that played on the car's ugliness and the Avis ads that proclaimed "We're Number Two," were extremely distasteful to clients and would surely have been nixed had they not already agreed to defer to the agency's decision.[18] Charlie Moss believes that "because it operated that way," DDB vastly increased the latitude within which creative people could operate.

For those talented people, it really gave them the strength of their convictions. It said, "Hey, look, if I really believe this, if I really think this is going to work for that client, I can push it, really, to the point of almost resigning the business." And what happened was, there were big ideas that would have normally been thrown right out, which prevailed. The Avis campaign was a very good example. It tested terribly, they hated the idea when they first saw it. Everything would have dictated these days that campaign would have been history.[19]

The reign of "groupthink" began to end, at least in the advertising industry, in the early 1960s. Freed to do what the agency thought best, DDB's creative teams would proceed to smash the advertising conventions built up throughout the age of organization.

alienated by the conformity and hypocrisy of mass society? have we got a car for you!

Bernbach's innovations in agency organization contradicted the prevailing management theories of the 1950s. But if his management style seems to have been designed to avoid the quagmire of "groupthought" and bureaucracy, his approach to advertising itself took mass society on directly, discarding the visual and verbal cliches of Madison Avenue, U.S.A., and saying the unsayable: consumerism has given us a civilization of plastic and conformity, of deceit and shoddiness. Bernbach's style wasn't so much promotion as it was cultural criticism, foreshadowing the postmodern meta-advertising of the 1990s discussed by Randall Rothenberg and James B. Twitchell.[20] And while DDB's less-hierarchical structure was copied in office towers across Manhattan, its characteristic advertising style was, by the end of the decade, pervasive across the sponsored surfaces of American public space.

The advertising that DDB began making for Volkswagen in 1959 is one of the most analyzed, discussed, and admired campaigns in the industry's history, studied in introductory marketing classes and included in advertising retrospectives of all kinds. Not only did it excite critics and incite commentary from every branch of the media, but it is widely believed to have made Volkswagen a competitive brand in America. The campaign's power derived from its blatant transgression of nearly every convention of auto advertising. And its success validated overnight the Bernbach creative philosophy, set a thousand corporations off in search of similar ads for themselves, and precipitated a revolution in ad-making. Within a few years, it had become a revered classic for an age at war with reverence and classicism. Randall Rothenberg enumerates the varieties of transgression that the campaign would unleash:

It changed the rules. Agencies were now no longer punished but *rewarded* for arguing with clients, for breaking the guidelines of art direction, for clowning around in the copy, for using ethnic locutions and academic references and a myriad of other once-forbidden formulae. Seemingly overnight, a great wave of originality engulfed the advertising profession, transforming agencies and agency-client relationships and, in turn, the impressions made on millions of Americans.[21]

chapter three

The history of consumer society is largely the history of the automobile, of the prosperity it brought to blue-collar workers, of the mobility and sexual freedom it permitted, and of the myriad consumer fantasies with which it was associated in the years after World War II. In the 1950s, the advertising of the three big Detroit automakers (which are always among the ten largest advertisers in the country) was the stuff of technocratic fantasy. Cars were designed and advertised to resemble the exciting hardware of the Cold War: streamlined, finned like airplanes, fitted with elaborate-looking controls, decorated with flashing chrome and abstract representations of rockets or airplanes. In ads, cars were posed next to jet fighters and radar dishes; Buick put holes in the side of its hoods to resemble airplane exhausts and named one model "B-58"; Oldsmobile offered "rocket action," built both an "F-85" and a "Starfire" (the actual name for the Air Force F-94); a 1958 Dodge advertisement invited readers to "take off" in a new model and declared that "the new Swept-Wing look for '59 is set off by thrusting Jet-Trail Tail Lamps."[22] Cars were markers of managerial efficiency in the worst Organization Man way. While the 1958 Edsel merely "says you're going places," ads for the 1961 Buick marked a pinnacle of other-directed boorishness:

What a wonderful sense of well-being just being *seen* behind its wheel. No showing off. Just that Clean Look of Action which unmistakably tells your success.[23]

Auto advertising of the 1950s redounded with empty phrases and meaningless neologisms, announcing cars with "radical new Turbo-Thrust" engines, "Quadra-Power Roadability," and "Finger-tip TorqueFlite."[24] The cars so trumpeted were always populated with idealized white nuclear families, manly husbands, fawning wives, and playful children. In television commercials, cars were objects of worship mounted on rotating platforms and, in one famous 1963 Chevrolet commercial, perched atop an insurmountable mesa and photographed from an orbiting airplane.[25] And every year cars' designs would change, the new models trumpeted in advertising ("All new all over again!" exclaimed those for the 1959 Chevrolet[26]) as the epitome of modernity, the old models and all their fine adjectives forgotten and discarded as surely as the cars themselves would be by the time they traveled 100,000 miles.

And each of these aspects of the car culture was, by the early 1960s, a point of considerable popular annoyance and even disaffection. Cars and their advertising, which brought together so many objectionable features of the era, were the aspect of the mass society most vulnerable

chapter three

to criticism, pounded with particular effectiveness in popular books by Vance Packard, John Kenneth Galbraith, and John Keats (*The Insolent Chariots*). Americans learned that the big three automakers changed styles every year in order to intentionally obsolete their earlier products and that their cars were designed to break down and fall apart after a certain amount of time. The car culture—and perhaps consumer culture in general—was a gigantic fraud. In his 1964 book *One Dimensional Man*, Herbert Marcuse describes the conflicted thinking of American car buyers of those years:

I ride in a new automobile. I experience its beauty, shininess, power, convenience— but then I become aware of the fact that in a relatively short time it will deteriorate and need repair; that its beauty and surface are cheap, its power unnecessary, its size idiotic; and that I will not find a parking place. I come to think of my car as a product of one of the Big Three automobile corporations. The latter determine the appearance of my car and make its beauty as well as its cheapness, its power as well as its shakiness, its working as well as its obsolescence. In a way, I feel cheated. I believe that the car is not what it could be, that better cars could be made for less money. But the other guy has to live, too. Wages and taxes are too high; turnover is necessary; we have it much better than before. The tension between appearance and reality melts away and both merge in one rather pleasant feeling.[27]

With the exception of the final three sentences, Marcuse might well have been writing copy for a Volkswagen ad. Although Volkswagen, no doubt, wanted consumers to experience a "rather pleasant feeling," their ads aimed to *push* the "tension between appearance and reality" to the point of breaking the bond between Americans and the Big Three, steering consumers toward what they repeatedly described as a "better car . . . made for less money."

Doyle Dane Bernbach's debunking campaign for Volkswagen began in 1959, puncturing the mythos of the American automobile in the very year of maximum tailfins on the GM cars. The ads, as a veritable army of advertising writers has noted over the years, defied the auto-advertising conventions of the 1950s in just about every way they could. While the American automakers used photographic tricks to elongate cars,[28] DDB photographically foreshortened the Volkswagen. The early ads were in black and white and were startlingly minimalist: the cars appeared on a featureless background without people or passengers; copy was confined to three small columns on the bottom of the page. The ads were always organized around a pun or joke, an extremely rare thing at the time, especially since the pun or joke usually seemed to mock the car's distinctive shape or its no-tailfin, little-chrome ugliness. Instead of boasting with Technicolor glare, the artwork for the Volkswagen campaign committed such bizarre heresies as including only a tiny picture in the upper left-hand corner of an almost blank page, depicting the car floating in water, drawn onto an egg, drawn onto a graph, dented in an accident, crossed out, crushed by a car-scrapping machine, or absent altogether except for a pair of tracks in the snow.

Aside from the Volkswagen ads' graphic distinctiveness, the "honesty" of their copy is their most often-remarked feature, and it is certainly the most striking characteristic when viewed in context, alongside conventional advertising from the 1950s. Gone is the empty claptrap Americans had learned to associate with advertising; gone are the usual buzzwords, the heavily retouched photographs, the idealized drawings. In their place is a new tone of plain talk, of unadorned simplicity without fancy color pictures and beautiful typefaces.[29] But what really distinguishes the Volkswagen ads is their attitude toward the reader. The advertising style of the 1950s had been profoundly contemptuous of the consumer's intelligence, and consumers knew it: in the wake of *The Hucksters*, *The Hidden Persuaders*, the quiz show scandals, and the various FTC lawsuits against fraudulent advertisers, consumer skepticism toward advertising was at an all-time high. The genius of the Volkswagen campaign—and many of DDB's other campaigns—is that they took this skepticism into account and made it part of their ads' discursive apparatus. They spoke to consumers as canny beings capable of seeing through the great heaps of puffery cranked out by Madison Avenue. As Jerry Della Femina admiringly observed, the Volkswagen campaign was "the first time the advertiser ever talked to the consumer as though he was a grownup instead of a baby."[30]

What made the Volkswagen ads seem "honest" are the curious admissions of (what appear to be) errors with which the ads are peppered. The sedan is "ugly" and "looks like a beetle"; the Volkswagen station wagon is "a monster" that "looked like a shoe box" with "a flat face and square shape"; an experimental model that never saw production was "something awful. Take our word for it." To make such admissions, even counterbalanced as they were with humor ("Could it be that ours aren't the funny looking cars, after all?") was a violation of fundamental principles of salesmanship. So were the campaign's occasional admissions that Volkswagen was, like everyone else, a profit-driven corporation: "since we have this burning desire to stay in business," etc.[31] This species of

chapter three

commercial "honesty" was a strategy DDB used to great effect in a number of other campaigns as well: Avis forthrightly declaring itself the "Number Two" auto-renter, Lowrey Piano confessing in 1965 that 1923 was "The year to be in the piano business," or Utica Beer admitting that "Our beer is 50 years behind the times." Within a few years, the technique was copied widely: creative superstars Wells, Rich, Greene's Benson & Hedges advertising focused on "The Disadvantages" of long cigarettes; J. Walter Thompson's ads for Listerine admitted the product's terrible flavor, exclaiming "I Hate It, But I Love It."[32]

But by far the most powerful feature of the Volkswagen ads—and a feature which one can find throughout DDB's oeuvre—is their awareness of and deep sympathy with the mass society critique. Not only do the authors of these ads seem to have been reading *The Hidden Persuaders*, *The Waste Makers* and *The Insolent Chariots*, they are actively contributing to the discourse, composing cutting jibes against the chrome-plated monsters from Detroit and proffering up Volkswagens as badges of alienation from the ways of a society whose most prominent emblems were the tailfin and the tract home with a two-car garage.

The foolishness of planned obsolescence was a particular target of DDB's Volkswagen campaign. Ads from the early sixties emphasized the car's lack of highly visible change and mocked Detroit's annual restyling sprees. Below one picture of the car, spotlighted as if at an auto show (a favorite Volkswagen target), runs the caption "The '51 '52 '53 '54 '55 '56 '57 '58 '59 '60 '61 Volkswagen." In another, headlined "How to tell the year of a Volkswagen," close-up photographs point out the minute changes the manufacturer has in fact made over the years (the picture for 1957 is blank: "No visible change"), each of them done not "to make it look different" but "only to make it work better." The ads appealed, as did the works of popular criticism which informed them, to a preconsumerist thriftiness and a suspicion of ornament and fashion. The Volkswagen boasted "no fancy gadgets, run by push buttons"; instead, ads spoke of the car's reliability, its solid construction, its ease of repair, and its efficiency.[33]

Later ads extended the attack to other aspects of the car culture. A 1964 ad took on the questionable and tasteless practices of car dealers, dressing up the anti-car in ludicrous sale decorations, wondering "why they run clearance sales on brand new cars," and faux-confessing, "Maybe it's because we don't quite understand the system." A 1966 ad assailed the vanity of cars as status symbols, comparing the efficiency of the "ugly little bug" to the fleeting looks of "a big beautiful chariot, drawn by 300 horses!" and quietly reversing the old Edsel slogan: "If you want to show you've gotten somewhere, get a big beautiful chariot. But if you simply want to get somewhere, get a bug." Another 1966 ad heaped scorn on "frivolous" automotive faddishness by asking, "Has the Volkswagen fad died out?" and confessing that, since it is so "completely sensible," "as a fad, the car was a flop."[34]

On occasion, DDB even encouraged readers to demystify the techniques of admaking. Volkswagen advertisements called attention to themselves as advertisements, and to the admaking philosophy that informed them. As one from 1964 put it rather disingenuously, "Just because we sell cars doesn't put selling at the top of our agenda." Another asked, "How much longer can we hand you this line?" (the "line" being the car's peculiar silhouette). So similar in format were the various Volkswagen print ads, and so familiar to readers, that in 1963 the company ran an ad with no picture, no headline, three blank columns, and instructions on "How to do a Volkswagen ad." But the ad's Volkswagen message was overshadowed by its pitch for DDB and the new style of advertising that acknowledged the audience's intelligence:

4. Call a spade a spade. And a suspension a suspension. Not something like "orbital cushioning."
5. Speak to the reader. Don't shout. He can hear you. Especially if you talk sense.[35]

The ad knocks Detroit's standard puffery in a way that Detroit could not possibly refute given its standard admaking style of the 1950s. In pretending to teach the reader to read ads critically, it naturally overlooks the new style invented by DDB: advertisers are liars, except, of course, this one. Conventional ad campaigns were incapable of responding in kind, since their appeal rested not on empowered readers but the fraudulent appeal of retouched photographs, dream-world imagery, and empty celebrity testimonials. For one of the Big Three's ads to admit to its ad-ness would be to undermine the various tricks that gave them whatever appeal they still had.

The Volkswagen critique was easily extended to the other objectionable features of consumer society. Even though it varied only little over the years, DDB cast it as a car for people who thought for themselves and were worried about conformity. A 1965 print ad confronts the issue directly, incorporating one of the standard icons of postwar order: a suburban street lined with look-alike houses, no trees, and tiny shrubs. But parked in the driveway of each house is a Volkswagen station wagon. "If the world looked like this, and you wanted to buy a car that sticks out a little," the copy advised,

> you probably wouldn't buy a Volkswagen Station Wagon.
>
> But in case you haven't noticed, the world doesn't look like this.
>
> So if you've wanted to buy a car that sticks out a little, you know just what to do.[36]

Volkswagen's television commercials went out of their way to lampoon various sacred rituals of the consumer culture. A 1967 spot mocks game shows, the glittering dream factories of daytime television whose charm has been undermined by a congressional investigation ten years before. "Gino Milano," a "little shoemaker" in awkward-looking glasses and bushy hair, answers questions about cars on a parody program called "The Big Plateau" while an audience of dowdy-looking women in pearls and cats-eye glasses watches anxiously. This quintessential middle American is eventually "done in by [questions about] the 1968 Volkswagen," failing to appreciate the nuances of the company's anti-obsolescence policy.[37]

Volkswagen's most incisive critique of American consumer frivolity came in a 1969 television commercial that lampooned the "1949 Auto Show," one of the great promotional fairs held in the year Volkswagen was introduced to America. Filmed in black and white to establish the setting, the spot focuses on the elaborate displays and misguided decorative designs of several defunct automakers. The Hudson display features three women singing, in the style of the Andrews Sisters, a little ditty that features the line, "Longer, lower, wider." A spokeswoman for Studebaker compares her car's peculiar styling to "Long skirts," which she assured her audience to "be the next look on the fashion scene." A DeSoto dazzles from a revolving platform. And a man in a white smock gestures toward his model (a Buick, although its brand name is not given) with a pointer and says, "So there's no doubt about it. Next year, every car in America will have [pause] holes in its side." Meanwhile, in an unadorned corner, without benefit of microphone, revolving pedestal, or audience, the Volkswagen spokesman delivers his simple talk about "constantly . . . changing, improving, and refining this car. Not necessarily to keep it in style with the times, but to make a better car." Not only is the industry's puffery transparently ridiculous in retrospect, but a number of its practitioners have actually gone out of business.

"1949 Auto Show" was a celebration of victory in two distinct ways. First, it trumpeted Volkswagen's spectacular sales success since 1949, the year in which, according to a 1960 ad, it had sold only two cars in America. Second, it signaled the victory of the Creative Revolution, of the DDB techniques over the empty puffery of the recent past. As the camera pans over the "1949 Auto Show," many of the standard postwar advertising cliches are represented: the glamorous singing girls, the Reevesian authority figure in spectacles and white smock, the handsome pitchman with a microphone, the car on the revolving platform. As a result of DDB's campaigns for Volkswagen, which first brought national attention to the new creativity, all of these selling methods are as obsolete as the tailfins, chrome, and portholes for which they were once employed. By 1969, none of the major automakers would dare to use such techniques: in just a few years, the DDB approach had made them stilted and old-fashioned, awkward emblems of a laughably outmoded past, so ancient that they had to be filmed in black and white to be properly distanced from the present.[38]

from nazi car to love bug

The Volkswagen campaign also marks a strange episode in the history of co-optation. Accounts of the counterculture generally agree on the Volkswagen (either "bug" or "microbus") as the auto of choice among the dropped-out. For many countercultural participants, the Volkswagen seemed an antithesis to the tailfinned monsters from Detroit, a symbolic rebuke of the product that had become a symbol both of the mass society's triumph and of its grotesque excesses. The Volkswagen was the anti-car, the automotive signifier of the uprising against the cultural establishment.

But "anti-car" was hardly a natural or normal signifier for the brand. In fact, at one time Volkswagen bore the ugly stigma of the mass society to an extent that American cars could never touch: in the fifties, the Volkswagen was known as nothing less than a Nazi product. George Lois, who worked on the Volkswagen account when it first went to Doyle Dane Bernbach in 1959, recalled some years later that

It was hard to forget that Hitler himself was directly involved in designing the Volkswagen. Even though the Fuehrer was helped along by the Austrian car engineer Dr. Ferdinand Porsche, the cute Volkswagen in 1959 reminded lots of people about the ovens. Julian [Koenig, who wrote the first round of copy for the campaign] was Jewish and wouldn't forget it.[39]

chapter three

Bernbach himself was Jewish as well, and it is one of the great ironies of the decade that his agency, which also produced celebrated advertising for El Al airlines and Levy's Jewish Rye Bread, was responsible for humanizing what Lois calls "the Nazi car."

That by the end of the decade the Volkswagen had acquired an image that was more hip than Nazi must be regarded as one of the great triumphs of American marketing. The irony that several of the creators of this image were Jewish was trumped by the irony implicit in that Volkswagen's hipness was a product of advertising, the institution of mass society against which hip had declared itself most vehemently at odds. The Volkswagen story, in other words, is the co-optation theory turned upside down, a clear and simple example of a product marketed as an emblem of good-humored alienation and largely accepted as such by the alienated.

DDB's ads for Volkswagen simultaneously attacked obsolescence in the world of automobiles and contributed to it mightily in the world of advertising, rendering ancient overnight the Madison Avenue dreams of the fifties. As a form of anti-advertising that worked by distancing a product from consumerism, the Volkswagen ads introduced Americans to a new aesthetic of consuming. No longer would advertising labor to construct an idealized but self-evidently false vision of consumer perfection: instead it would offer itself as an antidote to the patent absurdities of affluence. This, then, was the great innovation of the Creative Revolution, the principle to which Bernbach referred when he spoke so enthusiastically of "difference": the magic cultural formula by which the life of consumerism could be extended indefinitely, running forever on the discontent that it itself had produced. Hip was indeed the solution to the problems of the mass society, although not in the way its ideologues had intended. What distinguishes the advertising of the Creative Revolution is that, following Volkswagen's lead, it takes into account—and offers to solve—the problems that consumerism had created. In the hands of a newly enlightened man in gray flannel, hip would become the dynamic principle of the 1960s, a cultural perpetual motion machine transforming disgust with consumerism into fuel for the ever-accelerating consumer society.[40]

Thanks to the agency's signature visual style (simple photographs, minimalist layout, large, clever headlines), DDB advertising of the early sixties is generally easy to distinguish from the other ads in the glossy magazines where it appeared. Even more remarkable, though, is the consistency with which the agency referred to the mass society critique. Remarks about the fraudulence of consumerism and expressions of disgust with the system's masters run as a sort of guiding theme through virtually everything DDB did. Disgust with the consumer society was both the agency's aesthetic forte and its best product pitch, applicable to virtually anything: Buy this to escape consumerism.

The DDB critique is visible in such out-of-the-way places as a 1961 ad for "The remarkable Parker 61" fountain pen, which declares that "In this age of mass production and slickness (and sometimes, shoddiness), it's good to look upon a truly fine thing."[41] Or it can be seen, more openly, in a 1967 ad for El Al that cast the Israeli airline as a place free of the affected manners of the technocracy. Above a rather alarming photograph of a stewardess with a clownlike smile painted on her face is the declaration, "Maybe You Don't Want to Look at a Painted-on Smile All the Way to Europe." People are not robots or laboratory animals, and El Al knows it: "we feel our engines should turn on and off with a flick of a switch; not our stewardesses."[42]

Ads for American Tourister mocked, in typically self-effacing DDB style, virtually any aspect of the consumer culture that could be brought into contact with suitcases. Since the point was to demonstrate the product's resistance to clumsiness, accidents, and malicious misbehavior, the campaign provided ample opportunity for more "realistic" renderings of consumer life. People foolishly run over American Touristers in cars; they drop American Touristers from airplanes. American Touristers (like Volkswagens) are too durable to serve as status symbols: "The trouble with an American Tourister is nobody knows you've been around," a 1968 ad faux-confessed.[43] Even the jolly menials of the consumer world who were always romanticized in older advertising (the admiring butler, the compliant porter, the beloved Philip Morris bellboy) are lampooned in one 1970 American Tourister television commercial: a suitcase is tossed into a zoo cage, snatched up by a particularly violent ape who snorts and growls and smashes it about. Meanwhile, a placid announcer speaks of "savage baggagemasters," "clumsy bellboys," "brutal cab drivers," and "all butter-fingered luggage handlers all over the world." While in earlier spots such humble figures would have been rendered in friendly terms, here they are compared to apes.[44]

The most mockable institution of the consumer society was, of course, the deeply mistrusted practice of the advertising industry, and DDB took to the task with gusto. Many of their ads commented on previous advertising and knocked the deceptive legs out from under the older style. DDB played on the reader's cognizance of clutter, his boredom and disgust with advertising discourse. Before the 1960s, most ads ap-

chapter three

proached the reader as a neutral element of the "editorial" text that surrounds it: its intent to sell is rarely mentioned openly, the assumptions and processes by which it is created remain concealed. But the works of DDB would occasionally admit themselves to be and even discuss themselves as ads, aware of the medium by which they are presented and of the discourse into which they have been inserted. A 1964 ad for Chivas Regal whiskey typifies the agency's pseudo-hostility toward advertising: under the headline, "Don't bother to read this ad," the full page of copy below is crossed out.[45]

The agency's ads for Calvert Whiskey, which it dubbed "The Soft Whiskey," made a point of mocking more conventional whiskey advertising. After having come up with what may well be the most slickly meaningless product claim for a whiskey of all time ("soft" whiskey was supposed to be somehow "easier to swallow," a double-entendre of which the ads made much), the agency proceeded to denounce liquor advertising in general for its slick meaninglessness. "Is it just another slogan?" asked one of the campaign's 1966 headlines. Of course not: It required far more than "some sharp talk on Madison Avenue" to make the brand so popular.[46]

DDB's Calvert ads contained a streak of consumer populism as profound as those for Volkswagen. "It just so happens, you can't fool all the people all the time," one insisted, in the course of explaining why the advertising industry's tricks would be insufficient to sell the stuff. "One sip and you can write your own Soft Whiskey ad," proclaimed another, over a layout of product photos and blank lines. One 1964 installment actually depicted a consumer defacing one of the brand's special Christmas decanters by removing its label under running water, encouraging this anti-consumer practice on the grounds that "The people who drink it will know it's Soft Whiskey anyhow."[47]

Sometimes the DDB strategy of identifying products with public suspicion of advertising was more overt than others. As a 1966 print ad in the Avis rent-a-car campaign put it,

> People in this country don't believe anything they read in ads anymore.
> And with good reason.
> Most advertising these days is long on the big promise—a promise that the product doesn't always deliver.[48]

As a rule, advertising never acknowledges authorship or any other factors which would make clear its status as artifice; yet an Avis ad from 1965 openly proclaims itself to have been fabricated by a professional adman. "I write Avis ads for a living," the copy maintains. "But that doesn't make me a paid liar." The writer goes on to complain about an Avis car he rented which did not meet one of Avis's minor promises. Again the sponsor admits to a minor shortcoming, and again the end result is not the destruction of Avis's reputation, but its burnishing. Avis confesses—it's human, too—and its credibility is thus increased, as it is when the company forthrightly admits itself to be "Number Two." The anonymous ad writer even declares his professional reputation (that quality mocked by Victor Norman in *The Hucksters*) to have been threatened so severely by Avis's tiny oversight that it must never be allowed to happen again: "So if I'm going to continue writing these ads, Avis had better live up to them. Or they can get themselves a new boy." The ad concludes with a trick that seems to "prove" Avis's honesty by challenging them to "confess" their wrongdoing, "They'll probably never run this ad." And yet there it is, being run! [49]

The familiar spokesman models of the fifties, in their suits or lab coats, were a particular target of the DDB critique. In the Rosser Reeves era, the product pitchman had been a pretty predictable figure: a deep-voiced male whose authority was often augmented by spectacles and books, smiling when appropriate and always speaking earnestly and glibly of the product in question. Boring and respectable, he was a stock image of postwar order, an obvious symptom of the corporate world's problems with creativity and bureaucracy. And he was the target of several humiliating Doyle Dane Bernbach commercials. In a 1965 television spot for Campbell's Pork and Beans, the product's flavorfulness is demonstrated by a male spokesman, accompanied by his female assistant, who tastes the product while seated in a convertible with the top down and headed into a car wash. The spokesman carries on gamely through the soap and brushes, talking up the beans even as he is thoroughly soaked; his assistant insists, in the best product-demonstrator fashion, that despite the deluge "You can still taste the sauce!" At the spot's conclusion the car is filled to the brim with water, and the discomfited male is now unable to start the motor. "D'you think it's flooded?" asks his assistant, laughing uncontrollably. A famous 1968 commercial demonstrated the nonsagging qualities of Burlington Mid-Length Socks by showing them in action on the legs of a balding businessman in horn-rimmed glasses, white shirt, and narrow tie sitting in a minimalist modern chair. Everything about him is respectable, even distinguished-looking, except for the fact that he wears no trousers, only underwear and one of the socks in question. "We've asked you to put on a short sock the length most men wear," an announcer says, "and Burlington's new mid-length sock." The man is challenged to "make it fall down," and accordingly he begins to leap about the set, gritting his teeth, whirling around and waving his arms. Naturally, all his activity is for nought, the sock refuses to sag, and he abandons the struggle in exhaustion. The pant-less patriarch's humiliation is complete.[50]

Then there is the DDB commercial that won all the prizes—and still does, whenever a trade group or publication decides to designate the "top ads of all time." It is a 1970 spot for Alka-Seltzer that dramatizes the product by depicting, of all things, the making of a television commercial in which an actor is required to eat from a plate of spaghetti and exclaim, "Mama mia! That's a spicy meatball!" Unfortunately, the actor fumbles his lines again and again, and we hear a director's voice saying things like "cut" and "take fifty-nine." The viewer suffers through each attempt with short clips that appear to be actual outtakes from a filming session. The commercial was a masterpiece of the agency's long effort to turn public skepticism into brand loyalty: it recognizes advertising as artifice, and as a particularly ridiculous—and transparent—form of artifice as well. The actor is plugging an absurd product, a brand of ready-made meatballs that come in an enormous jar; he is filmed on an absurdly contrived set, with a smiling Italian mother type standing over him as he essays the dish; and when delivering his lines he adopts a grotesque Italian accent, which, of course, he drops when pleading with the director. Advertising itself—especially the prerevolutionary variety with its stock figures, its stereotypes, its contrivances, its fakery—is ridiculous stuff. Only Alka-Seltzer, which intervenes to rescue the long-suffering actor's tormented digestion, stands above the mockery. Consumerism, like Alka-Seltzer, now promised to relieve Americans from their consuming excesses.[51]

But the agency's best-remembered achievement was its 1964 election-year effort to sell none other than President Johnson as a symbol of opposition to mass society's greatest horror—the specter of nuclear war. Without giving Barry Goldwater's name, the commercial managed to portray the 1964 contest as a choice between automated holocaust and preconsumer innocence: a child playing with a daisy fades into a mechanical-sounding adult voice counting down to a nuclear explosion. Over the years, the commercial has been criticized as an unfair portrayal of Goldwater's views, and it is certainly true that Goldwater was not, strictly speaking, in favor of nuclear destruction. But the commercial's power has nothing to do with Goldwater, or with Johnson, for that matter. It aimed, rather, to case the election as an expression of the archetypal cultural conflict of the age. Its stark division of the world into flower-child and technocratic death-count couldn't have caught the mood of the nation more accurately or more presciently. And although it was run only a limited number of times (and DDB never did political advertising again), it summarizes the aesthetics and faiths of the consumer revolution more concisely and convincingly than almost any other document of the decade.[52]

chapter three

chapter four

THREE REBELS:

ADVERTISING

NARRATIVES OF

THE SIXTIES

There is a time in every man's education when he arrives at the conviction that envy is ignorance, that imitation is suicide, that he must take himself for better or worse as his portion. Insist on yourself. Never imitate. . . . Society everywhere is in a conspiracy against the manhood of every one of its members.

—VOICEOVER FROM "REEBOK LETS U.B.U." COMMERCIAL, LATE 1980S [1]

satirist

Just as Bill Bernbach inverted the standard advertising industry practices of the fifties, advertising memoirs and handbooks of the sixties flatly contradict those of the fifties on everything from the value of science to their depiction of daily life in the business. They usually begin, strangely enough, by acknowledging the mass society critique and agreeing with the criticism of the advertising industry leveled by outsiders like Vance Packard. The work of the nation's prominent Madison Avenue agencies, the authors of the sixties' three great advertising narratives were quite willing to admit, was degrading, insulting, and unconvincing stuff.

If the Creative Revolution can be said to have unleashed any genuine geniuses on American culture, the title would have to go to San Francisco adman Howard Gossage. The ads he made, for odd clients like the Irish Whiskey Distillers Association, Fina gas stations, Qantas airlines, and Eagle shirts, are gems of wit and friendly joking; published almost exclusively in Gossage's favorite medium, *The New Yorker*, they remain a pleasure to read forty years later. Although his ads never appeared on television, although he worked on the West rather than the East Coast, although his only book was published only in German (until 1987, when it finally appeared in English under the title *Is There Any Hope for Advertising?*), and although he died in 1969, Gossage inspired a following among American admen and practitioners of commercial art that persists to this day. This is curious, since Gossage produced as harsh an attack on American commercial culture as any generated by the Frankfurt School. In addition to being an adman, he was on the board of the leftist magazine *Ramparts*. He spoke out vigorously against the invasiveness of billboards and made hugely successful conservation ads for the Sierra Club (ads which, incidentally, were credited by some with having launched environmentalism[2]). His ad agency partner was Jerry Mander, who later wrote the anticonsumerism tract *Four Arguments for the Elimination of Television*. And his critique of the industry in which he labored and the consumer society which he had worked to build was biting in the extreme.

Is There Any Hope for Advertising?, which appeared in Germany in 1967, is an extended attack on the American advertising industry, to whose products Gossage applies in the course of two early paragraphs the words "fatuity," "objectionable," "degraded," "trivial," "boring," "uneconomical," and "the world's dullest show." Not only did the Reevesian repetition of simple USPs bore and irritate audiences, Gossage asserted, but it was a terrifically inefficient way to sell products as well, having caused over the years an "immunity" to develop in readers. "As the immunity builds up it costs more and more to advertise each year," Gossage wrote. "It's like narcotics, it must be taken in ever-increasing doses to achieve the same effect." The social order of which advertising was the preeminent expression was similarly deranged. In an article he wrote for *Harper's* magazine in 1961, Gossage described the affluent society itself as a sort of colossal Ponzi scheme. In the previous year's elections,

Both parties swore fealty to ever-expanding production; this presumably based on ever-expanding population and ever-expanding consumption. Not only are all of these terms plainly impossible, but unnerving as well. Put like that, our economy sounds like nothing so much as the granddaddy of all chain letters. All you can do is hope to get your name to the top of the list, or die, before something happens (like peace) and the whole thing collapses.

Just as academics were coming around to the forbidden joys of popular culture, leading admen were learning to shun them. And for ten years, at least, the makers of American advertising would rank among the country's most visible critics of the mass society.[3]

This skepticism would be the ideological point where the advertising of the sixties parted ways from its predecessors. In the gilded tableaux of so much of 1950s advertising, the world of consumer goods was a place of divine detachment, a vision of perfection through products. For Gossage, though, such ads were "shielded from real life," making no effort to "engage their readers on a direct basis or attempt to involve them." As with Bernbach and William Whyte, Gossage's solution was to speak meaningfully to readers—"not in advertisingese, but in direct, well-formed English"—and until admen did so, "we will never develop the personal responsibility toward our audience, and ourselves, that even a ninth rate tap dancer has." Of course, most ad agencies were prevented from speaking to readers in such a way by their layers of bureaucracy and their adherence to Reevesian theory; so, like so many other advertising writers of the era, Gossage posited an ideal adman who could circumvent entrenched ways. This was the "extra-environmental man," a figure who regarded advertising as an outsider, whose "mind isn't cluttered up with a lot of rules, policy, and other accumulated impedimenta that often pass for experience," who was "unable to see things in a normal fashion," who, like Gossage, regarded the American way of consuming as surpassing strange.[4]

The ads that Howard Gossage made are the best illustration of his ideas about the advertising industry. Like DDB's ads for Volkswagen, his campaign for Irish Whiskey, which began appearing in the *New Yorker* in 1958, was a studied effort to deviate as forcefully as possible from the predominant advertising styles of the day. Appearing as a long series of installments, each one consisted of a full page of words, densely packed and forbidding, and written in a long-winded Irish-sounding vernacular as distant from "advertisingese" as the campaign's eighteenth-century illustrations were from the immaculate, full-color renderings that accompanied the standard liquor advertising of the era. Although its copy refers again and again to the "dear" cost of advertising and to the "hard sell" in which the author apparently believes he is engaged, its method is decidedly soft—confiding, friendly, personal, and even a little hapless. Its layout is spattered with quaint effects like bracketed headlines and mail-in coupons for bizarre premiums. "Progress is perhaps our least important product," one ad even announced.

Gossage's campaign of 1961 for Fina gas stations seems to have been consciously invented to irritate Rosser Reeves. It was advertising, yes, but it was also a gorgeous satire of the pounding slogans and frivolous do-dads of the culture of consumption. Having discovered that most Americans scoffed at the various gasoline additives and other devices service stations then used to distinguish themselves, Gossage invented and then trumpeted to the skies a preposterous pseudo-USP: air for car tires that was dyed "premium pink." Succeeding ads in the series recounted how earnest Fina officials were struggling to get the pink air to their various outlets, they offered pink asphalt as a contest prize, and they each concluded with what must be, with all its exaggerated courtesy, the creative revolution's greatest anti-slogan: "If you're driving down the road and you see a Fina station and it's on your side so you don't have to make a U-turn through traffic and there aren't six cars waiting and you need gas or something, please stop in."[5]

scoffer

The quintessential managerial operation of the Creative Revolution is perhaps best summarized in the trait once attributed to adman Jerry Della Femina by journalist Charles Sopkin: he "managed to bring chaos out of order."[6] In place of Martin Mayer's objective and balanced prose style, Della Femina's 1969 memoirs, *From Those Wonderful Folks Who Gave You Pearl Harbor* (the title is taken from a joke about a Japanese client) address the reader directly, often veering into exclamations, hip slang, sarcasm, and obscenities. The story of his life on Madison Avenue is told as a series of winding anecdotes rather than as a precise exposition of advertising lessons. His purpose is not to demonstrate how well the big agencies do their business, but how badly. The book is a classic debunking: taking note of certain romantic portrayals of the advertising industry in the first chapter, he emphasizes with a cynical sense of humor the business's neuroses, the poor quality of most of its products, and the various ways admen's careers may be destroyed. The literature of advertising had come full circle: after years of industry denials of Wakeman's depiction, a successful advertising man was once again describing his profession in the terms made familiar by *The Hucksters*.

The corporate-style ad agencies that had been the heroes of Mayer's and Reeves's books are Della Femina's villains; the "large, bad agency" where decisions are made by account executives and businessmen rather than by people who actually make ads. Nor are the traditional agencies institutions of placid, calculated order, according to Della Femina, but madhouses of fear and constant danger. The book opens by describing such an agency on the day an important account is lost. Panic sets in quickly as the jobs associated with that client disappear and the various account men scurry to find another company to take the departed client's place. They boast of their friendships with people at comparably-sized businesses, their certainty of landing new accounts. And meanwhile they simply fire the "little people."[7] Della Femina devotes a whole chapter to the firing practices of the various agencies, noting in particular the instances of good workers being fired at the whim of an egotistical or deranged boss. Creative people are fired and replaced for a fraction of their salary by younger people. Entire departments are fired and refuse to discuss it with each other. Agencies hire special employees to do nothing but fire other employees. Presidents of companies are fired by officers they appointed. Other presidents fire everyone who stays at their agency for a certain duration to prevent anyone from becoming powerful enough to fire *them*. And when any of these people are fired, they find it very difficult to land another job. Fear, constant and mortal, is still the defining characteristic of the advertising business.

Della Femina's cynicism also extends to the type of work he himself does. The creative departments, where the actual work of making ads is done, are populated not by reliable organization men, but by eccentrics. "Advertising," he writes simply, "is the only business in the world that takes on the lamed, the drunks, the potheads, and the weirdos." Admen that he knows skewer telephones with scissors and try to throw their desks out windows. One insists on working from four in the afternoon until midnight. Alcoholism is rampant. Bizarre costumes are commonplace, as are "dilated pupils."[8] Della Femina is even more cynical about the actual work of the industry. He speaks of the various package goods—the staple clients of Madison Avenue—and the campaigns that promote them (including his own for a vaginal deodorant) in terms of frivolous, needless exploitation:

The American businessman has discovered the vagina and like it's the next thing going. What happened is that the businessman ran out of parts of the body. We had headaches for a while but we took care of them. The armpit had its moment of glory, and the toes, with their athlete's foot, they had the spotlight, too. We went through wrinkles, we went through diets. Taking skin off, putting skin on. We went through the stomach with acid indigestion and we conquered hemorrhoids. So the businessman sat back and said, "What's left?" And some smart guy said, "The vagina."[9]

Like Victor Norman, Della Femina is unable to internalize the seriousness with which admen like Rosser Reeves addressed the minutiae of product differences, the drama of brand competition. Of a Ted Bates commercial for Certs candy that declares, "It's two mints, two mints, two mints in one," he sarcastically comments, "Oh, it's a fantastic commer-

chapter four

cial, it is some claim to fame in the history of man. Two mints in one." If Della Femina was the zeitgeist barometer he clearly believed himself to be, by the end of the 1960s, the American adman was not a touchy defender of consumer excess but a jaded scoffer contemptuous of the institutions of consumer society, scornful of the imbecile products by which it worked, and corrosively skeptical of the ways in which the establishment agencies foisted them on the public.[10]

provocateur

"If you're not a bad boy, if you're not a big pain in the ass, then what you are is some mush, in this business," says George Lois.[11] A fervent proselytizer for the Bernbachian way since he worked at DDB during the late 1950s, Lois was a leading practitioner, a conspicuous success story, and a living symbol of the advertising revolution that began in the early 1960s. Since then he has been a Madison Avenue Jacobin, pushing the business revolution to its antinomian end. While Reeves, Ogilvy, and others were denouncing the self-serving and unproductive expressions of art directors who were not properly controlled by rules and theories, Lois was indulging his considerable artistic skills without heed for industry conventions and making effective advertising by so doing. When advertising texts of the fifties advised executives to suppress the dangerous artistic impulses of their underlings, people like George Lois must have been who they had in mind.

If Bernbach was suspicious of statistics and critical of the priority of research at most agencies, Lois was positively aflame with anger at the institutional procedures that, he believes, make for the epidemic of bad advertising that has long prevailed on Madison Avenue. "Advertising, an art," he wrote in 1991, "is constantly besieged and compromised by logicians and technocrats, the scientists of our profession who wildly miss the main point about everything we do, that the product of advertising, after all, is *advertising*."[12] Until the Creative Revolution, Lois insisted, the production of American advertising was smothered by rigid, repressive codes of dullness-inducing rules. The language he uses in his recent book to describe the prerevolutionary situation echoes the language of the mass society critique:

Advertising "instruction" available to artists could be loosely described as knee-jerk drills in constructing schematic advertising layouts. They were Prussian-style exercises, directed by hacks who preached the conventional wisdoms of advertising's early days: large illustration above a headline above a block of body copy with a logo in the lower-right-hand corner. Even today, most print advertising follows this vapid pattern. Small wonder that the least talented people in advertising, incapable of innovation, create advertising according to this gospel.

Lois countered this repressive tradition by writing, matter-of-factly, "Advertising has no rules—what it always needs more than 'rules' is unconstipated thinking." One chapter is titled, "To push for a new solution, start by saying no to conventional rules, traditions and trends."[13] For Lois, Bernbach's suspicion of rules was an archetypal conflict between repression and liberation, "Prussian" order and American-style heteroglossia, the anal-retentive and the "unconstipated." Bernbach celebrated difference; according to a 1970 profile Lois "can make the word normal sound like a social disease."[14]

According to sociologists Paul Leinberger and Bruce Tucker, the defining characteristic of post-Organization white-collar workers is a powerful artistic impulse.[15] For George Lois, advertising, as he practices it, is art. Lois is a graduate of Pratt; the dust jacket of his 1972 memoirs, *George, Be Careful*, depicts the hand and arm of Michelangelo's Sistine Chapel God reaching out to Adam; in 1977 he published a coffee-table art book called, simply, *The Art of Advertising*.[16] More important, Lois's professional practice seems to derive directly from Romantic ideas of the superhuman artist. He insists on the inviolability of his graphic productions, even though they are supposed to serve a commercial purpose. But artists were hardly comfortable in most places on prerevolutionary Madison Avenue, and Lois describes his life then as a constant war against the philistine managerial style of the fifties. According to his own 1972 recollections, he violently confronted superiors, whether other agency men or clients, whenever they edited or altered his work. Lois writes that when one ad he designed was changed without his approval, he felt "*Personally defiled*," and physically attacked the man responsible. While working for one large, bureaucratic agency in the mid-1950s, Lois discovered that his work, under evaluation by an important WASP account supervisor, had been spread out on an office floor and walked upon. Again he was enraged:

I kneeled down and swiftly rolled up my ads, column by column, until I had them all in a tidy cylinder under my arm. The diagonally positioned desk of C. L. Smith sat like a fortress in the far corner, behind me. I had salvaged my ads, but I was still

chapter four

in a blind rage, incensed at the way my work was defiled. I gripped the overhang of Smith's desk and with all the strength of my furious mood I flipped it toward Smith's corner. The fortress landed with a deadly thunk on its forward side as drawers slid open and were jammed back into the falling hulk. My cylinder of ads was safely tucked under my arm as all the debris from the top of Smith's desk crashed to the floor. My action was so sudden that a streak of ink actually surged from the desk's executive well and hit the wall like a Rorschach splotch. But I had my ads, my *work* —and without looking back I quietly walked out of the room.[17]

Even the symbols of traditional agency practice and authority aroused Lois's artistic ire. Like Jay Chiat snipping ties, Lois reveled in transforming the ink of fifties order into shapeless Pollock-like blotches.

Chafing under almost any sort of authority or hierarchy, Lois recalls how he broke again and again from the various agencies that employed him in the 1950s. In 1960, he left DDB to form his own agency with Fred Papert and Volkswagen copywriter Julian Koenig, the first shot in the long series of creative secessions that would define the decade. The sudden success of the trio's agency, dubbed Papert Koenig Lois (PKL) and specializing in creative outrage, signaled the changing dynamics of American admaking. The key to PKL's success, Lois insists, was its extreme organizational openness, its lack of constraints, bureaucracy, and established procedure, its allegiance to art rather than science. "The joint was unbefouled by mannerism," he wrote in 1972, "and nothing could stop us. . . . We worked late because it was painful to leave its carefree atmosphere." [18] Lois explains his agency's freedom in these simple terms:

"You start out by hiring people who are creative, then just give them room to do what they want," I said. "You just sit down and work with guys. Also we try to hire people who will disagree with us. . . ." [19]

Disagreement was just part of the climate at PKL, where, as at DDB, creative freedom encouraged every sort of activity other than "normal" business operations.

The title of Lois's 1972 memoirs is *George, Be Careful*, an admonition typical of the cautious advertising world of the 1950s. But George is never careful. He is an artist, and, as it has always been for artists in the twentieth century, outrage is the dynamic principle of his career. According to a 1967 issue of *Advertising News of New York*, Lois is "the archetype of the non-organization man," and the usefulness of defying convention in spectacular ways is the book's primary theme. Lois curses. He fights. He

chapter four

performs bizarre gestures to persuade clients to approve his outrageous ideas. He defies his superiors, rebels against conventional corporate order, and believes passionately, even violently, in the sanctity of his work as art. Whether standing up to recalcitrant clients or rankling under repressive account men, Lois refuses to live and work in conventional Madison Avenue ways. Lois recounts how his partner Koenig was pestered by a nosy client demanding to know how an ad would appear in a smaller format. "Julian held up the full-page layout and said, 'Here's how it would look'—and he tore it in half." Lois insists that all of the people hired by PKL were similarly irreverent, and he goes out of his way to emphasize their eccentric habits. None of them was a WASP, and none came from the comfortable classes that dominated the industry in the 1950s. Their ethnicity and supposed penchant for fisticuffs earned them the nickname "Graphic Mafia" in the business. Lois reports that when Carl Ally, who would later go on to found another of the decade's most successful creative firms, was interviewed for a job, he grew irate at Koenig's questioning and said, "Fuck you, I don't need this horseshit." This prompted Lois to hire him. Admen at PKL curse and fight one another. One day they shred a man's objectionable shirt while he is wearing it. Such tales would have been wildly out of place in the 1950s Madison Avenue accounts of either Vance Packard or Martin Mayer, but Lois recounts them with a certain pride.[20]

PKL was a dramatic success at first, with billings that grew from zero to $14 million by its third year, and it became the first advertising agency to sell stock publicly.[21] But the growth of the business was uncomfortable for Lois, and in 1967 to "kick the curse of bigness"[22] he walked out of PKL and set up another new shop. Lois's explanation of his move was that while PKL's success may not exactly have made it into an "establishment" agency, it had nonetheless been sufficient to transform him from a person who made ads—an artist—into a supervisor. "You know how much time I spent on creative work at PKL?" Lois complained to *Madison Avenue* magazine in 1968:

Between seven and nine each evening at home, because that was the only time I had to do it. The rest of the time, at the office, I was supervising the other creative people. It was different when PKL was billing 18 million. At that stage I was doing every stitch of the work.

Lois described the firm's climate with a word of some considerable negative connotation: "The feeling turned from a truly creative to more of a *normal* agency." [23] In the big establishment agencies of the fifties, management and client-relations had taken precedence over creative work. But Lois had no interest in administration. His new partner, James Callaway, summarized the sixties vision of agency operations when he asserted in 1968 that in other industries, upper management made critical decisions, but in advertising "the really important decisions . . . are made by the copywriter or art director who creates the ads, because the ads are what advertising is all about."

Lois's scheme for Lois Holland Callaway, the agency he founded in 1968, as he outlined it to *Madison Avenue* magazine, envisioned the Bernbachian managerial style taken to an anti-organizational extreme. The three principals of the new agency were to do all of the "important" work of admaking and hire others to do anything else that was needed. [24] The new agency was designed to be streamlined, to keep employees to an absolute minimum, and thus to maximize the creative freedom of the central trio. In a piece published five months after its founding, *Newsday* marveled at LHC's billings relative to the size of its staff. "The customary ratio of staffers to billing is 7 to 10 for every $1,000,000," the newspaper pointed out. "On this basis LHC should have something like 200 employees instead of 18." [25]

The free and wide-open workplace was not just a matter of Lois's personal preferences or his artistic disposition. He argues that openness is a necessary precondition to realizing the central element of his advertising style: outrage. His peculiar management beliefs and his shocking style are inextricably connected:

In order to be breakthrough, it [advertising] has to be fresh and different, it has to be surprising. And in order to do that, you need a talented art director and writer working together, who have some leeway and liberty to try to create advertising. [26]

In order for an ad to work, Lois argued in 1991, one had to cause outrage. Good advertising, therefore, is synonymous with rebellion, with difference, with the avant-garde's search for the new:

I'm always pushing for a creative idea that has more grit than one has a right to expect, that rubs against sensibilities, that drives me to the edge of the cliff. That's how you bring life to your work. The fact that something hasn't been done does not mean that it can't be done. Safe, conventional work is a ticket to oblivion. Talented work is, *ipso facto*, unconventional. [27]

Good advertising should "stun" the consumer, as modern art was supposed to shock, by presenting him or her with an idea that upends their conventions of understanding. When Lois presents his work to clients, he expects it to "cause my listener to rock back in semi-shock." Good advertising is like "poison gas": "It should unhinge your nervous system. It should knock you out!" Lois calls this the "seemingly outrageous," and when used properly it should drive the sales message home:

Advertising should stun *momentarily* . . . it should *seem* to be outrageous. In that swift interval between the initial shock and the realization that what you are showing is not as outrageous as it seems, you capture the audience.[28]

Lois's techniques necessarily militate against whatever happens to be acceptable at present. "The fact that others are moving in a certain direction is always proof positive, at least to me," Lois writes, "that a *new* direction is the only direction. Defy trends and don't be constrained by precedents."[29] The adman must live in perpetual rebellion against whatever is established, accepted, received. He must internalize obsolescence, constantly anticipate the new. It is not an exaggeration to say that there are *no* Lois ads that simply go through the conventional motions, like the ones studied by William Whyte back in 1952: in *every single one* an effort is made to assault the consumer's complacency, the sense of the usual that he or she has developed over a lifetime of commercial bombardment. Of course, after a few such ads the conventions and routines are entirely reformulated, and the struggle goes on. The Emersonian adage could be updated to fit the creative revolution: He who would be an adman must be a nonconformist.

A good example of the Lois technique is the LHC television campaign for the New York brokerage firm of Edwards & Hanly (1968). Before this campaign, brokerage advertising was sedate stuff, grasping for respectability with long columns of solid-looking words.[30] Edwards & Hanly, though, was a small and struggling firm, willing to do almost anything; at the same time Lois's new agency, LHC, was looking for a way to advertise itself with a startling, controversial statement. The resulting television commercials which Lois, Holland, and Callaway wrote in one day and produced in three weeks used the testimony of athletes, children, and other unlikely authorities to address people's basic need for brokers: to make money.[31] In one spot, the boxer Joe Louis, who had famously lost millions, looked unhappy and asked, "Edwards & Hanly, where were you when I needed you?" In another, Mickey Mantle said, "When I came up to the big leagues, I was a shuffling, grinning, head-ducking country boy. But I know a man down at Edwards & Hanly. I'm learnin', I'm learnin'."[32] Like other Lois campaigns, this one worked by pairing a serious subject with pop-cultural spokespeople. Lois described the episode in his usual manic style, exaggerating its offensiveness and celebrating yet another triumph of irreverence over stodginess:

> The minute [the clients] left, the three of us charged into the elevator, laughing insanely, mostly out of relief that we had come this far with our first wild campaign for the stuffiest industry of them all without getting stiffed by a frightened client. We ran through the Manhattan crowds like three stoned kids, laughing and whooping all the way to the bank on Fifth Avenue.

The New York Stock Exchange, which strictly regulates the advertising of its members, was not long in forcing Edwards & Hanly to withdraw a number of the spots. When Lois, Holland, and Callaway appeared to defend their work, the contrast between their free-swinging, ethnic ways and those of the guardians of the Exchange's honor was extreme. Lois quotes his partner Callaway's description of the showdown: "Two micks and a Greek were arguing about a TV spot starring a *schvaatza* in front of a bunch of WASP's."[33] The new capitalism was beginning to challenge the white pillars of order everywhere.

Perhaps Lois's boldest use of the "seemingly outrageous" came during a mid-sixties television campaign for the New York *Herald-Tribune*. The campaign's print ads used such volatile, mock-threatening lines as, "Who says a good newspaper has to be dull?" and "Shut up, whites, and listen." Its television side, Lois recalls, consisted of commercials that ran immediately before the eleven o'clock news on the New York CBS affiliate. During each one, an announcer would briefly discuss the next day's headlines, mention the newspaper's new appearance—and then attack the institution of television news! "There's more to the news than this headline," the voice-over would say, "*and there's more to it than you're going to hear on this program.*" "I couldn't believe that CBS was actually letting us get away with it night after night," Lois wrote. But again the ads' offensiveness caused the guardians of Organization to muzzle Lois's creativity: according to his 1972 memoirs, they were one day seen by CBS president William Paley who, duly outraged, put a quick stop to them.[34]

the utopian imagination of the Detroit automakers,

Oldsmobile, 1961. This is as neat a vision of consensus order as one will find anywhere in American culture: Norman Rockwell landscape, patriotic colonial architecture, confident man, fawning wife, mirthful children, jolly firemen, and reassuring reminders of the jet-age military. Five years later an ad like this would appear to be from a different country.

Champion
in its
field

CLEAR HEADS AGREE Calvert IS BETTER

Calvert

so banal it's surreal.

Calvert Whiskey, 1958. The headline suggests that most fanciful of product advantages: a whiskey that causes no hangover. But the art seems to be from a different ad–he's partial to football and boxing, not sports known for producing clear-headedness. The copy, which is a study in emptiness ("Something wonderfully satisfying about the flavor, isn't there?") seems to have been written for yet a third. And what's up with that giant glove?

The '51 '52 '53 '54 '55 '56 '57 '58 '59 '60 '61 Volkswagen.

Ever since we started making Volkswagens, we've put all our time and effort into the one basic model.

You can see we've had lots of practice. We've learned to make every part of the VW fit every other part so well, the finished car is practically air-tight.

The engine is so carefully machined and assembled, you can drive a brand new VW at top speed all day.

We don't make changes lightly. And never to make the VW look different, only to make it work better.

When we do make a change, we go out of our way to make the new part fit older Volkswagens, too.

With this result: An authorized Volkswagen dealer can repair any year's Volkswagen, even the earliest. (Why not? They use interchangeable parts!)

If you had to decide between a car that went out of style every year or two and a car that never did, which would it be?

enter doyle dane bernbach.

> *Volkswagen, 1961. Simple, elegant layout; simple, devastating sales pitch. The Volkswagen is never obsoleted, unlike those new American models that appear in the spotlights at the auto show. The light, humorous copy puts the ad's explosive message across easily: Detroit is a fraud.*

Has the Volkswagen fad died out?

Yes.

But it was an unnerving experience while it lasted.

Because after we introduced our completely sensible car, people ran out and got it for completely frivolous reasons.

The first people bought VWs just so they could be the first people to have one. And a lady in Illinois had one because

it looked cute beside her "real" car.

However, the faddists soon found out that the bug wasn't an expensive ($1574) toy, but a cheap ($1574) car.

As a fad, the car was a flop.

(When you drive the latest fad to a party, and find 2 more fads there ahead of you, it catches you off your avant-garde.)

But as a car, the VW was impressive.

If you had to go someplace, it took you. Even when some cars wouldn't. And when you got there, you could park it, in places where other cars couldn't.

Once people took the bug's good points for granted, it became the best-selling car model in history.

And that's when the VW fad ended.

volkswagen versus mass society,

1966. It's so practical, it inherently militates against faddishness and conformity. Notice the identification of the "avant-garde" with trendiness.

Soft Whiskey.
Is it just
another slogan?

f that were true, we'd be in big trouble by now.

But it just so happens, you can't l all the people all the time. And the people who taste Soft Whis- y and come back again aren't ying a slogan.

You see, it took more than some arp talk on Madison Avenue to ke Soft Whiskey soft.

It took time, money and thousands experiments that failed miserably fore we had it:

Tippecanoe and Tyler, too!

A whiskey that went down as easy as...well, Soft Whiskey.

But take heed:

That softness goes just so far.

After that, Soft Whiskey is 86 proof. Doing what any other respectable 86 proof whiskey can do.

(It's just that getting there is a whole lot easier.)

Naming Soft Whiskey was almost as easy as swallowing it.

One sip and you could have done it yourself.

the anticommercial whiskey,

Calvert Whiskey, 1966. Eight years later, with the giant glove nowhere to be found, DDB is selling Calvert whiskey as the antithesis of empty, "Madison Avenue" promises. After having come up with what may well have been the most slickly meaningless product claim for liquor of all time ("soft whiskey"), DDB proceeded to denounce liquor advertising in general for its slick meaninglessness.

MAYBE YOU DON'T WANT TO LOOK AT A PAINTED-ON SMILE ALL THE WAY TO EUROPE.

At El Al we feel our engines should turn on and off at the flick of a switch; not our stewardesses.

After all, we want you to feel at home.

And nobody walks around your home grinning at you like that for six straight hours.

Besides, six hours to London is one of our short hops. We also fly from New York to Paris, Zurich, Rome and Athens. And could you imagine being smiled at for ten and a half hours, all the way to Tel Aviv?

(That can be especially nerve-racking if you're the type who smiles back.)

So we teach our stewardesses how to pour wine, and how to warm baby bottles, and how to calm nervous grandmothers. And how to handle a thousand other little things that might come up, 30,000 feet up.

But giving big, warm smiles isn't always the first thing they think of.

That's why it's so nice every time they do.

El Al

the airline of authenticity,

El Al, 1967. Airlines, too, could benefit from the DDB makeover. There are no Stepford stewardesses on El Al. Like Volkswagens and Calvert Whiskey, their planes are affectation-free.

I hate conformity
because_____

Tell us your beef against society in
25 words or less and we won't send you
this Booth's House of Lords 'Protest' tie.
Anyone can give you a premium offer.
Booth's House of Lords gives you a
really fine gin and a chance to shoot
off your mouth with absolutely no risk.
All comments will be totally ignored.
Not a chance of winning anything.
Now that the competitive pressure is off,
why not take advantage of this
great opportunity? Do it today.
Or next year. It really doesn't
matter. There's no time limit on
taking a stand against conformity.
  You'll never be inspired by a faddist
gin. Instead try Booth's House of Lords.
Have it on-the-rocks, in a brandy
glass. We call it a Snifterini. But
you can call it anything you like.
That's one reason why many
people regard Booth's as the
non-conformist gin from
England.
Regardwise, it's the highest
we can be held in.

For $5, you may have four genuine Snifterini glasses, complete with Red Lion crest. Mail
check or money order to Made in England Co., 1197 McCarter Highway, Newark 4, N. J.

DISTILLED LONDON DRY GIN. 100% GRAIN NEUTRAL SPIRITS. 86 PROOF. IMPORTED BY AND BOTTLED IN THE U.S.A. FOR W. A. TAYLOR & CO., N.Y.

nonconformist gin,

> Booth's, 1965. By the mid-sixties, the zany creative style could be found even in ads
> for gin, the main ingredient of martinis. This ad for Booth's Gin, which ran in an
> advertising trade journal, mocks as many aspects of the Madison Avenue lifestyle
> (ties, mail-in offers, "competitive pressure," fads, martini glasses, the use of the
> suffix "-wise," and, of course, conformity) as one can in such a constricted space.
> (General Research Division, The New York Public Library, Astor, Lenox, and Tilden
> Foundations)

How to ignore the ad man when you buy stereo.

According to the latest unofficial count, there are 77 manufacturers of hi-fi and stereo who bring you the absolute ultimate in thrilling, realistic, three-dimensional sound.

That's what their ad men say in their ads.

Now suppose that you, an intelligent music lover without a degree in electronics, are actually shopping for the finest in radio-phonographs. Whose ad man should you trust?

No one's. Trust you own ears instead. They don't get paid for what they tell you.

Take your favorite record and make the rounds of the stores. Play it on as many radio-phonographs as you can. Listen carefully and compare. Then tune in a music broadcast on FM and listen some more. Also count the number of stations you can receive clearly across the FM dial. And have a good look at the cabinetry.

This particular ad man is confident that Fisher will stand out from all other makes in such a test.

But if you feel technologically insecure, do your shopping with an engineer friend. Or an electronics technician. Ask him what he thinks of the Fisher "Custom Electra" at $650 or any of the other Fisher stereo consoles from $400 to $2495. And if you don't want to rely solely on your own ears, maybe you know a professional musician who will listen with you.

Above all, ask your expert friend what he knows about Fisher and what the name means to him in comparison with others in the field.

After that, you'll read the stereo ads strictly as pop culture.

The Fisher
No ad man can do it justice.

Admen are liars,

but you are a discerning critic of pop culture, Fisher stereo, 1967. You can see through their puffery and falsehoods (if you can't, ask an unaffected, down-to-earth guy like an "engineer" to help you), and you can even see through this one, too!

savage parody

of the utopian style and frivolous auto design of just a few years before. Volvo, 1967. The "throw-away" culture for which the Detroit automakers are responsible is worse than Volkswagen has been telling you: it's actually "crazy." Even though tailfins had been dropped by GM and Chrysler in the early sixties, they continued to appear for years in critiques like this one as a standard symbol of everything that was wrong with consumer society.

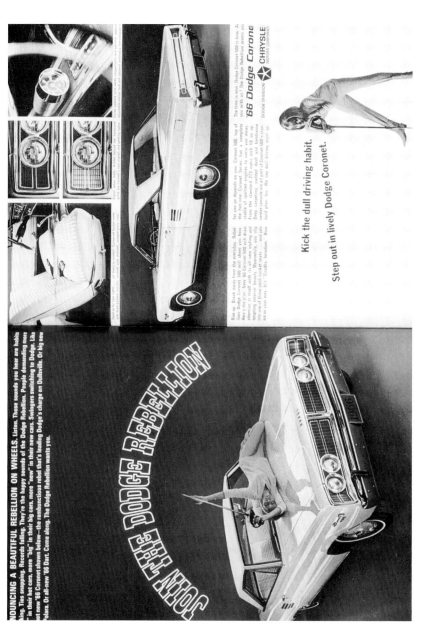

detroit strikes back.

Dodge, 1965. You say you've had it with Detroit-style consumerism? Then so has Detroit. Salvation is as easy as buying a new car: "Rise up. Break away from the everyday." Dodge is leading "the charge on Dullsville."

Desmond was afraid to let the cat out...until he got his Mustang.
Mustang! A car to make weak men strong, strong men
invincible. Mustang! Equipped with bucket seats, floor shift, vinyl
interior, padded dash, full carpeting, more. Mustang! A challenge to
your imagination with options like front disc brakes, 4-on-the-floor,
big 289 cu. in.V-8, you name it. Desmond
traded in his Persian kitten for an heiress named
Olga. He had to. She followed him home.
(It's inevitable...Mustangers have more fun.)

Best year yet to go Ford

MUSTANG!
MUSTANG!
MUSTANG!

the mustang transformation, 1965.

*Like the Dodge Rebellion, Mustang's promises to deliver consumers from ordinary life
were sexist, lighthearted and self-mocking. Later years would demand a more rigorous
critique of consumer culture.*

Today, millions of
Life readers
are getting
young ideas.
The '68
"youngmobiles"
from Oldsmobile
are here.

Call it different.
Call it individualistic.
Call it yours.
It's front-wheel-drive
Toronado '68. Drive it.

Young ideas:
Toronado has them inside, outside, under the hood. And these young ideas are backed up by all the values that have made Oldsmobile famous for 70 years. Oldsmobile quality. Oldsmobile prestige. Great Oldsmobile engineering.

Front view:
Toronado starts with front-wheel drive and takes off from there. A new 455 cubic-inch Rocket V-8, biggest in Oldsmobile's history, delivers greater efficiency with greater economy. A 400-hp Force-Air induction package is also available.

Exciting Styling:
Toronado has a burly-hooded, no-nonsense look that stands out from the crowd. Bold. Brawny. Massively male. Inside, more excitement. Rooms are flat. Carpeting is plusher than ever. Strato-Bench Seat with fold-down center is tailored in rich Morocceen. Buckets available, too.

Sporty Features:
Hideaway headlights that pop out at night. Windshield wipers that duck out of sight. Such optionables as instant-front disc brakes and a Tilt-and-Telescope Steering Wheel with a horn control all around the outside of the wheel.

Plus that famous Oldsmobile engineering and all the new GM safety features—including energy absorbing steering column, seat belts for all passenger positions, a host of others.

See Your Oldsmobile Dealer.

GM

youngmobiles.

By 1967 the obvious symbol under which all of these different strains of revulsion with mass society could be brought together was youth. Remember, it's the ideas that are young here, not the Oldsmobile owner.

buick populism,

1967. The documentary impulse in advertising. This corporation is an understanding friend, from their openness to your language to their gracious consideration of your needs to their realistic-looking models to their unadorned, sans-serif typeface.

Facts. Figures. Data. Reel after reel after reel. Wouldn't it be nice to have an Escape Machine?

It's here! 1970 Olds Cutlass Supreme, a totally new idea in elegance.

You and Cutlass Supreme, what a couple you'll make. We know because we checked it out on our computers. Here's what we found: You really go for elegant looks. Check. Those deep-comfort, double-padded seats—choice of buckets or bench. Check. That agile coil-spring ride. Check.

The no-draft Flo-Thru Ventilation System. Check. The anti-theft steering column lock. Check. The smoother, longer-lasting Rocket V-8 performance of Oldsmobile's exclusive new Positive Valve Rotators. Check. What do they do for you? They rotate the valves constantly—providing

better valve seating and perfect sealing for longer, more efficient engine operation. Check. And a price that will easily fit your budget. Check. Check. See your nearest Olds dealer soon and check out a Cutlass Supreme Escape Machine. It could be the start of something great.

Oldsmobile: Escape from the ordinary.

Protects you with energy-absorbing padded instrument panel, sideguard beams and stronger, longer-lasting bias-ply glass-belted tires, side marker lights and reflectors, anti-theft steering column. Pampers you with luxurious interiors, rotary glove box latch, easy-to-read instruments. Pleases you with Oldsmobile's famous quiet ride, responsive power, and contemporary styling.

"organization man" mutiny,

Oldsmobile, 1969. The promise is as simple as Volkswagen's, if the execution is poor (Oldsmobile just couldn't seem to get away from baffling terms like "Positive Valve Rotators"): this car rescues you from anonymity and bureaucratic malaise. Women, too.

There are some men a hat won't help

If you look anything like the fellow in the picture, you can stop reading right now. Wearing a hat won't do a thing for you.

No miracle happens when you put on a hat, but it can make the rough, competitive road between you and the top a little easier to travel.

You look more of a man with a hat on, and the men who run things have a deeply ingrained executive habit of reserving responsible jobs for those young men who look mature enough to handle them.

They may be right, or they may be wrong, but there's no denying that they're in charge. So it pays to humor them. Most business executives we've talked to prefer to hire men who wear hats.

We don't imply that going bareheaded marks you for failure. In the long run, it's what's under the hat that counts. Wearing a hat is just one of those little things that make it easier for a young man to get to where he wants to go.

Your age, you're in a hurry? Where's your hat?

A little friendly advice to young men in a hurry, published in the selfish interests of the hat industry by the Hat Corporation of America, 130 Fifth Avenue, New York 36, New York.

creativity yes, youth culture no.

Hat Corporation of America, 1961. A flippant, self-conscious ad in the DDB style, but distinctly craven toward the masters of mass society ("They may be right, or they may be wrong, but there's no denying that they're in charge") and hostile to rebel youth culture. The Beatnik pictured here is so dressed for failure that he even has a black eye. The hat industry started the decade striking all the wrong notes; by the end of the sixties it had been badly damaged.

youth culture, yes!

Love cosmetics, 1969. Hostility to affectation + suspicion of advertising + corporate populism + freedom, nature, honesty = Youth!

the uncola,

7-Up, 1969. Coke may have been the "real thing," Pepsi may have identified itself with the young generation, but 7-Up went just a little farther.

Note here the blurring of management theory and product pitch: by offering reproductions of its billboards, 7-Up is permitting "unrestricted creative freedom."

(© 7-Up and UNCOLA are marks identifying products of Dr Pepper/Seven Up, Inc. 1997. Courtesy of the John W. Hartman Center for Sales, Advertising, and Marketing History, Duke University Special Collections Library.)

Your car is out of style. Again.

And the money of it it, a big chunk of the money that you paid for your out-of-style car was used to bring out the very cars that put it out of style.

We make a car that hasn't been given a "big new look" in over 9 years. For 9 years we've been putting the money we save by not changing the way Volvo looks (a fortune in tail fins alone) into improving the way Volvo works.

Today, Volvo works like this: it lasts an average of eleven years in Sweden where there are no speed limits on the highways

and over 50,000 miles of unposed roads. It out-accelerates every other compact in its class. It gets over 25 miles to the gallon, even with automatic transmission.

What we're suggesting, of course, is that you buy something really new as a family car for 1967. A car that won't look old in '68.

Then you can quit trading cars so often and put the money you save into something that won't ever go out of style. Take a bank.

VOLVO

backlash, 1966.

Volvo. Now Detroit's promising youth, rebellion, and "Pizzaz," but they're still up to the same old tricks, and you're the loser by it. An unusual ad in that it actually pictures the relationship of reader and advertisement, proposes that advertising manipulates and victimizes consumers, and offers itself as a ready-made subversion.

With every pair of Mr. Stanley's
Hot Pants goes a free pack of short-
short filter cigarettes.

Now everybody will be wearing
hot pants and smoking short-short
filter cigarettes   ...almost everybody.

Camel Filters.
They're not for everybody.
(But then, they don't try to be.)

CAMEL

backlash, 1972.

Camel cigarettes. The sixties are over and now it's the pseudo-liberating, youth-
screaming styles of the Peacock Revolution that are the true markers of conformity—
and of a particularly effeminate conformity as well. The real rugged individualists
are . . . average guys.

chapter five

"HOW DO WE BREAK

THESE CONFORMISTS OF

THEIR CONFORMITY?"

CREATIVITY CONQUERS

ALL

Is creativity some obscure, esoteric art form? Not on your life. It's the most practical thing a businessman can employ.

— BILL BERNBACH [1]

resisting the usual

For all of the sophistication of recent cultural theory, many of its practitioners still tend to identify the sins of the consumer order as "homogeneity" or an obsessive logocentrism. In the advertising industry, that order's prime ideologist, however, these values were everywhere under attack by the mid-1960s. As a creative revolution followed in the wake of DDB's artistic and commercial success, the advertising industry began to recognize nonconformity, even more than science or organization or standardization or repetition or regulation, as a dynamic element of advertising and, ultimately, of the "permanent revolution" of capitalism itself. Early in 1970, a columnist for *Madison Avenue* magazine discussed the industry's realization of this principle. Although in "society" people "strive for . . . acceptance, conformity, anonymity," advertising necessarily militates against these values, offering consumers vicarious fulfillment of their "dream" to "stand out, to excell [sic], to be idolized, adulated." As Rosser Reeves had recognized, the basic problem much advertising faces is somehow to make products that are very similar to each other seem "unique." That advertising can only succeed if it, too, is made somehow to stand out from a blizzard of other ads, each vying for the consumer's attention. "To be successful," the magazine held, " . . . one must emerge from the mass, walk naked among the clothed, take that first step towards success, towards that dream fulfillment." The basic task of advertising, it seemed in the 1960s, was not to encourage conformity but a never-ending rebellion against whatever it is that everyone else is doing, a forced and exaggerated individualism.

> Every company is different and should look different. To be afraid to advertise in a way which talks about *real* problems or *real* differences is to be afraid to look in the mirror. To balk at communicating differently from competition is to balk at moving ahead of competition.[2]

Addressing the *"real"* problems of society and outlining *"real"* differences, then, would be the story of advertising in the 1960s.

As the decade progressed, Bill Bernbach's values of admaking and his revolutionary restructuring of the creative process spread rapidly through the sedate steel-and-glass boxes of Madison Avenue. The rage for creativity—which came quickly to mean an appeal to nonconformist rebellion against the mass society in ads as well as a nonhierarchical management style—was fueled partly by the demands of the admen themselves, who finally glimpsed liberation at the end of the corporate tunnel, but more importantly by the traditional buyers of advertising, the blue-chip clients of the big agencies who, impressed by the magic formula they saw in the Volkswagen (or Avis, or Calvert, or El Al) campaign, demanded similar work from their agencies. "'Let's get somebody like these guys and quit getting killed by General Foods,'" Jerry Della Femina imagines a Kraft executive reacting to a DDB ad. "The cry is going out all over town, 'Give me a Doyle, Dane agency, give me a Doyle, Dane ad.'"[3] The Creative Revolution may have questioned hierarchy, conventions of public speech, and the meaning of consumer culture, but it was fundamentally a market-driven phenomena. Remembering how his admaking philosophy was once denounced by the industry's press, George Lois says,

> That was the venom of the establishment. . . . Ninety-nine percent of the advertising came from the BBDOs and the J. Walter Thompsons, who were sitting there watching Doyle Dane's advertising and my advertising, and they were furious, because their clients were saying, "Why can't you do something like that?"[4]

After fifteen years of predictability and utopian fantasy, American capitalism suddenly developed an enthusiasm for graphic sophistication, for naturalism, for nonconformity, and for willful transgression. Dozens of

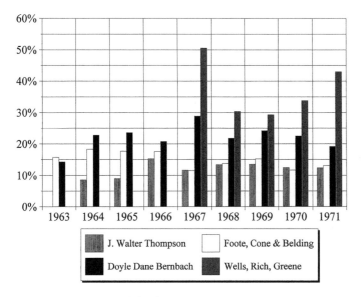

Profit Margins of Publicly Traded Advertising Agencies, 1963–71   fig 1

small, explicitly "creative" ad agencies appeared overnight, organized according to Bernbachian rather than the old hierarchical theories of management and promising to deliver the anti-establishment magic of the Volkswagen campaign. The large agencies scrambled to keep pace, reorganizing themselves into creative units, abolishing entire levels of hierarchy, and rushing to the corporate fore a caucus of young dissidents. The industry grew phenomenally during the decade. Expenditures in the six largest media (newspapers, magazines, radio, television, outdoor, and farm newspapers) grew from $4,736 million in 1953 to $7,164 million in 1960 to $12,237 million in 1970. The more meaningful indicator, though, is found in the relative profitability of the large, establishment agencies that had symbolized the industry during the fifties and the smaller, less hierarchical creative agencies. Figures for J. Walter Thompson and Foote, Cone & Belding (the successor to Lord & Thomas, the one-time employer of Frederic Wakeman) remain fairly comparable from 1966 on, hovering usually between ten and fifteen percent (see figure 1). During the same period, though, Doyle Dane Bernbach consistently posted profit margins above twenty percent while those of Wells, Rich, Greene, the superstar creative firm of the late sixties, actually exceeded fifty percent in 1967, their second year of operation. If only because of the blunt market logic of profitability, the age of organization was over,

chapter five

at least temporarily, on Madison Avenue; that of the small, flexible agency was beginning. And with the new trends in management would come a new cultural dispensation: it was to be the age of corporate hip.

ideologues of difference

Although there were always admen who disagreed strenuously with the admaking and management styles championed by Bernbach and Lois—the followers of Rosser Reeves spent the decade posturing as hard-headed businessmen under siege by romantic dreamers—by the mid-1960s the doctrines of creativity had swept the field. Admen from agencies large and small were producing articles, books, speeches, and, most important, ads that echoed or magnified Bernbach's hostility toward "science," to rules and to the priority of marketing data over creative inspiration. By 1965, the Creative Revolution had turned the industry's theories and management practices on their head as Madison Avenue entered a period of unrestrained rule-breaking and idol-shattering. One demonstration of the change came when Reeves was elected into the "Copywriters Hall of Fame" in 1965 and, with characteristic truculence, challenged the Advertising Writers Association of New York (AWANY, which sponsored the award) to define creativity. The organization's leaders fired back with equal conviction that "AWANY *must,* by its nature, come out against 'formulas' for advertising. By promoting individuality AWANY feels the standards of professionalism in advertising are raised."[5] That was hardly the harshest riposte faced by Rosser Reeves in those times, however. In February 1966, this quintessential adman of the fifties retired from his position as chairman of the Ted Bates Company, in a move that was interpreted by *Advertising Age* as a signal of changing ideas about creativity.[6] A later version of the story recounts the Reeves downfall as a much nastier bit of corporate skulduggery. In *Conflicting Accounts,* a 1997 book about the rise and fall of Saatchi and Saatchi, the British mega-agency that acquired Bates in 1986, advertising writer Kevin Goldman asserts that Reeves was sacked rather than retired—and that "the agency so wanted Reeves out that it paid him $80,000 annually for ten years to keep him away."[7]

By the mid-1960s the anti-principles of creativity had become rule-book stuff in their own right. In a 1966 handbook for copywriters, a Young & Rubicam creative leader instructs readers that "The first rule for copywriters is to be suspicious of rules. Rules have a way of turning into ruts."[8] Even more telling evidence of the new antinomian climate was a house ad for the Geer, DuBois agency, authors of the unremittingly hip campaign for Foster Grant sunglasses, that appeared in the *New Yorker* in 1967. Under a blank TV storyboard (a type of layout paper used to plan television commercials) are listed the classic steps to producing a television commercial of the standard Reeves style of the 1950s: "1. Open by getting attention. 2. Establish news value. 3. Briefly show what the product is," and so forth. After the eighth step, the copy reads, simply, "It's with good rules like these that bad commercials are made." The industry's storyboards were being symbolically wiped clean: a new beginning was at hand.[9]

The authority of "science" in advertising theory had also diminished considerably by the mid-1960s. In 1966, advertising writer Nicholas Samstag contributed a long essay to *Madison Avenue* magazine entitled "You Can't Make a Good Advertisement Out of Statistics." By then the argument that advertising was "more an art than a science" had definitely been won, he noted, but the traditional hostility of business for something as nebulous as art had made this difficult to put across: "the men who pay for advertising are ill at ease in the presence of artists." But, Samstag continued, "Don't let the pie-charts and research mumbo-jumbo fool you. An advertisement is a seduction," and "there are no objective standards against which the efficacy of a seduction can be measured in advance." Samstag's vision of the advertising revolution, which was replacing Reevesian science with Bernbachian aestheticism, could easily be read as a manifesto for the larger revolt against the constraints of the mass society.

> Marketing should be an emancipator. It should unlock locks and cut bonds by suggesting and implying, by hinting and beckoning, not by defining. It should be the agent that frees, not the agent that imprisons. . . .
>
> In brief, we need more and more affirmative, plastic, humanistic, refreshing research, less and less scientific authoritarianism. . . .
>
> Forward researchers! *You have nothing to lose but your dogma.*[10]

The passage is a remarkable document of the sixties, startlingly reminiscent in tone and language (it would be indistinguishable if the words "marketing" and "research" were removed) of the decade's other overheated celebrations of "emancipation" from "scientific authoritarianism."

The primary goal of unleashing all of this creativity was not to overthrow capitalism, of course, or even necessarily to make the workplace

chapter five

happier, but to jump-start the engine of change—the "permanent revolution"—that drove consumer culture. Following Bernbach's celebration of "difference," admen in the sixties awoke to the virtue of nonconformity. By the mid-1960s, talk about creativity and perpetual innovation was ubiquitous in industry literature. The ideologues of Madison Avenue now insisted, contrary to the standard practices of the preceding decade, that the adman internalize an automatic mistrust for received ideas. Arguing in 1966 that "the 'new' is inevitably the product of the impatient individual," Sherman E. Rogers of the Buchen agency advised his colleagues to understand "restlessness and discontent" for what they were: the wellspring of "the new." For Rogers, the good adman has nothing to do with "status quo-ism," or the agency types of the 1950s like the "play-it-safer" and the "hat-in-hander," those "who view the Jerk and the Monkey [popular dances] with wide-eyed alarm, who have not listened to Bob Dylan with the idealistic ears of the young."[11] Asserting that "we copywriters and art directors should be the most obvious disciples of change," Hanley Norins, Young & Rubicam's most fiery creative partisan, reaffirmed later that year the decade's commercial antinomianism, its skepticism toward whatever had already been decided. "What we need," he wrote, "is an attitude of distrust toward our own ideas. . . . As soon as you have an idea, try to disprove it."[12] Here, as in so many other aspects of the business, management theory spilled over unproblematically into the actual content of advertisements: Not only was this willingness to defy convention de rigueur for creative personnel, it made a fine brand image as well. For Chester Posey, creative director of the gigantic McCann-Erickson agency, creativity was defined as an embrace of what he called "the unexpected," a general contrariety that set an ad off from the masscult babble surrounding it. "I believe that our biggest risk in advertising is the risk of being *expected*," he wrote. "I believe that effective advertising must be incompatible with an indifferent opinion of a product. . . .that it must be interruptive, disquieting, challenging, surprising and unsettling." Nor was this a simple matter of announcing "all new all over again." Finding the unexpected meant constantly searching for unusual angles to "that good dull product that we deal with every day." It was "a philosophy and a way of thinking." And, like Rogers's "impatience," it was a concept he chose to illustrate with youth culture icons, a collection of which accompanied Posey's 1965 *Ad Age* article on the subject.[13]

By 1966, the new way had even triumphed at J. Walter Thompson, citadel of the advertising establishment. Concerned about the challenge from DDB and the other creative agencies, JWT circulated a series of

"Creative Forum Papers" within its offices, aiming to instruct its employees in the fine points of the new style. The installment for November,
1966, a short essay entitled "Conform with the Non-Conformists," written by associate creative supervisor R. Beverley Corbin, laid out the problems facing creative workers at big agencies. Since advertising has to "do
what everyone else *isn't* doing" in order to work, it was the adman's duty
to "do it differently" *and* to confront clients and co-workers who were
afraid to venture out of their gray flannel preserves, to "break these conformists of their conformity." In the past, admen had felt pressure to blend
into the organization, to resist showing individuality, to "seek out a technique of advertising someone else is doing successfully and latch onto it
like a Remora latches onto a Shark." But the days of conformity were
over, at least in theory. Corbin encouraged his colleagues to "try to stand
out like a healthy thumb amidst a bunch of sore fingers."[14] By 1966, even
Dan Seymour, the president of J. Walter Thompson, had been convinced.
"We are dedicated to constant discontent with the status quo," this head
of Madison Avenue's most status quo agency said. "We don't believe in
styles or schools. . . . The only thing we know for sure is that there is no
such thing as a J. Walter Thompson ad."[15] Nonconformity was fast becoming the advertising style of the decade, from the office antics of the
now-unleashed creative workers, to the graphic style they favored, to the
new consumer whose image they were crafting.

the creative workplace

As advertising theory increasingly reflected the Bernbach line, agency
organization and management made a sharp about-face as well. The Creative Revolution affected not only the way admen thought and the ads
they produced but their everyday business practices. If the rule-smashing
"New Advertising" (as one writer called it in 1970) that was then in
such demand—the antimarketing iconography of nonconformity, difference, and individualism—required decentralized, nonhierarchical anti-
organizations, then Madison Avenue would positively trip over itself to
deliver just that. If the advertising world of the 1950s was, as Randall
Rothenberg describes it, "a fundamentally conservative industry," an industry whose primary task was placating the whims of the client, that of
the 1960s would be dominated—symbolically at least—by the eccentric
creative genius, defying convention and going to the wall for his rule-
breaking ideas.[16]

chapter five

According to the heated industry rhetoric of the sixties traded back and forth through the pages of *Advertising Age* and *Madison Avenue*, the Creative Revolution was fought out along something resembling class lines: the division being between creative workers—art directors and copywriters—and the account men who communicated with clients. Jackson Lears maps onto this division his story of the endless war between managerial and carnival values in advertising. The books of Reeves, Mayer, and Ogilvy had all assailed dreamy and overcritical creative workers. But in the sixties, the tables would be turned. According to creative partisans, it was the traditional power of the account executives, who were said to know little about admaking itself, that made so much of their industry's product boring and ineffective. Not coincidentally, account men were also believed to be predominantly WASPs, wearers of gray flannel, and consumers of the famous "three-martini lunch." The terms with which George Lois excoriated "the hack marketing people" in 1971, are extreme, but they give a vivid idea of the hostility between the two camps:

They don't like the way we work, the way we talk, the way we dress. They don't know anything about advertising or how good advertising is created. They hold this business down. They help to create the bad advertising we are inundated with. [17]

Jerry Della Femina's chapters on agency dysfunction and the idiocy of such institutions as "creative review boards" are all aimed at account executives. And when questioned in 1968 by *Marketing/Communications* magazine about "the current state of the agency business," one particularly hip adman replied that

The creative spirit is dampened by account men in rep-tie blindfolds. There is much frustration. . . . a lot of creative people wasting their lives where their creative ability never gets by a plans board. I can see creative types going on strike . . . or a mass walkout of 200 or 300 creative types in this business. [18]

For Lois and others, the struggle between account-management and creativity was "war," an all-out conflict of lifestyles and philosophies.

It was a battle whose issues and outcome would define the industry throughout the 1960s. Creative workers denounced the science and research of the fifties and demanded instead freedom and autonomy in the workplace. At the same time, they insisted that their products and decisions be accorded the respect due the work of professionals. For some

chapter five

commentators in the 1960s, it appeared as though creativity might prevail unconditionally.[19] Demand was great for the new type of advertising; to meet it, an army of creative personnel broke away from the large firms to found their own less-structured agencies. The large "establishment" agencies began to reorganize themselves along the new lines as well. Young & Rubicam, the industry's second-largest agency, promoted Steve Frankfurt, a 36-year-old arts-oriented television director to its presidency. The other pillars of the "establishment" rushed to build creative cells, to shake up the tired ranks of their executive corps, to loosen up creative restrictions and rationalize the creative process. Martin Mayer had already noticed the magnitude of the change by 1965 when he wrote that while "in 1954 the nation's seven largest agencies were all run by 'businessmen'; ten years later, four of them had copywriters at the helm, and two of the others had moved 'creative' men into the heir-apparent positions."[20] In August, 1969, with the Creative Revolution in full swing, *Newsweek* estimated that almost a hundred new firms had been inaugurated in that year alone.[21]

Most of these new agencies, of course, would never grow to the size of J. Walter Thompson or Doyle Dane Bernbach. Nor would they provide all of the various services (media buying, research, testing, etc.) that larger agencies performed. But while they rarely represented blue-chip clients, these new, unstructured, and intensely creative agencies set the tone for the advertising of the decade. With struggling clients willing to try anything and little bureaucracy to hinder them, the creative shops—"boutiques" in the parlance of their doubters, "hot shops" in that of their supporters—expanded the boundaries of advertising, pioneered a thousand new techniques and formulas, and opened paths that their larger competitors would soon follow. And some of the firms founded in those years—Wells, Rich, Greene; Carl Ally; Scali, McCabe, Sloves; and Chiat/Day—did eventually become prominent industry fixtures.

Trade journal reports of the doings of the small, "hot" agencies invariably focused on three aspects of their work—three fantasies of corporate antinomianism that continue to define much of the language of advertising to this day (Dan Wieden's reminder to new workers that "chaos is creative" and that his agency functioned like a "slime mold" is more typical than it sounds). First, they were described as Theory Y havens, virtually unstructured organizations, places of anarchic lawlessness, frenzied rule-breaking, corporations that somehow did without intrusive, dragging bureaucracy. Thus photographer Onofrio Paccione complained to *Madison Avenue* in 1965 about the big agency experiences that had led

chapter five

him to strike out on his own. "Committees, committees, committees, and then you go back to your own office and solve the problem," he said. At Leber Katz Paccione, on the other hand, Paccione was able to develop ideas himself from start to finish, and actually took all of the photographs the new agency used in ads, a system which, the magazine noted, "gives him complete creative control over the execution of the ads. There is no distortion of an idea by having it pass through many hands."[22] "Establishing an environment in which creative people can flourish" was the theme of a January, 1966, article on Delehanty, Kurnit & Geller. Here, too, creativity was said to be privileged over organization. There were very few bureaucrats to interfere with true commercial inspiration, allowing one art director to sum up the creative process in these idealistic terms:

After knowing all he can about a product, the art director and the copy chief are ready to create a selling concept. The art director must then work in an environment where his intellectual and intuitive ideas may be expressed. Where his graphic skills and tastes can be appreciated. And where he knows his final product will not be destroyed by insensitive committees, frightened account executives or egomaniacal clients.[23]

A third agency even dared to de-organize itself to the point of defying Bill Bernbach's creative team system, the basis of creative agencies. It was just too structured, too orderly by 1966 standards. The agency president, Martin Solow, assailed what he called the

Fettish [sic] for teaming up creative people, such as an art director with a copywriter. We don't believe in rules. We simply work together. Maybe three copywriters will sit down and solve the problem. Our art directors have given us some of our best headlines. Bright things come out of bright people.

And the duty of the agency's management was simply to provide the surroundings and the materials in and with which those "bright people" could function best.[24]

Second, each of the small firms that dealt in creativity wore the aura of Bernbachian client-defiance. So intransigently did the new adman believe in the professionalization of his calling and the correctness of his creative judgment that he would rather resign an account than submit to the humiliation demanded by industry captains like Evan Llewelyn Evans. Thus, *Esquire* editor Harold Hayes notes in one of the blurbs on the dust jacket of George Lois's 1972 memoirs that relations between admen and clients have become much more volatile: "The image of the soul-rotted ad man, trembling before the wrath of his client in order to keep his ranch house in Westport, is not the image of George Lois."[25] Lois proudly recounts how he climbed out an office-building window in order to convince a recalcitrant Matzoh manufacturer of his advertising expertise and details his refusal to bow and scrape before the powerful head of Seagrams, Samuel Bronfman: "I wasn't about to play the foot-shuffling adman who swallows his pride and does a jig for a dozing client."[26] By the mid-1960s, Lois's defiance was commonplace among creative types. As one of his "nine statements for art directors," Georg Olden, the 1965 chairman of the New York Art Directors' Club, included this commandment: "I do not do everything I am told. Unless I agree."[27] Carl Ally, who left PKL to found his own agency in 1962, blamed the badness of mainstream advertising in 1966 (by then it was a fairly standard creative complaint) on agencies' traditional tendency to indulge clients' whims rather than stand up for what they know is the right approach:

The real flaw is lack of commitment. The well-they-won't-buy-that mentality. We don't ask what the client wants. We test everything on ourselves. If we like it, it's good. If we don't, it stinks.[28]

Scali, McCabe, Sloves, one of the most successful creative agencies launched in the 1960s, once took this adamantine stance toward clients to its logical conclusion, resigning an account when the client declined to take the agency's advertising advice. The agency made a practice of never offering "more than one execution of an ad or commercial to the client," *Madison Avenue* observed in 1970, and even then "when copy is to be changed for technical reasons, the writer who wrote it changes it, not the client." So when Scali, McCabe, Sloves disagreed with one of its largest clients about the nature and direction of a new campaign, the agency simply gave up the account rather than accept the client's dictation. As president Marvin Sloves recalled,

We [the agency people] talked it over. It took us five minutes to decide to resign the account. It wasn't anything petulant. We just disagreed with them and, since we regard ourselves as the experts, we had to stand up for what we believed in.[29]

Creativity's third identifying feature was, of course, the stunning divergence of its ads from the formulas of the 1950s, formulas which cre-

chapter five

ative admen believed, almost as a matter of faith, were still strictly enforced at the big agencies in the 1960s.

the establishment

The favored term among revolutionaries for the big agencies against whose bureaucracy and inspection they felt so much rancor was "establishment." Into the 1970s, creative admen continued to mount an array of accusations against them in the industry press: the establishment was the preserve of the repressed and fearful account men, where ads were still produced by what Jerry Della Femina called "the assembly-line method."[30] As he described it, copywriters at the establishment agencies were told the client's sales objective and churned out a number of possible headlines and pitches. These were then given to art directors to illustrate.

Now the art director is . . . chained to his desk; they don't want art directors roaming the halls at large agencies. . . . He usually is between forty and fifty years old but even if he's a young guy his mind is fifty. . . . The copywriter says, "We got to have a layout by this afternoon to show to the creative director." . . . It's in the hands of the creative director by that afternoon and that's it. There's little relationship between the art director and the copywriter. They hardly know each other.[31]

In "the establishment agencies" as elsewhere in the technocratic society, the artistic spirit was said to be imprisoned by the vast, impersonal organization, individuality was suppressed, and everyone was old. Creative partisan Robert Glatzer recounted in 1970 how corporate pusillanimity had given the large agency Foote, Cone, and Belding the nickname "Stoop, Prone, and Bending." Its abject willingness to please clients "has tended to attract docile, gelded Mad-Ave types to FCB, the security-minded androgynes of this malevolently sexual business, who would rather submit than fight a client bent on raping a campaign."[32] The accounts of both Glatzer and Della Femina were exaggerated, of course. But the "establishment" problems of the big agencies were acute enough to propel them into a revolution of their own.

As creativity became the most hotly-sought element of advertising, even the most factorylike, statistics-dominated firms gave in to the new wave and entered upon a frenzy of creative reconstruction. Large agencies "raided" smaller ones in hopes of luring away creative superstars with

more generous salaries; they established more or less autonomous creative
groups to produce material along DDB lines; they rejuvenated their management corps; and they leaped headlong into the endless theorizing
about the nature of creativity that fills the advertising texts of the period.

Jack Tinker & Partners, an experimental "think tank" that was developed by the enormous McCann-Erickson agency in 1960, was a small
group of advertising specialists headed by a veteran McCann copywriter
and charged with developing special marketing strategies for McCann
clients. But in 1964 Tinker began to make advertising on its own, for a
list of clients which eventually included Alka-Seltzer, Gillette razors, and
Braniff airlines. Launched on the antibureaucracy, antirules credo of the
hot, creative shops, the group was the first and one of the most successful
attempts to capture for a large agency the benefits of a small, unstructured
organization. The original Tinker Partners had been executives caught
up in the day-to-day supervision of others and unable to devote their time
to the actual stuff of advertising. One later recalled, "Jack was spending
80 per cent of his time in meetings, reviewing other men's work when he
should have been spending his time creating." The goal of the Tinker
experiment, then, was to find "if a small team of advertising executives
with proven ability, if sequestered from the committees, review boards
and daily mundane agency chores, could come up with fresher, brighter
and more creative solutions to advertising problems than seemed possible
under the normal agency structure." Naturally, the group's antihierarchical nonstructure was described in communitarian political terms that
sometimes marked the era's political attacks on the technocracy. One of
the partners, Myron McDonald, characterized the business as a "democracy." Jack Tinker himself described it as a "community in which outstand-
ing talents can exist together." Mary Wells, who first came to prominence
under Tinker's tutelage, voiced the group's suspicion of bureaucracy, a
standard creative complaint by 1965, the year her remarks appeared in
Madison Avenue: "We don't want eighteen people passing on information. The only effective way to do creative work is for the creative person
to see a commercial all the way through himself." [33]

The success of the Tinker group and its rapid imitation by every
other "establishment" agency marked a transition on Madison Avenue
equally important as the rise of the independent creative shops. It was
a declaration—first by McCann-Erickson and its gigantic parent company, Interpublic, then by the other corporate agencies—that the age of
Theory X had ended, that Organization was on its way to extinction, to
be replaced by a stripped-down, flexible, "democratic" arrangement that

privileged creative nonconformists. Before long, the new way had been adopted even by J. Walter Thompson, the great institutional foe of creative excess. In 1966, Thompson reorganized itself to meet the needs of "creative people, who almost instinctively rebel against the formal, structured organization," finally bringing art, copy, and television people together into one of six putatively autonomous "operating groups" where freedom was the order of the day. *Madison Avenue* magazine, ever optimistic about creative advance, hailed the change as "the replacement of the debilitating 'production line' atmosphere for a new sense of total involvement with each account."[34] At Benton & Bowles, the change required two separate waves of corporate radicalism, one in 1966 ("We came to the conclusion that for the best results our creative people should work together in an intimate relationship as *total* advertising people, working on creative problems together from start to finish," Al Goldman, the company's creative director, was reported to say) and another in 1970, when an outside "creative Messiah" was hired to clean hierarchical house in a flurry of firings and what today would doubtless be called "reengineering."[35]

In addition, many of the "establishment" agencies hired leading creative rebels away from the small shops where they had distinguished themselves, with each building what *Madison Avenue* columnist Jerry Fields called its "own brand of 'Tinker Toy' or Creative Island." But none of the changes made much difference to self-proclaimed *real* creative rebels, who, like Fields, continued to complain of being "emasculated . . . with many-splendored layers of creative review boards, committees, brand managers, product managers, and other filtering strata of management executives on the client and agency side" throughout the decade.[36] Although Jerry Della Femina publicly derided what he called the "zoo concept," he was himself acquired by none other than the Ted Bates agency, the hard-sell holdout from which Rosser Reeves would soon depart.[37] Tales of creative stars' defections to the big agencies and their subsequent unhappiness under the Organization's yoke are a standard trope of the literature of the period, an almost predictable cautionary tale for the new corporate age. After losing its top four creative workers to McCann-Erickson at one point, Delehanty, Kurnit & Geller president Shepard Kurnit said in 1969, "The offer was so good that if I didn't own the company, I would have gone along with them." None of the four stayed at McCann for long. Each went through a variety of positions at various agencies until two of them returned to Delehanty, Kurnit & Geller.[38] In 1968, J. Walter Thompson hired Ron Rosenfeld, one of

DDB's star copywriters, to construct a new creative group within the giant agency. A year later, Rosenfeld resigned from Thompson offering
advertising writers yet another opportunity to muse on the incompatibil-
ity of genius and hierarchy. Writing in *Madison Avenue* magazine, Bob
Fearon pontificated about the inherent conflict between the people who
create "an awful lot of the best advertising of late" but who "sense things"
rather than rely on research; and the rigid, overorganized agencies of the
corporate establishment who know simply "how to deliver an acceptable
product on time."

Being oriented to giving clients what they wanted, agency leaders tried to graft on a
free-spirited, gut-oriented creative quality to their already existing, highly-stratified
institutions. They brought creative names in. They said things were going to be different. In almost every case the chemistry was wrong. In almost every case the im-
port was asked to fit himself into the system. The system was not willing to bend.[39]

chapter six

THINK YOUNG:

YOUTH CULTURE

AND CREATIVITY

He sat on his inflatable plastic sofa, his beard curling over his turtleneck sweater, beads and Nehru jacket. Sitar music played over the loud speaker. He and the copywriter in the transparent blouse had just told the client what he could do.

— FRANCHELLIE CADWELL AND HAL DAVIS, 1968 [1]

In the early years of the advertising revolution, creativity meant minimalism. After the successes achieved with the simple layouts of Volkswagen and the no-background blankness used by George Lois, minimalism was an obvious choice for speaking to consumers made skeptical by years of stretched autos and glittering appliances. But in the mid-1960s, the look and language of creativity changed dramatically. The shift is plainly visible in the progression of the *Annuals of Advertising Art* published through the 1960s by the Art Directors' Club of New York. These volumes were yearbooks of the Creative Revolution, showplaces dominated by DDB, PKL, and their ever-expanding phalanx of followers. Until mid-decade they were also showplaces of clean, corporate minimalism, dominated by sans-serif typefaces and simple, uncluttered layouts. But with the volume covering 1966 (published in 1967), creativity finds a strikingly different graphic voice: the symbol for the 1966 Art Directors' show is a color photograph of a woman nude and supine for the camera, her body painted from head to toe with elaborate dayglo flowers and rainbows and the words, "46th Annual NY Art Directors' Show." Creativity had merged with counterculture. [2]

Virtually anyone who lived through the 1960s in America remembers advertising's strange and sudden infatuation with countercultural imagery, its overnight conversion to rock music and scenes of teenagers dancing their strange, indecipherable dances. Models in photographs and on television commercials became younger, gave up their clean-cut appearances for long hair and rebel garb, traded ingratiating smiles for serious stares at the camera. Typefaces and graphic design reflected new hallucinogenic styles as quickly as they could be invented. The fault lines of advertising discourse changed as well, seismically and suddenly. In conference after conference and article after article, admen counseled their colleagues in the fine points of hip slang, the varieties of rock music, the usefulness of psychedelic graphic effects. One day in 1967 Madison Avenue Man shed his gray flannel suit and leaped headlong into youth culture.

For countercultural participants and their admirers, advertising's change was co-optation, pure and simple, an effort to dilute a meaningful, even menacing uprising and sway a large body of consumers at the same time. But the appeal of hip to Madison Avenue derived as much from its kinship to the new understanding of consumer culture embodied in the Creative Revolution as it did from its demographic appeal. Counterculture, it seemed, was an ideal expression of the new vision of consuming that Theory-Y capitalism, with all its glorious flexibility, instant communication, and rapid obsolescence, was bringing into existence.

groovy

Looking back at the Creative Revolution in 1977, Bill Pitts, copywriter and co-author of the various George Lois books, characterized it as the development and eventual victory of a "counterculture [that] began to find expression on Madison Avenue," an insurgent movement with the same attitudes and enemies as the youth rebellion that overturned so many tired, conformist values in the 1960s and 1970s, a "new creative generation, a rebellious coterie of art directors and copywriters who understood that verbal and visual expressiveness were indivisible, who bridled under the old rules that consigned them to secondary roles in the admaking process under the dominion of noncreative technocrats."[3] Similarly, creative superstar of the 1990s Jeff Goodby recently hailed the work of Howard Gossage as an affirmation of the lifestyle revolution being conducted "just a couple of big hills away" from his San Francisco firehouse office. "Howard never seemed to judge or even acknowledge" the hippies themselves, Goodby remembers. "Yet looking back, he seems more like them than unlike them, a tiny, laughing, downtown outpost of it all."[4] The analogy between creativity and counterculture seems to be a natural one for those who participated in the corporate convulsions of those years. Youth culture became the industry's dominant fantasy almost overnight, converting not only the public appearance of advertising, but the trade discourse as well.

It was an odd symbiosis. Hip young people famously despised Madison Avenue and the plastic civilization for which it stood, and yet admen could never seem to get enough of their criticism, their music, or the excellent trappings of their liberated ways. A symptomatic document is *The Gap*, a book penned jointly during the summer of 1967 by a New York adman of the creative variety and his pot-smoking, Columbia-attending nephew. Each makes an effort to enter the world of the other: the adman smokes dope, the college student attends a martini-soaked client lunch at the Four Seasons. What astounds a contemporary reader is the inversion of generational roles that takes place. Ernest Fladell, the adman, is strangely candid and seems genuinely interested in the life of the mysterious young. He compares marijuana, with unmodulated admiration, to the alcohol he usually consumes:

The kids are on an entirely different kick. Sex isn't the object, nor is the ability to let go. They have both in reasonably good supply. Their groove is to feel more, see, taste, hear, enjoy more. The kids are hedonistic; we're puritanical.

But Richard Lorber, the hip twenty-year-old, is scornful and condescending and impossibly pretentious, recommending "experiments in expanded consciousness" to strangers and declaring that his uncle can't really have enjoyed marijuana (which "Many of my friends consider . . . to be an experience of sacred depth") properly after one try because "Pot is a learning experience and each time one turns on the effect is amazingly cumulative."[5]

But the scorn of Richard and his friends was for nought. Admen, especially of the new creative breed, could not come up with enough positive things to say and write about rebellious youth—some of them appearing even before the counterculture first came to the attention of the glossy mass-circulation magazines in 1967. In 1966, DDB published a study of youth whose conclusions anticipated Roszak and Reich by "predict[ing] a new image of and for American youth . . . based on *nobility, virtue, romanticism,* and *high purpose.*"[6] For all of the superlatives, these were actually fairly commonplace sentiments in the advertising trade literature of the time. According to adman and youth specialist Merle Steir in 1967, "The Now People" were perfect consumers for the age of creative rule-smashing, far out in front of their backward-looking elders: "Youth wants to see it and tell it like it is. Then People want to see it like it was."[7] Even Leo Burnett, the Chicago-based celebrator of middle-American values, applauded in 1967 what he called the "Critical Generation's" skepticism toward established values as potentially "one of the healthiest things that ever happened to the human race."[8] By 1969, *Advertising Age* was capable of publishing an all-out manifesto by creative leader Hanley Norins (who had gone from being a creative advisor to a countercultural enthusiast on the scale of Ralph Gleason) for the "individual revolution . . . for which the young people are the spearhead." Inviting his audience to marvel with him at the "wiggy words [rock lyrics] that feed your mind," the wild names of new rock bands, the endless variety of the new fashion in which "everyone [is] vying to be different," Norins celebrated the youth-led smashing of "the bondage of mass conformity." Admen should not be concerned with suppressing the youth revolution—which was impossible anyway—but with claiming a position in its vanguard:

The Individual Revolution is in full cry. It's not only coming. It's here. So why does anybody resist it at all? Above all, why don't we advertising men lead the revolution and help to make it a viable, positive one?[9]

It's not that admen like Norins or Burnett were unaware of the counterculture's mistrust of advertising or its hostility toward the consumerism of the World War II generation. Indeed, they saw in the counterculture a social embodiment of the mass society critique, complete with healthy skepticism toward Madison Avenue, that had done so much to define the advertising of the Creative Revolution in the first place. The counterculture allowed creative revolutionaries to say, "See, I told you so." E. B. Weiss, an *Advertising Age* columnist and a prominent celebrator of youth culture, recognized that "never has a young generation been so critical, and so mature in its criticism of advertising." Youth was, as he put it, "Junk[ing] the junk culture," that same junk culture junked in the Vance Packard books and the Volkswagen ads.[10] Even young people's most negative pronouncements could be transformed into a pitch for the more realistic style of the creative revolution. Referring to a Weatherman communique that accompanied a corporate bombing attack, Leo Bogart of the American Newspaper Publishers' Association was able to read the "skepticism of advertising messages" that youngsters expressed as just an-

other demand that the straightforward style of creativity replace the jack-
hammer puffery of yore.[11]

The standard explanation for Madison Avenue's almost embarrassing idealism about the counterculture is the size of the youth demographic in the 1960s. And it is undeniable that virtually all articles and speeches lauding the rebel young contain some reference to the giant youth market and insist that one must grant legitimacy to youth culture in order to speak the language of this mysterious but powerful new consumer. Almost every one of the countless articles or speeches on the subject of the youth culture mentions, in some form, the decade's favorite statistic: that half of the nation's population was, or would soon be, under the age of twenty-five; and its corollary, that young people had control of some $13 billion in discretionary spending dollars—$25 billion if the entire age span from thirteen to twenty-two was counted.[12] In addition, young people were widely regarded as economically powerful beyond their immediate means. They had become the decade's arbiters of taste, and advertising could target adults through appeals to their children. Articles and conferences and workshops offering advice on reaching this lucrative market proliferated wildly. A firm called Youth Concepts, which promised to unlock the mysteries of youth culture for the advertising world, put on a proto-counterculture exhibition for its clients in 1966 which featured a number of apparent demonstrators carrying signs that read, "We spend $12 billion a year" and "48% of the population is under 25."[13] And, as the firm's leader Merle Steir noted, "You can't communicate to people you are 'against.'"[14] Admen would have to make an effort to enjoy youth culture if they were to address its fans.

But the argument from demographics can only account for a part of the frenzy for hip that overtook advertising in the mid-1960s. First, it cannot explain why advertising completely ignored young people who did not take part in the counterculture. That admen were aware of this vast market of "silent majority" frat boys and football players is obvious from Leo Burnett's comments on the "Critical Generation," which, although it had captured the camera's attention at Berkeley and elsewhere, was clearly a minority among young people. Advertisers simply weren't as keen to appropriate the symbols of the crew-cut market segment. Second, the size of the youth market cannot explain why the symbols of rebel culture were applied to all sorts of products, even those aimed at older Americans. Car advertising was a particular anomaly, undergoing a youth-oriented image transformation in the mid-1960s despite contemporary statistics that put youthful car buyers at only 9 percent.[15] And, above all, the argument from demographics does not explain admen's glaring failure to successfully "speak to" the young consumer. Certainly the iconography of youth became the almost hegemonically dominant motif in the advertising of the period, and advertisers did everything they could to incorporate the new attitudes of the young into their works. But in the end, few among the counterculture's true believers were convinced. Trade journals repeatedly warned admen selling to the young against attempting to speak in youth's idiosyncratic idiom: older people could never get it quite right and would only end up arousing sneers and suspicion.

The size of the youth market is only a relatively small part of the explanation for Madison Avenue's curious infatuation with the counterculture. Viewed from a more encompassing perspective, the conversion of ads and the advertising industry as a whole to the look and language of youth culture only makes sense in the context of the Creative Revolution, its new understanding of consumer culture, and of the larger changes underway in capitalism as a whole. Admen equated creativity with counterculture; its language, its suspicion of advertising, its disdain for mass culture all seemed to reinforce the lessons of Bill Bernbach. As it would in the menswear industry, the counterculture provided advertising leaders with a language and a palette of symbols with which to express a new consuming vision that they had been espousing for a number of years already. It was no coincidence that *Advertising Age*'s most vociferous followers of youth culture were also its most extreme partisans of creativity: in their minds, the lessons of the new revolutionary youth culture were the same as the revolutionary tenets of creativity. "Think young," the advertising cliche of the day, did not simply mean to remember the youth market. It meant to think creatively, to embrace difference and nonconformity and, ultimately, to think like a consumer. Point number one of twenty that defined "The New Creativity" in 1968 for J. Walter Thompson employees was to adopt "a new tone of voice" that was "attuned to the idiom of today's affluent, hedonistic, youth-oriented society."[16] When *Newsweek* finally ran a cover story on "Advertising's Creative Explosion" in 1969, it openly equated creativity with Madison Avenue's new fascination with youth culture. Concentrating on the youthful faces then entering the business, the "bizarre modes of dress" favored by the creative types, and creativity's hostility toward the "establishment," the magazine constructed a portrait of the revolution that its readers were sure to recognize from its resemblance to the counterculture.[17]

And creativity certainly *appeared* to be countercultural, at least to judge by the look of younger admen in the later 1960s. Like counterculture, creativity seemed to be the province of young people, rebels who were identified with nonconformity and innovative thinking. In the industry as a whole, the stodgy middle-aged Organization Men of the fifties began to be overshadowed and replaced by a vast influx of younger copywriters and art directors in unmistakably with-it garb. Advertising had, of course, always been a profession in which people with bottomless energy, either still idealistic or nondisillusionable, had excelled.[18] But in the sixties, the prevalence of youth became so lopsided that it inspired concerned commentary in the industry press.[19]

By 1968, the notion that only rebellious young people could make good copywriters and art directors was so prevalent that E. B. Weiss, whose *Ad Age* columns oscillated between the decade's two burning topics of creativity and youth culture, entitled one effort "Is Creative Advertising a Young Business?"—a query which he answered in the affirmative: "I fully agree that the creative advertising function should be, indeed must be, monopolized by young people—not exclusively, but practically so."[20] But the question predated the countercultural explosion of 1967. In 1965, adman Jerry Fields had wondered, "Why are the creative Golden Boys . . . always young men in their twenties and early thirties?" and had asked what older admen could do to compete. He had concluded that the secret was less physical youth and more a matter of attitude:

Our solution to this problem is a very simple one—don't grow old. Think young. That's a pretty square and corny statement, but we mean it. We see old men of 35 walking into our office and we see young men of 50 coming in. It all seems to be based on a state of mind—a healthy enthusiastic approach to life in which you never seem to run out of *élan vital.*[21]

The refrain was a common one: creativity was a matter of young-mindedness, if not outright youthfulness. Even the soft-spoken, 59-year-old Bill Bernbach could be described by E. B. Weiss in 1970 as an "angry young man."[22]

By 1967, the countercultural overtones of creativity were undeniable as a thousand hip lifestyles flowered on Madison Avenue. Longer hair, beads, loud colors, and wide ties replaced the infamous "gray flannel suit."

Art director Stephen Baker noted that in 1967 "beards, whiskers, goatees, Van Dykes, manes became status symbols of the creative breed, symbolizing its schism from the business side of advertising, which is the Establishment."[23] Unusual clothing was sometimes taken by itself as a creativity index. Stephen Fox points out that at some agencies "clients were taken on pointed tours of the creative departments, to see the miniskirts and jeans, to smell the incense and other suspicious odors, as though to prove how daring and *au courant* the shop was."[24] In 1968, *Marketing/Communications* published a "Chat with an ad-man head" in which the creativity-enhancing powers of marijuana were thoroughly discussed.[25]

Hair was an important signifier of creativity. The locks of Tinker group creative superstar Gene Case were noted in the late sixties by one magazine to be long "even by Madison Avenue 'creative man' standards." A profile of Larry Dunst, the 28-year-old president of the very creative Daniel & Charles agency, was incomplete without commentary on his hair, which is duly noted to have "crept down over ears, eyes and neck, but it's styled":

> "Hair intimidates people, you know. You meet someone and they look you over; they figure this guy's got balls to let his hair grow that long. I wonder how long I'll let it grow before I chicken out." (For the record: A supervisor at Daniel & Charles, Jeff Metzner, has the Madison Avenue record. He shows only a nose-tip and has a pony tail.)[26]

A cartoon by a copywriter at McCann-Erickson that was printed in *Madison Avenue* in February, 1967, depicted the "Evolution of the Art Director" from square to hip. At the beginning, he is a simple "Mat Room Boy," with short hair, wide eyes, and a narrow tie. But as he works his way up the corporate ladder from "Paste-Up Man" to "Senior Art Director," new features appear: his hair lengthens, he grows a moustache and a beard, he begins to wear boots and loudly patterned clothes. As a "Senior Art Director," he is shown with glasses, a scowl, and a beard, his middle finger raised in defiance (or in command?). As an Executive Art Director, he is entirely overtaken by his hair and hairy poncho, and his face and body are no longer visible.[27]

Charlie Moss, copywriter, creative director, and finally president of Wells, Rich, Greene, surely the "hottest" creative agency during the late 1960s, recalls the businesslike way his penchant for unusual clothing was received in those years.

I remember I used to walk around in jeans and these flowery shirts . . . they were from England, there was this woman, and she used to make these wild, flowery shirts that you could see through, kind of gauzy things, that were really extremely fey. . . . One day Mary [Wells] called and said, "We've got to go down to Philip Morris right away, we've a big board meeting. . . ." I said, "Mary, I can't go like this, look at me!" And she said, "Don't be ridiculous, they expect you to dress like that." And so we went, and nobody even turned their head. I mean I had an afro out to here, and people really just basically accepted it, because I was, quote, creative, and it was allowed.[28]

Admen in the 1960s loved rock 'n' roll, or at least claimed they did. Throughout the literature of the period, one finds dozens of references to the music of the counterculture dropped by agency executives as though to demonstrate their cognizance of the hip underground. One magazine profile of the various brash young creative leaders written at the height of the revolution opens with assertions of the hipness of the "new rulers": "They dig rock and understand how it touches and turns-on a whole sub-culture." Jerry Della Femina "always keeps the record player going, loud and lusty rock music, in the office and at home." Larry Dunst is alleged to be "a fearless sort; sat near the stage at a Jimi Hendrix-Buddy Miles Express concert in Madison Square Garden."[29] Others claimed to be so intensely hip that they had been "into" the new music even before the rest of the world appreciated it. Andrew Kershaw, the president of Ogilvy & Mather, told *Madison Avenue* in January of 1970 that he had been "a Beatles fan . . . since before the time they became famous." Consequently, he suffered "no generation gap in my own family. . . ." Years later, Alex Kroll, chairman of Young & Rubicam, made almost exactly the same claim—premature Beatles fan; generation-gap immunity—for Hanley Norins, his firm's outspoken partisan of counterculture and creativity.[30] So rapidly did the rage for youth culture conquer Madison Avenue that it seems to have taken a number of "establishment" figures by surprise. One famous story that made the rounds in the sixties had the head of a large, institutional agency, now at a disadvantage and under pressure to produce "creative" work, calling a pep rally for its employees. There, the agency chairman gave a rousing speech encouraging his employees to broaden themselves creatively by attending the theater, going to movies, and listening to rock music like that of Bobby Dylan, mispronouncing the star's name ("Dile-in") egregiously.[31]

One of stranger victories of the Creative Revolution was the conversion to the countercultural style of none other than Dr. Ernest Dichter of the Institute for Motivational Research, the sinister "depth-probing" villain of *The Hidden Persuaders*. In the sixties, it seems, Dichter moved on to something else even more illuminating than statistics. In 1967, he issued a report which suggested that admen learn from (those who had learned from) LSD, undertake "mind expansion," use "animation with psychedelic colors and motion," and "bring the product alive with new, more exciting meaning."[32] Nor was Dichter alone in his semi-enthusiasm for psychedelics. A September, 1967, article in *Madison Avenue* agreed on the advertising value of psychedelics. The authors, two creative people from the stodgy Campbell-Ewald agency, did not encourage their fellow writers to indulge in the drug specifically, but its effects, then being widely discussed in the media, could provide "psychedelic advice for the creative adman." LSD, it seems, approximates the sensitivity the copywriter or art director must have in order to provide maximum dramatization of an otherwise mundane product, and the authors compare various statements made by tripping people to high-literary prose. Even though he may or may not take acid, "*a great writer is on one long 'trip' from the beginning of his life to the end of it.*" The secret to the "heightened sense perception" that is the province of "great writers" and LSD users is, again, the willingness to violate the conventions of perception. And, as violating conventions was the central premise of the Creative Revolution, any good adman should have been able to summon up drug-induced delirium at will, even without actually consuming acid:

Will you go through a day looking for yellow . . . on Madison Avenue, in the office, at home? Will you feel yellow, will you count how many yellows, will you try to imagine what yellow should smell like or sound or taste like? . . .

You don't need LSD for this; you just need the guts to *live*. To shake the embalming fluid out of your thinking.

This was sensitivity training for the former architects of commercialism, a rudimentary version of the sort of phony spiritualism that would soon sweep the bourgeoisie of California in a flurry of chanted "Oms" and beads and bubbling hot tubs. Just as the adman of the 1960s was expected to be hostile to "rules" generally, the exercises the givers of "psychedelic advice" prescribe for developing a great creative talent are a matter of simple transgression of everyday routine, a rebellion for its own sake against whatever variety of conformity to which the reader happened to belong.[33]

The adman was fast being saddled with a new image: no longer was he the other-directed technocrat, the most craven species of American businessman, but the coolest guy on the commuter train, turned on to the latest in youth culture, rock music, and drug-influenced graphic effects. It was a stereotype used by creativity's enemies as well. "The lunatics began to take over the asylum," is how Rosser Reeves described the sixties in 1970 from his new position as head of the appropriately named Starch research organization. "A new type of copywriter appeared—with . . . shoulder-length hair, bell-bottom trousers, chains, medallions and sandals," wrote this quintessential man of the fifties with obvious disgust. "And to my amazement, a group of otherwise sane, senior advertising marketing men began to believe that this group is 'with it.'"[34] The Creative Revolution in general, he believed, was a symptom of the industry's precipitous decline.

The most sophisticated partisans of the revolution might well have agreed with Reeves's condemnation. Heavy reliance on overt youth-culture references were but a "creativity-substitute," as Jack Tinker star copywriter Gene Case put it in 1967. The best way to appeal to the young and young-thinking was to adopt the same techniques and values of agency organization that had, a few years before, been touted as the techniques and values of creativity. Even when they were writing specifically on the youth market, the advice admen proffered each other was phrased as suggestions on improving admaking generally, on updating agency operations to reflect that the old ways were fatuous, unconvincing, and dull. Steir's praise for "The Now People," for example, hailed their "redoing and reconsidering" the various stultifying institutions of society as a way of praising his colleagues' efforts to overthrow the creativity-restricting constraints of the large agencies. In order to deal with the rewarding youth market, Steir wrote in 1967, advertising would have to adopt certain attitudes that had already been the bywords of creativity since the late 1950s: "Businessmen will have to be outrageous," he insisted. "Being in step today is to be out of step tomorrow. The initial premise for the search might be: We must be doing something wrong. . . . The business climate is now so stultified and rigid that any innovation and meaningful contact with the youth market will be rewarded." Even though stultification and rigidity had already been blasted for a number of years in favor of outrage and difference, Steir still phrased his 1967 article on "The Now People" in terms of a battle between the noble youngsters who were bringing "revolution" and "the Then Generation [which] attempts to retard change in order to enjoy material satisfaction

chapter six

in the old way. . . ." Just as big agency bureaucrats and account men were pilloried for resisting the new, oldsters were cautioned against hostility to youth culture. Steir even described the victory of "the Now People" as a lesson in the basic fact of marketing: "Youth *has* won. Youth must *always* win. The new naturally replaces the old."[35]

Not coincidentally, the techniques of admaking said to be useful in the age of the hip were the same as those pioneered by Bernbach ten years before. Hanley Norins's 1969 recommendations for getting out in front of the "individual revolution" were substantially the same as the ones he had trumpeted during an earlier phase of the Creative Revolution: His model advertisement was a 1959 Volkswagen ad. "Some of us oldtimers might call this 'soft-selling advertising,'" Norins wrote, using the term which had once been used to describe (and disparage) the works of Bernbach and others, "but that's the message of the Individual Revolution, and the kids call it 'cool.'"[36] Counterculture and creativity were essentially one and the same, with identical heroes and villains. John A. Adams, Detroit manager of the (large, "establishment") Grey agency, repeated the argument in 1971 when he was reported to have insisted that "the old bombastic, pound-it-home-again approach does not reach them [the young]." Instead, the advertiser's voice was said to be the most critical factor in commercial persuasion, a realization which, again, pointed directly to the very features that had distinguished Doyle Dane's advertising since the late 1950s: "Humor—the product is not a matter of life or death; candor—the company admits some imperfections; simplicity—the company does not try to list the most product points in a single ad."[37]

A most remarkable exposition on this subject, written by businessman Lee Adler and published in the quasi-academic journal *Business Horizons* in February, 1970, posited a "new consumer" arising whose "moral, social, and cultural values," regardless of his age, were defined by the new worldview associated with the counterculture. The values of this new American may be different, but his consuming potential was just as great, perhaps even greater, than that of his parents. The "Implications for Advertising" that Adler perceived arising from the development of the "new consumer" were each features that had been emphasized by DDB and its imitators since the late 1950s; only one was new. Since "The under-30 generation loathes sham and hypocrisy" and "'Tell it like it is' is the touchstone," Adler suggests that admen take the more "honest" tone associated with creativity. Adler went on to list all of the various "new approaches in copy and art" that allowed business to speak "memorably and persuasively with the new consumer," including "low-key appeals," experimental, "nonlinear presentations of information," "more wit, honesty, verve, self-deprecation, [and] irreverence," and "cautious use of the more ephemeral elements of today's under-thirties subculture." All except the last were standard features of the Creative Revolution, and that single exception would be quickly adopted in the mid-1960s. The ads with which Adler illustrated his theories naturally came from certain much-lauded creative campaigns: Jack Tinker's spots for Alka-Seltzer, Wells, Rich, Greene's work for Benson & Hedges, McCann-Erickson's ads for Opel and Coca-Cola.[38]

If the wonderment of Ernest Fladell is any indication, many mature admen regarded sixties' youth culture with bewilderment. And, as one would expect, a number of firms took advantage of the situation by setting themselves up as youth-culture specialists. Merle Steir's group was called "Youth Concepts" and produced "now shows" for a variety of establishment advertisers interested in rejuvenating their image. The humorously named Spade and Archer agency, founded in 1966 as youth market specialists, produced ads designed to persuade this problematic group of consumers. It received attention in trade publications and general magazines like *Newsweek* as both an intensely creative shop and as a countercultural stronghold. Spade and Archer was given to dazzling potential clients and industry rivals with demonstrations of its countercultural cognizance, like the elaborate one *Advertising Age* covered in April, 1968, which featured "A rock group, the Group Image, plus dancing girls and strobe lights, a body-painted model, a consumer panel of young housewives 'who were weaned on the Beatles' and an assortment of miniskirted and Nehru-jacketed associates." The advice the agency's principals offered on admaking, unsurprisingly, reaffirmed the critical style of the Creative Revolution. Above all, the kids were exactly the sort of consumers Bill Bernbach had been positing since the late fifties: smart and extremely skeptical toward conventional advertising. "Honesty" and its inevitable Bernbachian corollary, a sense of humor about the product, were what was required in order to sell the young.[39]

For some, the counterculture represented a sort of creative epiphany, a culminating vindication of the revolution in which Madison Avenue had immersed itself. Hanley Norins believed that creativity and counterculture were both part of a larger historical insurgency: the "Revolt of the Individual," a vast uprising "expressed most openly by the young people, but [which] is really deep down inside all of us."

chapter six

It's the revolt of the individual against the very systems which we here in this room have been so influential in devising—the American systems of mass education, mass communication and mass conformity.

... It's the problem of mass conformity that's mostly getting us down. And that's what the revolution is going to destroy.

Fortunately, the revolution against conformity was most definitely not a revolt against consumerism or the institution of advertising. In fact, according to Norins, the best ads—like the Volkswagen campaign—do not just react to the new revulsion to convention; they provoke and even "anticipate it." Mass society was now the target of a generalized revolt and hip was becoming a widespread cultural style, but, provided it stayed on its toes and embraced the mass society critique, Madison Avenue could ride the waves of unrest to new heights of prosperity. The counterculture was, ultimately, just a branch of the same revolution that had swept the critical-creative style to prominence and that many believed was demolishing Theory X hierarchy everywhere, from Vietnam to the boardroom.[40]

counterculture / consumer culture

The use of youth culture and youth imagery in advertising was not, of course, an entirely new thing in the 1960s. It had appeared extensively, if sporadically, since the 1920s. But "youth" marketing has always been a little confusing. Much of it has indeed been designed to speak to young people. But even more frequently, "youth" has served as a marketing symbol, an abstraction of commercial speech, a consuming vision for Americans of all ages.[41] Obviously, the actual "youth market," the vast number of consumers under thirty, or twenty-five, or twenty-one, or nineteen (depending on the definition at hand) was important to admen in the sixties, and the demographic significance of the baby boom has been amply recognized by cultural historians. What is less frequently recognized is the basic marketing fact that "youth" had a meaning and an appeal that extended far beyond the youth market proper. This point is driven home again and again in the trade press of the era: The imagery and language of youth can be applied effectively to all sorts of products marketed to all varieties of people, because youth is an attractive consuming attitude, not an age—an attitude that was preeminently defined by the values of the counterculture. By "youth," Madison Avenue meant hip, often expressed with psychedelic references, talk of rebellion, and intimations of free love.

Youth markets come and youth markets go; so do youth styles and youth movements, and sometimes without ever drawing the attention of a single adman. But this one was different—and not merely in terms of its size. When creative admen looked at the counterculture, they saw what they chose to see. The industry's privileging of the antimaterialist youth over their conformist brethren—of the hip over the square—marked a crucial step in the development of a new ideology of consumption that arose with the Creative Revolution. With simple black-and-white photographs, gentle humor, and straightforward-sounding copy, DDB had sold Volkswagens as a solution to the ills of mass society; now admen were discovering a ready-made symbol for the cultural operation Bill Bernbach had taught them to perform. In the eyes of the American ad industry, the counterculture was special—it appeared to be a broad social affirmation of the very values that had launched the admen themselves into the new era. The counterculture seemed to have it all: the unconnectedness which would allow consumers to indulge transitory whims; the irreverence that would allow them to defy moral puritanism; and the contempt for established social rules that would free them from the slow-moving, buttoned-down conformity of their abstemious ancestors. In the counterculture, admen believed they had found both a perfect model for consumer subjectivity, intelligent and at war with the conformist past, and a cultural machine for turning disgust with consumerism into the very fuel by which consumerism might be accelerated.

"Youth" was a posture available to all in the sixties. Admen clearly believed that the marketing potential of youth culture far transcended the handful of people who were actively involved in the counterculture: as Mary Wells Lawrence recalls, "It didn't matter what age you were—you had to think young." [42] Youth was the paramount symbol of the age, whether in movies, literature, fashion, or television. For admen "youth" was a sort of consumer fantasy they would make available to older Americans. Jerry Fields noted in a *Madison Avenue* article entitled "Think Young" that appeared in February, 1965, that "the maintenance of a young, fresh appearance has become a primary concern of our population which looks back wistfully at their thirty-fifth birthday." [43] In 1967, the magazine quoted an adman who noted that "the youth market has become the American market. It now includes not only everyone under 35, but most

chapter six

people over 35."[44] Edward Gorman, sales and merchandise manager of J. C. Penney was reported in *Advertising Age* in 1966 to have said that

the youth market not only encompasses teens, but everyone up to 35 and "most of the people older than that." He explained that the appeal to the young is heard by many who are in their 30s and 40s. They even buy the cars that were designed for the young. "Like the Pontiac GTO," Mr. Gorman said.[45]

The name given by admen to the market thus targeted was the "young thinking," a rubric under which advertising people could classify almost everybody. "To be young is to be with it," ruminated Martin R. Miller in a 1968 editorial in *Merchandising Week,* the journal of the electronic appliance industry. "Everywhere, our mass media push psychedelia with all its clothing fads, so-called 'way-out' ideas, etc. Youth is getting the hard sell." And the benefits from this were clear to his readers: "the fountain of youth has spilled over into new areas and is revitalizing the buying habits of some older, more affluent customers."[46] A 1970 *Business Week* article reached similar conclusions. Noting the across-the-board effectiveness of the young-thinking theme, the magazine predicted that "The 1970s promise to become the decade when youth becomes a state of mind and overflows all traditional age boundaries." And "whether they are marketing to youth or to youthfulness, businessmen find the prospects exhilarating."[47]

Madison Avenue's vision of the counterculture was notoriously unconvincing to many who actually took part in the movement—and for a very simple reason: they were not necessarily the primary target of such campaigns. If youth was an attitude rather than an actual age, it would have to be expressed in a manner understandable to much older people. Thus, through the proliferation of psychedelia, Milton Glaser imitations, and "yellow submarine art"; all the photographs of self-assured young iconoclasts and body-painted women, advertisers were careful to speak a language that sounded hip but got a message across to young and old alike. The size of the "young-in-spirit" market, art director and *Advertising Age* columnist Stephen Baker counseled, made it "important that youth language is made to be understood not only by the under-aged chaps and chicks but also those who want to stop the clock and can afford to do so."[48] A 1966 study conducted by BBDO (the "establishment" agency responsible for the Pepsi Generation) stated the facts even more directly. Images of youth were simply not appropriate for the youth mar-

ket, it found: these consumers already *knew* they were young. Youthfulness was best used as an appeal to older consumers:

Since the need of a "younger" image appears quite suddenly (at about 25), it should
probably be kept in mind that in selling to people under 25, the "youthful" appeal
may not be effective. A proper appeal to [the] youth [market] might actually emphasize a topical appeal.[49]

Again, the slogan "Think Young" is illustrative: consumers could not all
be young, but they could all be encouraged to think as though they were,
to assume the attitudes of the young revolutionaries. The function of
"youth" in advertising was symbolic, an easy metaphor for a complex new
consumer value-system. The really remarkable fact about co-optation
isn't that Columbia records ran pseudo-hip ads in "underground" publications; it's that a vast multitude of corporations ran pseudo-hip ads in
Life, Look, and *Ladies Home Journal.* Madison Avenue was more interested in speaking *like* the rebel young than in speaking *to* them.

There were, of course, other symbols for the new antinomian consumerism available during the 1960s—both spies and jaded jet-setters
were common before 1967. Admen settled on the counterculture as the
signifier of choice for hip consumerism at least partially because they believed, contrary to the assertions of countercultural theorists like Roszak
and Reich, that the hip young were good potential consumers. Despite
their suspicion of advertising and material accumulation, and despite the
standard claims that the movement's privileging of nonconformity and
heterogeneity opposed it automatically to consumer capitalism, admen
used the external markings of their culture to represent new consuming
values because, admen believed, it had already internalized those consuming values. Like Christopher Lasch and Irving Howe, Madison Avenue found in the ideas of people like Jerry Rubin a continuing—even a
heightened—commitment to the values and mores of the consumer
society. Caught up in the frenzies of the Creative Revolution, admen
looked at the counterculture and saw . . . themselves.

Madison Avenue's favorite term for the counterculture was "the
Now Generation," a phrase that implied absolute up-to-dateness in every
sense. It also intimated what admen felt was the young's most important
characteristic as consumers: their desire for immediate gratification, their
craving for the new, their intolerance for the slow-moving, the penurious,
the thrifty. Admen believed they had found an entire generation given

chapter six

over to self-fulfillment by whatever means necessary—which would, of course, ultimately mean by shopping. Grey's John Adams made what is perhaps the bluntest statement of this perception, having been reported by *Advertising Age* in 1971 to have said

There is nothing to support the contention that the youth are anti-materialistic. "They are in the peak acquisitive years," he said, "and their relative affluence enables them to consume goods and services at a rate unheard of for their age level."[50]

In 1968, creative partisan Bob Fearon penned an impressionistic appreciation of the young for *Madison Avenue*. Written in a curious colloquial style that was probably meant to demonstrate his familiarity with the intricacies of youth culture, the article aims to enlighten advertising men about the tastes and anti-advertising predilections of the inscrutable young ("They talk to him. They tell him things like that. And he listens. He doesn't condemn. . . . And he ends up knowing.") Perhaps the most important feature of the young people Fearon discusses, despite their hotly professed antimaterialism and their suspicion of consumerism, is their heightened appetite for the new. Unlike their parents, the hip new youth are far more receptive to obsolescence; buying goods for the moment, discarding them quickly, and moving on to the next:

"When the new generation buys they want it for now. They're not interested in how long it will last."
These young people have a different idea about thrift. They have a new definition of value. They accept obsolescence. They want the new, improved version tomorrow. Very important words. New, improved. More than ever before. Everything is instant. Now. Everything is faster.[51]

Not surprisingly, the same texts that praised the counterculture for its questioning of conventional ways usually came around to the counterculture's single worthiest point: its revolutionizing of America's *consuming* ways. Older Americans had been reluctant to spend, had guarded their money jealously, would only spend on the basis of a hard, demonstrable product superiority—and sometimes not even then. It was for overturning this antiquated, depression-induced, even puritanical attitude that youth culture received its greatest plaudits. Merle Steir wrote:

The Then Generation didn't know where its next dollar was coming from, so it paid attention to getting lots of dollars stashed away. But if you realize you are always able to make a living you begin to wonder what else you might want to do. This is par- ticularly true if you noticed that for all the money around older people don't appear very satisfied. . . . So the Now Generation says: "If I have choices, I want to be satis- fied as well as housed and fed."[52]

This was consumerism for a new age, consumerism that began where the old variety left off—the anomie, conformity, and meaningless of plastic mass society. It was to escape these qualities, to be fully "satisfied," that the "Now Generation" would do its consuming.

The craving for deeper satisfaction, wrote E. B. Weiss, would lead inevitably to accelerated lifestyle experimentation, something admen— and businessmen generally—were anxious to encourage rather than to suppress.

[I]n 1971 these youngsters spent more on travel than the entire older generation spent on travel ten years ago. They spend more on stereo than their parents spent on phonographs. They may furnish their first home more simply than was true decades ago, but they will replace their initial home furnishings much sooner and much more often. Disposables—not "forevers" are their thing. . . . True—their lifestyles will differ on a larger scale, but isn't changing lifestyles what marketing is all about?[53]

American advertising took the side it did during the cultural revolution of the 1960s not simply because it wanted to sell a particular demo- graphic, but because it found great promise in the new values of the counterculture. Conformity, other-direction, contempt for audiences, and Reevesian repetition were good neither as management styles nor as consuming models, the creative revolutionaries had proclaimed; now, it seemed, here was a broad cultural upheaval validating their vision of hip consumerism. Thus did the consumer revolt against mass society, which had begun with the selling of a sturdy car that defied obsolescence, come into its own as a movement of accelerated obsolescence.

the now agency and the end of the plain

Wells, Rich, Greene (WRG) was the agency whose history most clearly traced this trajectory from creativity to hip, from criticism to outright secession from the boring everyday of mass society. Founded in 1966 by three prodigious creative talents who had worked on ads for Braniff and Alka-Seltzer at Jack Tinker Partners, WRG was the instant beneficiary of

chapter six

a deluge of blue-chip accounts looking for the selling magic that the new hip advertising seemed to promise. By December, 1967, *Madison Avenue* was able to claim that "no agency in history has grown so big so fast. Nor acquired such an array of talent in the process."[54] The firm proceeded to skyrocket to $100,000,000 in billings in a mere five years, a feat duly noted by *Advertising Age* in 1971 to have been "undoubtedly, the most astonishing growth record in advertising history." For products like Benson & Hedges, Braniff airlines, and Love Cosmetics, the agency seemed to work commercial magic. Articles in the industry press treated Wells, Rich, Greene like a hip, updated version of Doyle Dane Bernbach that managed to achieve the same prosperity in just a few years that DDB spent a decade acquiring. The agency's president, former DDB copywriter Mary Wells, quickly established herself as the industry's most glamorous figure as well, marrying the head of one of her client companies and attracting the attention of society columnists nationwide as she jetted between the hangouts of the world's wealthy.[55]

No company in America was hipper than Wells, Rich, Greene. It brought together in a dynamic, explosive combination the two great themes of advertising in the 1960s: creativity and the new system of values being ushered in by the youth culture. In campaign after campaign, WRG produced memorable, often hilarious ads that combined hip sensibilities with uncompromising sales messages and high production values. The agency's work at its best was as characteristic of the late 1960s as DDB's had been for the late 1950s and early 1960s: introducing differently colored airplanes for Braniff ("The end of the plain plane"); the "Try It, You'll Like It" and "I Can't Believe I Ate the Whole Thing" ads for Alka-Seltzer; the astonishingly successful campaign for Benson & Hedges that focused on fanciful disadvantages of longer cigarettes. "This is our moment," said Mary Wells in 1966. "In every era, some agencies come along to set new trends, to illuminate the industry in some way. In our case, we are completely geared to our time. We are terribly aware of the current sounds and fears and smells and attitudes. We are the agency of today."[56]

Looking back in 1990 on the period she once claimed to personify, Mary Wells Lawrence (she was married in 1967 to Harding Lawrence, the president of Braniff) describes the ethos of WRG as a strain of creativity supercharged by the omnipresent rebel spirit of youth. The title of her *Advertising Age* retrospective, "Baby Boom, Creative Boom" draws connections between the two great forces, and throughout it she links youth insurgency with creative insurgency. "I think in the '60s, it [the advertising business] was a very adolescent thing," she recalls.

Adolescence is pulling away, doing things in a new way. It's revolutionary, and the '60s were revolutionary, in every way.

. . . And the advertising that stands out, that you remember, was very revolutionary. It was like a bomb dropping into what had been a very stilted, limited kind of world.[57]

Youth was also critical to the creative attitude at WRG. When *Advertising Age* accused the agency of having entered the "agency world 'establishment'" in 1971, Wells Lawrence replied that WRG intended to retain a youthful attitude that put creative performance above organizational stability:

I don't think they [WRG employees] feel very "establishment." They feel they're sitting on a hot seat all the time. It's the responsibility of an agency's management to stay very young and very hot. The minute you get smug you're dead.[58]

And to at least some outside observers, WRG had the look and feel of a countercultural outpost. Scripps-Howard writer Robert Dietsch visited the new agency in 1967 to take in all of the big-city weirdness for his readers back in the provinces. The new, creative agencies, he explained, "are managed and directed by far-out people, not the traditional marketing and research-oriented conservatives." He was particularly taken with the shop's decoration and the sartorial tastes of its employees:

There is a psychedelic "LOVE" poster in the foyer. The guest chairs are rattan or bamboo and they have baby blue pillows which sink you down deep. The receptionist is from Haiti with just the right amount of accent and chocolate thigh.

It follows that les girls beyond the white foyer wall are mini-minded, but a couple are wearing pants. Their eyeglasses are four inches across and cigarette holders are "in."[59]

Naturally, early accounts of WRG also emphasize its use of the stripped-down principles of agency organization that had spread over the decade outward from DDB. Talent, not organization, was the key to the advertising business, Mary Wells insisted, and the less organization the less interference there was in the truly important creative work. "Agencies should be sleek," she wrote in *Newsweek* in 1967. "Fat agencies tend to move slowly and dully. They waddle through confusions caused by their complex organizations."[60] At WRG, "we don't want to be cluttered with lots of mediocre people. We don't want lots of underlings around, hired to take our clients to lunch."[61] William Whyte couldn't have put it better: the ethos of the Organization necessarily militated against the brilliant.

The key to WRG's zeitgeist-mastery was a slightly updated version of the model consumer posited earlier in the decade by Bill Bernbach. The consumer was no longer merely skeptical of mass society, but positively *hip*, young-minded, wise to television's tricks, drawn to the alienated filmmaking of the era, and only reachable through the coolest of advertising agencies. "He's a very hip, aware character," executive vice president Herb Fisher said in 1968:

spearheading an attitude, an awareness, that is more open, more expansive and more inquisitive at all age levels.

A second key fact: He is bombarded on all sides with news, sensation, art and all manner of stimuli that are explosive and exciting. . . . Exposure to the bombardment produces skepticism. Today's consumer . . . has developed a sophistication about, an imperviousness to, the "big sell" . . . [62]

One of the most difficult problems facing the ad industry in the late 1960s, then, was identical to one that it faces today: consumer cynicism toward the clutter of mass society. As Wells herself put it in 1966, "People have seen so many promotions and big ideas and new products and new advertising campaigns and new packaging gimmicks, and they've heard so many lies and so many meaningless slogans and so many commercialized holy truths that it's getting harder and harder to get their attention, let alone their trust."[63] But, as Bill Bernbach had realized, public jadedness also provided advertising with unprecedented opportunities.

WRG simply upped the ante on the decade's violence against advertising convention: it would discover whatever was the usual way of pitching a given product category and then seek to do just the opposite. In order to come up with ideas for a campaign, Wells writes, the agency would ask, "Consider what you can't do, then do it."

Like with cigarettes, you could never mutilate them, they were touched by God. So we broke them in the Benson & Hedges campaign.

We took Alka-Seltzer, which was then used strictly in the bathroom, in the dark, by people ashamed of themselves, and we made it the current, the hip thing to do to need an Alka-Seltzer. If you didn't need an Alka-Seltzer, you weren't alive; it meant you weren't eating good food, you weren't drinking wine, you couldn't afford good things.[64]

Instead of men in lab coats repeating transparently insignificant USPs, cars on rotating platforms, or animated characters singing cigarette jingles, commercials made by WRG often used bizarre vignettes of things going horribly wrong to dramatize a product's characteristics. A famous Alka-Seltzer spot that the WRG principals had done while still working for Jack Tinker established the genre, picturing a series of human bellies being terribly mistreated: those of workmen hanging over jackhammers, those of boxers being pummeled, those of obese office workers in conversation.

In 1966, WRG used the formula to promote Benson & Hedges, a new brand of cigarettes. Somehow the agency settled on the astonishing slogan, "Oh, the disadvantages" as the best way of drawing attention to the cigarette's then-unusual length. The best-known commercial from their campaign for that cigarette (and one that is still referred to frequently today in the industry's all-time best-of lists) was made up of a number of humorous, three- or four-second shots of the faintly ridiculous problems encountered by smokers of longer cigarettes: a man's cigarette is caught in elevator doors; another is bent on a telephone; a third burns a man's beard during a conversation; and an exasperated hand is shown holding a cigarette case from which the unwieldy product protrudes sloppily. The campaign must have been the first to actually make a product seem attractive by depicting the ways in which it put one at odds with the conventional world. WRG steered Benson & Hedges directly into the teeth of the old "personal efficiency" pitch, promising not to make the consumer more successful but actually to saddle him with "disadvantages" and make him *less* efficient—and it is remembered as one of the most successful cigarette campaigns ever. A print ad from 1968 brought the idea full circle by proclaiming that their length also made them difficult to advertise—they wouldn't fit onto a standard-size magazine page. So antithetical was this cigarette to mass society that it even shortcircuited advertising.[65]

The theme of hilarious social dysfunction could be applied to almost anything, it seemed. In one 1968 spot for the American Motors Rebel, WRG dramatized the car's durability by showing the terrifying experiences of a driving instructor whose pupils come from every class of bad driver. The car is driven over a fire-hydrant and through a construction site; student drivers grind its gears and steer it recklessly through traffic. In a famous late-sixties spot for Alka-Seltzer, a sophisticated fellow is victimized by a waiter at a quaint ethnic restaurant of some kind who has reassured him about an unfamiliar item, saying, "Try it, you'll like it"; the diner uses Alka-Seltzer to recover from the nasty dish that is foisted upon him. A commercial for the 1968 American Motors Javelin muscle car impresses upon the audience the car's power and sportiness by depicting a day in the life of a Javelin owner who is not interested in power and sportiness. For all of his well-demonstrated timidity and carefulness (at one point he declines to race another driver, saying "I've got a bowl of goldfish in the seat") though, the man cannot suppress his car's anarchic destiny: eventually he turns it over to a parking lot attendant who promptly races away, tires screeching.[66]

One of the most visible markers of youth culture's progress on Madison Avenue was Mary Wells's adoption of the slogan, "love power" in 1967 as a description of her agency's amusing style.[67] By conceiving of the consumer with affection rather than the contempt that seemed to emanate from so many of the ads of the fifties, WRG aimed to produce enjoyable, entertaining commercials that it believed consumers were happy to watch. Charlie Moss explains how Wells's "love" philosophy worked in the actual creative sense:

What Mary always used to talk about was, "Get them to like you, get them to like your product." Be sympathetic, be "buyer friendly," I suppose. At the time . . . this philosophy was in the middle of a bunch of advertising from the old days that was basically pretty hard sell. . . . Her point of view and philosophy was, we've got to entertain people, we've got to make them like us, we can't bore them to death with our advertising, we don't want them looking at the screen, saying "Oh, that commercial again, yech," and getting up and leaving the room.[68]

"Love" was a strategy that transformed cynicism into consumer responsiveness. Here, as in so many other places in this story, business theory spilled over into actual advertising. As it turned out, "Love" also had a very concrete meaning for Wells, Rich, Greene. In 1969, pharmaceutical manufacturer Menley & James hired the agency to devise a name, packaging, and a marketing strategy as well as advertising for a line of cosmetics, and the agency promptly came up with "Love." Love Cosmetics was thus a product created in its entirety by the advertising climate of the late 1960s. Another instant success story (Love sales finally fell off and the brand all but vanished in the mid- to late-1970s), the Love campaign was

celebrated both in the industry and the popular press as a shining example of the power of countercultural, "hippie-looking" advertising, with
packaging and store displays that used psychedelic designs and rendered
the word "Love" in birds and flowers.[69] Many hip campaigns during the
sixties, of course, made use of such psychedelia. But the ads WRG prepared for Love cosmetics went much farther, actually striking a strangely
authentic-sounding note.

Love cosmetics were anti-cosmetics, makeup for a time—and a generation—at war with the pretense and falsehood of makeup. "This is the
way Love is in 1969," the premier ad's headline announced: "freer, more
natural, more honest—more out in the open." Nonetheless, "most cosmetic companies" remained ignorant of the new ways and "are laboring
under the delusion that love and girls are the same as ever." It was a
strange, even paradoxical claim for a brand of cosmetics to be making,
but it seemed to work: while older brands were said to mask and conceal
the user's selfhood, Love enhanced her individuality, allowed her real nature to come to the surface: "You've got a complexion worth seeing. You
don't need make-ups that blank you out. Ours won't. Ours can't."

Love was transparent, and so was the company that was selling it.
The makers of Love had, they announced, moved beyond the huckster's
trickery of the past. They had the reader's best interests at heart. "We're
not going to sell you a lot of goo you don't need," as do the square cosmetics companies, no doubt, "or ideas and formulas as ancient as the
hills." The products themselves came in radically simplified packages,
basic cylinders rather than the elaborate faux-crystal decanters of other
brands. They bore whimsical instructions printed on the bottles in earnest, sans-serif typefaces. The ads, furthermore, asked readers to question
advertisers—and then to find this particular advertiser to be their generational ally rather than another arm of the establishment. "What gives us
the audacity to tell you what you do and don't need?" the ads asked.

> We're young too.
> And we're on your side.
> We know it's a rough race.
> And we want you to win.

The Love ads appeared to be concerned with young people as exclusively as anything that appeared in the decade: they were illustrated with
photos of youngsters in long hair and peppered with lines like, "You're
young. You've got healthy skin oils. You don't need a grease job." But the

youth appeal was clearly only skin-deep. The ads ran in mainstream journals like *Life* and *Harper's Bazaar*. They referred to martinis as a beverage that readers were familiar with. And the party in Paris that WRG threw to launch the brand featured superannuated luminaries like the Duke of Windsor, Gloria Swanson, and Diana Vreeland.[70] As Mary Wells Lawrence said soon afterwards, "The products are created for a woman with a specific attitude about herself rather than of a specific age."[71] "Youth" was primarily being used here as shorthand for the new, anti-technocracy consumer ideal, the pictures of hip young people filling the same space once occupied by distant aristocratic beauties.[72]

chapter seven

The CYBERNAUT generation is intrinsically anarchistic, endlessly antiauthoritarian and hates corporate America. Therefore, this is not an ad for Coke. We repeat, this is not an ad for Coke.

— ADVERTISEMENT FOR COCA-COLA, 1996

Ads, not only admen, became hip during the 1960s. As the theories and organizational style current at American advertising agencies went from the overorganized, account-man fifties to the rule-breaking sixties, the ads themselves changed too, following a parallel trajectory from a USP-hammering and cliche-ridden style to one that positioned products as bearers of nonconformity, escape, resistance, difference, carnival, and even deviance. Roland Marchand has demonstrated that advertising before World War II advised consumers in navigating the complex and hazardous ways of modernity; advertising in the sixties and afterwards counseled consumers on maintaining individuality and purpose in a time that sought to deny individuality. The move to this more hip style was fully established by 1965, well before the counterculture had made its national media debut (by my own count fully 70 percent of automobile advertising appearing in *Life* magazine in 1965 was distinguishable as hip, as was 55 percent of all advertising in six product categories—see appendix). And in the later years of the decade, when youth and counterculture became the paramount symbols of this new sensibility in ads, hip became virtually hegemonic, almost extinguishing the older, square style altogether (the high point came in 1968–69, when hip advertising hit 79 percent in *Life's* auto ads and went above 70 percent in all ads). Hip advertising ran the entire width and breadth of the corporate spectrum. It was produced by agencies big and small, "creative" and conservative, for clients that manufactured almost every sort of product for every demographic. Hip was, in a very real sense, the new consuming paradigm, and its rise to preeminence in advertising was one of the most important changes in the visual landscape of the American 1960s.

To understand the omnipresence of the hip new advertising, though, it's important to stay away from blatantly countercultural ads like the famous "Man Can't Bust Our Music," and to examine instead the representations of hip that so filled the pages of mainstream publications and the commercial time of the three networks. On most such occasions, countercultural references were strictly superficial, with little relation to the product or a larger marketing strategy. This was the case when the formerly cute Campbell kids were decked out in Nehru jackets, beads, and day-glo colors in 1968; when S & H Green Stamps announced that "With this little square you swing"; when a collection of Raleigh bicycles was photographed in front of a family whose members are wearing oversized headbands; when Buick announced its 1970 models as cars that "Light your fire"; and when the staid retailer to middle America, Montgomery Ward, declared in 1969 that Wards was now "unexpected" and offering non-middle-American products.[1] When ads for women's clothing patterns made by the Simplicity company pictured female protesters and shouted, "Lower the sewing age; sew your own thing" and "You don't let the Establishment make your world; don't let it make your clothes," they were merely utilizing opportune, ready-made slogans; no deeper relationship between the company and the counterculture was envisioned.[2] Similar examples can be tallied up endlessly. The St. Regis Paper Company, makers of all manner of packaging, ran a Peter Max-style drawing of a rock group in *Forbes* magazine in 1969 under the headline, "Stodgy old paper company wraps it up for 'The New Colony Six.'"[3] Vaco products, makers of a variety of hardware, chose to dramatize themselves in 1969 with the slogan, "Join the Tool Revolution!" and with such lines as "Vaco says down with dull tools," "Wrench free," and "Riveters arise."[4]

In 1967, Clairol cosmetics announced what it called "The Great Beige-In!" to commemorate the launch of "3 psychedelicious beiges frosted for lips and nails," which it described in terms that confused counterculture with protest ("Redheads! It's Your Right to be Different").[5] Talk of youth culture, rule-breaking, and the hip uprising was even deemed appropriate in as mundane a field as cleaning products. In 1967, Dash laundry detergent began to use as its slogan, "Somebody had to break the rules," seeking to associate Dash's "breakthrough" qualities with those of a series of models dressed in the more outre styles of the period (miniskirt, "geometric haircut").[6] Top Job kitchen cleaner aired a commercial in which a woman decked out in an overdone hip costume rolls around on her kitchen floor and speaks in an indeterminate European (stage) accent. She wears a loud print pantsuit, uncomfortably heavy makeup (including white lipstick and heavy eye shadow), and sports a painted or tattooed floral design on one bare foot. Her dialogue reveals her to be a member of the hippest cognoscenti:

For a woman, the look is in. But for your kitchen floor, the look is passé. Now there's a *wild* new way to tell if your kitchen floor is really clean—you feel it. . . . And Top Job gets your kitchen floor so clean you can feel it. Wild![7]

As adman Ernest Fladell could testify, alcohol was not only not the preferred drug of the counterculture but a basic marker (martinis especially) of the generation gap. Despite this fact—perhaps because of it— a number of liquor campaigns got aggressively hip in the latter part of the decade. Gordon's gin got off to an early start by comparing itself in 1967 to "The Liverpool Sound," which it illustrated with a photo of a rock band, "vibrant and rollicking." Ads for one brand of premixed cocktails spoke of "the new free spirit in liquor" and of "uninhibited drinks from Heublein" while Gilbey's gin offered hints on how to "make" the "martini scene." Meanwhile Wolfschmidt vodka (post-George Lois) invited readers to "turn on, tune in." In 1970, Smirnoff vodka inaugurated a curious (curious because its longstanding "Leaves You Breathless" campaign had been so successful) countercultural approach that seemed to equate the beverage with LSD. In the place of businessmen and cocktail parties the brand shows a gathering of young people in liberated clothing who seem to be doing nothing but simply contemplating flowers, staring into a pool of water, or playing guitar. "Leaves you breathless" had been aimed at businessmen who drank during lunchtime; now the ads burst with pseudo-profundity and play up the drink's appropriateness for "change" and for the whims of individual expression:

Only Smirnoff is subtle enough to go wherever your soul moves you. If you change your mind. Just change your mix. Smirnoff can get together with just about anything.

Again the drink was flavorless but now that quality bore more profound virtues than simple lack of smell: "Joyful. Gentle. Honest."[8]

chapter seven

The point here isn't simply to catalog ads and commercials that used countercultural imagery—a task which would be almost endless—but to demonstrate how normal that imagery was given the tasks of sixties advertising, how it fit the decade's existing commercial themes. Thanks to the Creative Revolution, hip consumerism had been firmly established on Madison Avenue well before the counterculture presented itself to the nation. The countercultural ads of the late sixties, so easily condemned as shallow co-optation, were in fact a continuation of the new hip consumerism that had dawned with Volkswagen. The central theme that gives coherence to American advertising of both the early and late sixties is this: Consumer culture is a gigantic fraud. It demands that you act like everyone else, that you restrain yourself, that you fit in with the crowd, when you are in fact an individual. Consumer culture lies and seeks to sell you shoddy products that will fall apart or be out of style in a few years; but you crave authenticity and are too smart to fall for that Madison Avenue stuff (your neighbors may not be). Above all, consumer culture fosters conventions that are repressive and unfulfilling; but with the help of hip trends you can smash through those, create a new world in which people can be themselves, pretense has vanished, and healthy appetites are liberated from the stultifying mores of the past. Conformity may have been a bulwark of the mass society, but in the 1960s it was usurped by difference, by an endless succession of appeals to *defy* conformity, to rebel, to stand out, to be one's self. Advertising in the 1960s taught that the advertising of the 1950s had been terribly mistaken, that people should not consume in order to maximize their efficiency or fit in or impress their neighbors. Instead, consuming was to derive its validity from the impulse to be oneself, to do one's own thing. The appeal of hip consumerism, with its reverence of the outsider, is obvious on the simplest commercial level: The vast majority of brands are not "number one" in their respective markets, are not pleased with the status quo, and they quite naturally came to adopt nonconformity as a central element of their corporate vocabularies.

Inflections of nonconformity appeared in a variety of forms in advertising during the 1960s. In many cases it was simply stated, straight out, that the users of a particular brand were individuals. While advertising had once been a running graphic testimonial to the happy consensus world of

the fifties, in sixties advertising virtually nothing is "normal." In 1967,
Oldsmobile introduced the Toronado by confessing, "Frankly, Toronado
is not for the average man." Alternatively, ads suggested that particular
products or retail outlets would empower individuality. A Chicago-area
furniture chain called Colby's suggested that "The real you is alive and
hiding out at Colby's," that "you might find you" in one of their many
decorating styles.[9]

A 1974 commercial for Barney's Men's Store done by the creative
firm Scali, McCabe, Sloves demonstrates how this theme, combined with
the individualist impulses of the Peacock Revolution in menswear, persisted long past the date usually believed to mark the end of the counterculture and the Creative Revolution. The spot depicts moments in the
life of an other-directed man who suffers through the years of conformity,
forced to wear the clothes that others have dictated he wear. Brief vignettes detail the various "people [who] have been dressing you": his
mother, the big kids at school, an angry sergeant in the army, the salesman at a clothing store that only stocks black or dark gray suits. But at
Barney's, this hapless character is finally able to determine his own personality by choosing his own clothes, by going to a store where they
"think you're big enough to dress yourself." Clairol and Reebok, Barney's
took as its slogan, "We let you be you," echoing DDB's 1971 slogan for
Clairol Nice 'n' Easy hair coloring ("It lets me be me") and anticipating
Chiat/Day's famous slogan for Reebok of the late 1980s ("U.B.U."). And
in the final vignette, the man, this time with longer hair and sideburns,
tries on a wide-lapel jacket at Barney's. When he asks the Barney's salesman, "What do you think?" the man replies, "What do *you* think?," thus
transforming him into his own man.[10]

Suzuki, manufacturer of no less a symbol of defiance than motorcycles, had a fairly obvious and unproblematic interest in the credos of
hip consumerism. The company's 1969 print campaign promoted the
brand as a means to "Express Yourself." "Freedom," announced a one-
word headline from that year. The copy continued this theme in hip
prose:

To move. To grab at the wind. To get out of the "where-it's-at" bag. . . . Suzuki has
the power to free you.

Suzuki motorbikes were countercultural machines, enabling resistance
and permitting individuality. "Suzuki takes on the country," the slogan

the company began using in 1970, implicitly set the bike off against the mass society, but their gigantic headlines could hardly have left any doubt: "Suzuki expands life"; "Suzuki conquers boredom."[11]

The nonconformist theme was often expressed by referring to the masses from which the individual consumer was distinguishing himself. In 1970, Bell & Howell engaged the political spirit of the age by encouraging consumers to "Break away from the silent majority" (with a home movie camera that recorded sound). Old Gold cigarettes used the direct line, "Get away from the crowd." And Van Heusen shirts were dramatized in the late 1960s with a photograph of a lone Van Heusen wearer, usually attired in one of the loud colors then fashionable, standing amid a group of lifeless, colorless papier-maché statues (who were often wearing hats). The company's slogan promised to differentiate the consumer from the square herd, confiding that "When you come on in a Van Heusen shirt the rest come off like a bunch of stiffs."[12]

Since artists were preeminent exponents of the orthodoxy of transgression and the cult of the new, they became suddenly visible in the advertising of the creative revolution. Andy Warhol appeared in George Lois's famous commercials for Braniff and directed some ads of his own; the aging Salvador Dali appeared for both Braniff and Datsun. A television commercial from 1973 pictures the latter product in a Dali-esque landscape; the master himself loads his canvases into the rear of the Datsun and appears odd with his long hair. As the commercial closes, he pronounces the car "Absolutely original, different, sensational" in his halting, heavily accented English—characteristics that Dali, if anyone, should be authorized to recognize.[13] Again, management theory had spilled over into the advertisements themselves: art figures became appropriate pitchmen as Madison Avenue veered away from the rigorous certainties of "science" and toward the unrestrictiveness of "art."

More numerous were campaigns for brands that permitted consumers to become self-expressing artists themselves. For products like the Polaroid Land Camera, such a strategy was obvious. The self-developing film, as a 1964 ad put it, allows the consumer to "express yourself," to try again and again until he or she creates "a masterpiece." For something like Tappan gas ranges, the "revolutionary new . . . art" pitch was more of a stretch, but it was made nonetheless in 1968. "Suddenly you're not just cooking," ran the ad's copy. "You're creating!"[14]

A hilarious variation on the nonconformity theme appeared in the 1965 campaign for Booth's House of Lords Gin, "The non-conformist gin from England," whose ads were made by the creative Daniel & Charles agency. One ad consisted of a large headline reading, "I hate conformity because _____" and a photograph of a tie (emblem of conformity) with the legend "Protest Against the Rising Tide of Conformity" painted on it in whimsical, nineteenth-century poster-style lettering. Advertising being well known as one of the primary engines of conformity, the copy naturally mocks conventional advertising premium offers and the "competitive pressure" that was believed to drive consumerism:

fill in the blank spaces and we won't send you this Booth's House of Lords "Protest" tie. Anyone can give you a premium offer. Booth's House of Lords gives you a really fine gin and a chance to shoot off your mouth with absolutely no risk. All comments will be totally ignored. Not a chance of winning anything. Now that the competitive pressure is off, why not take advantage of this great opportunity? Do it today. Or next year. It really doesn't matter. There's no time limit on taking a stand against conformity.

Appropriately, the ad appeared in a variety of trade magazines where it was read by businessmen and professionals, the subjects of the "gray flannel suit" critique. So popular did the Booth's "nonconformist" campaign become that the company eventually sold posters of the ad to private individuals.[15]

By 1970, the idea of such a nonconformist mail-in contest was no longer an in-joke among businessmen. Smirnoff Vodka actually encouraged general readers that year to write to the company about their personal strategies of flouting social convention. The brand's "Break a Silly Rule" contest was avowedly not about politics, but aside from that, entrants were supposed to come up with "the silliest rule of social behavior" they could think of and describe how it should be smashed. Smirnoff explained its hostility toward the rules that "stop people from having fun" as a matter of liberating the individual and his or her tastes:

We're talking about the silly conventions that cramp your style. The who-knows-where-they-came-from customs standing between you and a more entertaining, rewarding life.

Like the rule that says you've got to squeeze into your most uncomfortable clothes to attend the dullest party of the year. Or the rule that says white wine goes with fish and red with meat.

Smirnoff was striking a blow for fun, enjoyed by people "at their own pace. In their own way." At war with those troublesome conventions that kept people from consuming at their best, Smirnoff counted itself an enemy, not a beneficiary, of social conformity. And if the great struggle of the sixties was that of the individual against the tyranny of social convention, Smirnoff wanted the people to know which side it was on.[16]

you rascal you

A favorite mode of dramatizing the contrast between the age of bureaucratic self-restraint and the uninhibited present was to depict consumers behaving madly for (or because of) particular brands, tossing decorum to the winds—and then sometimes assuming a voice of pseudo-authority and pretending to counsel readers against such impropriety. In the mid-1960s, Lucky Strike smokers wore hats from which they had somehow been forced to take a bite; Tareyton smokers, famously, "would rather fight than switch" and appeared in ads beginning in 1964 with black eyes. A 1964 ad for Nabisco Shredded Wheat confided that it's perfectly all right to eat eighteen Nabisco Shredded Wheat biscuits, but consuming nineteen is extremely dangerous and is likely to send the consumer, like the man pictured in the ad, rocketing from his chair: "Exercise self-control." Similarly, in a 1967 ad placed by National Steel to encourage readers to buy American cars, a "quite, conservative, feet-on-the-ground solid citizen" is shown leaping in the air, the markers of his respectability (hat, spectacles, tie, shoes) flung from his body because he has bought a new car.[17]

A variation on this theme imagined consumers to be so enamored of a given brand that they were driven to violate restrictive rules and social mores in order to consume it. In 1969, Teacher's scotch faux-scolded drinkers in humorous legalese for consuming the brand on "days other than Tuesday" after the company has duly settled, "in strictest point of fact, . . . on Tuesday as the official, approved day for drinking Teacher's." Consumption on any other day "must be technically considered unauthorized." A television commercial for Heinz spaghetti sauce made by the Grey agency pictured a variety of people driven to commit the grave faux pas of dipping their bread into other people's spaghetti sauce. "Man," the announcer says, "Heinz spaghetti sauce is so thick and rich, you just gotta dip your bread in it." An award-winning 1967 Doyle Dane spot for Gillette razor blades dramatized the embarrassment of a Soviet diplomat returning to his repressive homeland after a tour of duty in the United States. A Communist superior enters the diplomat's hotel room unexpectedly while he is packing and proceeds to scrutinize the contents of his luggage, chiding him for the various luxuries he is transporting back with him: ties, pornographic magazines, and Gillette razor blades. The diplomat has an excuse for each one ("I want to show the people how decadent the Americans have become"), and for the razor blades he delivers a product pitch. But then the superior discovers an enormous quantity of the blades in the diplomat's suitcase, and the small man, now facing disgrace for his capitulation to the temptations of consumerism, confesses: "Comrade Boobinsky, so I've gotten a little spoiled." Communists are favorite advertising foils because of their supposed hostility toward pleasure and the lockstep totalitarianism they are said to endure. Here their inability to obey their own strict regulations serves to reinforce a central sixties advertising lesson of the final demise of hyperorganized puritanism.[18]

the triumph of the antispokesman

During the Creative Revolution, the stock spokesperson of the 1950s was replaced by a variety of unconventional and unusual product representatives, rule-breakers instead of besuited men of order, deviants instead of conformists. This was the era in which the "Frito Bandito," moved by his love of corn chips, pilfered bags of the snacks from their rightful owners; and in which "Zoltan, the Gypsy Chief," demonstrated his fondness for L & M cigarettes by offering to swap livestock for them. An otherwise unremarkable 1965 print ad for Kellogg's Corn Flakes designated as a "Kellogg's Corn Flaker" a small boy eating his cereal seated at a piano while an old man in suit and bow tie—the long-suffering piano teacher—holds his forehead in despair next to him, all in a quaint Norman Rockwell-style rendering.[19]

George Lois was the master of choosing peculiar figures to represent products, which he did (and does) in order to heighten the "seemingly outrageous." His 1962 television commercial for Xerox showed a chimp using a photocopier; for the brokers Edwards & Hanly, he used children; for Braniff, he paired art figures with heroes of popular culture like Andy Warhol and Sonny Liston, Whitey Ford and Salvador Dali, Mickey Spillane and Marianne Moore. Commercials of the late 1960s for Wheatena hot cereal featured a number of odd sixties figures endorsing this most conventional of products. A surfer balances his surfboard on his head and says, "I'm not sure of many things in this world, but I'm sure I feel better

chapter seven

on days when I eat Wheatena." In another, a scowling young woman delivers a particularly strange (feminist?) variation on this theme, "I know I feel meaner when I eat my Wheatena." Lois's ads for a similar product, Maypo oatmeal, featured weeping superstar athletes pouting, "I want my Maypo." An early 1970s spot for Lestoil household cleaner that Lois executed reminds one of nothing so much as a Monty Python ad parody. It pits "Mr. America," a bodybuilder who flexes his muscles and rotates for the camera, armed "with an ammoniated household cleaner," in a stain-removal contest against "Barbara Brenner," an ordinary person, who uses Lestoil. An excited announcer narrates the contest as "the extraordinary Mr. America works with his cleaner" and Barbara Brenner with hers. Despite Mr. America's glamorous fabulosity, the humble homemaker with her Lestoil quickly prevails.[20]

Criminals and criminal behavior were another sixties advertising staple, from the ubiquitous ads for Foster Grant sunglasses, which encouraged consumers to imagine themselves as all manner of stylish lawbreakers, to the 1966 ad which alerted readers that the chief communists in the Kremlin were readers of the *Wall Street Journal*, to a 1969 campaign that promoted Scripto pens with a graffiti contest. The theme can be detected as early as 1963, when Howard Gossage promoted Land Rovers by noting "the growing popularity of the Land-Rover in the commission of grand theft." Land Rovers make good escape cars, not only from the police but from mass society. A mail-in coupon that accompanied the ad is headlined, "Bored with your present life?" It can also be seen in as mundane a commercial as a 1967 Canada Dry spot in which the soda is promoted by a host of women dressed up as Prohibition-era gangsters, miming stilted working-class accents ("Da ginger ale wit da jolt!") and posing with machine guns in traditional gangster attire.[21]

anti-status, anti-obsolescence

The quest for status, another oft-criticized characteristic of fifties consumer culture, was another target of sixties consumer culture as products promoted themselves for their authentic qualities ("It's the Real Thing") rather than for the impression they would permit consumers to make on others. House of Stuart, a lower-priced brand of scotch whiskey, advertised itself in 1967 as "the Scotch for people who don't have to prove anything to anybody." Curiously, by insisting that people only bought House of Stuart because of its taste, the ads were able to revive the impressiveness pitch from the rear, as it were: the photograph of the "people who don't have to prove anything" leaves little doubt that they are extremely wealthy people, wandering about on the lawn of their estate.[22]

Planned obsolescence was a particularly noxious element of the car-based consumerism of the past, and a number of brands sought to establish their praiseworthy distance from the superficial styling that permitted the practice. Whirlpool humorously dramatized the longevity of its washing machines in 1967 by trumpeting in national magazines the infinitesimal fact that a nondescript and insignificant replacement part from its 1928 model year was being discontinued. That the manufacturer was only beginning to obsolete its 1928 line was, of course, said to be evidence of the best sort for the durability of Whirlpool's products. The makers of Westclox alarm clocks made a similar appeal in 1969 by pseudo-confessing that "sixty years ago we made a clock that lasted too long," and that "we're still making the same mistake." Even dishwashers could get in a few jabs at the auto industry and its notorious practice: a 1966 ad for the Kitchen Aid "convertible" dishwasher announced that "you won't trade this convertible in every three years."[23]

hidden persuaders exposed

A favorite tactic of the sixties was to draw attention to an ad with headlines that seemed to be confessing some sort of error, a strategy learned from the success of DDB's Volkswagen and Avis ads. It functioned both to mark a sort of commercial honesty—we're not just using superlatives automatically—and to build readership with startling words. Renault, joining a list of foreign carmakers that already included Volkswagen, Volvo, and Fiat, used a particularly aggressive version of this tactic in its 1966 ad campaign. One headline for the French brand admitted nothing less than that "our customers are dissatisfied!" As it turns out, they're only dissatisfied because they think Renault hasn't been advertising enough. But maybe the scare headline had been used because Renault had some actual confessing to do: a few months later, the company began admitting to some more serious-sounding flaws. Under the interesting headline, "The Renault for people who swore they would never buy another one," copy written in a humorous poorly-translated-from-the-French style confesses to having actually sold lousy cars a few years before, but assures the public that Renaults are now very fine vehicles indeed.[24]

Before long, the scare-headline technique was in such widespread use that whatever honesty points it had once earned were no doubt dissipating fast. In 1966, Chiquita bananas had used the strategy to draw attention to their quality-control capabilities, with photos of misshapen bananas and headlines reading, "Mistakes we make. But we don't label them Chiquita." Similarly, the 1967 headline, "You miss a lot when you take Contac," referred to the fact that, with the cold remedy's help, you "missed" sneezing and various other symptoms. Philco televisions, which came with a "fancy cabinet," were promoted with the line, "A fancy cabinet doesn't do a single thing to improve color tv viewing"; GE dishwashers offered to "treat your dishes like dirt." Pontiac also got into the shock-headline business in 1967. One ad used the line, "It's a great car to get rid of," under a picture of that current year's model, a strategy that must have been truly disheartening for some Pontiac buyers but by which the company simply meant that Pontiac's resale values were high. Toward the end of the year, the company even indulged in the headline "Wide-Tracking leaves a lot to be desired," then quickly made clear that what was "desired" was, in fact, a brand new wide-track Pontiac.[25]

A close relative of the faux-confessional style was the denunciation of the advertising industry, a strategy widely used in ads for foreign cars, like Volkswagen, Volvo, and Fiat's 1964 ad, which equated American car advertising with "brainwashing." It is surprising, though, how widely the suspicion of advertising and selling generally spread from these origins. "Be suspicious" of salesmen was the message of a 1967 ad for Sanforized products: "Don't let the smile blind you," it advised, or "the watch hypnotize you." And be sure the salesman, that conniving trickster, doesn't somehow prevent you from being sure of the "Sanforized" label. The 1967 campaign for Fisher stereos actually carried the slogan, "No ad man can do it justice." One installment was particularly hard on "the 77 manufacturers of hi-fi and stereo" and their "ad men." The ad encourages readers to "ignore the ad man when you buy stereo" by trusting no ads and only their ears and the advice of experts. "After that," it concludes, "you'll read the stereo ads strictly as pop culture."[26]

critics' choice

So bleak was the representation of American consumer culture produced in Volvo advertising during the sixties that the car's ad agencies appear to have been positioning the brand as the choice of the alienated. Ads for the Swedish car, done until 1967 by Carl Ally and after that by

Scali, McCabe, Sloves (both creative firms in the forefront of the revolution), closely resembled those of Volkswagen. Featuring minimalist
black-and-white photographs of the car, they did without fantasy back-
grounds, close-ups, and photographic stretching techniques, and remarked on the product's durability, efficiency, lack of changes, and even
its odd appearance. But Volvo replaced Doyle Dane's humor with a
darker, more despairing vision of American life. Volkswagen had used
mirthful ridicule; Volvo used acid cynicism, describing America's dream
culture as a landscape of absurdity and futility. Gone was the idealized
vision of a happy family in their "merry Oldsmobile": the car culture from
which Americans hoped to derive such joy was empty and meaningless,
the product of malicious robber barons and their unscrupulous Madison
Avenue minions, all of whom were endlessly scheming to bilk the public.
More than any other campaign of the decade, Volvo's ads spoke to consumers who were aware of the discourse of advertising, of the marketing
strategies of the Big Three, and, most important, of the mass society critique and its understanding of consumer culture as a vast fraud.

A 1963 Volvo ad set the tone: this was not going to be a campaign
about the wonders of Volvo per se but about escaping from the clutches
of the American automakers and embracing a brand that connoted (as
they would put it years later) "an honest car at an honest price." Four
headlines from other campaigns (Valiant, Rambler, Corvair, and Falcon)
have been torn from their respective ads and displayed next to one another on a black background, so that their slogans, each blustering and
fatuous ("The New Shape of Quality"; "It's Exciting!"), are reduced to
empty puffery. Below, the Volvo's various qualities are listed in minute
type, concluding with the line, "Now if we could just come up with a
slogan . . ." Volvo offers everything but the superficial.[27]

Volvo ads never tired of portraying the American car culture as deranged and the Detroit manufacturers as malevolent and deceitful beings.
Buying new cars every few years was an unhealthy and illogical "habit,"
Volvo suggested in one 1964 ad. "How often do you buy a new car?" asked
another. "That's too often." Volvo also repeatedly recalled readers' attention to the failed fads of the past. "Remember compact cars?" asked one
ad in 1967. They were briefly popular; "then Detroit got the idea that
more is better and came out with 'super-sized' versions that weren't popular with anybody." Another ad alerted readers that Detroit was up to no
good again: "Now those compacts are being souped up with big engines,
slicked up with fast-back roofs, daubed up with chrome, and the carmakers are advertising them as high-performance rally-type cars . . ." Nor

chapter seven

could the Big Three, hamstrung by bureaucratic ineptitude, as every reader of *My Years with General Motors* or *Organization Man* knew, include one standard Volvo feature because they "were still having committee meetings on the idea."[28]

Exposing the perfidy of the American automotive establishment continued in the brand's television commercials. A 1967 spot opens with a close-up of a car door being slammed, voices speaking disparagingly of its inadequate sound, and an announcer's voice-over explaining how, "over the years, smart car buyers" have come to judge cars by the sound of the door being slammed. Gradually the camera pulls back to reveal the owners of the critical voices, three men in authority figures' white smocks slamming the door—which is not attached to any automobile—and studying its sound. "So naturally, smart car makers, being even smarter than smart car buyers," the announcer continues, "spend a lot of time perfecting just that." One of the men produces a hammer and gives the door a sudden blow. This alters its sound when slammed, causing one of his colleagues to comment, "Now that sounds like a quality car." The scientists who had been so beneficent in the Rosser Reeves style of the 1950s were now defrauding the consumer rather than protecting him, using their technological know-how to investigate his car-culture folk beliefs and perfecting a deceptive, disembodied door.[29]

Planned obsolescence, though, was Detroit's worst transgression of public confidence, and for deflating it Volvo reserved special wit. A particularly cruel ad that ran in 1967 included beautiful publicity pictures of the 1957 Plymouth, Chevrolet, and Ford Fairlane, over the headline, "The exciting new cars of 11 years ago. Where, oh where, are they now?" But Volvos "don't change much," they aren't "new and exciting for 1968. So [they] won't be old and funny-looking for 1969." Even more savage in its deflating of consumer culture was an ad that ran the next month suggesting that Americans might as well buy "paper cars": it's "a logical next step in a continuing program of planned obsolescence." Logical, that is, if the madness of consumer culture is overlooked:

You think the idea is crazy? Sure it is. But trading cars every couple of years is a little crazy, too. And what difference does it make if you're a little crazy or a lot crazy?

The paper car referred to is depicted, complete with foot-high tailfins and beautiful model, the car's hood sagging under her weight. So sinister was the American car culture that one Volvo ad from 1966 dared to suggest a sort of consumer death-wish. Out of a single illuminated window in a row of dark townhouses, a man looks at his chromed, finned American car. This is not pride of ownership, however: he is "hoping someone will steal [his] car." But, as the copy continues, "Forget it." Not even a thief would want such a "big pain in the pocket."[30]

Volvo buyers, on the other hand, were said to be people who didn't really care much about the frou-frous, the chrome, and the souped-up engines that the Big Three made for Americans. "This car is for people who don't like cars," read the headline of a 1964 ad. Another addressed itself to "those of you who couldn't care less" about cars that won various races. "Bring up the subject of cars to a lot of people and they'll tell you cars are a pain in the neck," began another ad's attack on the car culture.

They'll say you have to tinker with them; lay out money for repairs; buy gas, gas, gas; trade every two or three years, lose money on the deal and make payment after payment, year after year after year.[31]

A Volvo television spot of the late 1960s took this hatred of cars to a gritty, depressing conclusion. A thirty-second, wordless vision of automotive hell, it depicts with grinding close-ups and through an oily rain the daily work of the man who runs the crane at the car crushing plant, the end of the line for the foppish vehicles in which Americans psychically and financially invest so much. Volkswagen had boasted of the snowplow driver who got to work in a VW; here Volvo shows us the man who destroys cars for a living and drives home in a Volvo.[32]

cultural dopes

On occasion, Volvo would extend its critique of consumerism to consumers themselves: the people who have bought American cars are colossal suckers; a monstrous fraud has been perpetrated on a gullible people. The consumer who actually fell for the tricks of the "hidden persuaders" and Detroit's planned-obsolescence strategy was the target of a particularly poisonous 1971 Volvo commercial. The spot presents itself as a testimonial of some kind for a large, unspecified American car; not until several seconds into it does the viewer realize that the qualities of which it boasts are hardly desirable ones. A man speaks to the camera as he washes his car in the driveway of a typical suburban house. "I've been driving nineteen years," he avers,

and I've had twelve of these! Why, as soon as this one's paid for, I'm gonna get another one! Just in time for the '72s! Yes sir, I'm hooked. I wouldn't drive anything else. Look at that color—peacock blue! If it wasn't such a great car, why would I buy so many of them?

The man is self-evidently ridiculous, a consumer out of the most pessimistic pages of Vance Packard. But not everyone is such a sucker, of course. As the man looks uncomfortably around, his own gullibility perhaps beginning to dawn on him, his neighbor drives up in a Volvo, and a voice-over announces that "If the logic of this argument escapes you, you're ready for a Volvo."[33]

Given the preponderance of ads, especially in the automobile categories, that made youth-culture appeals, it should hardly be surprising that Volvo eventually ran an ad concerned with the hapless folks who fell for all of the campaigns and promises of liberation discussed here. A slump-shouldered man on a dark street stares into a brightly lit auto showroom in one 1966 Volvo ad; only his pathetic silhouette is visible. Over his head are posted a variety of new-car encomiums, lettered in standard car-dealer script and larded with the language of rebel youth then being used by all the American automakers: "The New Fun Look of Youth," "Join the New Rebellion Now!" "Get Out Front with the Long Lean Low Forward Look for '67," and "More Pizzazz for '67." The man's dejection is summarized by the ad's powerful headline: "Your Car is Obsolete. Again." Hip is not a form of resistance to Detroit's annual march of style but the very force that has victimized this hapless consumer. "And the irony of it is," the copy reads, "a big chunk of the money that you paid for your obsolete car was used to bring out the very cars that made it obsolete."[34]

The Creative Revolution had made all aspects of fifties-style consumerism fair game for mockery. But as youth culture increasingly became the metaphor of choice in advertising, as hip slang shouted from a thousand billboards, it was inevitable that the values of creativity would conflict, if rarely, with the less corrosive values of the counterculture. On most of the occasions when consumerism was to be mocked, of course, it was consumerism as understood by the critics of the mass society: a regime of unthinking conformity and look-alike suburbia. But in certain extraordinary instances admen mocked consumerism by going after its new imagery of rebel youth rather than lonely crowd. Madison Avenue was acutely conscious of its own developing understanding of youth culture, so when the "Madison Avenue" worldview was to be knocked, on rare occasions it was youth culture that stood in as whipping boy.

Public service ads for the Peace Corps made in the late sixties by creative giant Young & Rubicam were bitingly hostile to youth culture. Seeking to encourage selflessness rather than the purchase of products and thus actually aiming to mock consumer values, these spots used the imagery of the hipster as a negative, rather than a positive, model. One memorable Peace Corps commercial that ran in 1968–69 barely makes any point at all about the Peace Corps: its intention seems to be simply to deride the counterculture, to cast its pursuit of enlightenment as idle, hedonistic frivolity. The commercial opens with a disembodied head of a long-haired young man looking about at a superimposed background of stars to the strains of the anthem from *Hair*, "Age of Aquarius." As the song mentions that "the moon is in the seventh house" a poorly animated moon swims across the screen; but as if to emphasize the tawdriness of hippie spiritualism, the moon is surprisingly similar to the Procter & Gamble logo. The rest of the song's references are also illustrated with noticeably shabby special effects: Jupiter and Mars align clumsily, asteroids emit squeaks and blip about the screen. The man's head develops a multicolored halo as he watches the proceedings; eventually, his face takes on the psychedelic multicolored appearance familiar from posters for the musical from which the song is taken. But the man's transformation is a false enlightenment. His head is literally in the stars; he marvels at special effects that appear laughably poor to the viewer. As the voiceover at the end declares, "It's one thing to predict the future [as the song's lyrics do]; it's another to help make it." Hipness is idleness, a part of the Procter & Gamble consuming universe, while the Peace Corps accomplishes real-world tasks.[35]

The message was made more explicitly in a 1968 radio spot that Young & Rubicam developed for the same Peace Corps campaign. The ad features two voices, that of a down-to-earth but idealistic young man and his shrill, trendy mother. But instead of the stereotypical activist child admonishing his complacent parents, the listener hears the opposite: the mother berates her son for refusing to demonstrate, even denounces him in new-leftish style. Protesting, the ad implies, is not only conformist but is tainted by stylishness as well, by the participation of fashionable oldsters busily "thinking young." "Look, Marvin, why can't you demonstrate for peace like everybody else?" she demands; the child responds that he "doesn't like crowds." The ad world's usual calculus is here inverted: protesting is not an act of rebellion but of conformity to the ways of parents and "crowds." "Your father, with his flat feet, marched thirty-seven blocks last weekend," the mother continues, "and he was carrying a sign and chanting!" And when the son announces that he would rather join the Peace Corps because "I wanna do something—something that counts," the mother responds that a commitment to peace is a matter of correct appearances, not substance:

> The Peace Corps! What kind of a crazy way is that to demonstrate for peace? You've gotta carry signs, and chant slogans, and wear sandals! [singing] "We shall overcome. . . ."

This last, which is sung in a ridiculous falsetto, further demonstrates the depthlessness of what many Americans probably believed was the counterculture's favorite pastime. The spot ends with the mother saying to her son, "You're a troublemaker, Marvin, you know that? Anybody that would join the Peace Corps is a troublemaker." As usual, the parents represent consumer foolishness, conformity, and superficiality, but this time they have fallen for nothing less than the think-young promises of the Creative Revolution.

By 1972, the triumph of commercialized hip was so complete that when Camel cigarettes organized a campaign around the theme of individualism, they were careful to assert that hip was merely another implement of faddishness and the real rebels distanced themselves from the now-mainstream ways of the pseudo-hip. While Camel's new slogan, "They're not for everybody," would certainly have been illustrated a few years before with a defiant hipster rising up against mass society, now he is contrasted against figures whose commitment to the revolutions of the sixties make them appear distinctly buffoonish. In one ad, a balding, middle-aged man in a polka-dot shirt is shown being measured for a pair of velvet shorts, an imaginary product of the Peacock Revolution. Far from being a genuine rebel, though, this man is a conformist of the worst kind:

> With every pair of Mr. Stanley's Hot Pants goes a free pack of short-short filter cigarettes.

Meanwhile the true individualist, the smoker of Camels, avoids the preposterous trends the sixties have unleashed on the land. Creativity has come full circle: to resist mass society one must dress unremarkably and smoke the most mainstream of cigarettes.[36]

power to the people

If the consumerism of the past had been a fraud conducted by malevolent industrialists, the consumerism of the sixties was an expression of the popular will (a fundamental tenet of free market theory as well as sixties advertising). Now products had the characteristics they did, not because of somebody's depth research, but because that is the way the people demanded it. The Lark cigarette slogan of 1965 was typical, appealing to public approval as validation of its superiority: "You decide for yourself . . . but for me there is nothing like a Lark." While the other GM lines were declaring themselves for escape or youthful excitement, Buick took a different strategy against the auto pitches of the past. Buick was, it decided in 1967, a practitioner of corporate populism, a philosophy it explained under the slogan, "Now we're talking your language." Rather than dictating to the consumer, this year Buick decided to give the people what they truly wanted. "We changed the Skylark from front to rear, we gave it a whole new look," one ad pointed out, "simply because we believe you want a car like this." The generous people at Buick "also refuse to limit your choices," permitting all manner of variety in details and color schemes. Later Buick campaigns extended the theme, announcing that the 1970 models were "the cars you've been asking us to make."[37]

A curious variation on this theme envisioned products as the subject of protest, the contested terrain of revolution, and the objects of, literally, popular demand. The makers of Coronet Brandy appealed to the democratic temper of the times by announcing in 1969 that "Brandy surrenders," that they were abandoning "aristocratic snobbishness" to sell liquor to "the people." In another ad from the same year, a mother and her three children stare angrily at the camera under the headline, "We demand equal air," a reference to the brand of air-conditioner being pitched. And George Lois's early-1970s campaign for Olivetti typewriters semifacetiously encourages "Olivetti girls" to "form a sort of Olivetti underground. And convert your friends to the Olivetti cause."[38]

women's liberation

The advertising of the sixties was, by and large, astonishingly sexist stuff, from the hapless Dodge "rebel girl" discussed below to the clinging females who populated the ads of cigarette brand Silva Thins. While it may have questioned and criticized other aspects of the mass society, sexism was one arena in which advertising made virtually no advances until the end of the decade: the stereotypes of femininity in which it dealt were, for the most part, forthrightly repellent, without subtlety or regard for female tastes. But then everything changed, and quite suddenly, in 1969 and 1970. Faced with an articulate popular uprising that looked to be as widespread and as powerful as the revulsion against the mass society, industry leaders quickly changed course. Liberation was their stock-in-trade, and they scrambled to align the Creative Revolution with this latest wave of cultural dissidence.

This was hardly the first time that advertising had superficially allied itself with feminism. Through an elaborate and much-studied campaign in the 1920s, Lucky Strike cigarettes had managed to make itself a badge of female emancipation. *Madison Avenue* recapitulated the standard industry interpretation of the event in 1969: "This campaign turned Luckies from a loser into a winner and helped make smokers of American womanhood. You might say that this was another plank in the platform of women's emancipation or entrance into the American male's world."[39] So remarkable was the Lucky Strike windfall that it continued to mold the industry's understanding of feminism many years later.

During the late sixties, there was such a rush among advertising writers to hail women's liberation as a freeing of consuming potential that it became an almost monotonous theme in industry commentary. The abandonment of certain ideas of feminine restraint, one reads again and again, will make women into much better consumers than had been their mothers. Laurel Cutler, a senior vice president at McCann-Erickson, described the revolution for readers of *Madison Avenue* as a shift from the age of the "understated" woman of the 1950s—who was reluctant to use certain products ("Rouge was out. If she colored her hair she was embarrassed about it.") to the "age of options," when "the American woman is free to look like a lady or a tramp" or "like herself or anybody else." This freedom promised, among other things, vastly increased consumption of certain goods:

Does anyone care anymore whether only her hairdresser knows for sure? Not if she can have more fun as a blonde. Forget color. Much of the time the hair we're wearing is not our own. And we wear more jewelry at once than our mothers wore in their whole lifetimes.

Transgression of outdated social convention was directly linked to increased consumption; the liberated woman was to be welcomed because she was a "heavy user." Cutler laid out the basic cultural operation of hip consumerism for her readers in no uncertain terms:

Many women like many writers and movie directors are romping in the ruins of the old censorship. They are throwing out the old forms. They are challenging every institution in our society. At the least, they are questioning all the traditional values. At the most, they are rebelling against the old authorities. Not only Church. State. Family. But also Fashion. Propriety. Modesty. And that great establishment Lady.
    Isn't this new woman, this free and loving-every-minute-of-it woman, the heavy user every industry must find and cultivate and multiply?[40]

Feminism, as it was understood by the industry in the late sixties and early seventies, was an almost perfect product pitch, and toward the end of the decade the ads of a great number of products specifically marketed to women took on overtly liberationist themes, even when the product had clearly been developed according to less liberated notions of femininity. A particularly counterintuitive example was the array of new vaginal deodorants introduced in the late 1960s. Ad campaigns for virtually every single one, regardless of its manufacturer or agency, touted the product as an accoutrement of women's liberation. A 1970 advertisement for FDS, "the first feminine hygiene deodorant spray," declared in mock-liberated fashion, "The age of FDS began with understanding. Understanding you . . . today's young woman . . . committed to *total* femininity . . . entitled to *total* confidence."[41] Massengill Feminine Hygiene Deodorant Spray advertised itself as "the freedom spray" and pictured the product's container next to a political button reading "freedom now."[42] One make of "Feminine Hygiene Deodorant" called "Pristeen" ran ads that featured long testimonials from various celebrated women of the 1960s under the headline Ms. X "talks about woman's new freedom." The various women who appeared avoided absolutely any discussion of the product; instead they talked at length about new fashions, counterculture and, once again, the importance of defying rules. Gossip columnist Suzy Knickerbocker asserted that "the most significant new freedom of today's woman" was her liberation from propriety, her new ability to evade traditional social constraints (strange for a product that was designed to eliminate "troublesome odors"): "What's really significant is that there is no longer so much concern with what is proper, how a woman should lead her life. That's outmoded today." Mary Quant, "the high priestess of young fashion," further promoted the brand by attesting that "Now all the rules are gone. . . . There is no such thing as what's in and what's out." "Rules" would indeed have to be broken in order for American women to accept such an unnecessary product; suspicions of such clearly cosmetic items—suspicions both traditional and of the sort being encouraged by Vance Packard and in ads for Volvos and Volkswagens—would have to be overturned.[43]

In 1969, J. Walter Thompson made a fairly successful effort to adapt the feminist image strategy to Pond's hand lotion, a product grounded almost fatally in preliberated social conventions. Up until that year, the lotion had been promoted with a series of ads stressing ladylike appearances and featuring photographs of elegant women who used the product. A 1963–65 campaign, for example, offered teenage girls advice on appearances and pleasing boyfriends. But in 1969, the company did a sudden about-face: conventional ideas of fragile femininity and demure womanhood were now to be scoffed at, as were the advertisements and products that catered to such notions. Now Pond's sold itself as an accoutrement of liberation instead of beauty; its superiority over other brands phrased in terms of the superiority of women's lot in the present over that of the past.

One 1969 print ad described the Pond's consumer as a skeptical, liberated nonconformist who easily saw through the very sort of advertising Pond's themselves had been using until that year. After referring to nineteenth-century feminist Amelia Bloomer, the ad noted that

the suffragettes who whip into the store for today's Pond's creams are strictly 20th Century.

They're a whole new genre of unfettered, free-spirited, savvy women who know how to cut through the phony baloney of the beauty business and get right down to basics.

The woman chosen to illustrate this "unfettered, free-spirited" individual is laden down with hip markers like a pantsuit, a derby hat, and rings on every finger.[44] Other ads depicted the new female consumer as a creator of modern art rather than a churner of butter, a breaker of rules rather than a compliant traditionalist. Pond's feminist campaign juxtaposed derisive comments about the orderly, repressive past with fantasies of the present-day American female as a skilled but rule-breaking craftsman (much like the creative admen themselves). In one ad she was a mechanic, working on her motorcycle (eternal symbol of hip rebellion), with copy that sneered, "You need another pale, white, virtuous hand lotion like you need another apron." In another she was a sculptor with a blowtorch, accompanied by copy that emphasized her defiance with these words: "You need another pious, lily-white, Lady Jane hand lotion like you need a whale-boned girdle." In each, the notion of "dishpan hands" as woman's great scourge was ridiculed, as were the advertisements that continued to cater to such a "housewifey" female. Whiteness was now a mark of shame in the corporate canon, not virtue (the new Pond's lotion was pink), and the "prim" and "prissy" female of the 1950s had been banished forever.[45]

The best-known feminist campaign of the 1960s was crafted by the all-American firm Leo Burnett (the company responsible for the Marlboro cowboy, the Jolly Green Giant, and the Pillsbury Doughboy) for Virginia Slims cigarettes, a new Philip Morris product that had been specifically invented to appeal to the new attitudes of women. These new cigarettes were longer ("you've come a long way") and narrower than usual, but their real difference, as with all cigarette brands, was an image defined by advertising. This image was concocted of varying quantities of militant feminist rhetoric mixed with some less radical aspects of American femininity (like makeup and fashionable clothes). It incorporated a great many of the aforementioned themes: the oppressive cigarette establishment, nonconformity, self-determination, and the liberating power of the youth counterculture. One of the campaign's first television spots opens on a woman dressed in an overdetermined, old-fashioned costume standing alone in the middle of an uncluttered set. A male voice addresses the viewer while restrained flute music is played:

chapter seven

It used to be, lady, you had no rights. No right to vote, no right to property, no right to the wage you earned. That was back when you were laced in, hemmed in, and left with not a whole lot to do. That was back when you had to sneak up to the attic if you wanted a cigarette. Smoke in front of a man? Heaven forbid!

As it was in so much of the advertising of the 1960s, the past was an unhappy time of repression both sartorial and consuming. But while the announcer is speaking, the woman has produced a pair of scissors and, with a coy look at the camera, begun to free herself from this past by cutting her costume apart. And behold, when stripped of her conformist costume, she is not demure at all, but wears stylish striped stockings. Within seconds, she has transformed the old-time dress into a contemporary poncho-like drape. And then, since liberation is a matter of consuming, she lets her hair down, dons earrings, and applies mascara. Similarly, the flute music is replaced by the brand's rock 'n' roll jingle, to which the woman begins to dance: "You've come a long way, baby, to get where you've got to today." As the Marlboro cowboy symbolized the promise of individualism, so the stylish female of Virginia Slims, always contrasted in print advertising with her repressed forebears, came to identify the brand with the promise of women's liberation.[46]

the dodge rebellion, the pontiac secession, and youngmobiles

The automobiles of the 1950s, with their garish tailfins and chrome, had been mocked by Nikita Khruschev and excoriated by the analysts of mass society. They were the target of popular books by both John Keats and Ralph Nader, and it is appropriate that hip consumerism's attack on the conventions of car culture was launched with a sustained barrage by foreign car manufacturers Volkswagen and Volvo. Yet while the marketing practices of American automakers may have been the most prominent symbol for everything that creative advertising declared was wrong with the world, that fact hardly deterred the Detroit automakers from embracing creativity and the commercial critique of the mass society that it implied. In fact, the advertising of the American automakers was itself revolutionized quite thoroughly by the end of 1965. Almost no American car manufacturers were still using the idealized, white-family-at-play motif by that year. And with the exception of luxury lines (Cadillac, Lincoln, Chrysler), virtually every car being marketed in America introduced its

1966 model year as an implement of nonconformity, of instant youthfulness, of mockery toward traditional Detroit-suckers, or of distinction from the mass society herd.[47] There was, of course, the Mustang, the decade's great automobile success story, which was promoted with ads facetiously claiming to have transformed ordinary people—"born loser[s]," in one ad's formulation—into owners of exotic, daring lifestyles: bullfighters, socialites, gamblers, star musicians. There was also Rambler's "Rogue" and "Rebel"; the "big, new-generation Comets" from Mercury; the Plymouth Fury, which was evidently "for getting off the beaten path. And making your own"; and the Corvair, "a most unusual car for people who enjoy the unusual."[48]

The critique of mass society leveled by the American automakers, was noticeably different from that of Volkswagen and Volvo. The ads of the Big Three automakers were not concerned with evading planned obsolescence, but with discovering for annual style changes a more compelling meaning. Where Volkswagen and Volvo emphasized authenticity and durability, Detroit stressed escape, excitement, carnival, nonconformity, and individualism. It is a cleavage that goes to the heart of the commercial revolution of the sixties: every brand claimed to be bored, disgusted, and alienated, but for some these meant the never-changing Volkswagen and blue jeans; they steered others toward the Pontiac Breakaway and the Peacock Revolution.

The transformation of Oldsmobile advertising from the 1950s through to the adoption of the "Youngmobiles" slogan in 1968 is illustrative of the industry's change. Oldsmobile television commercials during the 1950s featured all of the standard devices of prerevolutionary car advertising: cars and disembodied engines on revolving platforms; smiling male announcers with deep, authoritative voices; meaningless descriptions like "futuramic," "the linear look," and "rocket" engines; graphs with no notation on either axis; an unchanging jingle about "merry Oldsmobile" that dated from the prewar period.[49]

By 1964, Oldsmobile commercials had begun to invent a more distinct brand image for the line and to speak to particular—and decidedly unyouthful—market segments rather than simply specify the cars' features. A man with gray hair who plays polo finds "high-spirited high-fashion in this Olds 98." He is a "man of action and discernment" and Oldsmobile is, quite simply, "Where the action is!" Throughout the mid-1960s, the line's commercials emphasized the action, adventure, and daring that Oldsmobile made available to such affluent consumers. In 1965, Oldsmobile enlisted the announcing services of John "Shorty"

Powers, whose well-demonstrated familiarity with the exciting world of jet aircraft reinforced the car's daring image. Then in 1966 Oldsmobile began to go from Cold War cool to counterculture (from the first sixties cultural obsession to the next, as it were). Commercials from that year used a guitar and tambourine soundtrack in place of the earlier jazz orchestra. Psychedelic graphics appeared: whirling flowers and fields of dayglo color moved rapidly about the screen as Shorty Powers drove around in his 442 convertible, the features of its suspension demonstrated with animation.[50]

Then in 1967 the Oldsmobile company turned openly to youth culture. To make the comparison especially clear, the cars were now referred to as "Youngmobiles," their features repetitively described with the words "young ideas." "Youngmobiles" were to be implements of resistance to the conformity and sameness that mass society apparently demanded: "Call it different. Call it individualistic. Call it yours," read Toronado ads. They were also cars with a distinctly countercultural air. One commercial mixed footage of surfing, waves washing over the camera, and a distorted electric guitar soundtrack to establish the correct atmosphere. "1968 is happening," says the announcer. Something young is happening."[51] The "young" theme, though, was not meant for actual young people. In another commercial, a married couple discuss cars in bed at night. "Harry," says the wife, "I just dreamed we bought a 1968 Youngmobile from Oldsmobile." In her dream, she and her husband, who wears a business suit, examine the car in question at a dealer's showroom. "The styling, the lines," she says.

So fresh. So young. . . . So young inside, too. Young ideas everywhere you look. . . . The way it performs—so young. . . . And such a young spirit.

Naturally, she dreams of driving the car to the beach, where a number of attractive young surfers are in attendance.[52]

For all of their references to youth and their libidinal engagement of youth culture, the first "Youngmobiles" ads exhibited little comprehension of the counterculture's social critique. Later advertisements, though, more fully embraced the new values. Oldsmobiles were not only "young," they were hip: emblems of nonconformity, agents of distinction from and rebellion against the dull sameness of mass society. The company's 1968 slogan promised an "Escape from the ordinary." One ad appealed to consumers' feelings of hostility toward everyday routine by asking, "Run-of-the-mill cars got you feeling grounded?" and "Want to really send the ordinary into a tailspin?"[53]

Oldsmobile's 1969 campaign was a truly extraordinary effort to link the mass society critique to a brand identity. The "youngmobiles" line had been dropped, replaced by classic and more familiar (for Oldsmobile buyers) images of anonymity and bureaucratic malaise derived from the world of white-collar work. In the background of the company's print ads, people toil away at a line of identical desks or tend to ranks of sixties-era computers; in the foreground is posed a 1970 Oldsmobile. This was the answer to the monotony of corporate life: "Facts. Figures. Data. Reel after reel after reel. Wouldn't it be nice to have an Escape Machine?" The solution to the meaningless drudgery of mass society was a consumer product.[54]

Dodge advertising of the mid-1960s, made by BBDO, called on consumers to join the "Dodge Rebellion," a cheerful revolt against the mass society malaise. Under slogans like "Rise up," "Break away from the everyday," and "Move away from the crowd," the automaker offered its products as a solution for conformity. Dodge was no longer the line of gigantic, meaningless tailfins that it had been a few years before, but a bearer of revolutionary differentness, the liberator of suburbia, "the rambunctious rebel that's leading . . . [the] charge on Dullsville." A BBDO executive explained the campaign to Victor Navasky in 1966 as "designed to blast the stodginess image."[55] But the company had yet to get its signifiers straight. In these ads, which appeared toward the end of 1965, insurgency was symbolized by a female model that the trade press called the "rebel girl," who appeared in a hipster's dark tights and turtleneck and brandished a sword, flintlock, or similarly antique weapon. Not only is the rebellion in which the "rebel girl" is engaged thus whimsically ancient, but her doings are hapless and ineffectual. In one 1966 ad, she points a gun at her own head. In television commercials, she crashes airplanes, accidently detonates a railroad car full of dynamite on which she is riding, and she is sexually submissive, falling helplessly from on high into the back seat of a moving Dodge convertible. However it promised to deliver consumers from "the herd," the Dodge rebellion was pretty tame stuff.[56]

In 1967, BBDO sharpened Dodge's rebelliousness, reformulating the brand as a more active anti-establishment agent. The new campaign focused on "Dodge Fever," an imaginary malaise brought on by the sight of Dodge cars which caused square over-forty men to botch weighty social responsibilities. In one television commercial, a new Dodge causes a jeweler to smash a "two million dollar diamond"; in another a chemist with a German accent frets, "Ze Dodge Fever—please, not now!" "I'm so nervous," the jeweler confides. "What if I got—Dodge Fever?" He is rightfully worried. He is a quintessential Organization Man, the antithesis of Dodge-ness: he wears old-fashioned spectacles, mops his forehead with a handkerchief, uses bowdlerized pre-sixties expressions like "boo-boo," and is closely supervised by a worried, overweight capitalist. The chemist, who is balding, also wears tiny round glasses and a lab coat. While these figures of precision and order attempt to perform their tasks, a young woman in miniskirt and boots is pictured driving about in a Dodge car, which in one case is called the "Swinger 340," the automotive equivalent of the counterculture: a "young new compact with a wild new personality." The appeal of Dodge's wild youthfulness is irresistible, demanding immediate gratification. As the female model says, "Some things just can't wait."

The Dodge compulsion to consume immediately and without moderation comes naturally to the hip young, like the car's driver. But for repressed, other-directed men like the diamond cutter and the German chemist, the liberating call of the wild Dodge is threatening indeed, a "fever" which they must not "catch." Of course, at the moment of gravest importance both men look out their windows and glimpse the woman with the Dodge car. The jeweler shatters his diamond; the chemist causes his laboratory to explode. Order is reduced to rubble by the merest suggestion of consumer freedom. And the pathetic Organization Man is left to ponder his certain punishment: "Oh boy, am I gonna get yelled at," despairs the luckless diamond cutter.[57]

The upgraded menace of this more subversive tactic in the Dodge rebellion is clearly demonstrated in a 1969 television commercial for the Challenger, a powerful muscle car. Again the car's desirability is established by a confrontation between a ludicrous and overdetermined square figure and a young, reasonable character whose car offends postwar propriety; again we admire its features because of the degree to which they annoy the Man. This time, though, the square is no less than the counterculture's great foe—the Pig: an overweight policeman with a pronounced stage-Southern accent. He has pulled over the (young, white, more generic-sounding) driver of the Challenger and, chewing a cigar, addresses him in the derisive manner supposedly unique to Southern lawmen: "Boy, you're in a heap of trouble." The young man is charged with symbolically disrupting the order this unpleasant figure is paid to protect by "operatin' a racing-type vehicle inside the city limits." Of course, the driver of the Dodge pleads that an injustice is being committed, that the Challenger is a stock consumer product like any other, that its various attractive features (tires, racing stripes, enormous motor, peculiar shift stick) are not illegal. But the stout bearer of authority will not be placated. The car challenges the Establishment, and he even threatens the young man with further charges if he continues to protest: "Careful, boy. I'll book you for sassin' a law officer." A young female announcer appears at the commercial's conclusion to drive home the ad's message that the virtue of Dodge cars lay in the ways they discomfit men of order. "If you can handle the way people react to your 1970 Dodge Challenger," she says happily, "You could be Dodge material." [58]

This commercial's challenge to authority did not consist merely of a simple fictional confrontation of youth and the law; it also rebelled dramatically against the conventions of automobile advertising. If policemen appeared at all in earlier commercials for cars, it was as benevolent, admiring figures. Here he is pig, a stock buffoon borrowed from *Easy Rider* and bent on repressing the very brand of car being advertised. Dodge's unflattering portrayal of the policeman was no doubt offensive to the "silent majority" then proclaiming its support for local police forces in their running post-Chicago battle with the cadres of the revolution. But evidently Dodge did not care: as for so many business spokesmen in the 1960s and since, the restrained, conformist values of postwar convention were contrary to the consumer attitudes Dodge wished to encourage. In the battle between counterculture and Establishment, Dodge came down solidly on the side of the rebels. [59]

Throughout the early sixties, Pontiac ads had emphasized the car's wideness ("wide-track Pontiac") in an attempt to identify the brand as a master of troublesome nature. But when Dodge began to speak for the Rebel, Pontiac aligned itself with another stock sixties character, the Outsider, giving voice to an even deeper sense of dissatisfaction. The automaker did this, however, with only a few overt references to the counterculture, the most forceful exponent of such angst. Instead, commercials used more distant icons of alienation like gangsters. Dodge may have mocked the upholders of law and order, but Pontiac went them one better, identifying their products with actual—not wrongly accused—lawbreakers. A 1968 ad, which appeared soon after the success of *Bonnie and Clyde*, mimicked the movie closely and signaled corporate America's approval of what is usually understood to have been a landmark inversion of the traditional Hollywood conception of justice. The spot features a group of gangsters who emerge from a bank they have robbed in clothes almost identical to those worn by Warren Beatty and Faye Dunaway in the movie, climb into a 1930s Packard, and drive away. Cheerful banjo music plays throughout the commercial, as it did in the film. The group quickly discards its Packard for a new Pontiac Firebird convertible, which is in turn abandoned for a Pontiac station wagon, establishing the simple point that Pontiac is the getaway car of choice for America's outlaws, with whom the viewer was encouraged to identify: "If you're particular about the car you drive," as bank robbers no doubt are, "there's a particular kind of Pontiac for you."[60]

In 1968, Pontiac stated the new theme more openly. "Pontiac announces the great break away!" declared its print ads. The familiar "wide-track" theme was redefined: "wide-tracking" was no longer a matter of mere performance, but an existential operation, a secession "from humdrum driving." Pontiac extended its invitation to rebel to everyone: in its television commercials, even golf-playing businessmen were alienated from the civilization of business. One 1968 commercial opens with Jack Nicklaus and two young women proclaiming their hostility toward the world of conformity and denial and averring that Pontiac is the car for their disaffection. "I broke away because I got teed off," says one woman, looking stern and angry at the camera. "I broke away because I wanted to swing," says the other. But again their alienation is harmless stuff. The trio climb into a Pontiac Firebird and spend the rest of the sixty seconds driving around a golf course.[61]

A 1969 spot for Pontiac's GTO, now known as "The Humbler," was much less benign. If the "Bonnie and Clyde" spot had signaled Pontiac's acceptance of new values exalting the alienated and even violent outsider by focusing on stylized gangsters from a distant, cartoonish past, this later commercial purposefully starred a genuinely threatening character from the present—the juvenile delinquent. The setting is the familiar site of teenage contestation, the hamburger stand, crowded with young people in by-now-commonplace long hair. The action is simple wordless drama. Unaccompanied by a female, the anti-hero drives up in his Pontiac GTO and cruises the restaurant's parking lot, which is filled with other muscle cars. He stares menacingly, revs his engine, opens his exhaust, and finally roars away. Despite the other powerful motors sitting around, his Pontiac is the subject of everyone's quiet stares of awe, its superiority universally recognized. In place of the usual announcer, the car's various features are hymned by a surprisingly hard rock band who resemble the once-revolutionary Detroit group MC-5. And the words

with which these features are described speak openly to the antisocial
sentiments that delinquents are supposed to harbor. "Wheels," they sing,
"tough as leather. Big and bad and black. Pipes, open wide, don't hear no
one talkin' back." In 1969, "Big and bad and black" must have conjured
images of black militancy, and indeed one black couple is shown at the
hamburger stand nodding approvingly as the GTO loner drives by. That
the "Humbler" is said to be "bad," and that the loudness of its "pipes"—
that is, an exhaust system that can be made to circumvent the muffler
(and the law)—are an attractive feature reveals how far hip had come
by 1969. Ten years before, each of these values would have been considered negative and even dysfunctional. At the commercial's conclusion,
the traditional authority, the deep-voiced male announcer, actually en-
dorses the free-floating hostility of the unpenitent Pontiac outsider: "The
humbler is here. This is the way it's gonna be, baby."[62]

the uncolas

Another product category that was quite thoroughly given over to hip
advertising was soda, a cheap, disposable product bought largely by young
people themselves.[63] Even so, the best soda ads stressed the *values* of the
counterculture rather than simple countercultural appearances—footage
of long-haired youngsters or rock soundtracks. 7-Up and Dr. Pepper, for
instance, both used overtly countercultural messages but less rock music
and day-glo illustration than one would expect. Even here, with products
specifically targeted to young people, hip consumerism was a more complex phenomenon than "co-optation" would imply, a larger shift in the
values of business culture than a momentarily expedient dalliance with
the rebel doings of the young.

Campaigns for Dr. Pepper have proclaimed the soda's uniqueness and
vaguely subversive "differentness" since the late 1960s, but without making many overt references to the counterculture's embrace of these same
values. When Young & Rubicam took over Dr. Pepper's advertising in
1970, the drink was tagged memorably with the term so frequently applied to errant youth in those years: "misunderstood." Strangely, though,
the campaign commented mainly on business values, which it addressed
in language almost identical to that used by the young cultural insurgents.
The most famous commercial from that era is basically a dramatization of
the problem faced by Dr. Pepper's ad agency—persuading people to remember what Dr. Pepper was. It depicts a group of Dr. Pepper employees

standing around a loading dock in their Dr. Pepper jackets and pondering the problem. One of their number arises to address them, reflecting the era's romanticization of popular democracy. "Men," he shouts, arms waving, his accent that of a Southern preacher. "There's people out there that don't understand us. . . . Now what are we going to do about that?" A comrade shouts, with revolutionary fervor, "Make 'em understand us!" At the commercial's conclusion, an announcer says in a distinctly working-class accent, "Dr. Pepper may be America's most misunderstood soft drink, but with guys like we got, it won't be for long." Even without long hair and electric guitars, the struggle to make one's uniqueness "understood" could be easily translated into commercial imagery.[64]

Later ads for Dr. Pepper enlarged on this corporate-protest theme, moving from "misunderstood" to a more specific, but still-hip adjective: "original." Commercials from this campaign used a variety of situations to illustrate a single metaphor, the transformation of the square through the intervention of Dr. Pepper, the nonconformist soda (what Ford today calls a "serious attitude adjustment"). One television commercial of the early 1970s is particularly illustrative of the brand's ongoing confusion of hip and corporate values. A group of businessmen are shown ordering lunch to eat during a board meeting. The boss asks for a "cola," and in a scene reminiscent of *The Hucksters*, each of the men seated at the long table call out, "Me too, sir." A lone young person, though, refuses to be a corporate yes-man. In defiance of business protocol and decorum, he leaps up onto the table and sings, "Oh no, not for me, sir. I need originality, sir. Give me innovation, variation, Dr. Pepper"; soon, of course, the entire august group has been won over.[65] In another, a number of Dr. Pepper consumers, who are in the majority this time, confront a bookish librarian, quintessential enforcer of logocentric order, coaxing her to "Have some excitement." After tasting "some originality" in the form of Dr. Pepper, she is instantly liberated and begins to cast off her various sartorial restraints; removing jacket, glasses, scarf, letting her hair down, and joining in the carnivalesque Dr. Pepper dance.[66]

The lemon-lime soda 7-Up stayed closer to the actual counterculture but still managed to produce a fairly serious commercial critique, equating the tyranny of mass society with the cola-monopoly. During the 1960s, 7-Up had for some time run a distant third in sales to cola giants Coke and Pepsi. Late in that decade its agency, J. Walter Thompson of Chicago, tagged the beverage as the "Uncola" and successfully hitched the product to the rising star of nonconformity. The campaign brought together the ad world's Creative Revolution with the new values sweeping the land: nonconformity in admaking, as it turned out, dovetailed nicely with nonconformity as a brand image. As John Furr, presently Thompson's Worldwide Director of Training, recalls, the sixties saw a changing of the guard at the ad world's most "establishment" agency, a change that was driven by the demands of anxious clients like the people at the 7-Up corporation. At the time when 7-Up asked Thompson for a new and more aggressive campaign, the agency

was undergoing a massive reinvention of itself. So it was a very interesting coincidence, that here was a client who was trying to reinvent its brand or challenging what it was, coming to an agency that was very much doing the same thing, in terms of its own . . . creative persona.[67]

During the early 1960s, advertising for 7-Up cast it as a good mixer with liquor or as an appropriate accompaniment to certain foods rather than as a beverage in its own right. And although its ads used obligatory soft-drink lines like "It's got the sparkle that swings!" they often paired the drink with people engaged in stilted upper-crust activities like tinkering with a Ferrari or playing with a pet falcon.[68] In response to 7-Up's desire to remake its image, in 1966 J. Walter Thompson inaugurated a new campaign around the more hip-sounding slogan, "Wet and Wild." Commercials from 1967 pair avant-garde filmmaking techniques with a new rock 'n' roll jingle: the goal seems to have been to establish the drink's "wildness," to identify 7-Up with the tide of liberation, particularly sexual, that was then beginning to draw the attention of the mass media. But for all its rock music, its graceful camera work, and its suggestively posed female models, this attempt to identify the soda pop with the emerging counterculture was too superficial to be convincing. As John Furr notes, the campaign suffered from one of the perennial problems of the Creative Revolution: artistry obscured message. "Wet and Wild didn't work," he recounts. "It was visually dramatic, it was an art director's dream come true, it was very striking advertising, but it really didn't . . . reposition the brand."[69] The commercials may have used countercultural signifiers, but they had no countercultural content to speak of.

The Uncola campaign, inaugurated in 1968, accomplished the company's goals much more effectively. Discovering through research that consumers only identified brands of cola as "soft drinks," JWT decided to confront the public's basic perceptions of what soda was. 7-Up needed to actively encourage defiance of established cola tastes, and the idea of "uncola" suggested itself as a means of dissent. From its inception, the campaign was cloaked in an aura of transgression, of taboo-smashing and establishment-challenging activities. As Furr tells the story, an art director at Thompson "Got a cola glass and poured 7-Up in it. And it was like heresy! 'You mean, 7-Up is a cola?!'" The first round of Uncola commercials "was such a violation and departure that the bottlers were furious."

> It was a shocking campaign, . . . the first several commercials that were done. When it was shown at a bottlers meeting, that I believe took place here in Chicago . . . [late 1968 or 1969], I'm told, about half the bottlers got up and walked out. They were so outraged. They were incensed about this advertising.

Unlike soda campaigns of the past, the Uncola effort was organized not so much around particular product claims as around what Furr calls "an attitude." The Uncola was anti-establishment, the outsider beverage, the negation of America's traditional tastes in soft drinks. It not only identified the product with the youth uprising, but it managed to accomplish the company's marketing needs by doing so:

> We were still struggling to try to get out of Vietnam, and there was this whole anti-establishment everything. . . . The timing was brilliant, because it allowed the younger people to, in effect, say, "this is my soft drink," and it allowed us to violate taboos that were very much part of the generation that was there. . . . So the advertising didn't look anything like ordinary soft drink advertising, which was also fortuitous, because we were being outspent, even then, by Coke and Pepsi by a measure of probably ten to one.[70]

7-Up used youth culture both to speak to its largest target market and to reposition itself against the very-much-established colas.

The Uncola campaign made extensive use of countercultural imagery. 7-Up billboards and print ads consisted of vibrantly colorful Peter Max-style renderings of the product as an electric guitar or a butterfly, surrounded by the omnipresent rainbows and birds and hearts and flowers of the psychedelic era. In 1969, the company sponsored Chicago performances by counterculture favorites like Blind Faith, Creedence Clearwater Revival, and Crosby, Stills, and Nash.[71]

But the first round of Uncola television commercials, aired in 1968, contained no countercultural or youth imagery at all: here the anti-establishment "attitude" was conveyed simply through clever attacks on cola as the drink of unenlightened mass conformity. "Uncola" was more an attitude about consuming than it was an appeal to a particular market

segment: cola is sameness, dreary homogeneity, while 7-Up is the beverage of differentness, daring, and rebellion. Even the announcer's hesitat-
ing voice—continually interjecting "um" and "uh"—serves to under-
score the Uncola's distance from the establishment hard sell. Three
brown bags are shown at the opening of one commercial, each with an
unspecified bottle of soda inside. "Uh, these are the three largest-selling
soft drinks," the announcer says. The first two are identical: "This one's a
cola too. It's brown, like a cola; it's sweet, like a cola." But the third is
decisively different: "And this one is the uncola. It doesn't look anything
like a cola, it doesn't taste anything like a cola." In another commercial,
the colas' sameness is damned as an element of oppressive conformity.
After noting, Avis-like, that 7-Up is the number-three-selling soda, the
modest announcer suggests that maybe it would sell better if it addressed
the conformist fears of consumers: "Uh, it could be one of the two largest-
selling soft drinks if only the Uncola *looked* like a cola." To address this
imaginary anxiety, the announcer facetiously offers a "Security Kit" consisting of two test-tubes of brown fluid which, when mixed with 7-Up,
give it a cola color. "You see?" he says in a tone of mock reassurance. "If
the uncola makes you feel un-secure, well, there's your answer." But then
conformity is undone: a hand brusquely removes the "Security Kit," replaces it with a bottle of 7-Up, and the announcer delivers the punch
line. "So now you know, we could make it look just like a cola, if we
wanted to, but we don't."[72]

A later (1973) commercial dramatized this message with classic images of machinelike monotony disrupted by the beverage of unconfor-
mity. A succession of empty cola glasses are being filled with ice, seized
by hands, and filled by a machine with a brown fluid. The glasses appear
rhythmically one after another to the accompaniment of generic machine noises, faster and faster and faster, until the cola assembly line is
brought to a sudden halt by 7-Up. Ice bounces off the top of a glass instead of falling in. The machine noise stops. A hand turns the glass
upside-down; its opening is on the other end. Everything moving slowly
and reasonably now, the inverted glass is filled with 7-Up and placed in
front of a row of colas. "For years, the colas had things pretty much their
own way," the announcer explains. "But then came the Uncola. And
ever since, the fresh, clean taste of 7-Up has been turning the Cola world
upside down."[73] The inversion of values of the 1960s and 1970s was
not a threat to 7-Up or its agency, but the opportunity of a lifetime. As
J. Walter Thompson remade itself along creative lines, its client could
challenge the market leaders on grounds of philosophy, not just image.[74]

chapter seven

chapter eight

CARNIVAL AND COLA:

HIP VERSUS SQUARE

IN THE COLA WARS

Pepsi and other such companies have been more interested in the term segment as a verb than as a noun. They have segmented markets, rather than merely responded to a market segment that already existed. There was no such thing as the Pepsi Generation until Pepsi created it.

— RICHARD S. TEDLOW, *NEW AND IMPROVED*

One of the most dramatic confrontations of the new hip consumerism with its predecessor took place in the 1960s on the battlefields of what has been called "the cola wars." While the near-universal hegemony of Coca-Cola was a product of an earlier marketing paradigm, the rapid rise of Pepsi during the 1960s was made possible by an ad campaign that made skillful use of the subversive, anarchic power of the carnivalesque and of the imagery of youth rebellion. Ever since the invention of the Pepsi Generation in the early 1960s, Pepsi has offered not just a soda but a vision of its consumers as impudent insurrectionaries, sassy upstarts flouting the dull, repressive mores of the past. As with 7-Up, enlisting youthful vitality and insurgency was a natural strategy for Pepsi, locked in a difficult battle with longstanding market leader Coca-Cola. The Pepsi-Cola Company wanted Americans to question the "establishment" in the most real sense of all, to turn away from established tastes and preferences.

Both Coca-Cola and Pepsi were invented in the American South in the late nineteenth century, and both were originally dispensed as patent medicines in soda fountains. Both are made from similar ingredients, namely, sugar, water, and a flavoring derived from the African kola nut; and both taste remarkably alike. But owing to its earlier start and its more aggressive marketing, Coca-Cola long dominated the soft-drink world, with Pepsi-Cola, the imitation beverage, lagging far behind. Pepsi only became a real competitor in the 1930s, when, with the colorful Walter Mack as its president, the company began to offer twelve-ounce bottles for the same price as Coke's six-ounce package (backing the effort with a catchy radio jingle). But in the meantime, Coca-Cola had become a veritable symbol of all things American under the guidance of its deeply religious founder Asa Candler and his successor, conservative Southerner Robert Woodruff.

Both giants of the soft-drink industry are and have long been very much concerned with the production of advertising. Since soda is not a basic necessity or a traditional beverage choice, and since the soda consumer chooses between many brands with almost indistinguishable flavors, advertising alone must make the product appealing.[1] Image—established with massive advertising campaigns—is the name of the game in the soda industry. So much so that officials associated with both cola giants have made almost identical public statements attesting to the priority of advertising to product at their companies.[2] But it was not until the 1960s that Pepsi hit upon the images that would make them the second soft-drink superpower.

Since the sixties, Pepsi's advertising strategy has aimed to identify the drink with a certain model consumer, an ideal with which the viewer was encouraged to identify himself.[3] As Alan Pottasch, Pepsi's senior vice president in charge of marketing, once put it, "one of the best ways to separate our product from the competition was to differentiate our users."[4] Officials at Pepsi and its advertising agency, BBDO, often explain this strategy by comparing brands of soda to men's ties, nonessential items which are worn for decoration only, chosen to make a statement about the wearer's (drinker's) personality rather than to serve some utilitarian purpose.[5] Thus Pepsi aimed for an image that described the user in some meaningful way rather than the product ("Join the Pepsi People" rather than "Pepsi refreshes") and sought to spell out through advertising the various features of the ideal Pepsi consumer.

Given these imperatives, BBDO invented a campaign that, in many ways, epitomized the commercial culture of the 1960s as effectively as did DDB's ads for Volkswagen: in 1961 they invented a fictional youth movement, a more wholesome version of Mailer's hipsters but still in rebellion against the oppressive demands of mass society. With the fast-moving antics of the "Pepsi Generation," Pepsi would inscribe the binary system that still characterize American thinking about the sixties onto the bipolar cola universe: Pepsi is hip, Coke is square; Pepsi is youthful, Coke

is fogey; Pepsi smashes rules and inhibitions, Coke is hopelessly entangled
in the stultifying postwar order; Pepsi is for individualists, Coke is for
conformists.

When speaking of the Pepsi Generation, agency and company executives are always careful to assert that they were not focusing narrowly
on the youth market. "It wasn't youth, it was attitudinal," says Allen
Rosenshine, later chairman and CEO of BBDO. "It was attitudinal youthful." Rather than a particular physical age, he noted, "there are attitudes
and styles which we wish to make signals of or synonymous with the
brand."[6] Although the youth market was vast and important, Pepsi was
looking for a potential consuming base to rival that of Coca-Cola; that
is, one which included virtually everyone in America. Thus Pepsi cast
itself in ads from a 1961–63 campaign as the drink for "those who *think
young*," who embraced a nebulous "new outlook," "a modern enthusiasm for . . . getting more out of life."[7] Others reassured the public that
"Thinking young is a state of mind. Any age can join in. Today you see
it everywhere. . . ."[8] As James Forkan wrote in a 1980 *Advertising Age*
retrospective on Pepsi advertising, "the youth market remains the biggest
consumer of soft drinks, but age is not the real focus on the many Pepsi
campaigns created since the late 1960s. The Pepsi generation, signifying
a state of mind, transcends age groups, as well as changing hair, apparel,
and music styles."[9] According to Pepsi, as well as many other advertisers
who used youth appeals during the 1960s, youth was an attitude toward
living—and particularly toward consuming—rather than a specific age
group.

The preliminary and fundamental defining attribute of what Rosenshine calls "Pepsi-ness,"[10] is what it is *not*, what it defines itself
against—namely, Coke-ness. As industry analysts J. C. Louis and Harvey Z.
Yazijian have noted, in the cultural battle between the two cola giants, a
constant awareness of "the competition" is always present in advertisements as they struggle to define themselves as diametrically different from
the other.[11] And what was the Coca-Cola Company? It was venerable, it
was conservative, it was established, it was number one. Tom Dillon,
president of BBDO, remarks that Coca-Cola "had an old-fashioned
bottle, an old fashioned trademark . . . it ran very dull television stuff. . . .
The whole atmosphere of the [Coca-Cola] company was staid, traditional, it was [like] an old bank."[12] When in the early 1960s Bill Backer
of McCann-Erickson (Coca-Cola's agency) tried to persuade the Atlanta
giant to begin using rock 'n' roll music in their advertisements, he encountered serious resistance:

chapter eight

"Rock music was considered dirty and low-class," Backer said, referring to this condescending attitude of the late fifties. . . . He well remembers the thick, heavy silence of those meetings with the Coke leadership during the early sixties when he desperately tried to dispel the fears born of that ancient, inbred prudery that suffused so much of Coca-Cola.[13]

As the nation entered the decade of youth and revolution, the Coca-Cola company still clung to a vision of consuming more appropriate to an earlier time. In many ways, it had no choice: according to business historian Richard Tedlow, Coca-Cola was inextricably identified with the mass-marketing paradigm that was quickly coming to an end during those years. It offered one uniform product, distributed worldwide in one uniform package, and closely identified with all things American.[14] For all its great marketing achievements, it was a dangerously vulnerable product in an age of convention-smashing and market-segmenting, and its image of restraint, sobriety, and what Pepsi-Cola President Roger Enrico calls "rock-ribbed American values"[15] would be hard-pressed in the hip advertising climate of the 1960s.

Pepsi's strategy was obvious. It would imbue its model consumer, its Pepsi Generation, with characteristics that were at odds with, if not outright antagonistic to, the paradigmatic personality of the Coke order: nonconformity, daring, enthusiasm for the new, and a passion for individual liberation through product choice. Pepsi would identify itself with cultural dissent. As Volkswagen had just a few years before, Pepsi took up the cultural cudgels against mass society for hard-headed corporate reasons. And in its attack on the cola of conformity, Pepsi soon gained an ally in the social ferment then taking place. While the hairstyles, the clothing, the music, and above all the attitudes of the counterculture may have signaled a serious threat to some, Pepsi knew better. The soft-drink giant literally made itself by deploying the generation gap and its rival worldviews as a cola gap. "I think the greatest thing that Pepsi-Cola ever did was make Pepsi the official drink . . . of young America," comments former BBDO vice-president John Bergin. "The other drink is for those generation gap people called Dad and Mom. That's right! Loathesome."[16] Alan Pottasch, Pepsi's vice-president in charge of marketing, makes an even grander assertion of Pepsi's role in the "cultural revolution" of the 1960s, referring to the "25 million kids that we named and we claimed as our own with a big, sweeping invitation to live life to its fullest."[17]

Pepsi's identification of itself with the youth culture of the 1960s goes further than mere "claiming" and "naming." The Pepsi Generation were bearers of new values as well, values distinctly at odds with the universe of which Coca-Cola was a part. As Pottasch puts it (in reference to a Pepsi campaign from the 1970s), Pepsi represents "a new and very powerful urge to be oneself, to be an individual, and not be just a number. To think for oneself, to act like oneself, to choose for oneself, to be free to be yourself."[18] A jingle during the 1970s laid out the Pepsi values explicitly, "Free to choose a new way, free to stand up and say, you be you, and I'll be me. . . ." In the 1980s and 1990s, Pepsi would symbolize itself with then-daring stars like Madonna and Michael Jackson, monarchs of massified hip; images of Ray Charles and the "Uh-Huh Girls" defying repressed nerds and stuffy authority figures; and grunge kids moshing on a beach and mocking sedate oldsters under the stripped-down slogan, "Be Young." Pepsi consumers were and are rebels—"innovators," in Forkan's words[19]—overturning the restricting mores of the past (and Coca-Cola) and ushering in a new era of unrestrained liveliness. Whether playing wildly at the beach, speeding on motorcycles, or dancing to rock music, the Pepsi Generation was acting out 1960s notions of both youth rebellion and corporate America's vision of the model consumer.

That Pepsi's fictional liberated generation, sketched out in national magazines and television commercials as early as 1961 (the actual words "Pepsi Generation" were first applied to it in 1963), anticipated the actual youth movement of the 1960s is one of the more curious aspects of the cultural history of that decade and also one of the most revealing facts about the development of the new consumerism. Clearly the standard explanation for countercultural advertising like Pepsi's—that Madison Avenue simply mimicked what (it believed) the young were doing in order to sell them—does not explain the Pepsi Generation or the larger shift in corporate thought of which it was a salient particular. Some who were closely associated with the making of the campaign imagine a much grander historical role for the makers of Pepsi advertising: that in its haste to encourage youthful defiance of convention, Pepsi may somehow have contributed to the divisiveness of the late sixties. Tom Anderson, a producer and music director at BBDO, recalled in 1984 the effects he believes Pepsi advertising had on the young:

I used to . . . especially in the late '60s, early '70s, started to go through the guilts of maybe having caused this preoccupation with youth, maybe even have contributed to some of the rebelliousness that was going on within the country. Yeah, I thought it was that impactful [*sic*], that perhaps we may have done something wrong. It very definitely was a prototype campaign in expressing and possibly even developing lifestyles. And I truly believe that.[20]

serious fun

The Volkswagen campaign had attacked the conventions of American car culture by puncturing its illusions and speaking to its skeptics; Pepsi cast doubt on the entire culture with which Coca-Cola was inextricably linked by dramatizing the carnivalesque, the anarchic cultural mode whose genuinely subversive qualities are celebrated by so many social theorists. The order against which the Pepsi Generation rebelled was also an order that Pepsi itself had some experience in constructing. Through much of the 1950s, Pepsi advertising had offered glimpses of a well-heeled group called "The Sociables," a group of well-to-do society people who chose Pepsi for the lame but typically fifties reason that it "refreshes without filling." The campaign sought to overcome the brand's leftover 1940s stigma as a bargain drink by picturing bottles of Pepsi in the company of beautiful people, their expensive accoutrements, and America's social betters. The artwork apotheosized affluent suburban life, with spare, idealized drawings (never photographs) of smart-looking couples enjoying Pepsi in a variety of sedate, luxurious settings. Whether depicted at the fashion show, horse stables, beach, ski slope, or simply entertaining amid fine furniture and great silver bowls of Pepsi on ice, the stylishly drawn Sociables closely resemble fashion illustrations from department store ads. But snob appeal did little for Pepsi's sales, and in 1960 Pepsi dumped "The Sociables" and shifted its advertising account to BBDO.[21]

Pepsi's new agency produced a dramatic shift in direction that presaged the vast change that would characterize the new decade, turning away from adult, sedate, suburban society and embracing action, vitality, and youthfulness. The first articulation of the new carnivalesque ideal, produced by BBDO in 1961, came under a clumsy but all-inclusive slogan: "Now It's Pepsi for Those Who Think Young." Pepsi drinkers are no longer snobs: now they are "young thinking" and hyperactively dedicated to novelty and leisure pursuits. The words "modern," "new," "today," and (obviously) "now" were heavily, even repetitiously used in the campaign's print ads. A typical installment defines "thinking young" as "enjoying new pleasures, seeking modern ideas." In others, it means "a modern enthusiasm for getting outdoors, getting more out of life," joining "today's active people" in leading "the livelier life [which] is more popular than ever today." Despite the thick layering of cliches, a new definition of Pepsi-ness was beginning to emerge: Pepsi meant *vitality*, a colorful call to recreation, excitement, daring, and fun. In stark contrast with the elegantly posed Sociables, the "Think Young" characters are an extraordinarily lively bunch, always "on the go," fancying peculiar (and costly) pleasures like "flying to a picnic." The ads speak repeatedly of their "enthusiasm" and their "activities," which are "varied."

The liberation from a confining past is borne out in the "Think Young" campaign's technical execution as well. While the earlier campaign had used catalog-style drawings and subdued colors, the new ads employed close-up photographs of happy couples in full, vivid color. Copy was squeezed into the margin at the bottom of the ad and printed in a sans-serif type in one of a number of bright colors, instead of the traditional black newspaper font that had been used in the "Sociables." Although the Pepsi drinkers are still clean, immaculately groomed, and well-dressed, and the women are still mostly blond, the difference in plausibility between the idealizations of the 1950s and those of the new decade is immense.[22]

In 1963, Pepsi streamlined the cumbersome "Think Young" slogan with a memorable consumer call to arms: "Come Alive! You're in the Pepsi Generation." In the place of unsubtle appeals to "think young," BBDO simply used the magic word "generation," implying youth but actually modified with "Pepsi," opening membership up to anyone who consumed the beverage. Again the copy emphasizes "lively," "life," and "getting a lot more" from it. And the concept of a generation defined by its taste for daring recreation is made more clear: "Who is the Pepsi Generation? Livelier, active people with a liking for Pepsi-Cola. . . . The Pepsi Generation? It's a whole lot of people like you!"[23]

Commercials from the 1963–66 "Come Alive!" campaign, which was Pepsi's first to make heavy use of television, follows young people engaged in some kind of fast-moving and often exotic entertainment: riding a motorbike, driving an amphibious car, piloting a sailboat with wheels across a desert. After the jingle is sung, an announcer delivers standard Pepsi lines about "active, livelier people," "the young view of things," and "the official drink of today's generation." The commercials also use dark hints of danger to establish the Generation's daring and vitality. Each one opens on an ominous, puzzling musical chord and a striking or disturbing visual. In "Motorbike" the airborne camera zooms

chapter eight

closer and closer to a road on a hillside. When it seems a crash is certainly imminent, a young couple burst out from behind the hill on a scooter and the camera flies away in another direction. In "Amphicar," another group go racing down a road and drive their vehicle straight into a lake. In "Sand Sailing," four members of the Pepsi Generation are mounted on dangerous-looking contraptions which zoom about and tilt precariously to one side. In each case, the unsettling atmosphere is abruptly ended after only a few seconds when the jingle begins, the words "come alive" are sung, and the viewer suddenly recognizes that it is a Pepsi commercial he is watching.

Carnival may be dangerous, but it is not work. The Pepsi Generation's liveliness, its frenetic racing about, is aimless and unproductive. Although they are almost always depicted using some kind of transportation, the Pepsi Generation are never going anywhere in particular. To these modern youngsters, the tools that others use to get from place to place are implements of pure pleasure. Jackson Lears has pointed out that American advertising oscillates constantly between images of carnival and those of "personal efficiency," and it is significant that, while Pepsi was constructing its apotheosis of fun, Coca-Cola was producing a series of ads which touted Coke's power to assist working Americans perform taxing workaday tasks.[24] Under the slogan "Things Go Better With Coke" Coca-Cola was describing itself as the drink of workplace order, while Pepsi was the beverage of leisure-time anarchy, of pure consuming.

The speed and excitement of the action in the "Come Alive!" spots is also heightened by execution that replicates the distinctive techniques and appearance of French New Wave cinema, features which at the time connoted gritty realism and up-to-the-minute savoir-faire. It was also new to American television, not to mention American television advertising. Cameras swing wildly, shoot from unusual angles, zoom in and out extremely quickly, and there is abrupt, rapid cutting from shot to shot. The effect is to dramatize play to make it seem like a meaningful challenge to the Coke order rather than a frivolous blow-off.

the official drink of today's generation

From 1964 to 1966 the nascent counterculture was remarkably similar to the youth culture of Pepsi's imagining: emphatically harmless, it was led by rock stars singing sugary love songs and wearing frivolous, eccentric costumes and self-consciously boyish hairdos. For a time, it even seemed to be as deeply committed as Pepsi to establishing the importance of frolicking happily on the beach and in the surf. Its cinematic representations, like the Beatles's film *Hard Day's Night* and the Monkees's television show, closely resembled the manic visual effects of the early Pepsi spots. But by 1967, the counterculture was a much more serious thing, and it soon became clear that Pepsi's fantasy generation had hit a terrible obstacle: youth no longer looked anything like this. The music that accompanied the "Come Alive!" jingle, for example, aged quickly. Today, its jazz orchestra and piccolo sound, which probably once signified excitement and daring, hail from an unfamiliar, even quaint, pre-rock era. As William Munro of Pepsi said in 1969, "overnight, those tanned, frolicsome, happy-go-lucky people of the Pepsi generation began to become advertising anachronisms. They became square to the very people we were aiming at." [25] And if there was one image Pepsi had to avoid, it was squareness, the absolute negation of "Pepsi-ness."

In the mid-sixties, therefore, the simple liveliness of the Pepsi Generation began to take on a more serious demeanor. Pepsi vitalism, with all of its daring overtones, was recast as Pepsi hip. This shift was already evident during the mid-1960s, in the eager mimicry of youth culture in phrases like "the lift that turns you on" (from a "Come Alive!" television spot) and the final "Come Alive!" print ads. By 1966, these last no longer had to explain who the Pepsi Generation was—the reader already knew that images of youth meant Pepsi-Cola, just as pictures of cowboys meant Marlboro cigarettes. Now the copy is smart-alec tone rather than inviting, and the overt explanations of "Pepsi-ness" are replaced with hip phrases and anti-establishment wit. An ad depicting surfers describes them as "Board members / of the Pepsi Generation." Another featuring skiers offers similar establishment-tweaking: "Summit meeting. / Pepsi Generation-style." [26]

But still Pepsi had problems adjusting itself to the actual doings of the counterculture. From 1967 to 1969, the brand briefly reverted to a product-oriented campaign, aiming to establish that it tasted better than Coca-Cola. The new campaign's print ads did little more than picture blonde kids on beaches with bottles of Pepsi frozen in great chunks of ice, but television commercials continued to focus on young people at strenuous outdoor play. The most noticeable difference is that the Pepsi youngsters' frivolity has become emphatically exotic, as though by pushing good clean fun to some sort of extreme Pepsi could somehow reclaim

American youth, now largely lost to a much more menacing real-life carnivalesque. One commercial depicts members of the Pepsi Generation and being hauled along the ground on wheeled skis by giant multicolored parachutes. In another, they play in the surf while one of their comrades does stunts in a biplane overhead.[27]

At some point during this 1967–69 campaign, Pepsi produced a peculiar psychedelic commercial, a fragmented, impressionistic montage of hip urban nightlife that is as naive and rosy a rendering of the counterculture as anything written by Roszak or Reich. The commercial is very dark throughout with only city lights and a variety of glowing emblems shining through the gloom. Figures are always dim, lit from one side only, or illuminated by a flashing strobe lamp. No one speaks through the entire commercial; even the Pepsi jingle, which drones throughout in a Byrds-like rendering, has to go without lyrics. The spot is held together by the sporadic appearance of a woman wearing fashionably short hair and a sequined minidress. As it opens she is striking poses for the camera; perhaps she is a model of some sort. Then she is having her face painted with a fluorescent flower design. After shots of Times Square, marquee lights, and a large Pepsi logo rendered in sequins, she is shown drinking from a cup marked with the glowing word "Pepsi," holding an oversized lollipop, and dancing to music being played by a rock band.

This obviously experimental embrace of countercultural emblems serves to bridge the sun-and-beach fun of the earlier commercials with the more threatening, more erotic pastimes of the youth movements that had rendered Pepsi's own youth movement so square. The model's orderless doings are not athletic or even wholesome in a conventional sense. Yet Pepsi encourages us to accept them regardless as the new and even more liberated version of good clean fun. The lollipop the woman carries eases the transition by making hip seem less dangerous, much as the earlier commercial's visual effects made Pepsi play seem *more* dangerous. Also remarkable is the obvious role of psychedelic drugs in this commercial, from the model's glazed stare to the curious visual effects used by the ad's producers. But no drugs appear in the spot—the only thing consumed (other than the lollipop) is Pepsi, whose logo is shown several times in psychedelic renderings. Pepsi had once been marketed as a pharmaceutical, and it appears here in the place normally reserved for LSD or marijuana in longer films that use these effects.[28]

In 1969, Pepsi introduced a new campaign that revived the consumer-focus of the earlier years and placed a revamped and more obviously countercultural Pepsi Generation back in the center of the screen. This time Pepsi was careful to make much more serious philosophic claims for the generational beverage and the meaning of play generally. "You've Got a Lot to Live, and Pepsi's Got a Lot to Give" ("Live/ Give") is a unwieldy phrase when spoken, but became quite elegant when put to its soaring rock-anthem jingle. Live/Give is remembered by Pepsi and BBDO executives for its power as a message of national reconciliation, its optimistic cheerfulness during an otherwise dark time. While celebrating happy nonconformity and real-life otherness, it was also openly patriotic. Both carnivalesque and commercial, naturalistic and contrived, Live/Give sought to heal the nasty fissures of 1968—but not by returning to the blithe, idealized world of the sociables. It did so with what was by then explicitly countercultural language and imagery. Oddly enough, at the same time, Coca-Cola was offering a thematically identical campaign, organized around the authenticity-grabbing declaration that "It's the Real Thing" and a popular folk-rock jingle that proclaimed multicultural harmony; peace and love under the aegis of the universal product. Starting from opposite sides of the American cultural divide, Pepsi and Coca-Cola had somehow met in the middle: the counterculture was now all-American.

"There's a whole new way of livin', Pepsi helps supply the drive," went the first line of the Live/Give jingle, identifying Pepsi as the fuel of the decade's cultural revolution. "It kind of was a generation gap campaign," comments John Bergin. "[W]e did something we thought was kind of with it." [29] And, from its mimicry of the grandiose rock sound of the day to its images of long-haired men and liberated women, Live/Give exemplified corporate America's eagerness for the big change that was freeing people from the restrictions of the past.

It also showed exactly how far advertising could carry its countercultural pretensions and where corporate sponsors would draw the line on revolution, creative or otherwise. For all their carnivalesque frenzy, the "Life/Give" commercials were a much diluted version of the original proposal. The idea for the campaign had been suggested by a BBDO employee, a person, as Bergin puts it, "as close to being a hippie himself as anyone on this earth," who envisioned it as a tribute to the hardest-core of the movement. Bergin summarizes this individual's ideas:

[T]he first one he came up with was "I want a mob of real crazies. I want them gathered in Central Park, I want all the protesters, all the hippies, all the long hairs,

chapter eight

and all the beads and beards, I want them all gathered in some central place like Central Park, and I want to do this song as a kind of an anthem to them."

But for all of its enthusiasm for youth culture, there were some lines Pepsi would not cross. The aim of the Pepsi Generation had been to create a nonexclusive image of youthful consumers with which mainstream America could identify, not one which would send them running in fear. Bergin continues,

I said to him, "My God, you are missing the boat here, friend. This is a song that seems to say, 'C'mon we love you, do more, burn more, attack more, go after the institutions of our society more.'" It was a bad piece of advertising. Pepsi-Cola would no more have sponsored that than they would have sponsored the Vietnam War.

Equating the brand with LSD was one thing; violence was quite another. "The guy who wrote the original line," Bergin recalls, "his idea really was to whip the flames of protest. Ours was to soothe them."[30] Still, the idea did make it onto film, and with a number of revisions, Pepsi relaunched its updated youth movement in 1969.

The "Live/Give" commercials are composed of rapidly flickering montages of what appear to be unrehearsed scenes in which people do all manner of energetic things. The usual Pepsi vitalism but with one crucial, effective difference: the activities depicted are things one could actually do without expensive accoutrements, and they zip past with such speed that the effect is one of sheer anarchic profusion. A commercial called "School," for example, goes through fifty-nine separate images in sixty seconds. Live/Give is polymorphous perversity as consuming ideology: all is frenzy, all is real-life authentic, and all images are random. There seem to be only two rules to Live/Give: first, that no one shall be shown at work. Almost everyone depicted in the campaign is engaged in some sort of leisure-time play or consuming. Second, nothing here is "normal." Each of these latest members of the Pepsi Generation is hilariously, passionately ecstatic, laughing robustly, running drunkenly, smiling broadly. The campaign constantly uses images of odd, unusual, or irregular human behavior; images that were rarely, if ever, associated with nationally advertised products before. Comical, inscrutable, or especially frivolous doings which put familiar objects to odd uses or somehow break the rules of play are emphasized.

A 1969 spot called "Young America" flickers past a series of inscrutable or bizarre images: two laughing children in a single raincoat,

a woman carrying a skeleton, a woman on a beach holding a flower
waitress-style which she drops when struck by a wave, a young couple
pelting each other with snow, a young man feeding a young woman with
a pair of sticks, another couple running and then tripping and falling on
a beach, a child feeding a horse from a mug, a man with no shirt being
tossed on a blanket, two boys with food smeared on their faces who look
up from eating some messy substance without utensils, and a little girl
spilling pieces of watermelon on her dress. The images that flicker by in
"This Happy Land," a commercial from the same year, are aggressively
antipretentious. A man squatting in a stream and shaving with a straight
razor as he looks into a mirror held by a squatting woman. A man with a
beard and bandanna rappels down a rock face, a woman with unusually
long hair and beads plays poorly at frisbee, a couple clutches each other
and spins, a girl holds a tambourine, a number of people are shown wearing hippie clothing, and a woman points a camera directly at the viewer.
In "Leisure Time," a child sticks his tongue out at the camera, another
lays down in a creek, and a woman rides on the handlebars of a bicycle.
"Big Town USA" depicts many different couples laughing ecstatically
and children playing in the traditionally forbidden water from a fire
hydrant.

Previous Pepsi Generations had always enjoyed expensive toys; the
group that populates "Live/Give" is an embodiment of disorder, a living
rebuttal of organization, even of organized play. The commercials seem
to bound off in every possible lifestyle direction, depicting the absurd, the
whimsical, the odd, proclaiming them all OK. A print ad from the campaign echoes this theme, with copy over a picture of people with their
motorcycles reading "Flat out and free. That's the way to live. There's so
much to do, to see, to try."[31] "You've got a lot to live" is fundamentally
about plenitude, about the vast multiplicity of choices available to Americans in an affluent consumer society. The seeming disorder and everyday-
ness of the activities depicted in "Live/Give" make it immediately a more
realistic campaign, and also much better attuned to the values of the new
youth culture.

However "Live/Give" may have aimed to reunite Americans, it did so
not by embracing the "silent majority" or returning to the advertising
styles of the fifties. Instead, it mimicked the live-and-let-live language of
the late-sixties counterculture. And, naturally, overt countercultural signifiers were an important part of the campaign. Pepsi described the "Live/
Give" jingle to its bottlers (who paid much of the media-placement bills)
with these words:

Exciting new groups doing out-of-sight new things to, and for, music. It's youth's bag and Pepsi-Cola is in it. With a song composed for the "now" sound. With lyrics that make this generation's "thing" our "thing" like never before.

"There's a whole new way of livin'" and Pepsi's supplyin' the background music. . . .

It's a radio package that obliterates the generation gap and communicates like a guru.[32]

Images of young people with long hair, in which they are often wearing flowers, are included in virtually every "Live/Give" television spot. In many, people are shown holding long-stem roses, which were no doubt supposed to mark them as flower children or sympathizers with the liberating youth culture. "Portrait of America" flicks through the obviously significant image of a person on a motorcycle in the desert, then a drag race, and a jazz band. People clearly intended to be recognized as hippies are shown, and a woman swings around a large sign marked "Love" with the sun directly behind her. Several spots picture rock bands, and "After Dark" echoes the psychedelic commercial of a few years before with a flashing, disorienting strobe effect, aerial pictures of carnival lights at night, a nocturnal pool party, people dancing crazily, a DJ, and a stylized Pepsi logo. It also includes a helicopter shot of the Capitol Records building in Los Angeles, world headquarters of commodified hip.[33]

But neither Pepsi's earnest embrace of a purportedly subversive way of life, nor its approving depiction of behavior chosen for its transgressiveness subverted or contradicted the ads' commercial intent. "Live/Give" is, in some ways, classic co-optation, a panorama of hip images without radical content, devised by an establishment advertising agency for a soda manufacturer. Understood in the context of the creative revolution, with all of its naturalistic impulses, as part of the long-running Pepsi Generation campaign, and as one shot in the symbolic cola war, however, the "Live/Give" commercials are something quite different. Certainly the newly countercultural Pepsi Generation was a sanitized and depoliticized version of the real thing. BBDO officials have affirmed, as usual, that the object was to appeal to people far beyond the youth market. "As a marketing idea we were appealing to the people in the . . . little houses with the white picket fences, and on the farms, and the teachers in the classrooms, and on and on and on," John Bergin recalled years later of the "Live/Give" commercials. "And we may have turned off some of the more serious protestors, flower children, whatever you want to call them."[34] The object was not to somehow subvert countercultural radical-ism or even primarily to speak to the alienated young. "Live/Give" was, rather, a grandiose cultural manifesto in an age of grandiose cultural manifestoes, a vision of countercultural carnival as an all-American myth for the new commercial age.

chapter eight

chapter nine

FASHION AND

FLEXIBILITY

And let it be said that these [retailers] are no idealists who see the revolution in terms of pure fashion. Far from it. What good is fashion, pure or otherwise, unless it is planned, programmed, projected and serviced for continuity of image, more stock turns and better profits?

— CLARA HANCOX, FASHION COLUMNIST, *DAILY NEWS RECORD*, 1972

all the patriarchs join in

According to theorists like David Harvey, fashion is the cultural bulwark of late capitalism. Its endless transgression of the established defines recent economic history. According to observers of the clothing industry like sociologist René König, fashion is an immutable part of human nature, the product of a "permanent disposition for change." And yet, until the 1960s, the central feature distinguishing men's from women's clothing was fashion's absence. From roughly the time of the French Revolution until the 1960s, men's clothing styles for the most part remained subdued, dark, and static. While women's wear could vary radically from season to season, men's attire evidenced very little change in design or appearance. The dark business suit was a mandatory middle-class male item, with a few more or less significant alterations, from early Victorian times.[1]

The uniformity of men's clothing was also an important element of the mass society critique and its countercultural corollary. Nothing, after all, better exemplified the stasis and conformity of the "technocracy" than the way respectable men dressed. Criticism of men's clothing spanned the spectrum from *Life* magazine, whose photos of uniformly clad and hatted commuters came to typify the fifties malaise, to the "Whiteman" comics of R. Crumb, in which a business-suited character is tormented by the zany antics of people less repressed than himself. The

185

men's "traditionally conservative" clothing industry, as one *New York Times* columnist called it, should have been a prominent victim of the lifestyle revolution of the sixties. And yet no branch of the American "establishment" was more sanguine about the counterculture and the changes it seemed to promise than manufacturers and retailers of men's clothing. Like Irving Howe's vision of the 1960s, in which "the sophisticated middle class" reacts to "the rebels of sensation" by "moaning, 'Oh, baby, *épatez* me again, harder this time, tell me what a sterile impotent louse I am and how you are so tough and virile,'" menswear professionals thrived on the condemnation of their business by the counterculture.[2] Here, too, the story was more complicated than the co-optation theory would suggest. Yes, the menswear industry underwent astonishing changes in the late sixties, and it did so while explicitly imitating the styles believed to have been pioneered by hip young people. Certainly on its surface the story was a simple one: in the late sixties prosperous, middle-aged men commonly wore flashy clothes that bore a superficial resemblance to those favored by their offspring, but which they purchased at elite shops. Even so, to parse the story in such a way is to overlook entirely that, in a manner even more pronounced than in advertising, the changes in the menswear industry were largely unrelated to the youthful demographic. The garment industry threw itself headlong into revolution for reasons of its own: the counterculture merely happened along at precisely the right time with what the industry believed to be the right attitudes toward clothing and the right palate of looks.

One can study the "Peacock Revolution" that ensued through any number of theoretical lenses: the glory of the ever-shifting sartorial signifier; the way style filters through society; the long, slow, perhaps terminal decline of the business suit and the triumph of casual. But to do so is to risk missing the less exciting (but possibly more meaningful) facts that menswear faced in the 1950s, problems similar to those faced by other culture industries like advertising, that its leaders understood those problems through yet another commercial version of the mass society critique, that they had embarked on what would become the Peacock Revolution well before the counterculture had materialized on the scene, and that when the great rebel youth culture finally made its appearance they hailed it as at least a symbolic solution to their problems. As it happens, the changes in menswear also had much more ambiguous long-term results than those in advertising: while its short-term success was remarkable, for many of the manufacturers and marketers that had been its most ardent supporters, the Peacock Revolution ended in defeat and even disaster. For a much smaller group of others, it marked the beginning of trends in menswear that have proven immensely profitable.

The traditional narrative of the Peacock Revolution goes something like this: in the late sixties responsible, middle-class men of all ages abandoned the somber tones and severe stylings of conventional clothing to follow the examples of the rebel young and their rock 'n' roll celebrities. An astounding succession of flamboyant garments began to appear: the Nehru jacket, accessories like beads and chains, exaggerated Edwardian coats, the leisure suit. And by late 1968, the Peacock Revolution was far enough advanced to merit a cover story from *Newsweek* magazine, which duly noted that the new styles had arrived "with the Beatles, the hippies and the student revolts. In short, when a new era of social expression was born in the United States, the dark ages of male fashion began to die. . . . Hipped on color and cacophony, whether it's psychedelic art or discotheques, young people dress to fit their milieu—and their elders are picking up the beat."[3]

The key to the Peacock "beat" was change. Trade journals spoke of borrowing the sales and production techniques of women's wear, of rapidly changing tastes, of an accelerated fashion cycle, and above all of the boom that accompanied these new conditions. Suddenly, it seemed, all sartorial conventions were dead; all taboos violable. According to the trade literature, men were suddenly becoming enthusiastic for the latest thing, for up-to-the-minute looks. "Things are moving mighty fast in a field where change has always been measured in quarter-inches per decade," observed *Life* magazine in 1966.[4] The editors of *Gentlemen's Quarterly*, a monthly men's magazine concerned predominantly with clothing (and referred to universally as "*GQ*"), observed in 1971 that their publication's

existence . . . is based on its reflection of change. For, what is fashion but a continuous evolution of new ideas? So, if a fashion publication is even halfway responsible in the job it's doing, it is, of necessity, a vehicle imbued with change.[5]

In place of a standardized dress code, men were suddenly favoring rapid and extreme change; diversity instead of uniformity; flux over stasis.

Like the creative revolution in advertising, the Peacock Revolution was grounded in a commercial understanding of the problem of conformity that owed much to the critique being popularized by William Whyte, David Riesman, Paul Goodman, Norman Mailer, and Vance Packard. While management literature generally was growing concerned

chapter nine

with declining creativity and the human cost of Taylorist overorganization, that of the clothing business was going from complacency to worry about the problems of style stagnation. Through the fifties, the menswear industry experienced a very real lack of movement. Business men were almost universally expected to wear the traditional American "sack" three-button suit with a white shirt and tie. Sales of tailored clothing, the industry's staple products—suits, jackets, trousers—declined steadily. Certainly the image of the gray flannel uniform is an exaggeration; suits and ties (and even shirts, depending on the environment) could show considerable variation in color and pattern. There was also experimentation at the industry's margins, particularly in sportswear. But in comparison with the manic pace of change and the tastes for loud, garish designs that was to come, the fifties were indeed a time of dull colors and motionlessness. An interesting glimpse into the industry's difficulties is provided by a short article that appeared in *Fortune* in 1952, in which various labor spokesmen (!) pointed to the mass migration to suburbia as the cause of a shift toward less formal and less stylish clothing. The magazine quoted approvingly from a report issued by the Textile Workers of the CIO, which criticized the industry's "antiquated designing and merchandising practices." Management had done nothing, the union charged, to acclimatize itself to the fact that

the tastes of the buying public had shifted from the dressy styles of the early postwar period to casual wear more suitable in an era of television-viewing and suburban living . . . Most textile mills continue to turn out the old staple fabrics, with minor changes in weave or color patterns marking the limit of their experimental spirit.

"In effect," *Fortune* concurred, "textiles, which once led the way in yearly change, have lost the secret of American capitalism—the permanent revolution."[6] The advice was in vain. Throughout the decade, questions of fashion were eclipsed in the pages of *Daily News Record*, the leading journal of the textile industry (and a product of the Fairchild publishing empire), by accounts of such down-to-earth developments as strikes, tariffs, and corporate personnel shifts.

But toward the end of the 1950s, while advertising writers worried about creativity, menswear writers began to express increasing concern over the problem of fashion. Their publications spoke openly of accelerating cycles of obsolescence and discussed how fashion could be introduced to the American market. A symptomatic document is the 1959 document by advertising man Henry Bach that was excerpted in *Men's*

Get Younger—Men's Suits Get Older." According to Bach, the industry's
problems were attitudinal and cultural: men had simply not yet been persuaded to accept fashion, with its rapid changes and extreme variation.

The industry still has not found within itself the mechanism or the power to ef-

fect style obsolescence to the degree that it becomes self generating . . . two key

obstacles . . . consumers' lack of style-consciousness and his attitude toward com-

pleteness of stock.[7]

The article laid out both the challenge of the 1960s—to find a cultural
carrier for the idea of fashion, to discover the language, the referents, that
would make "style obsolescence" palatable to a mass market—as well as
its solution, the imagery of youthfulness.

The conventional date given as the dawn of the Peacock Revolution
is 1960, the year in which Pierre Cardin became the first important designer to enter the men's business, producing his trademark suits with
their shaped, two-button jackets and narrow, flared trousers. An equally
reasonable date might be 1957, the year in which *Gentlemen's Quarterly*
began publication, subsuming an industry journal called *Apparel Arts*.
The new magazine, then published by the mass-circulation *Esquire*, was
the first journal concerned primarily with menswear to be aimed at the
consuming public rather than an industry audience. Subtitled "The Fashion Magazine for Men," GQ dedicated itself to a monothematic cause:
the introduction of fashion to the slow-moving world of men's clothing.
By 1965, the magazine had generated a definitive vision of the man at
which it was aimed: the fashion consumer was to be a nonconforming
individualist, a creature of incessant excitement and change. An article
that appeared in February of that year featured a full-page illustration of
the famous "man in the gray flannel suit" in his familiar dust-jacket pose
with an "X" drawn through him. The magazine's ideal male, "the GQ
reader," could never tolerate such conventional garb; "if he dressed one
invariable way day after day he would be bored." The orderly look of
gray-flannel "is stultifying to a man with any creative urge about his visual personality." This new man chooses his clothes to "express himself"
rather than conform to the mandates of his surroundings. "What we
would like to see," proclaimed GQ, "is men dressing more to the limits
of their own personality and inventiveness instead of following the patterns of dress set by other men in their professional or social milieu." Still,
for all of its fire-breathing individualism, the magazine's suggestions to

the man who "would demand something a bit different" raised only a modest challenge to the sack-suit orthodoxy:

He would take that dark suit and one day he'd wear a light blue shirt with it, then a yellow shirt, then a striped shirt, then a shirt with white collar and cuffs and a red-striped front. His ties, his handkerchiefs would also vary; his shoes would reflect contemporary styling. And when he shopped for a new suit, he would look for a lighter grey, or a check or plaid, or a one-button model, or a new lapel design. . . .[8]

Then, after years of slow progress, men's fashion exploded in 1966 with the arrival in America of "Mod," the Carnaby Street stylings favored by the Beatles, the Rolling Stones, the Who, and their youthful followers. The word "peacock" became suddenly pervasive as the flamboyant, overstated, and brightly colored looks of Mod were snapped up and displayed by department stores across the country. For industry organs, this was clearly the break that they had been waiting for. Throughout the beginning of 1966, Mod styles were featured on the front page of *Daily News Record,* and comments like "Modism is Modern Volume Fashion" (the consensus of a number of retailers surveyed by the paper) and "THIS COMBINED REVOLUTION AND EVOLUTION HAS TO BE TRANSLATED INTO A GREAT, NEW FASHION DIRECTION" characterized the industry's enthusiasm.[9] With its distinctive and unusual double-breasted jackets, loud patterns printed on virtually everything, long hair, wide belts, and tight low-rise trousers modeled after American jeans, Mod was the first complete look to be identified with sixties youth culture. As such, the industry's fashion ideologues, like GQ contributor Jason McCloskey, would later point to Mod as "the birth of the counter-culture, the first visible evidence in America that the young were drifting away from the solutions of their fathers."[10] More significantly, Mod was also the first style of the 1960s to bring with it a new vision of men's clothing generally, linking a heightened sense of individuality to external appearances. With its greater emphasis on the new, on quick obsolescence, and on the attitudes of the consumer, Mod was the first glimmer of the revolution in consumption that characterized male clothes buying in later years. As a columnist for GQ put it in September 1966,

there is no one look that is Mod: on the contrary, Mod is a spirit of individualism. The shops on Carnaby Street and King's Road are showing new things monthly, even weekly, and young men are continually shopping the stores to find items that appeal to them and putting them together in fresh ways, so that individual expression is allowed a new latitude.[11]

Mod was introduced to America with an unprecedented media flurry, including a cover story in *Life* magazine. But its wilful, even pointless, extremism and juvenile looks were pushed too aggressively on a skeptical American adult market, making the sudden collapse of the Mod bubble in late 1966 even more spectacular.

Mod's sudden demise seems to have persuaded almost no one that fashion was dangerous stuff. The enthusiasm of the industry press continued unabated through 1967. Not only would Mod influence its successor looks, but the designing and consuming attitudes that it had brought forth would remain and would continue to power fashion for years to come. As one designer remarked in 1967, "the name ['Mod'] may be dead, but that doesn't matter. It's going to keep spreading in men's wear; men are going to become more elegant—*much more elegant.*"[12] It was even argued that the transience that made Mod obsolete overnight was exactly the phenomenon the industry should be encouraging. That retailers and manufacturers were hurt by the public's sudden abandonment of Mod merely indicated that they needed to make their production and buying techniques more flexible to accommodate the vagaries of fashion. As one retailer opined in March, 1967, "Mod was a sellout in July through September. . . . The only mistake stores made was buying the same thing twice."[13] Throughout 1967, the year in which the counterculture's colorful doings became a media obsession, the descendants of Mod began to filter into the mainstream. It would be the last year of the narrow tie.

In February of 1968, Johnny Carson wore a Nehru jacket designed by Oleg Cassini on "The Tonight Show," precipitating an overnight mania for the garment. The changes that followed constitute one of those highly visible and instant mass shiftings that are so often pointed to as distinguishing one historical era from another: square middle America became hip almost overnight. Sartorial propriety seemed to vanish in many social circles and years of stasis gave way instantly to a plethora of fantastic garments. Beads and chains with large pendants were worn with the Nehru, as were square silk scarves. Nehru was soon joined by the Edwardian look, with its tight-fitting, double-breasted jacket, and then coats with the enormous "Napoleonic" collar. Printed patterns allowed diversity amidst diversity. Flared trousers appeared. *Men's Wear* ran a feature on

"Trans-Sexual Fashion," in which writer Jack McCloskey noted the rising popularity among the young of "flowing scarves and look/alike vests, psychedelic prints, and perhaps even he/she caftans, serapes, djellabahs and burnooses."[14] Brightly colored shirts with exceedingly long collar points began to eclipse the standard white shirts, and what *Men's Wear* referred to as "Bodyline" began to alter the shape of conventional suits, which were now being designed to fit much more closely to the body.[15] And, as in the advertising industry, a parade of creative heroes known as "designers," passed across the nation's sartorial stage—one of them, Ralph Lauren, bringing with him the loudly decorated, four-inch-wide tie.

The succession of new garments that flickered through the pages of industry publications in the four years that followed was dizzying. Change, in seemingly any direction as long as it took men conspicuously away from the status quo ante, became the hallmark of a once cautious industry. In early 1969, *Men's Wear* trumpeted the "Cool Conservative" or "Individualist" look, which, despite its name, bore very little resemblance to the standard attire of just a few years before: it featured jackets with extremely wide lapels, extremely wide ties, extremely wide trouser cuffs, and bright colors and vivid patterns on everything.[16] And 1970 brought the introduction of the tieless "vestsuit," the "tunic suit," the "shirt suit" and the "sweater suit," in which a very wide belt was worn over a matched shirt (or sweater or vest) and trousers.[17] The leisure suit, introduced as the "sport suit," an item of tailored, high-fashion clothing, followed in July. The American Institute of Men's & Boys' Wear chose this time to change its name to the Men's Fashion Association of America.[18] In 1971, *Men's Wear* breathlessly narrated the "Kaftan Revolution" and hailed the "revolutionary" "NewSuit," which encompassed "youth suits, coat suits, knicker suits, special suits. . . ."[19] The revolution was whirling implacably onward and no strongholds of the old regime were secure.

By 1972, the trade paper *Daily News Record* was able to point out with satisfaction that even in the establishment stronghold of Palm Beach the best retailers had gone over to fashion. "Worth Avenue is still a long way from Carnaby Street," it noted, "but the ultra conservative men's wear retailers are being forced to sharpen their image or move out." Sulka, a bastion of traditional attire, had closed. The Cove, home of the "blue blazer-and-white flannel business for the last 25 years, was quiet all through the holidays." A salesman at one of the hipper shops, which were apparently doing fine business with double-knit suits and high-fashion items, was observed by the *Daily News Record* reporter to mildly rebuff a

are no good any more," he told her. "Not even on Worth Avenue."[20]

Even when the passion for outrage subsided in the 1970s and many of the more divergent looks were vanishing, garment trade writers continued to insist that fashion itself was alive and well, that the revolution had successfully and permanently accelerated industry cycles. Throughout 1972, *Daily News Record* promoted a look it called "Classic" or "Layered," consisting most notably of a jacket, sweater, shirt, and tie all worn at the same time. But when a *New York Times* article in March of that year interpreted the new dispensation as a sign that the "Peacock [Was] Pulling In Its Feathers," that a fashion thermidor would soon put an end to the rapid pace of change and have men clad again in gray-flannel uniforms, fashion writers bristled with indignation. *Daily News Record* ran a page-one response that reassured retailers and consumers that the "new classicism" was merely another step in the ongoing fashion revolution, which, in the course of its endless wanderings, would inevitably alight briefly on vaguely familiar looks:

> Sure, we in the trade talk about "classics" and "new traditionalism." Unfortunately, names and terms are necessary to categorize certain looks. But classicism in men's wear for 1972 doesn't mean a return to what was. The men's wear industry latched onto fashion a few years ago and isn't about to let it go that easily.[21]

fashion as industry

"Calculating, industrial society is obliged to form consumers who don't calculate," writes Roland Barthes; "if clothing's producers and consumers had the same consciousness, clothing would be bought (and produced) only at the very slow rate of its dilapidation; Fashion, like all fashions, depends on a disparity of two consciousnesses, each foreign to the other."[22] Barthes's observation may seem matter-of-fact, but it touches on the most explosive topic among students of fashion. Everyone knows, of course, that the apparel industry, like any other, does have a trade literature; and that participants in that literature tend to describe fashion the way Alfred Sloan described style changes in General Motors cars, as something subject to the same calculations as the products of any other industry. But historians, sociologists, and journalists of fashion generally regard it as somehow unsporting to acknowledge that trade literature when discussing fashion. Fashion, it is sometimes argued, is an expression of the consumer marketplace and, as such, is democratic in some deep sense. To suggest otherwise in any way is to participate in a sort of conspiracy theory.[23] Not that any of them believes the fashion industry itself to be benevolent and democratic. On the contrary, they generally take the industry's manipulative tendencies for granted, pointing out instead that, since not every manipulative effort succeeds, the industry's intentions are irrelevant.[24]

But irrelevant to whom? While it is plain that public tastes are not mere products of industry dictation, it is also obvious that the business decisions, the experiences, and the thinking of apparel trade leaders are worth studying in their own right, regardless of what consumers ultimately decide to buy or not buy. This is especially true when the subject at hand is the meaning and power of cultural dissidence. It is fruitless to speculate about corporate America's interest in hip or its strong desire to force people into some sort of "homogeneous" mold without consulting the literature of corporate America directly.

Like the history of women's clothing, the story of men's fashions in the 1960s is littered with failed ideas and products that were extravagantly promoted but didn't catch on. But in contrast with women's wear, where fashion is taken for granted and the main site of contestation is the primacy of particular looks, in menswear, the question with which the industry was faced was far more basic: should or should they not welcome the very institution of fashion itself, with all of its uncertainty and acceleration of stylistic change. The answer was an overwhelming yes. The menswear industry did not regard the demise of stasis unhappily. From the beginning, the industry's trade press rallied behind every development that appeared to have potential to advance the fashion revolution. Despite their countercultural flavor, the new looks of the Peacock Revolution, if the trade press is to be believed, met with virtually unanimous approval from the garment industry.[25]

And for a very simple reason: whether or not industry leaders got to act as cultural dictators, fashion looked to be more profitable than stasis. The sixties were boom years for makers of men's clothing. Looking back over the years of revolution in 1970, Robert C. Forney of the textile fibers department of E. I. du Pont de Nemours & Co. outlined the direct relationship of fashion to industry growth:

In 1959–64, when fashion meant very little to the average guy and we still had drawers full of white shirts and racks of narrow ties, men's wear had a growth rate of 2.7 per cent a year compared with 4.2 per cent a year for women's clothing. In

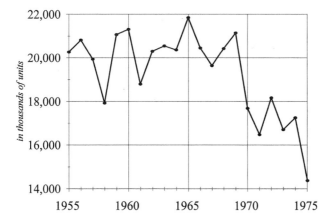

Cuttings of Men's Suits, 1955–75   fig 2

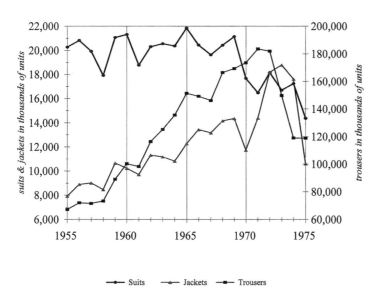

—●— Suits   —▲— Jackets   —■— Trousers

Cuttings of Men's Tailored Clothing, 1955–75   fig 3

1964–68, when men were learning about fashion and color, the men's wear growth rate increased to 3.7 per cent year, compared with 4.1 per cent for women's wear.[26]

After fluctuating throughout the 1950s, the sales of suits, traditionally the most important data for the industry, reached a plateau in the 1960s, an all-time apogee in 1965, and another peak year in 1969 before falling off disastrously in the early 1970s. Sales for all tailored goods (suits, trousers,

chapter nine

and jackets) shifted less dramatically, but still reached a high plateau during the 1960s and fell off in the mid-1970s.

The industry not only welcomed the arrival of fashion; it hoped and pleaded and planned for fashion well before the explosion of 1966. As early as 1965, menswear executives were speaking of "fashion consciousness" and new designs that "are expected . . . to generate consumer buying enthusiasm for the fall season far out of proportion to the usual sales." Robert Turner of suit manufacturer Albert Turner & Co. commented to the *New York Times* on the profitability of speeding up the cycles of change in men's clothing in that year:

> There is no such thing in men's wear as a one-year change obsoleting what went before. . . . It's a six- or seven-year change that makes a suit old-fashioned. If we could speed that change to two or three years, it would benefit the whole business.[27]

And this was not just conjecture. The arrival of fashion brought a dramatic shift in the fortunes of the men's clothing industry. The *New York Times* equated fashion, liberation, and dramatically increased sales in early 1966 in no uncertain terms:

> Freed from the restraints of traditional attire and encouraged by the willingness of consumers to spend more for apparel, the clothing makers produced about 22 million men's suits in 1965, an 11 per cent gain over the previous year's level.[28]

In 1968, the *Times* reported a further 17 percent increase in production of men's suits over the previous year.[29] Increases like this, which continued throughout the late 1960s, briefly reversed the slow downward slide of suit production that had prevailed since the mid-1950s.[30] Lawrence M. Nathan of the Bruce Hunt store in Washington, DC, was even more explicit when he predicted that "in 1968, retail men's wear sales should show an increase of 3 to 4 per cent on the price level alone. . . . And if we don't add another 5 per cent or so to that on the basis of fashion, then we're not doing our job right."[31]

One of the most objectionable features of mass society, attacked most notably by Galbraith and Packard, had been planned obsolescence, the stylistic features of cars and other products that would make them seem antiquated and undesirable just a few years after having been manufactured. It is deeply ironic, then, that a movement purporting to be a revolt against the conformist sartorial codes of mass society wound up providing

such a powerfu! fuel for nothing other than obsolescence. But obsoles-
cence was, nonetheless, the key word in industry literature during the
Peacock Revolution. As Leonard Sloane, the menswear writer for the
New York Times, put it in 1969,

This trend toward obsolescence—as any customer who once bought a Mod tie or a
Nehru jacket must agree—is largely why the industry had record retail sales of
$17.7-billion last year. And all indications point to more of the same movement, to
one degree or another, toward high-fashion merchandise with a short life span in
the future.[32]

The acceptance of new looks automatically made older styles undesirable
overnight. Quinn Meyer, who was a vice president of Rubin Brothers, a
Canadian suit manufacturer deeply involved in the Peacock Revolution,
remarks that the women's fashion business currently does,

conservatively speaking, 10 times as much in dollar volume, than the men's business
does. Because it's a changing industry, and they obsolete themselves. It was just
women's ready-to-wear brought into the men's clothing industry. . . . Back in those
days the women would lower the hemline, raise the hemline, emphasize the bosom,
de-emphasize the bosom, big-shouldered look, no-shoulder look. It was always a new
look, a reason to buy a wardrobe. We just translated that into the men's business.
And the market was ready for it.[33]

While certain advertising campaigns (most notably those of Volkswagen and Volvo) were mocking obsolescence in cars, obsolescence in
clothes was actually an occasional selling point in advertising aimed at
clothing consumers. J & F Suits ran a series of advertisements in GQ in
1965 and 1966 that appealed to men's fear of being out-of-date. "Do you
still put your pants on over your shoes?" demanded the headline, over
copy that continued, "Don't admit it if you do. You shouldn't be able to.
Any suit that calls itself new should have tapered pants so narrow you
have to put your shoes on last." In order to avoid the stigma associated
with such an embarrassing practice, the ad recommended that readers be
careful to buy a legitimately "new" product next time they shop. But
recognizing how difficult it is for some to "check the cuffs, length of
jacket, vents, lapels, buttons, colors, etc." of a new suit, the J & F company had thoughtfully marked the design year on their products, "like
cars," a product with which men are traditionally comfortable: "You can

buy the 1965 models now." The advertisement makes no claim that the new models are in any way superior to the old; it even recognizes that certain people may not like them. The sole selling points of J & F suits is that they are the latest thing and that even people not conversant with fashion can easily determine that they are the latest thing by the date with which they are clearly emblazoned.[34]

The new emphasis on obsolescence made for a dramatic acceleration of production and marketing cycles. Prior to the Peacock Revolution, retail outlets and manufacturers had been accustomed to buying and producing only two lines a year, neither of which ordinarily showed significant revisions of models that had come before. Where even the smallest changes had once taken a decade to accomplish, they now proceeded at a rapid clip. New Jersey retailer Sid Schlesinger commented to *Men's Wear* magazine in 1966 on the increasing instability that accompanied the Mod look, remarking that "the market is so volatile and moves so rapidly you have to buy only for the moment. . . . It's like the women's business . . . you can't buy twice a year—rather twice a week."[35] By 1970, the trend toward acceleration was so undeniable that *Men's Wear* entitled a survey of large retailers in that year "No More Seasons." "Cycle or seasonal buying is at an end," declared one Miami retailer. "We'll buy only on a steady basis."[36] In 1972, Chester Kessler of the Clothing Manufacturers Association told the *New York Times* that, although the pace had slowed somewhat, the accomplishments of the sixties were remarkable indeed: "You know, it took the industry about 15 years to reduce the width of coat lapels from 5½ inches to 1⅞ inches and then we reversed that trend in a year and a half."[37]

As in the advertising business, where the Creative Revolution was led by "boutique" agencies capable of great flexibility and uninhibited by Theory X corporate strictures, the preeminent retailing sites of the Peacock Revolution were the hundreds of small menswear boutiques that sprung up across the country in the 1960s and positioned themselves as purveyors of the new, institutions of sartorial rebellion. While the daring of the great department stores was limited by their size, boutiques were able to carry clothes unavailable elsewhere, garments (like the products of Rubin Brothers discussed below) designed especially for a particular shop. Boutiques were hothouses of obsolescence and of managerial flexibility, places where rapid turnover and a continual changing of styles were cloaked with a hipness that bigger stores could only dream of achieving. "THERE ARE NO SEASONS HERE," *Men's Wear* columnist Amy Teplin wrote of the boutique business in 1970.

For the retailer who would like his fair share of the action, it means CONSTANT BUYING, always being out on the market, always being open to new ideas and re-sources and always being controlled enough to change gears right in the middle of the ball game.[38]

As *Men's Wear* pointed out again and again, boutique retailing could be, like fashion generally, immensely profitable. But not just anybody could do it. According to Teplin, only small entrepreneurs could muster the "hip" required to keep up. Big established stores, by contrast, were too inflexible to achieve the countercultural savoir-faire necessary for boutique-style fashion success:

The [First National Boutique] show proved that this business has become conta-gious. What it failed to show to the masses of department store buyers ordering tie-dye and T-shirts by the ton is that boutique-ing is not just a matter of stocking the right tops and bottoms and calling yourself "funky" or "groovy" or a "head shop."
It's much harder to be hip when you're big.[39]

As the menswear industry would discover in the seventies, though, obsolescence had its down side as well. As the new styles grew more and more distant from the familiar looks of the 1950s, many consumers began to complain and to cease buying. An article on slowing suit sales that ran in the *New York Times* in January, 1972, pointed to accelerated fashion as one of the causes of the slump.

At the same time [the recession of 1970 and 1971], a lot of clothing companies were making such radical and rapid style changes that retail customers were confused, concerned—and unwilling to buy—when obsolescence seemed to be right around the corner.[40]

One consumer's disaffection with fashion was so pronounced that the *Times* printed his grumblings in October of 1970. Malcolm C. McMaster, who described himself as an affluent consumer from Vermont, blamed that year's slump in the menswear industry on fashion and "overstyling," which he obviously believed had been artificially constructed by the busi-ness to encourage consumption. "Maybe the manufacturers are in error if they think that they can involve men in something like the mini-midi-maxi controversy," he wrote. "Who will want to wear this stuff in three years?" Significantly, this irate consumer pointed to the disproportionate

chapter nine

influence of European designers and countercultural figures for the frenzy of obsolescence and fashion.

> Most of it [the clothing advertised in the *Times*] seems to originate in Italy or France. Are there no American designers? I gather that most of the shops won't even let one in the front door unless one's hair is down to the shoulders.

Although McMaster's complaint read like classic fashion-as-conspiracy grumbling, the marketplace was hardly democratic for this consumer nonetheless: fashion was an imposition, for all of its language of liberation. Stores' "unwillingness to carry standard items" was particularly irksome, as the fluctuation of fashion made strange items seem suddenly omnipresent and familiar articles seem suddenly unavailable.[41]

Rubin Brothers Clothiers, Ltd., of Montreal, makers of men's tailored clothing (suits, jackets, trousers, and topcoats), was a firm that exemplified the industrial shifts toward flexibility and transgression that David Harvey finds at the center of postmodern business enterprise. Having incorporated a number of manufacturing innovations in their assembly procedures during the 1960s, the company found themselves capable of producing virtually any number of variations on a basic garment in an extremely brief period. Fashion, constant change, perpetual obsolescence, and the value of differentness were natural selling points for such an operation, and the company quickly found itself at the forefront of the revolution.

A profile of Rubin Bros. that appeared in *Men's Wear* in July, 1971, highlighted the firm's "unique" "flexibility of operation" and its "faster cycling of fashion," both products of its highly specialized plant, located in Victoriaville, Canada. Ronald Hipps, the company's presciently named chief executive officer and general manager, described its remarkable abilities:

> Our plant is so constituted that it can readily provide a store with virtually anything it wants in the way of fashion. We can give a merchant his own lapel design, any button, any back, any pocket treatment or any lining he desires. . . . And yet, at the same time, we produce 1,100 coats and 1,300 pairs of pants a day.[42]

Quinn Meyer, who was an executive at Rubin Bros. charged with opening the U.S. market during those heady years, recalls that the factory was "modeled after an automobile plant, where they had a basic body, and they could add things like lapels or pockets, just as the automobile manufacturers added fenders and grilles to differentiate among the various models."[43] The company also employed a designer who, in Meyer's estimation, "was responsible for the Peacock Revolution more than any other person." The result was a capacity for variation and accelerated production unrivaled in the industry. *Men's Wear* noted that Rubin Brothers' "delivery cycle, from order to receipt of goods, normally ranges from six to eight weeks, in contrast to the 12 to 15 weeks it ordinarily takes its competition south of the border to complete an order."[44]

Looking for a selling point with which to penetrate the U.S. market, Meyer remembers, Rubin Bros. offered retailers more daring, up-to-date looks than they had previously been willing to buy. One of the keys to the garment business's traditional sluggishness had been the danger of speculating on unusual products which would not be delivered until many months later, when whatever force had compelled the order may well have vanished: in the "worsted market," Meyer recounts, "it had to necessarily be dull, because the pipeline on the worsted market was two years long, and nobody wanted to take a chance. So, you know, you're dealing with navies and grays." But suddenly, he recalls, his employer made different looks available at minimal risk:

We went to a lot of stores . . . and we said, "Look, you don't have to make a commitment 6 to 9 months away, here: it's 6 weeks. Why don't you buy a little bit, try it, and if it sells, we can give you a 6-week reorder time. Certainly you'll be able to tell in the first week if it sells." So that was how we were able to insert . . . these wild looks, in a market that was very, very static and used to no change at all. The big idea back then was that you would go from center-vent to side-vent in the course of three years, and very, very dull fabrics. And the suit was meant to last a long time, and we developed the idea of disposable fashion.

The most critical factor, of course, was that many American consumers, anxious to distinguish themselves from the crowd, were ready for just the sort of "different" garments that Rubin Brothers was offering. And so the distinctive suits sold. To keep them selling, Rubin Brothers embraced another idea from the auto industry—obsolescence. As Quinn Meyer recollects,

We were really marketing ourselves all the way from the production to the changing the models and everything after the automobile industry, which was so very successful at that time, and we would purposely obsolete ourselves. Because we had hold of a buyer who had to have the "dernier cri," the last word. A very small segment of the market was what prompted this whole thing, and they were self-made people, extravagant people, rather gauche, and open to anything that was new. And so our idea was to, twelve months from now, present a totally different look, so you've got to throw everything away. Never let anything wear out: obsolete it out.

With this marketing strategy, Meyer explains, Rubin Brothers focused on producing clothes that were *different*, in almost any way. "The whole idea was to be as different as you can, and do it in the short cycle, with small quantities ordered, where the retailer wasn't taking that much of a chance." So with their plant's immense potential for variety, Rubin Brothers designs took off in every imaginable direction.

we got to the point where we were taking a lot of ideas from outerwear, and incorporating suede lapels, and buckles on pockets, and leather trims. . . . We had this marvelous plant, that we could do just about anything [with], so we started doing just about anything. And typically, whereas the average clothing line would have maybe five models, we would come out four times a year with up to 50 models, realizing that, if we were lucky, 8 of them would be meaningful [sell well], and the rest we could throw away. But we got to the point that we found out 20 of them were meaningful. . . . So the retailer started buying very little depth, but tremendous numbers of models, because he found out the market was ready for it.

Salesmen were instructed, Meyer says, to "find ideas anyplace, anywhere, buy them and send them in," so they could be copied. Rubin Brothers began to design their own fabric, using unusual colors and textures: "We started incorporating lavenders, and pinks, and roses, and shrimp colors, and teal greens, and . . . just anything to be different," Meyer recalls. "We just changed for the sake of change." Unconventional details were added to garments, then abandoned in favor of other unconventional details: "we went from leather applications to braid applications. And we would copy old English tennis jackets, with the braid piping on the pockets and lapels. And the next year after the braid, we did piping copying military jackets, with the backs out of military jackets." The company offered silk-screened prints on tweeds, psychedelic amoeba designs, and burgundy gabardines. The potential for distinctive, visible variation was virtually infinite:

At one time it was figured out on a computer we had a potential to produce something like 2 million variations. Because we developed a way to put a different pocket with a different lapel with a different back treatment and with a different sleeve treatment. . . . Our motto was "Options Unlimited," and you could literally design anything from scratch, because the sleeve would come out of a separate shop, and the pocket would come out of a separate shop, and the lapel would come out of a separate shop, and the back would come out of a separate shop, all to be assembled at a final point. And we had a tremendous variety of buttons, we used to seek out the women's market to find different button treatments, and different lining treatments. And then we got started with the contrast stitching, which was a very big thing at one time, then we went to double-track stitching, and triple-track stitching. We had navy blue suits, if you can believe it, with red piping one row, white piping one row, and sky-blue piping in another row. All you've got to do is look at a 1971 Cadillac and figure the guy who'd buy that was open to anything.

The rise of fashion was profitable for Rubin Brothers and the retailers who carried their products. Meyer cites a 300 to 400 percent growth in sales during the Peacock Revolution and notes as well that

we came to be the highest profit supplier that any retailer had. Because he bought in small quantity. He was turning his money 6 times a year, whereas in the industry the average was one and three-quarters—1.74—turns. We were turning money 6 times. And we told the retailer to double the markup, because after all, either it was going to sell at that price or you couldn't give it away.

Along with garish styles, inflated prices were one of the Peacock Revolution's most striking and remarked-upon features. Even though elaborate and expensive tailoring was being abandoned in the 1960s in favor of more ostentatious marks of status, prices continued to climb. Quinn Meyer remembers how

I saw retail salesmen selling suits that were priced 3 times more than they should have been. Because they looked different. "Well, yeah, but the reason this suit is worth so much is because the buttons are the same color as the fabric." I mean, there was no intrinsic value. The suits were all glued. There was no tailoring in them. . . . It was the same thing Detroit was doing. Those cars weren't worth half the money they were selling them for at that time. But they looked *different*. And the proof of the pudding was that the car depreciated 30 percent the minute it left the show-room, and the only cars that maintained their value were the ones that were the wildest of all. And we were doing the same thing in clothing.

For Rubin Brothers fashion arose from the flexibility permitted by new technologies, from a capacity to produce variety on a scale previously unimaginable. Borrowing techniques and the concept of obsolescence from the auto industry and the women's wear business, menswear manufacturers were able to introduce rapid stylistic change, to transgress established modes. But the most important prerequisite for fashion would be Barthes's second "consciousness," the public's attitudes about consuming.

chapter ten

HIP AND

OBSOLESCENCE

Become an imposter. *The yippies try*
to liberate people by getting everybody
to change their clothes. As a
transitional stage towards
Communism, the yippies demand that
everybody change his job and his clothes
every few months. Everybody should
interchange roles with others so that we
can all share our experiences.

          — JERRY RUBIN, *DO IT!*

Men of the world, arise! The revolution
has begun and fashion is at the
barricades. Charge into Chapman's
shops for men and lead the way to this
new found freedom in men's clothes.

      — RETAIL ADVERTISEMENT, 1968

Charles Reich found world-shaking significance in most aspects of the counterculture he discussed in *The Greening of America,* but he reserved special praise for the liberating effect the youth uprising was having on men's clothing. The new garments then becoming available were more comfortable than their predecessors, he testified, permitting a freedom of movement absent in the traditional business suit. Bell bottoms, for example, "give the ankles a special freedom as if to invite dancing right on the street." The new clothes, Reich insisted, were also profoundly expressive of the individual's inner nature and irreducible selfhood, rather than molding his features into a uniform appearance.[1]

Reich might as well have been writing copy for the menswear industry, so similar were his epiphanies to those of the trade press. When, as almost all observers insist, the 1960s saw America polarized into two hostile camps (or "consciousnesses"), the men's clothing industry, former purveyors of conformity, joined the nation's young rebels at the barricades in their battles with the "Establishment." The official voices of the menswear industry did not recoil from or seek to suppress the new looks: on the contrary, in the trade's publications, the new clothes and the new "consciousness" they bespoke were both the subject of almost incessant praise. The revolution in menswear and the revolution of the young were essentially the same thing to the clothing industry, and both were welcomed as harbingers of a new fashion awareness.

In 1959, the menswear industry had not yet happened upon a cultural combination powerful enough to communicate the nascent fashion sensibility they wished to encourage. During the 1960s, they would discover just such a theme in the widespread sentiments of rebellion against the "mass society" of postwar America. When the industry first raised its voice in dissent in the mid-1960s, the counterculture had yet to be noticed by the nation's media, and the industry's visions of rebellion had to be expressed without such helpful symbols as long hair and drug references. But by the decade's end, the new consuming vision of GQ, Daily News Record, and Men's Wear was entirely a matter of countercultural hip.

"Revolution" was probably the most overused word of the 1960s. There was a Creative Revolution in advertising as well as the Peacock Revolution in menswear, a sexual revolution, a revolution in rock music and agriculture and filmmaking and furniture design and fiction writing. For members of the New Left, Todd Gitlin recalls, the word became a "supreme talisman."[2] A similar fetish for the language of radical transgression was fully in place by 1966 in the trade literature of the men's clothing industry. Although they had yet to take on the look and content of the youth uprising, invocations of "revolution" were commonplace. An advertisement for Dexter shoes that ran in Men's Wear in March of 1966 pictured a number of rather plain-looking slip-on shoes perched on a spherical bomb with a lit fuse; both shoes and bomb being exemplars of "The Spirit of '66," as the headline reads. The shoes are touted as "Dynamic, revolutionary, explosive. An entirely fresh concept in men's casuals that in every way captures the aggressive, independent mood and spirit of '66." These were not only new and hence revolutionary products, they were the sartorial evocation of the anti-organization man, the inwardly directed and "independent" rebel against mass society.[3] Gulf Stream slacks sounded a very similar theme, calling upon men's retailers to "Join the Revolt Against Conformity." The company used a pod of peas throughout its 1966 advertising campaign to symbolize the mass man, the Theory X automaton in the "lonely crowd," the kind of person nobody wanted to be. "Maybe this is the time to be a leader and not a follower," the ad counseled. With this particular brand of trousers, it maintained, men could affirm their individuality and free themselves from the confines of oppressive tradition. "Sure, it takes courage to break with the past. But what are you, a man or a greenpea?"[4] The issue of Men's Wear in which the ad for Dexter shoes ran also carried a curious call to "Join the BIG YANK revolution," to abandon "work clothes" in favor of "permanent press utility apparel." Three middle-aged blue-collar men are pictured wearing the items advertised and holding signs as protesters often did during those years. The ad seems strange not only because of its mixture of "rebel" signifiers with such ludicrously unhip products and models, but because it evokes the name of "revolution" without making any references to the new sensibility. Awkward and unconvincing, it testifies only to the appeal of the word, to the power of "revolution" over the minds of marketers.[5]

The hero of such accelerated times was, of course, "The Rebel," a figure who dominated the men's clothing trade literature during these years, much as he would come to be the idée fixe of the mass media generally in the latter half of the 1960s. In the early 1960s, the only reference to rebels or proto-hippies one was likely to find were distinctly negative. One advertisement, run by the Hat Corporation of America in *Life* magazine in 1961, featured a large photograph of a beatnik in a characteristically insouciant slouch, under the headline, "There are some men a hat won't help." The ad is a classic of the advertising style that Jackson Lears has called "personal efficiency": wearing a hat, it promises, will make one a more effective achiever. Because the executives "in charge" like hats, hats "can make the rough, competitive road between you and the top a little easier to travel." Beatniks, on the other hand, having no place in the world of the people Vance Packard called the "pyramid climbers," are figures of consumer horror rather than ideals for consumer emulation. It is appropriate that the ad ran on behalf of the hat industry, one of the most conspicuous casualties of the sartorial revolution of the decade which followed.[6]

But by 1967, the rebel had become a paragon of consumer virtue. His intolerance for the ways of the corporate status quo had gone from being dangerous folly to being a proud symbol of the values of fashion. The menswear industry now rallied unanimously against the problem of conformity, which was not only a terrible social dysfunction but a barrier to fashion as well. Industry writers quickly erected a cult of the archetypal resister of conformity. The change from 1961 to 1967 could not have been more dramatic: while the earlier ad actually discouraged rebels from reading further, a December 1967 *Men's Wear* column by Stan Gellers named "The Rebel" the "Man of the Year":

THE REBEL . . . ISN'T THIS THE WORD THAT REALLY DESCRIBES THE MOOD . . . THE ATTITUDE . . . AND THE LOOKS DEVELOPING IN ALL PARTS OF THE MEN'S WEAR MARKET?[7]

chapter ten

Coincidentally, the act of rebellion with which the industry was most enamored was exactly the twisting of signification that also draws the admiring gaze of so many recent academics: what "rebels" did was "break the rules." This most elemental act of defiance became a sort of fashion mantra during the decade, a rallying cry for the sartorial antinomianism the trade press seemed to advocate. For the menswear rebel, as he was glowingly delineated in trade publications, customs were something to be violated rather than obeyed. "IN SHORT . . . AND IN DEPTH . . . ," Gellers continued in 1967, "THE REBEL IS MAKING UP A COM-PLETE NEW SET OF FASHION RULES THAT TRY HARD TO BREAK THE RULES."[8] Gellers continued to flesh out his vision of sartorial insubordination in later columns.

As soon as a rule is made it's shattered by the new Contemporary Man who's off in a different direction. And it's all for individuality. Today the real rule is irreverence.[9]

Antinomianism recurred constantly in the language of clothing industry writers in the 1960s and 1970s. Toward the beginning of 1970, *Men's Wear* insisted that the garments of the new decade "All express a new sense of freedom for clothes that will be breaking as many rules as the people who have started to wear them."[10] And in 1972, the magazine was still declaring, "The new rule is no rule!"[11] Naturally, many of the particular garments and looks of the Peacock Revolution were described in the trade literature as implements of rebellion against rules of all kinds, symbols of one's resistance to conformity—even when the clothes in question were formal. An article entitled "Break the Rules" that appeared in *Men's Wear* in August 1966 recounted how "the vacationing college crowd" recently "brightened the resort scene with striped shirts, boldly patterned jackets, many shapes in bows" and so on. The swimwear of surfers was described in June 1968 as "breaking the mold," and its wearers as "independent, unpredictable" people who "refuse to remain part of the herd."[12] The Nehru jacket and its many progeny were reverently described as especially revolutionary garb, smashing the monopoly of the traditional business suit and clearing the way for unusual styling of all kinds.[13] Scarves were spoken of in GQ as garments beyond regulation: "the hippest, happiest thing about them is that they have no rules."[14] *Men's Wear* columnist Amy Teplin insisted that what she called the "NewSuit" was a bona-fide establishment-tweaker, garments which "boldly proclaim they're being different from the standardized styles a guy's father once wore." Not only were they rule-breaking and nonconformist, she continued, but, amazingly, obsolescence-proof as well. "There are no rules where this customer is concerned," she continued, " . . . no establishment ethics are going to make these suits obsolete."[15] Manufacturers of men's clothing pursued the same themes in their advertising, proclaiming their products enemies of established convention, breakers of rules. Although in 1961, beatniks had been figures of derision for the Hat Corporation of America, by 1965 clothing ads celebrated men who defied the mores of the technocracy. A series of ads that ran in GQ in 1965 and 1966 pictured Monte Cristo suits being worn by a variety of people who, the reader is told, actually break the law. "He's a notorious jewel thief," read one, a man who actually engages in "impersonation of the affluent, sincere businessman of good taste." In others, he was "an international spy," "a card shark," "a cad." In each case, the ad laments suggestively, "Too bad his character doesn't live up to the suit. Does yours?" For the reader, of course, the equation is reversed: in a Monte Cristo suit the "affluent, sincere businessman" was actually being permitted to dress like a notorious, fashion-conscious outlaw.[16] Nor was the sartorial rebel-ideal of the mid-1960s necessarily a young person. One 1967 advertisement, for clothing purportedly made by "The Iconoclastic Count Crespi," exhorted buyers to follow the traditional menswear leadership even as it anticipated the era of resistance to mass society. This Crespi was supposed to be "a noble representative of the new breed of Italian cosmopolites who have become restless with traditional edicts and are searching out contemporary tailors and designs."[17]

By mid-1968, industry ads for products that enabled wearers to signify their defiance of convention, their hostility toward rules and tradition were commonplace. The Tyson Shirt Company ran an advertisement which declared, provocatively, "We hope these shirts destroy our image." What this peculiar statement meant, in its self-deprecating Creative Revolution style, was simply that "Whenever we hear of somebody who still thinks of Tyson as that quaint old traditional shirtmaker, our corporate heart breaks a little."[18] Lamplighter knitwear ran an ad whose headline proclaimed, "Revolutionizing It!" in large letters.[19] In 1969, Resilio ties were marketed as the product that "goes beyond the traditional. . . . In wildly flamboyant colors for the adventurous male." "This is not a conventional coat," was the slogan of Harbor Master raincoats.[20] "Pizzazz '70" was the slogan for Phoenix Clothes, "a wow of a word that immediately takes you away from the ordinary, the trite, the cliché."[21] Moss shirtmakers invited readers to enlist in nothing less than "The Moss Mutiny," assuring them that "Our old ideas have been thrown overboard

chapter ten

and we've run up the colors of a buying generation . . . "[22] Even ads for fabrics, usually pragmatic and matter-of-fact, would occasionally appeal to transgressive hip. The makers of Kodel polyester asserted that "the male of the species continues his spectacular flight from the ordinary in shirts for Spring 1970."[23] Dacron polyester echoed the same themes in a sixteen-page cartoon insert that ran in Men's Wear in March 1969. It portrayed "the new affluents" as hip, individualist nonconformists, fans of rock 'n' roll and parachuting, rendered in loud colors against a black and white background. One panel depicts the target consumer in a colorful plaid outfit taking an enormous stride to the right of the page while behind him a long line of briefcase-toting, hat-wearing drudges trudge to the left: "They don't want to Sing Along With Mitch."[24] By 1970, even a brand of pipe could be promoted with this theme: "the first pipe to break with tradition and find something better for its bowl. Pyrolytic Graphite."[25]

So anxious were advertisers to declare themselves different that, at one point in 1969, two makers of men's toiletries were on the verge of launching new campaigns when they were informed by Men's Wear that both were using the same theme: the words "The Different Drummer." The line, which, as Men's Wear recounted, was derived from "the hippie enclave's poet hero, Henry David Thoreau," was also used by "a swinging New York City boutique." As the magazine noted, "It seems that in the age of the new individualism the masses are swinging to the sound of a different drummer and that to be truly different one will have to quit marching and start running."[26] There was also a complete array of menswear products called "rogue." Not only did that rascally appellation grace an Atlanta boutique profiled in Men's Wear, but it also designated a shirt made by Sero, a variety of Interwoven socks, and a line of overcoats, the "WeatheRogues" by Genesco, which promised "a fast getaway from tradition."[27]

rebels young and otherwise

In the literature of the menswear industry, the importance of revolution, rebellion, nonconformity, and rule-breaking had been well established by the end of 1966. What it lacked was a unifying symbol to give it coherence and meaning. During the last few years of the decade, the industry found exactly the figure they required in the youth movement that was busy denouncing the establishment and declaring its desire to do its own thing. Though neither *Men's Wear, Daily News Record,* nor *GQ* could have counted many actual young people among their readers, "youth" was still a perfect, ready-made shorthand for the fashion rebellion, and it quickly became an almost inescapable theme in the discourse between manufacturer and retailer that filled those journals. In the defiant deeds of the counterculture—occasionally conducted in clothes similar to those they were promoting—the industry saw a reflection of its own cultural battle. Change for the sake of change thus sought to make common cause with a movement that, on its surface at least, recoiled in disgust from the shallow materialism of fashion and planned obsolescence.

Just as with the advertising industry, the trade journals of the menswear business were very concerned with the great youth market of the sixties. But here, as in advertising, the youth market's size was only part of its significance. It also demanded the attention of the industry because the tastes and buying habits of the young seemed to be setting the pattern for the tastes and habits of their elders. The mainstream press almost unanimously attributed the Peacock Revolution to the influence of youth.[28] While standard theories of fashion place aristocrats and the very wealthy at the top of the emulative pyramid, in the 1960s men are believed to have looked to the hip young as sartorial, as well as attitudinal, sexual, and rhetorical leaders.

But when writers in *Men's Wear* and *GQ* referred to "youth" as fashion leaders, they were almost always speaking metaphorically. Even though trade journals offered article after article scrutinizing the innovations of every imaginable subdivision of rebel youth culture—from rock stars to students to hippies to surfers—the young were hardly the primary consumers of the Peacock Revolution. Young people were generally unable to afford the products of the high-end manufacturers. Who was the typical Peacock consumer? Nora Ephron of the *New York Times* discussed him in a 1968 article about yet another designer to cross over to menswear from women's clothing, Bill Blass. "What is significant about Blass," she wrote, "is that his clothes appeal to a group of men who have hitherto been resistant to fashion change—a group which, in fact, includes the stockbrokers and undertakers, who can well afford to pay the extra premium for colorful, well-tailored, tasteful clothes but want nothing to do with ruffled blouses and love beads." Among other satisfied fans of the designer, Ephron noted with obvious astonishment, were a Cincinnati pharmacist, *"the dean* of a Colorado business school," and "A *Sacramento real estate man."* None were bomb-throwers in any way; none were hippies; none were young.

The typical man in the Bill Blass suit is an affluent suburbanite who once owned a Madras jacket, plays golf at his country club, drives a Thunderbird which he thinks is a sports car, and brings a bottle of liqueur back from the islands every February and makes all his friends drink it. "He's over 30," said Blass. "He's tall, a little thick in the middle and heavy in the legs. He's apt to be a business type. Sounds awful square, doesn't he?" [29]

The meaning of "youth" to fashion industry thinkers was clearly stated in a 1966 *Daily News Record* interview with Richard Ohrbach, a decorator, painter, and general connoisseur of the arts. "The present and future look is clean-lined and it's young," he pointed out. And, as the famous Pepsi ads of the early sixties would also insist, "Youth is an attitude, not an age, nowadays." The foremost attribute of this 1960s notion of "youth," and clearly the feature that made it so appealing to the industry (and to Madison Avenue as well), was its openness to and its taste for difference, change, and otherness. "What's catching on," Ohrbach noted, "is the use of the unexpected . . . like the greater use of the old next to the new . . . the French Provincial chair next to the modern table." [30] "Youth" was that quality in art, in fashion, in consuming, that insisted on breaking the rules, on changing for no other sake than for change alone. "Youth," in other words, was the antinomian spirit of fashion itself.

The promise of youth rebellion was a theme that would be repeated again and again in industry discourse, both advertising and editorial, over the next seven years. Turtlenecks were said to be a discovery of "youth power," as were new designs in socks ("a Youth Powered attempt to shake the black hose syndrome"). [31] "The Toiletries Boom" of 1967 was also discussed as a product of "Youth-Power." [32] A 1967 article on jumpsuits recounted a contest held by Du Pont, makers of synthetic fibers, that aimed "to see how student designers interpret this generation's desire for individuality . . . its revolt against conformity in clothing." That the jumpsuit emerged as the apparent choice of the young was hardly cause for alarm at *Men's Wear,* which noted with equanimity that

That's exactly how the Now Generation feels about clothes for the '70s. They enjoy breaking the traditions . . . the wornout rules that keep men in buttons and belts . . . suits and suspenders. [33]

Even trends in the traditional clothing market were explained in terms of youth's rule-breaking influence. "Traditional clothing is ready to lead the fashion pack again," *Men's Wear* exulted in March 1969, "because young thinking is back and taking over." Even in the "natural shoulder" realm, insurrection was becoming orthodoxy and the establishment was on the run:

Rather than confuse "traditionalism" with a way of life, these young businessmen [retailers] are making the world of natural shoulder swing. Why not, they reason, their customers are. And that's been the problem of traditional clothing and selling during the past five years. Today's young men have taste and they hardly need the sober respectability of a sack suit. They welcome change and want a contemporary approach to clothes that really meshes with their way of life. In short: Their lives aren't dull and they don't want to dress that way.[34]

The hat industry, on the other hand, suffered from a consistent inability to recast itself in youthful terms. While "fashion has turned to youth for inspiration," *Men's Wear* noted in June 1967, " . . . hatters still follow the father-to-son road," commercial poison in the age of the lifestyle revolution. As a solution *Men's Wear* recommended "a move to *jeunesse* in dress hats." "The new direction must be youth-identifiable," columnist Kevan Pickens wrote. "Good taste with 'Hippeal.'"[35] And less than a month after these words of warning were printed, advertisements appeared in *Men's Wear* for new models of Stetson hats bearing impressionistic names like "Now" and "Skyhawk."[36]

In 1967, the menswear industry discovered the perfect symbol with which to unite its fantasies of youth and rebellion: the counterculture. Advertisers began to make heavy use of hip imagery to buttress the revolutionary claims they had been making and to convince retailers of their products' rebel authenticity. Ads were suddenly populated by rock stars (or people who looked like rock stars), hippies, protesters, and young rule breakers of all sorts—clad, of course, in the latest products of the Peacock Revolution. An ad for Kazoo pants that ran in *Daily News Record* in that year featured a photograph of several serious-looking youngsters holding signs with emblems such as "Freedom of the Press NOW" and "Join the Crease Corps." Copy demanded that readers "Give in to the Lean-Age Revolution."[37] Petrocelli sport coats were promoted in 1968 with the slogan, "Tune in. Turn on. Step out."[38] In 1969, Jantzen hired a rock band and dressed them in its "Extension" line of clothes to validate its claim that "People who know where fashion is going will find Jantzen is already there."[39] Anvil Brand slacks demonstrated its familiarity with hip by issuing a group of "the zaniest, grooviest" psychedelic stickers and by running an ad in which a long-haired youngster asks a befuddled salesman where to find the trousers in a seemingly incomprehensible jargon.[40] Jockey sportswear portrayed its consumers at a suburban living room "recital of sitar music."[41]

By 1970, the imagery of the counterculture had become such a pervasive theme in the ads that appeared in *Men's Wear* and *GQ* that older lines like "revolutionary," "rebel," and "nonconformist" were entirely recast in the character of the insurgent youth movement. An advertisement for Male Slacks pictured a bare-breasted woman in a headband and bell-bottomed trousers staring distractedly into space and breaking the rules by throwing one leg carelessly over the arm of the chair in which she is sitting. The copy that accompanies this image is impressionistic, arty, and hip, clearly intended to suggest an LSD experience and to establish Male slacks as implements of personality fulfillment and revolutionary longing.

I want to be me. / Sitting in a time / When I am not here. / Past these timeless days. / Where the air is so strong. / And the feeling's so wrong. / So I put on / The other part of me. / Male. / They fit the times and my mind. / And help me drop / Into a maze. / Hue. / Like a colorless daze. / Traveling on a trip / To a meeting in my mind.[42]

Lee slacks also used the leg-over-the-arm-of-the-chair motif in its "Get a Leg Up With Lee" campaign. Here the brash young nonconformist wears sunglasses and long hair, and the furniture for which he shows such contempt is an elaborately carved wooden chair, symbolic of the ages of tradition which he defies.[43] "Young Turks" was how Hickok belts described their insurrectionary products: "Belts that take over. The in rage for fashion rebels. The far outrage youth has a yen for."[44] Readers were also radicalized, no doubt, by an advertisement for Tads pants, which exhorted them to "Do Something Revolting in Tads" and pictured a group of topless women in headbands and a variety of models of bell-bottomed trousers carrying signs that read "Down with the male chauvinist PIG!" and "Impeach Miss America" and "If you're a sex object—OBJECT!"[45]

The industry's libidinal fantasies toward youth culture were so powerful that they were willing to continue embracing the movement even after the unpleasant episodes of the late sixties (the Chicago Democratic Convention, Altamont, Weatherman, Charles Manson), which

are widely believed to have permanently soured the public's feelings toward counterculture. Just as Dodge went from the happy Dodge rebellion
to the lawbreaking challenger, menswear trade journals willingly upped
the ante of hip as the provocations escalated. Revolution was no longer
just fun; it was serious business, and the reader was challenged to match
his revolutionary talk with a revolutionary stock. A line of clothes called
"Expressions" by Campus were illustrated in 1970 by photos of unsmiling
young people dressed in a variety of unconventional looks and staring
menacingly at the camera. The ads' prose was unrelentingly hip:

The wildest of The Wild Life.
An imaginative bag of right-on things to wrap around a body.
    Colorful. Rebellious. Daring.
    And like that.

In another a sober-looking crowd of youngsters in such diverse garments
as a poncho, a buckskin jacket with fringe and a headband, and a mohair
vest stare out from under text that prods the reader to declare his allegiance to the movement here and now:

Well, let's say you're coming to S.F. You're going to be seen when you get off the
plane. Who are you going to look like? Us? Or them? Think about it.[46]

By 1970, most affluent Americans had thought about it—and they had
elected Richard Nixon. Nonetheless, the menswear industry stuck by its
guns and by its determination to side symbolically with the counterculture.

the fashion underground

The most coherent manifesto of fashion as liberation was GQ magazine,
which by 1970 had changed from a guide for corporate man on his way
up into a particularly fiery advocate of countercultural hip. Although it
was still technically a publication dedicated to directing consumers down
the precarious paths of good grooming, by the end of the sixties, GQ had
given itself over almost entirely to the revolution—not just in fashion,
but in culture generally, remaking itself intentionally as a glossy cousin
of the radical underground press. A harbinger of the publication's new
trajectory came in February 1970 when GQ sported a cover designed

by Peter Max.[47] The cover story of the next issue, "Aquarius Rising," offered a history of the Peacock Revolution as an emphatically genuine countercultural insurgency.[48] By February 1971, the magazine had gone considerably further, its cover adorned with a long-haired, bell-bottomed, pot-smoking Uncle Sam. Inside, the patriotic gent was pictured on a motorcycle with the distinctive long handlebars and extended fork that marked Peter Fonda's countercultural cool in *Easy Rider*. An article in the same issue on radical "street fashion" was illustrated with a four-page R. Crumb knock-off depicting an array of people walking along in many different, distinctively wild costumes. Only one, who emits a thought-balloon with words in Cyrillic script (surely Russian is the mother tongue of repression), wears a tie and jacket. The rest strut across the page in fez, flares, star-spangled cape, "shirt suit," unruly hair-and-headband, zoot suit, and propeller beanie decorated with peace symbols.[49]

Did this early-seventies GQ mark the zenith of co-optation? Or was there something slightly more complicated going on? Strangely enough, during its hard-core hip phase there were surprisingly few obvious false notes in GQ. The magazine was in earnest: it seems to have been less interested in the visual symbols of the counterculture as a means of making itself credible to the youth market than genuinely excited by the new world of hip. During this period, it featured regular stories on leaders of the revolution like Creedence Clearwater Revival, Joe Cocker, and Iggy Pop, and published writers with credentials little more elaborate than that they understood the Movement and could explain what it meant for clothes. Jason McCloskey, who wrote the March, 1970, cover story on "The Men's Fashion Revolt" (McCloskey was later described as "a free-lance writer, Aquarian brother, mystical realist and constant reporter of the thoughts, fashions, music and dreams of Americans on campus"[50]) was at least as deeply committed to the revolution in manners as were Charles Reich and Theodore Roszak. He characterized the considerable changes that had shaken the clothing industry during the 1960s as no less than a revolution in "gestalt," "a national change of consciousness" brought on by the insurgent hip: "For some—the young—it was easy," he wrote.

> But the transition from a conditioned, receptive, Ivy-oriented, drinking, middle-brow national *gestalt* in the U.S. during the Sixties to the heady freedom and spontaneous bliss of doing your own thing (staying young forever) was to create a

the man in the grey flannel suit had been dispelled by the undeniable look of funky cats and frontier princes, and the millions who followed Moses out of Egypt were to catch a glimpse of a brand new Promised Land.[51]

McCloskey narrates with great reverence the various steps to enlighten-ment that the decade brought—along with their sartorial equivalents: Mod, rock music, the march on the Pentagon in 1967, the various upris-ings of 1968, the moon shots, the enormous antiwar protests of 1969, and Woodstock. "By the time the Nehru crest had subsided, it was only a matter of time until the nation witnessed a growing acceptance of the real presence of what the new theologians, the astrologers, called Aquar-ian America," McCloskey observes. "A new kind of cat was walking the land."[52] And for this new cat the monotone uniform of the past would never do. He must have garments that expressed his liberation, his new consciousness.

While this revolution was being programmed through rock, it was manifest through fashion; the American fashion industry was one of the first to move to accommodate the change on a national level. Thus, the view through the lens of the men's fashion revolt in the Sixties provides a quick fix on the means and method by which one of the most reactionary industries was radicalized.[53]

McCloskey envisions the rise of the new age as a rejection of the con-sumer order that drove (via advertising) the nation's "elders" to "accrete the available modes of security: money, stock, property, cars, fashionable goods and social status." But he also characterizes it, significantly, as a groundswell of demand for *new* products:

It had become clear that the American economy, structured and geared to the con-sumer's appetites, was up for change. The revolution had passed the point of no re-turn. Many products long taken for granted would have to be overhauled or face outright rejection.[54]

Other GQ writers were equally committed. In October 1970, GQ columnist John D. Golden praised what he called "Stoned Fashion," the plethora of new looks available which, he argued, "is proving that it's a movement attempting to correct the ills of our society." Echoing Charles

Reich, Golden asserted that the clothes of the counterculture, with their "body consciousness" and "individuality" were pointing the way to a youth-led epiphany that would correct the grinding madness of the organized society: "This fashion is saying that there's hope—a revival of sanity throughout youth." But even as he saw men rejecting "manufacturers who produce fashion as the arbiters of their fashion moods," Golden clearly associated the new age with the exploding array of consumer goods of the Peacock Revolution. "Individuality," for example, was not associated with "one-of-a-kind merchandise, but rather [with] the diversity that's suddenly being offered." And the immediate product of the counterculture's uprising would not be salvation, but an enhanced receptiveness to the New: "Soon we'll become so amenable to change that we won't really notice it."[55]

The cover of GQ's September, 1970, issue boasted two stories that linked the new offerings of the menswear industry to the exciting world of radicalized youth, "The Fashion Activist: His Revolutionary Clothes; His Hair's New Freedom; His No-nonsense Apartment" and "The Campus Counter-Culture: Its New Fashion Image; Its Volatile Attitudes." Both repeated the magazine's fervent ongoing endorsement of the counterculture and its hostility toward conformity as an engine of fashion consciousness. The article on "The Fashion Activist," notes that the sixties' liberation of the individual has helped men overcome traditional fashion reticence. Each of the three personalities that are profiled, "Contemporary," "Hip," and "Funky," are sartorial rebels: their devotees have abjured "Traditional fashion values" and are comfortable in a wide variety of extraordinarily nonconventional clothes.[56] Elsewhere, GQ's publisher, Bernard J. Miller, celebrated the power of youth-driven fashion and the new consuming attitudes that accompanied it:

Fashion is eternally young—and for the eternally young. And since the spirit of the times influences the way we dress and look, a refreshing emancipated attitude towards fashion exists today among men of all ages. There's a good deal more individualism and less inclination to meld with the masses.

Indeed, the men's fashion picture has never been more exciting—or revolutionary, for that matter.[57]

Central to this conflation of counterculture and fashion was a nuance-free notion of the pre-1960s past, a binary stereotype of repres-

chapter ten

sion and liberation that is shared today by many accounts of the decade.
"The Fashion Activist," as GQ called him, militated against a backdrop
of repression and monotony: "A man might have desired the freedom of,
say, a casual suit, but found his yearning repressed by demands that he
don a garment not unlike what his father wore."[58] In order for 1970s
"radical fashion left" of boutique designers to have any credibility, they
had to "become the new outcasts, feeling the same Establishment backlash that greeted the signature designers not so long ago."[59] The "Establishment" resisted change, it was (and is) argued; the revolution of the
counterculture was profoundly disruptive and deeply threatening to its
consumerist ways.

Thus Jason McCloskey, GQ's house ideologue of the new age, begins his account of the fashion rebellion with a glimpse of the sartorial
and spiritual dark ages that preceded the dawning of Aquarius. With
the promising exception of John F. Kennedy, he remembers, the world
leaders of 1960 wore voluminous, ill-fitting clothes that signaled their
allegiance to the rule of mass society. When Eisenhower and Khrushchev
met at Camp David in that year, "The President wore a massive suit
jacket, sagging pants and a vest. The Premier wore a tent-like jacket
and cuffed slacks several inches too short."[60] The menswear industry
itself, which would soon be turned on its head, resisted change and
basked in stasis. "The men's fashion industry was a stagnant but reasonably profitable and moderately socially acceptable means of liveli-
hood for a group of predominantly second and third-generation Jewish
manufacturers," McCloskey wrote; "it turned out the equivalent of fan
belts."[61] John Golden's "Stoned Fashion" was only understandable as a
movement "mocking the almighty Establishment,"[62] and in a column
printed in GQ's Summer, 1970, issue he traveled to Cincinnati solely to
deride the backwardness of its stolid Midwestern businessmen ("An all-
encompassing inspection of my hotel lobby showed no fashion in Cincinnati. It was a parade of crew cuts, ankle-length pants and half-inch ties.")
and to encourage the insurgent young who, with their single Cincinnati
boutique, were valiantly subverting the drab order of their elders.[63]

The cover of the March, 1971, issue of GQ announced an article on
"The Corporate Guerrilla: Overthrowing Business Drag," which was illustrated by a photograph of a leisured-suited, tieless man standing on a
city corner amidst a crowd of men in business suits. The actual article, by
Thomas M. Disch, was subtitled "There's Them and Then There's Us"
and outlined the various shifting fronts of the Peacock Revolution. While

at some corporations sartorial rebels were routinely punished for their daring, at others, particularly the advertising and entertainment businesses, men were permitted to express themselves through unusual clothing. In this saga of the "Peacocks" versus the "Penguins," he wrote, "There are parts of the country, whole sprawling prairies, where the Penguins are sadly entrenched and seem to be in no present danger." In provincial places like Detroit and Kansas City, Disch noted, stiff resistance to the new products and the attitudes that accompanied them was the order of the day. "In Texas," where, he mused, "it is still officially 1954," corporations persist in directing their employees' garb along strict, conservative lines. He quoted at length from a clothing mandate of the Electronic Data Systems Corporation to demonstrate "what life was like before the Revolution," to remind GQ's readers how far they had advanced, sartorially and attitudinally, beyond their benighted, pre-sixties past.[64]

By 1971, the world of men's clothing was polarized into two rival camps: the hip and the square. While the former embraced the multitude of offerings of the Peacock Revolution, the latter clung to the antiquated, unchanging, and increasingly difficult to find products of the pre-1965 past. As Alison Lurie notes in The Language of Clothes, men from different age groups (different "consciousnesses" would have been more accurate) dressed so differently in those years that when they appear together in "family pictures" they often "seem to be members of different cultures or even different nationalities."[65] And although there was clearly a substantial market for both looks throughout the decade, the official voices of the garment industry chose unanimously to side with the countercultural one. Nowhere is this division—and the business's opinion of it—made more plain than in a GQ photo essay called "At Home" that ran in March, 1971. In each of the dark, serious, black-and-white photographs that comprised the feature, a young man clad in long hair and a leisure suit or some other distinctive product of the Peacock Revolution is shown sitting or standing next to his parents, who wear "conventional" clothes. The juxtaposition of rebel and conformist was undoubtedly meant to be extreme. As is GQ's custom, the relevant designer, price, and retail information is given for the son's outfit. But the corresponding data for dad's three-button suit and narrow tie is conspicuously absent. Only the hip son's wardrobe is worthy of the GQ reader's attention and emulation; dad is included simply for contrast, to demonstrate by his squareness exactly how obsolete, how distant, the old ways are.[66] The men's clothing industry was not an impartial observer to this shift in public tastes, nor did it defend the looks it had produced in previous years. Entrenched and "established" though it was, this branch of capital spoke out forthrightly for the counterculture's revolution in consciousness and the resulting revolution in the way men bought clothing.

chapter ten

chapter eleven

HIP AS OFFICIAL

CAPITALIST STYLE

abandon the creeping meatball!

The recessions of the early 1970s put an abrupt end to the great postwar boom and with it the enthusiasm for experimentation that had so revolutionized the advertising and menswear industries. Suddenly the blue-chip clients whose excitement about creativity in the 1960s had brought such changes to Madison Avenue were no longer willing to take chances. Young & Rubicam removed creative leader Steve Frankfurt from its presidential post in November, 1970; a short while later Doyle Dane Bernbach lost the Alka-Seltzer account for which it had made what is widely regarded as the single best television commercial in industry history. *Madison Avenue* ceased publication in 1970, and in the next year both Young & Rubicam and DDB announced they would no longer enter most of the advertising art competitions that they had dominated throughout the preceding decade. *Advertising Age*, never much of a creativity partisan in the first place, took to declaring the creative era at an end.[1] At the same time, the industry faced a host of external critics who demanded that it submit to federal regulation and that it adopt a more factually accountable style. The Federal Trade Commission took legal steps against particularly misleading ads, and the National Organization for Women leveled well-deserved accusations against certain advertisers of constructing degrading female stereotypes.[2]

225

Through most of the sixties, creative admen had warned that Americans were becoming more skeptical toward advertising, and they had written their ads with that skepticism in mind. But now, with advertising under outright attack from those same skeptics, and with the economy in recession, creativity was losing its appeal to a more narrowly focused hard-sell. Although Bernbach, Lois, and other creative leaders were hardly ready to concede the battle to the statistics and marketing experts, the industry press seemed positively gleeful at their newfound discomfiture. The scoffers now had the upper hand and hip consumerism seemed to be on the retreat; even the Pepsi Generation was replaced for a time in the 1970s with a product-oriented campaign featuring "The Pepsi Challenge," a purely Reevesian routine designed to demonstrate the drink's marginally greater tastiness when compared in blindfolded tests with Coca-Cola.

For the partisans of Peacock, the end was even more abrupt. Having racked up a remarkable total in 1969, sales of suits dropped off precipitously in the next few years, entering a long-term decline from which they have never really recovered. In September, 1971, GQ declared that "The Costume Party is Over," distancing itself from the "extremes of the fashion revolution," which it had featured in the past, and the following spring the New York Times officially announced the movement to be in its final phases. Most of its innovations, true to their self-obsoleting design, didn't survive the decade.

But in other respects the Peacock Revolution never really ended at all. While fashion cycles slowed considerably from their late-1960s peaks, they have never returned to their snail-like 1950s levels.[3] Designers like Ralph Lauren and Bill Blass, who came to prominence during the 1960s with certain startling designs, were able to remake themselves completely, in classic fashion-industry pattern, from arbiters of revolution into arbiters of tradition. Fashion never receded far enough to threaten the life of GQ, the revolution's chief journalistic promoter, and today it, along with its Gen-X imitator Details, dominate the men's magazine market niche with their incessant calls for sartorial and lifestyle rebellion. Even the more staid magazine Men's Wear, retitled M (then M Inc.), was able to transform itself from an industry sheet into a general audience publication and prosper for a time with a transfusion of some more radical 'tude.

And in two respects Peacock's legacy has been profound. Male dress codes never properly recovered from the beating they took at the hands of their former promoters during the 1960s, and the result was an explosion in casual wear. Although the lower retail prices of jeans and sports-wear prevented them from receiving proper coverage in industry papers, their sales figures, still driven by fashion, accelerated throughout the 1970s and 1980s. The curious aesthetic known as "retro," the whimsical rehashing of styles from past eras that made up so many of Peacock's looks (the Napoleonic and Edwardian looks, Civil War costumes, suits pat-terned after those worn in 1930s gangster movies, etc.), also survived and prospered through the decades to come. Retro's vision of the past as a floating style catalog from which we can choose quaint wardrobes but from which we are otherwise disconnected is, in many respects, hip con-sumerism's proudest achievement: it simultaneously reinforces contem-porary capitalism's curious ahistorical vision and its feverish cycling of obsolescence. As retro has become our favored means of understanding history, it is fitting that the decade most thoroughly scavenged—and hence rendered most cartoonish—is the orderly 1950s. Fifties retro began in earnest even before the lifestyle revolution had ended, with Sha Na Na appearing at Woodstock and Men's Wear magazine rediscovering that "magic" decade in May, 1971, reducing the "Fifties" to an era of mystical fashion heroes like cheerleaders, high school athletes, and—gasp!—"the Madison Avenue image of The Man in the GRAY FLANNEL SUIT."[4]

If imagery from the utopian fifties appears in contemporary advertis-ing at all, it's in the same role invented for it during the sixties: emblems of consumer idiocy, mindlessly smiling foils from the generic past against which we can measure our own hipness. As it turns out, creativity in advertising—or the hip consumerism for which it was the vanguard—was never even partially abandoned by its partisans. For all of Advertising Age's joy in the difficulties that beset some of the creative agencies in the early 1970s, it is the ideas and deeds of Bernbach, Wells, Ally, Lois, and Gossage to which the prominent admen of the 1990s pay homage; it is the pseudo-science of Reeves, Hopkins, and Ogilvy at which they con-tinue to scoff.[5] Snipping off clients' ties and wandering aimlessly through nonhierarchical, non-dress-code loft offices, admen of the nineties con-tinue to imagine the marketplace as a site of perpetual revolution, a cer-tain jaded rebel hipness as the ideal consuming posture, and consumerism itself as a machine propelled madly onward by no less plentiful a fuel than popular disgust with consumerism.[6]

In contemporary American public culture the legacy of the consumer revolution of the 1960s is unmistakable. Today there are few things more beloved of our mass media than the figure of the cultural rebel, the defiant individualist resisting the mandates of the machine civilization. Whether

chapter eleven

he is an athlete decked out in mohawk and multiple-pierced ears, a policeman who plays by his own rules, an actor on a motorcycle, a movie fratboy wreaking havoc on the townies' parade, a soldier of fortune with explosive bow and arrow, a long-haired alienated cowboy gunning down square cowboys, or a rock star in leather jacket and sunglasses, he has become the paramount cliché of our popular entertainment, the preeminent symbol of the system he is supposed to be subverting. In advertising, especially, he rules supreme.

The language of menswear remains particularly beholden to talk of style subversion, now routinely supercharged with academic-sounding phrases and suffixes. Even when it became clear that the tastes of the various prominent menswear designers for fall 1997 were veering ever so slightly toward more traditional looks (tweed, pinstripes, gray flannel, camel hair), the *New York Times*, while freely acknowledging that the "clothes reeked of currency," still insisted on describing them in the language of revolution. These are clothes, *Times* writer Amy Spindler asserts, about "turning cash into the ultimate tool for rebellion. . . ." Even the most "transgressive" designers agree about affluence's subversiveness, Spindler points out. She also notes that designer Tommy Hilfiger had an alternative rock band and a rap group performing at his show and quotes the editor of *Details* asking himself, "how is a man rebelling today?"

On the other side of the coin, of course, are the central-casting prudes and squares (police, Southerners, old folks, etc.) against whom contemporary advertising, rock stars, and artists routinely cast themselves. "By now it should be obvious," writes historian Rochelle Gurstein, "that there is something fraudulent, if not perverse, in the endless rehearsal of arguments that were developed to destroy nineteenth-century Victorians in a world where Victorians have been long extinct."[7] But the cliches persist nonetheless, thriving on some cultural logic of their own: rebellion is both the high- and mass-cultural motif of the age; Order is its great bogeyman.

And in many ways, our standard binary understanding of the 1960s revolt as the negation of the "conformity" of the 1950s is but the historical rendering of this nonstop pageant of rebellion against order, a PBS version of one of those commercials in which the individualistic Red Dog defies the martinet dog. We believe in the rebel sixties, in the uprising against the humorless "establishment," like we believe in World War II as "the good war."

Yet, through it all, capital remained firmly in the national saddle, its economic and cultural projects unimpeded even though the years of conformity that had given way to those of cultural radicalism. What changed during the sixties, it now seems, were the strategies of consumerism, the ideology by which business explained its domination of the national life. Now products existed to facilitate our rebellion against the soul-deadening world of products, to put us in touch with our authentic selves, to distinguish us from the mass-produced herd, to express our outrage at the stifling world of economic necessity.

The counterculture came out of its brush with hip consumerism changed as well. While its symbols, music, and lingo were transformed safely into mass culture, many of its participants turned to a more adversarial understanding of their experiences. Abbie Hoffman's *Steal This Book* is a handbook of politicized theft. Appearing in 1971, after events like the Chicago police riot, Kent State, and the various Weatherman bombings had polarized the movement, the book had no place for the softer, gentler counterculture of 1967. Lifestyle was most definitely *not* revolution, and the epiphany of Charles Reich was not what Hoffman was aiming for.

Smoking dope and hanging up Che's picture is no more a committment [sic] than drinking milk and collecting postage stamps. A revolution in consciousness is an empty high without a revolution in the distribution of power. We are not interested in the greening of Amerika except for the grass that will cover its grave.[8]

The book is profoundly hostile to the consumer order: the majority of its content describes various ways to steal the things one needs to live, and a host of publishers rejected it because the title, emblazoned in enormous white letters on a black cover, promised to subvert the fundamental operation of book publishing (Hoffman ultimately had to have it printed by himself). Its cover blurb, "Everything You Always Wanted for FREE," mocked the slogans and material dreams of the mass society, and the author's photograph depicted him stealing from a bookstore. Years later, Hoffman wrote of this call to theft as a sort of consumerism in reverse, a politicized anti-shopping:

It's universally wrong to steal from your neighbor, but once you get beyond the one-to-one level and pit the individual against the multinational conglomerate, the federal bureaucracy, the modern plantation of agro-business, or the utility company, it becomes strictly a value judgment to decide exactly who is stealing from whom. One person's crime is another person's profit. Capitalism *is* license to steal; the government simply regulates who steals and how much.[9]

chapter eleven

Abbie Hoffman's counterculture of thieves may have prefigured certain characteristics of later varieties of American consumerism—its exaggerated hedonism, for example—but he clearly conceived of it as a direct subversion of the affluent society. This ambivalence informs much of the counterculture's larger self-understanding as well. Even as it provided business with a cultural vehicle for its new understanding of consumption, even as it introduced a new array of mores appropriate to new modes of accumulation, many of its participants understood it as a diametrical opponent of the commodity fetishism in which consumerism is grounded. Feminist writing from the 1960s was particularly conscious of consumerism's power to create the narrow boundaries within which American women were forced to live. A 1970 essay by Alice Embree specifically confronts the various "feminist" campaigns discussed above in observing that

the mass media molds everyone into more passive roles, into roles of more frantic consuming, into human beings with fragmented views of society. But what it does to everyone, it does to women even more. The traditional societal role for women is already a passive one, already one of a consumer, already one of an emotional nonintellectual who isn't supposed to think or act beyond the confines of her home.[10]

The counterculture as envisioned by people like Hoffman and Embree grew from an instinctive revulsion toward the fundamental assumptions of consumerism. Money was not the measure of all things; under no conditions could products (even drugs) bring happiness; culture and government should not be the exclusive provinces of business; ownership of goods was a chump's game. This revulsion, appearing in different, more or less sophisticated forms, has informed American writing on consumerism from Veblen's day to the present. Hoffman believed that the counterculture represented a real-life acting-out of this impulse, and in certain of its manifestations it clearly did. Regardless of its usefulness to business, the counterculture gave rise to an enormous corpus of works that seek to understand the nation's mass-cultural operations without succumbing to the platitudes of affirmation or elitism.

the uses of hip

The changes in the worlds of advertising, fashion, and business in general during the sixties were a greater part of the cultural upheaval of the period than is customarily acknowledged. From the management theory of

Douglas McGregor to the advertising-criticism of Bill Bernbach, leading businessmen made a deliberate attempt to smash the idealized but stagnant consensus of the postwar years, and one can trace the cultural trajectory that sixties historians describe with terms like "unraveling" and "coming apart." But from the perspective of almost forty years, the efforts of American businessmen to break the brittle conventions of the fifties seems more like a first step in the creation of a new ideology of consuming, one we live with still. Not only does hip consumerism recognize the alienation, boredom, and disgust engendered by the demands of modern consumer society, but it makes of those sentiments powerful imperatives of brand loyalty and accelerated consumption.[11]

It's a circular cultural operation that works through a variety of media. Mark Crispin Miller finds it in television programming, functioning to prevent the very sort of viewer elusiveness so beloved of certain cultural theorists. According to Miller, the moments of carnivalesque and patriarchy-mocking that are so typical of contemporary television are less the concessions to popular resistance that some believe them to be and more an integral part of broadcast strategy. "TV preempts derision by itself evincing endless irony," he writes.

Thus TV co-opts that smirking disbelief which so annoyed the business titans of the Thirties. . . . TV protects its ads from mockery by doing all the mocking, thereby posing as an ally to the incredulous spectator.

For Miller, television's pseudo-subversiveness is an essential element of the way it works. Unlike the telescreens in *1984*, which demand that people revere authority (and which made up the central symbol for one of the all-time greatest installments of commodified hip, the famous commercial that introduced the Macintosh as an implement of counterhegemonic empowerment in 1984), television gains their assent by mocking authority, leaving only itself. "TV would seem to be an essentially iconoclastic medium," Miller notes; "and yet it is this inherent subversiveness toward any visible authority that has enabled TV to establish its own total rule—for it is *all* individuality that TV annihilates, either by not conveying it or by making it look ludicrous." One can detect the first glimmerings of this strategy of preemptive irony, of advertising that works by mocking advertising convention, in the early Volkswagen advertisements that launched the creative revolution. And, as Miller observes, this strategy has proven particularly lucrative as countercultural participants became prime middle-aged consumers in their own right:

chapter eleven

Through such easy irony the generation that upset the Sixties now distracts itself with an illusion of exceptionalism; for it is that generation, or its wealthiest subgroup, that maintains the spectacle today, both as its authors and as its most esteemed consumers.[12]

But there is another, even more fundamental cultural rationale for business's ongoing hunger for rebellion. In the battle between Warren Susman's two "moral orders," the ideology of hedonistic consumerism may have prevailed in certain public spaces, but its victory cannot alter the fact that portions of the earlier, more repressive system of values remain necessary to economic production. Daniel Bell finds in this a terrible "contradiction": the workplace still demands the earlier values of diligence and sublimation, while as consumers we are taught the opposite virtues.

What this abandonment of Puritanism and the Protestant ethic does, of course, is to leave capitalism with no moral or transcendental ethic. It also emphasizes not only the disjunction between the norms of the culture and the norms of the social structure, but also an extraordinary contradiction within the social structure itself. On the one hand, the business corporation wants an individual to work hard, pursue a career, accept delayed gratification—to be, in the crude sense, an organization man. And yet, in its products and its advertisements, the corporation promotes pleasure, instant joy, relaxing and letting go.[13]

But hip consumerism resolves the "contradiction," at least symbolically. However we may rankle under the bureaucratized monotony of our productive lives, in our consuming lives we are no longer merely affluent, we are *rebels*. Efficiency may remain the values of daytime, but by night we rejoin the nonstop carnival of our consuming lives. As it turned out, the mass society critique was one with which American capitalism was singularly well prepared to deal—which is why it sometimes seems we will never be rid of it. Hip and square are now permanently locked together, like the images of Coke and Pepsi, in a self-perpetuating pageant of workplace deference and advertising outrage. Our celebrities are not just glamorous, they are insurrectionaries; our police and soldiers are not just good guys, they break the rules for a higher purpose. And through them and our imagined participation in whatever is the latest permutation of the rebel Pepsi Generation, we have not solved, but we have defused the problems of mass society. Impervious to criticism of any kind, and virtu-

ally without historical memory, hip has become what Norman Mailer
predicted: the public philosophy of the age of flexible accumulation.

find your own historical consciousness

How dark things must have seemed on Madison Avenue back in 1992, with riots breaking out in Los Angeles, nasty wars flaring up all over the just-freed East Bloc, and some unpleasant new things called "class" and "poverty" giving the lie to the happy platitudes that had defined American consuming life throughout the eighties. How fervently the diviners of the American public mind must have wished for some new mass-cultural dispensation, some array of symbols and celebrities that would make them relevant again, that would reestablish their leadership in the great corporate race to stay forever hip. How they must have cursed the fates that had saddled them with such transparently fake frontmen as M. C. Hammer, Vanilla Ice, the New Kids on the Block, and Madonna.

And how they must have rejoiced when the leading minds of the culture industry announced the discovery of an all-new angry generation, the "Twenty-Somethings," complete with a panoply of musical styles, hairdos, and verbal signifiers ready-made to rejuvenate advertising's sagging credibility. Armed with quickly produced books and informative cover stories in *Advertising Age*, *Business Week*, *U.S. News*, and *Newsweek*, admen were eager to take on the inscrutable "Generation X."

The strangest aspect of what followed wasn't the immediate onslaught of even hipper advertising, but that the entire "Generation X" discourse repeated—almost mechanically and yet without betraying the slightest inkling that it was doing so—the discussions of youth culture that had appeared in *Advertising Age*, *Madison Avenue*, and on all those youth-market panel discussions back in the sixties. The boomers had been said to be extraordinarily cynical and savvy about advertising, impervious to the blunt techniques of the fifties and responsive only to clever pitches that shared their skepticism about mass society: so was Generation X. "Traditional advertising sometimes does not work with twentysomethings," runs a profile of a Gen X advertising agency in the *New York Times*. "Excessive exposure to glad handing salesmanship early in life, the theory goes, has made them less susceptible."[14] *Business Week* concurs. "They are very savvy consumers. . . . far more knowledgeable about and suspicious of advertising than earlier generations passing through their twenties." "They are media savvy but are said to feel alien-ated from the mainstream culture," agrees *Advertising Age*.[15] As it turns out, the consequences this time around are said to be exactly what they were in the sixties. Exactly like the boomers, the "X-ers" are said to respond well to "honest" advertising. "Honesty policy," explains *Business Week*:

> Buster cynicism about blatant product pitches has . . . shaped Nike, Inc.'s marketing. Says [the] global marketing manager for the footwear maker's women's division: "That's one of the reasons we decided to be as honest as possible. . . ."

Even the old self-mocking ads of the 1960s were given a new lease on life by the supposed tastes of the "baby busters."

> Busters respond best to messages that take a self-mocking tone. What works, says market researcher Judith Langer, is "advertising that is funny and hip and says, 'Hey, we know.'"

Most important of all, the twenty-somethings really go for "irreverence."

> Recent TV ads for the Isuzu Rodeo off-road vehicle tap into busters' feelings of rebellion. One begins with a little girl in a classroom being urged by her teacher to color only between the lines. In the next shot, she's a twentysomething who aban-dons the traffic lanes and roars off the highway onto a dirt road.[16]

As the discovery of the rule-breaking boomers merely cemented the vic-tory of the creative revolution, so the discovery of their rebel successors in the 1990s has breathed new life (and new imagery) into the basic wis-dom established during those years: hip is the cultural life-blood of the consumer society.

Business seems to find whatever it chooses to find in youth culture, and any creative lifestyle reporter can think of a dozen pseudo-historical platitudes to rationalize whatever identity they are seeking to pin on the demographic at hand. What's strange is that business always seems to want to discover the same thing. Regardless of its objective "content," and regardless of whether it even exists, rebel youth culture will always be found to fit the same profile, will always be understood as an updating of the 1960s original. Its look and sound must continually vary, but its cultural task does not change. No matter what the kids are actually doing, youth culture as we see it in ads, television, and mass circulation maga-

zines is always a flamboyant affirmation of the core tenets of hip consumerism. Regardless of whatever else the newest "generation" is believed to
portend, it is always roughly synonymous with that human faculty known
as "skepticism"; it is always described as hostile to mass culture, as a foreign, alien group not as easily convinced as others have been, as a standing challenge to marketers who believe, like Rosser Reeves, in repetition
and continuity. The fact of "generations," then, always requires the business response of "credibility," which almost always turns out to be a question of hip. And hips, by no coincidence, is a faculty only enjoyed by
"creative" businessmen.

The sixties are more than merely the homeland of hip, they are a
commercial template for our times, a historical prototype for the construction of cultural machines that transform alienation and despair into
consent. Co-optation is something much more complex than the struggle
back and forth between capital and youth revolution; it's also something
larger than a mere question of demographics and exploitation. Every few
years, it seems, the cycles of the sixties repeat themselves on a smaller
scale, with new rebel youth cultures bubbling their way to a happy replen-
ishing of the various culture industries' depleted arsenal of cool. New
generations obsolete the old, new celebrities render old ones ridiculous,
and on and on in an ever-ascending spiral of hip upon hip. As adman
Merle Steir wrote back in 1967, "Youth *has* won. Youth must *always* win.
The new naturally replaces the old." And we will have new generations
of youth rebellion as certainly as we will have new generations of mufflers
or toothpaste or footwear.

chapter eleven

appendix

It seems more than a little perverse and maybe even slightly silly to quantify a cultural revolution that proclaimed itself at war with quantification and with all of the IBM-card, bean-counting ways of the social sciences. At the same time, the subject of hip as a commercial style could surely use a thorough statistical going-over. Existing accounts of advertising's Creative Revolution are mythical concoctions recounting the deeds of brave individual defiers of hierarchy, lone shamans of the popular mind, solitary artists in frenzies of mercantile inspiration. Furthermore, advertising industry literature is maddeningly vague on precisely those aspects of the subject where historians require solid data. Not only does their insistence on understanding the decade as a fable of the creative elite against the bureaucratic herd prevent industry writers from giving their readers any idea of exactly how far the revolution progressed in the Madison Avenue establishment (very far, as it turns out), but they usually fail to provide correct dates with the ads they are discussing: everything just seems to have taken place in a foggy, featureless past until one day agency X did that great ad for product Y and all hell broke loose. How widespread was the creative revolution? What part of the advertising environment did it affect? Did it really disappear with the end of the sixties? Memory, it seems, is a slippery faculty for many advertising people.

To answer these questions, I decided to look (with the help of an assistant) comprehensively through the constantly shifting advertising facade of the decade and to divide it into categories of "hip" and "square." The vehicle of my inquiry would be ads from six product categories as they appeared in two popular magazines of the period, each directed to a different and distinct middle-class demographic. The product categories were automobiles and cigarettes (where a large chunk of the nation's advertising dollars are spent), appliances (mainly stereos, refrigerators, dishwashers, and air conditioners), soaps and detergents, and two very particular categories—toothpastes and breakfast cereals. (The last two generated almost no significant data). The magazines surveyed for these ads were *Ladies' Home Journal*, a monthly read by an audience of suburban homemakers, and *Life* magazine, a weekly that, as the preeminent voice of consensus reason, was the great advertising showplace of the 1950s and 1960s (it was also a prominent victim of the decade, ceasing publication in 1972). For the weekly, my assistant and I chose one issue per month to evaluate; for the monthly, we looked through each one. We read both magazines from 1961 to 1970, with one year from the fifties and one year from the seventies to give context to the overall picture. I intentionally avoided studying a magazine specifically targeted to young people.

My strategy for reading the ads had two obvious and unavoidable problems. Since each issue of *Life* magazine to be evaluated was chosen at random (out of four possible weekly issues per month), there was always the possibility of reading issues that contained fewer ads, or more square ads, or more hip ads, and thus not being a purely representative sampling. A second problem arose from the very effort to label ads "hip" or "square"—the judgments would have to be entirely subjective. Generally speaking, I used five criteria to distinguish hip ads from square ads, criteria that include not only the award-winning creative ads but lame creative ads as well; in fact, everything influenced by creativity. In order to be hip, an ad had to do one of the following:

- show evidence of minimalism or graphic sophistication, as in the early-sixties ads of Bernbach or Lois (the use of sans serif typefaces was a giveaway in the early sixties);
- speak flippantly of the product in question or show it damaged or defiled in some way, as in the Volkswagen or Benson & Hedges ads;
- mock consumer culture or address the problems of mass society, as in the Volvo ads;
- speak of "escape," defiance, resisting crowds, rebellion, or nonconformity;
- use the imagery of the counterculture (not just any youth culture, and not just any reference to "generations" was sufficient).

On the other hand, ads that spoke seriously of the product as a means of impressing others or of establishing the consumer's social status were square. Humorlessness, straight product demonstrations, scientific-sounding features, and exaggerated portrayal of the product, as in prerevolutionary auto ads, were reliable markers of squareness. Difficult as these criteria may sound to apply, in practice, distinguishing between hip and square becomes remarkably easy, a matter of what might be called personal distance. Creative advertising is close: it addresses the reader as a friend or confidante, speaks to his unhappiness with consumer society and his suspicions of advertising. Advertising of the earlier variety is more stilted and formal: it seems to issue from a distant land of consumer perfection in which products are more Platonic ideals than mundane goods.

Some explanation of the results are in order. While brands tended to stick with a given campaign or theme for long stretches of time, and thus be consistently either "hip" or "square," the larger product categories seemed to change very suddenly. Advertising for autos in *Life* magazine hit a high point in the mid-1960s, dropping off afterwards as television replaced the magazine as the preeminent advertising showplace. Likewise, cigarettes were prohibited from advertising on television at all in 1970, which caused them to increase their presence in magazines dramatically.

Although my methodology was utterly and admittedly subjective, three results of the study are noteworthy. Creative advertising arose earlier, was more pervasive, and persisted longer than previous accounts have maintained. By 1965, it had spread from Volkswagen and Volvo to become a dominant style in auto advertising, with Dodge sponsoring a "Rebellion" and the Mustang advertised as an implement of personal transformation. By the end of the decade, the creative style was almost universal in auto advertisements, falling off only slightly during the early 1970s. Cigarette advertisers were slower to catch on, but by 1968 hip was standard for this product category as well, from Wells, Rich, Greene's ads for Benson & Hedges and Leo Burnett's for Virginia Slims to the "night people" of Parliament and the amputated and roughly reattached filters of Tareyton. Cigarette makers were also quicker to abandon the style, turning en masse during the early seventies to matter-of-fact claims about low tar and special filters. Strangest, perhaps, is that the creative approach, as defined here, even made its way into ads for such unromantic products as Carrier air conditioners and Fisher hi-fis.

appendix

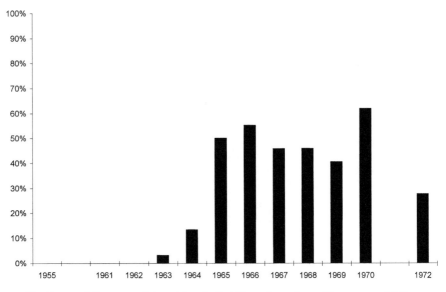

chart 1   Hip Soap and Detergent Advertising, *Ladies' Home Journal*, as a Percentage of All Soap and Detergent Advertising, 1955–72

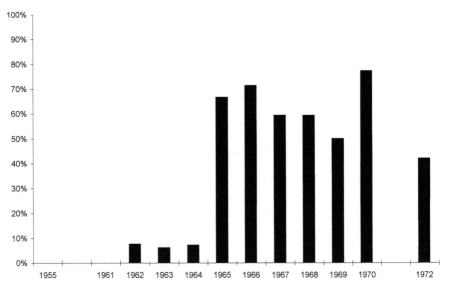

chart 2   Hip Appliance Advertising, *Ladies' Home Journal*, as a Percentage of All Appliance Advertising, 1955–72

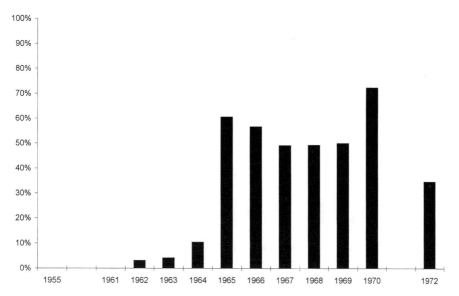

Hip Advertising, *Ladies' Home Journal,* as a Percentage of All Advertising, 1955–72   **chart 3**

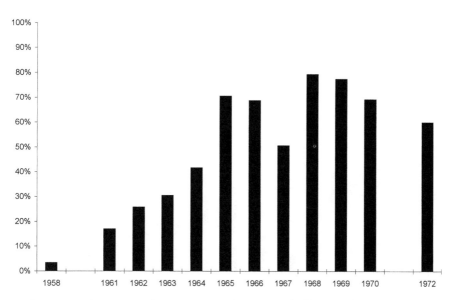

Hip Auto Advertising, *Life* Magazine, as a Percentage of All Auto Advertising,   **chart 4**
1958–72

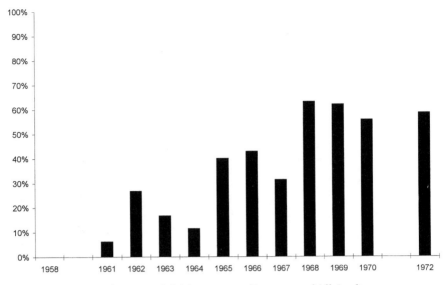

chart 5   Hip Appliance Advertising, *Life* Magazine, as a Percentage of All Appliance
           Advertising, 1958–72

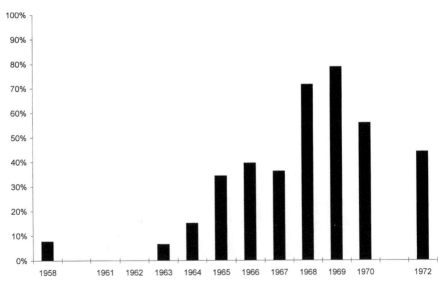

chart 6   Hip Cigarette Advertising, *Life* Magazine, as a Percentage of All Cigarette
           Advertising, 1958–72

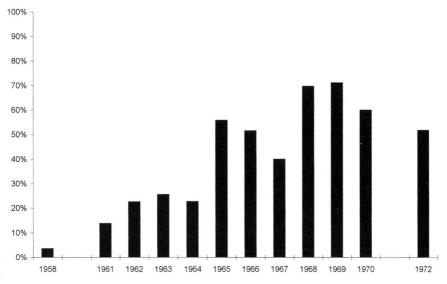

Hip Advertising, *Life* Magazine, as a Percentage of All Advertising, 1958–72   chart 7

notes

chapter one

1. Allan Bloom, *The Closing of the American Mind* (New York: Simon and Schuster, 1987), pp. 320, 314, 316n.

2. Bork is particularly determined to pin the blame for everything he dislikes on "the sixties," running down the list of contemporary evils and noting that each has its roots in the hated decade. See Robert Bork, *Slouching Towards Gomorrah* (New York: HarperCollins, 1996), p. 13. Compare this with Jerry Rubin, *We Are Everywhere* (New York: Harper & Row, 1971).

3. Peggy Noonan, "You'd Cry Too If It Happened to You," in *Backward and Upward: The New Conservative Writing,* edited by David Brooks (New York: Vintage, 1996), p. 150.

4. Fred Barnes, "Revenge of the Squares," *The New Republic,* March 13, 1995, p. 29. Counterculture and Great Society are linked almost whenever Gingrich speaks of the decade. "His enemy is 'the Great Society counterculture model.' In other words, the 1960s," writes Fred Barnes (p. 23).

5. Bork, *Slouching Towards Gomorrah,* p. 53.

6. "California Clem," direct-mail flyer produced by Jerry Weller for Congress, 1996. Photocopy in collection of author. The Democrat in question is Clem Balanoff, who lost the election.

7. See Tom Engelhardt, *The End of Victory Culture* (New York: Basic Books, 1995), pp. 274–80.

8. The Nike-Burroughs and Fruitopia campaigns are discussed in Leslie Savan, "Niked Lunch," *Village Voice,* September 6, 1994, pp. 50–53; those for cars, beer, and fast food in Thomas Frank, "Just Break the Rules," *Washington Post,* June 11, 1995, page C1–C2; those of R. J. Reynolds and Nike-Heron in Thomas Frank, "Selling Power," the Chicago *Reader,* November 17, 1995, p. 10.

9. Rick Perlstein, "Who Owns the Sixties?" *Lingua Franca,* May/June 1996, p. 32.

10. The exceptions are David Farber, who tells the stories of city authorities in

Chicago '68 (Chicago: University of Chicago Press, 1988) and Jane and Michael Stern, who include a chapter on suburban tastes in *Sixties People* (New York: Knopf, 1990).

11. Nicholas von Hoffman, *We Are the People Our Parents Warned Us Against* (Chicago: Ivan R. Dee, 1989 [reprint of the 1968 book]), p. 261.

12. The American Social History Project, *Who Built America? Working People and the Nation's Economy, Politics, Culture and Society* (New York: Pantheon, 1992), pp. 581, 580. Abe Peck, *Uncovering the Sixties* (New York: Pantheon, 1985), chapter 11. Attentive readers will notice that, while the ad is supposed to have been deceptively placed in underground publications, it is in fact reproduced from the pages of *Rolling Stone*. The ad ran there December 7, 1968. A few more recent versions of the co-optation theory include Richard Goldstein, *Reporting the Counterculture* (Boston: Unwin Hyman, 1989), p. xix; and Stuart Ewen, *All Consuming Images* (New York: Basic Books, 1988), pp. 248–49. "During the 1960s, and at other moments since then," Ewen writes, "the rise of alternative subcultures has generated renegade styles—verbal expressions, ways of dress, music, graphics—which particularly captivated young people, traditionally seen as the most lucrative sector of the style-consuming public. This sense of having fallen behind, and the attempt to catch up, shows up in the trade literature of the style industries."

13. David Riesman, with Nathan Glazer and Reuel Denney, *The Lonely Crowd* (New Haven: Yale University Press, 1973 [1950]), p. 21.

14. William H. Whyte, Jr., *The Organization Man* (New York: Simon & Schuster, 1956).

15. Andrew Ross, *No Respect: Intellectuals and Popular Culture* (New York: Routledge, 1989), p. 60. See also Allen J. Matusow, *The Unraveling of America* (New York: Harper & Row, 1984), pp. 7–8.

16. On this see Todd Gitlin, *The Sixties: Years of Hope, Days of Rage* (New York: Bantam Books, 1987), p. 19.

17. Daniel Bell, *The End of Ideology: On the Exhaustion of Political Ideas in the Fifties*, rev. ed. (New York: Free Press, 1962), p. 35.

18. Norman Mailer, "The White Negro: Superficial Reflections on the Hipster," reprinted in *Advertisements for Myself* (New York: G. P. Putnam's Sons, 1959), passim. This enormously important essay has never been adequately recognized for what must either be counted its remarkable influence or its remarkable prognostication: Mailer here managed to predict the basic dialectic around which the cultural politics of the next thirty-five years would be structured. One must also note Mailer's astonishingly backwards racial views: although expressed in terms of admiration rather than fear or hatred, his identification of black Americans with bodily pleasure, lack of inhibition, and sexual prowess conforms rather neatly to standard stereotypes and racial myths.

19. Jackson Lears, *No Place of Grace* (New York: Pantheon, 1980), p. 32.

20. Daniel Bell, among others, has made the argument that the counterculture represented the democratization of modernist impulses. Daniel Bell, *The Cultural Contradictions of Capitalism* (New York: Basic Books, 1978), pp. xxvi–xxvii, 79.

21. It is important to note that, according to virtually every observer, the counterculture was a phenomenon distinct from the New Left. As Jack Whalen and Richard Flacks, two veterans of the New Left, insisted in 1989, the "moral framework" of the counterculture "emphasized personal rather than social change. In the code of the counterculture, what was valued was self-liberation—freeing impulse and emotion from social repression and psychic inhibition—and the fostering of persons aware of their needs and desires, and capable of expressing them." The split between the New Left and the counterculture was obvious to all but the most hostile polemi-

cists (one thinks of Gingrich, who promiscuously associates the counterculture with virtually every political movement to which he is opposed) at Woodstock: while the promoters and the rock stars enjoyed a success of mythical proportions, the pavilion set up for "the Movement" went largely ignored. See Jack Whalen and Richard Flacks, *Beyond the Barricades: The Sixties Generation Grows Up* (Philadelphia: Temple University Press, 1989), pp. 11, 13.

22. *Life* magazine, April 21 and 28, 1967, on Esalen, July 12, 1968.

23. Theodore Roszak, *The Making of a Counter Culture* (New York: Anchor, 1969), pp. 50–51, 265, xiii.

24. Charles A. Reich, *The Greening of America* (New York: Random House, 1970, pp. 236–37, 237, 243. Interestingly, Mailer had also portrayed the ways of the Hipster as a new form of consciousness. Airy pretension seems to have been the inescapable literary mode when the subject was the counterculture.

25. For books on the sixties, see: Andrew Jamison and Ron Eyerman, *Seeds of the Sixties* (Berkeley: University of California Press, 1994), and Meta Mendel-Reyes, *Reclaiming Democracy: The Sixties in Politics and Memory* (New York: Routledge, 1995).

26. W. T. Lhamon, Jr., *Deliberate Speed: The Origins of a Cultural Style in the American 1950.* (Washington, DC: Smithsonian Institution Press, 1990).

27. A PBS documentary series which commits itself to *Making Sense of the Sixties* begins by delineating the "rules" of being young in the fifties. The show's narrator comments authoritatively: "One of them was: obey authority; don't ask questions. In the '60s, millions of young people would renounce that one. . . . Another rule: fit in with the group; don't stand out; conform in your actions and your appearance. In the '60s, great numbers of young people would, quote, 'Do their own thing.'" Transcript of "Seeds of the Sixties," part 1 of *Making Sense of the Sixties* (aired over PBS on January 21, 1991), p. 4.

28. This aphorism, more frequently found in British accounts of the sixties, is sometimes misattributed to Plato, though the sentiment fits. Note *Republic IV*, section 424: "The introduction of novel fashions in music is a thing to beware of as endangering the whole fabric of society, whose most important conventions are unsettled by any revolution in that quarter" (trans. Francis Macdonald Cornford, 1941).

29. Ralph J. Gleason, "It Ain't Really Funny" (*Rolling Stone*, January 4, 1969), reprinted in *The Age of Paranoia* (New York: Pocket Books, 1972), p. 412.

30. Roszak, *The Making of a Counter Culture*, pp. 42, 44.

31. "Beat, the Christmas tree of Hip," he wrote, "arrived with Kerouac, and because it is sweet and odd-ball, a cross between folklore and fairy tale, Madison Avenue took it up, they had to, this was the first phenomenon in years to come out of the Great Unwashed which Madison Avenue hadn't rigged, manipulated, or foreseen" (Mailer, *Advertisements for Myself*, p. 278).

32. "Some of the attempts to co-opt the rhetoric of the revolution . . . have been pretty funny," Gleason continued. "There was a commercial for Thom McAn shoes (aren't they the ones who went through that phase with Ravi Shankar and World Pacific Records hustling the shoes?) in which the announcer talked about how odd it is that everything 'we' dig 'they' are against, and it turned out (not on) that he was rapping away about silver buckled shoes or some other lame idea." See Ralph J. Gleason, "So Revolution Is Commercial," reprinted in *The Age of Paranoia* (December 21, 1968), p. 408.

33. Roszak, *The Making of a Counter Culture*, pp. 71, 72, 38.

34. They are also commonplace to the point of hoax. See Alan Sokal, "Transgressing the Boundaries: Towards a Transformative Hermeneutics of Quantum Gravity," *Social Text* 46–47, pp. 217–52.

notes

35. John Fiske, *Reading the Popular* (Boston: Unwin Hyman, 1989), pp. 17, 19, passim, 5, 8. Italics in original.

36. One noteworthy exception is Christopher Newfield, *The Emerson Effect: Individualism and Submission in America* (Chicago: University of Chicago Press, 1996).

37. Warren Susman, *Culture as History: The Transformation of American Society in the Twentieth Century* (New York: Pantheon, 1984), pp. xxiv, xxviii, xx. There has been, of course, a great amount of commentary on the subject of this shift, generally siding with Susman and perceiving it as a change within capitalism, not a fundamental threat. See, for example, Daniel Bell, *The Cultural Contradictions of Capitalism* (New York: Basic Books, 1976), p. 70.

38. William Leach, *Land of Desire: Merchants, Power, and the Rise of a New American Culture* (New York: Pantheon, 1993), pp. 385, 381, 290, 291.

39. Art Kleiner, *The Age of Heretics: Heroes, Outlaws, and the Forerunners of Corporate Change* (New York: Doubleday Currency, 1996), p. 10.

40. A typical such "summoning up" occurs in the January 8, 1996, issue of *Newsweek*, in which a photograph of a roomful of men in gray suits, white shirts, and horn-rimmed glasses is given the caption, "The myth of perfect management: Corporate executives meet in 1967" (pp. 28–29).

41. Alfred P. Sloan, Jr., *My Years With General Motors* (New York: Doubleday, 1990 [originally published 1963]). See, in particular, Sloan's hilariously phlegmatic account of how he and GM reacted to the American entry into World War II (p. 185).

42. *Fortune*, February, 1951, p. 176. On the title's origins, see p. 70. "U.S.A. The Permanent Revolution" was later reissued as a book by Prentice Hall.

43. Whyte, *The Organization Man*, p. 397.

44. Joseph G. Mason, *How to Be a More Creative Executive* (New York: McGraw-Hill, 1960), p. 10.

45. Douglas McGregor, *The Human Side of Enterprise* (New York: McGraw-Hill, 1960), pp. 61, 246.

46. See Kleiner, *The Age of Heretics*, p. 46.

47. Leary: "Letter from Timothy Leary," dated September 18, 1970, *Weatherman* (n.p.: Ramparts Press, 1970), p. 518.

48. Robert Townsend, *Up the Organization* (New York: Knopf, 1970), pp. 11, 10, 9, 98, 71, 10, 53, 142.

49. Richard S. Tedlow, *New and Improved: The Story of Mass Marketing in America* (New York: Basic Books, 1990), p. 6.

50. Tedlow, *New and Improved*, pp. 346, 103, 104.

51. Ibid., pp. 371–72. It is important to note here that no one considers Tedlow a conspiracy theorist or even a follower of Adorno for making such claims.

52. Stanley C. Hollander and Richard Germain, *Was There a Pepsi Generation Before Pepsi Discovered It?: Youth-Based Segmentation in Marketing* (Chicago: NTC Business Books, 1993), pp. 101, 109. On the inherent desirability of youth to marketers, Hollander and Germain write: "It may well be that the entire general experience (the *gestalt*) of the youthful years has a profound influence on subsequent dispositions. Moreover, early product and brand choices, especially if frequently and satisfactorily repeated, will establish barriers, but by no means impervious barriers, to rival options. Simultaneously, the high value accorded to youthfulness in the American culture will give the decisions of subsequent generations considerable weight in overcoming these barriers."

53. David Harvey, *The Condition of Postmodernity: An Enquiry into the Origins of* *Cultural Change* (Oxford: Basil Blackwell, 1990), pp. 287, 285.

54. Kleiner, *The Age of Heretics*, p. 20.

55. Cf. Art Kleiner, whose book explicitly grounds contemporary management theory in the revolutionary doings of the 1960s, both in the boardroom and in the streets of Haight Ashbury.

56. Irving Howe's essay, "New Styles in Leftism," in *Selected Writings, 1950–1990* (New York: Harcourt Brace Jovanovich, 1990), is probably the best-known embodiment of this critique.

57. Delmore Schwartz, "The Present State of Poetry," *Selected Essays of Delmore Schwartz*, edited by Donald A. Dike and David H. Zucker (Chicago: University of Chicago Press, 1970), p. 45. This essay originally appeared in 1958.

58. Michael Harrington, "We Few, We Happy Few, We Bohemians," *Esquire*, August 1972, pp. 164, 99.

59. Earl Shorris, "Love Is Dead," *New York Times Magazine*, October 29, 1967, p. 114. IBM was a frequently used symbol of old-line corporate thinking.

60. Warren Hinckle: "A Social History of the Hippies," *Ramparts*, March 1967, reprinted in Gerry Howard, ed., *The Sixties: Art, Politics, and Media of Our Most Explosive Decade* (New York: Paragon House, 1991), p. 226. Marshall Berman: "Sympathy for the Devil: Faust, the '60s and the Tragedy of Development," *American Review*, January 1974, reprinted in Howard, *The Sixties*, p. 496.

61. Ross, *No Respect*, pp. 96, 101, 96.

62. In this sense corporate use of rebellion helps to defuse what Daniel Bell calls one of the leading "cultural contradictions of capitalism," linking leisure time in a sort of inverted relationship to work-time. "On the one hand," Bell writes, "the business corporation wants an individual to work hard, pursue a career, accept delayed gratification—to be, in the crude sense, an Organization Man. And yet, in its products and its advertisements, the corporation promotes pleasure, instant joy, relaxing and letting go." Hip consumerism encourages consumers not just to "let go," but to consume as a means of rebelling symbolically against the work order. See Bell, *The Cultural Contradictions of Capitalism*, pp. 71–72.

63. See especially Michael Lewis, "The Rich: How They're Different . . . Than They Used to Be," *New York Times Magazine*, November 19, 1995, pp. 65–69.

64. See Perlstein, "Who Owns the Sixties?," pp. 30–37.

chapter two

1. The gender-charged term "Adman" will be used throughout because that was the standard parlance of the period. There were, of course, many women in advertising in the 1950s and 1960s, and some rose to positions of great prominence (most important, Mary Wells of Wells, Rich, Greene, Phyllis Robinson of Doyle Dane Bernbach, and Shirley Polykoff of Foote, Cone, and Belding, the author of the Clairol "Does She or Doesn't She" campaign). But, by and large, most admen were, in fact, male.

2. Frederic Wakeman, *The Hucksters* (New York: Rinehart, 1946). The epigraph is from pp. 295–96; the quotations are from pp. 88 and 294–95.

3. As Frederic Wakeman's former employer, Fairfax Cone of Foote, Cone, and Belding (the company that once handled the Lucky Strike account), wrote in 1969, "Even in 1946 advertising agency practice had gone far beyond the creation of a slogan, which was the principal contribution of Wakeman's hero to the beauty-soap

advertising around which the story revolved. *Love that soap* might indeed have been used by one of the soapers, but it would have required support based on a carefully built and researched selling proposition to back it up, and this was entirely omitted in the novel." Quoted from Fairfax Cone, *With All Its Faults: A Candid Account of Forty Years in Advertising* (Boston: Little, Brown and Company, 1969), p. 165.

4. Sloan Wilson, *The Man in the Gray Flannel Suit* (New York: Simon and Schuster, 1955).

5. Jackson Lears, *Fables of Abundance* (New York: Basic Books, 1994), pp. 138, 162, 197, 217, 216.

6. Claude Hopkins, *Scientific Advertising* (Chicago: Advertising Publications, Inc., 1966), p. 213.

7. Edward Bernays, "The Theory and Practice of Public Relations: A Resumé," in *The Engineering of Consent*, edited by Edward Bernays (Norman, OK: University of Oklahoma Press, 1955), p. 4.

8. Vance Packard, *The Hidden Persuaders* (New York: Cardinal editions, 1958), pp. 1; 2–3, 4, 207.

9. Packard, *The Hidden Persuaders*, pp. 4, 2, 207. James B. Twitchell, *Adcult USA: The Triumph of Advertising in American Culture* (New York: Columbia University Press, 1996), pp. 111–16. According to Twitchell, Ogilvy & Mather once "found that 62 percent of the public believed that subliminal ads do exist and that 56 percent believed that such ads worked in motivating other people (not themselves, of course) to buy unwanted things" (p. 116).

10. Martin Mayer, *Madison Avenue, U.S.A.* (New York: Harper & Brothers, 1958). DDB is an exception to both rules; Rosser Reeves and David Ogilvy both continued to write copy as agency heads.

11. Ibid., pp. 29, 76, 280.

12. Ibid., pp. 13, 30. Wakeman himself, Mayer suggests, was part of the "disgruntled" creative legion that have "given the industry the unfortunate part of its reputation."

13. "J. Walter Thompson Company," *Fortune*, November, 1947, pp. 223, 97, 223, 101.

14. David Halberstam, *The Fifties* (New York: Villard Books, 1993), p. 226.

15. Rosser Reeves, *Reality in Advertising* (New York: Knopf, 1961). Advertising history is crowded with successful campaigns based on such a strategy: "It's Toasted" for Lucky Strike (all cigarette tobacco is toasted); Schlitz beer bottles were "Washed with live steam," as were all other beer bottles, etc.

16. Mayer, *Madison Avenue, U.S.A.*, p. 49.

17. Reeves describes his strategy for discovering a USP thus: "When an agency turns loose a group of qualified scientists, when broad-scale, open-end research and testing are started, it is astonishing how many radical differences come swimming to the top—differences either in the product, or in the use of the product, which had not been suspected before" (Reeves, *Reality in Advertising*, p. 54). The summary of the Reeves style is from *Advertising Age*, February 14, 1966, p. 40.

18. Ted Bates Historical Reel of television commercials at the Museum of Television & Radio (MT&R), New York. Mayer wrote: "Bates's advertising, with its heavy emphasis on medical testimony, vastly irritates creative people at other agencies; the standard objection runs: 'You can always tell a Bates ad by the white coat.' And a high executive of one agency, showing deep distaste, described the Bates technique as 'the philosophy of the uncheckable claim'" (Mayer, *Madison Avenue, U.S.A.*, p. 50). Reeves quoted in *Advertising Age*, February 14, 1966, p. 40.

19. Quote from Reeves, *Reality in Advertising*, p. 72; the anecdote appears in Mayer, *Madison Avenue, U.S.A.*, p. 35.

20. David Ogilvy, *Confessions of an Advertising Man* (New York: Atheneum, 1963) pp. 31, 46, 93, chapter 6 passim, 123–24, chapter 9 passim.

21. David Ogilvy, "Standards for Judging the Graphics of Print Advertisements," in *Advertising Directions*, edited by Edward M. Gottschall and Arthur Hawkins (New York: Art Directions Book Company, 1959), p. 39.

22. As Larry Dobrow has written of four of Ogilvy's more successful print advertisements (for Schweppes, Hathaway, Puerto Rico tourism, and British tourism), all "are just about identical in appearance. They adhere almost slavishly to Ogilvy's rigid requirements for building readership." See Larry Dobrow, *When Advertising Tried Harder. The Sixties: The Golden Age of American Advertising* (New York: Friendly Press, 1984), p. 37.

23. Ogilvy, "Standards for Judging," p. 39, and *Confessions*, p. 121.

24. Ibid.

25. Reeves, *Reality in Advertising*, pp. 106, 116, 122.

26. Reeves could barely restrain his rage at such contests. "Recently, an advertising magazine asked the creative people of twenty-five top agencies to pick the three worst TV commercials of the past several years," he wrote in *Reality in Advertising*. "These men and women picked (*as the worst!*) two of the most dramatically successful commercials of the past twenty years. One had introduced a new product, and in just eighteen months had swept aside all competition. . . . The second commercial, in another field, had done almost the same thing. The reasons given by this panel were almost as odd as their choice: 'No trace of cleverness or brightness,' said one writer. 'Unoriginal,' said a second. 'Dull,' said a third. 'I am glad I did not write them,' said a fourth. And these people are advertising men! And advertising men are supposed to be salesmen!" These were almost certainly Bates ads, made according to Reeves's principles. See Reeves, *Reality in Advertising*, pp. 114–15.

27. These ads appear in the February, 1951, issue of *Fortune*, which featured the "Permanent Revolution" articles.

28. John Furr of J. Walter Thompson, Chicago, interviewed by Thomas Frank, July 6, 1993, at his office in Chicago. Mr. Furr is presently Worldwide Director of Training for JWT.

29. William H. Whyte, "The Copywriters Speak," *Fortune*, September 1952, pp. 188, 190.

30. "J. Walter Thompson Company," *Fortune*, November, 1947, p. 210.

31. Reeves, *Reality in Advertising*, p. 119.

32. Ogilvy, *Confessions*, p. 20. Ogilvy's quote is not attributed.

chapter three

1. On how admen see the prerevolutionary past, see Jackson Lears, "See Spots Run," *In These Times*, April 15, 1996, p. 27, and Randall Rothenberg, *Where the Suckers Moon: The Life and Death of an Advertising Campaign* (New York: Vintage, 1995), p. 217. On Jay Chiat, see Tom Frank, "Rebellion Ad Nauseam," *Chicago Reader*, June 23, 1995; on Wieden & Kennedy, see Rothenberg, *Where the Suckers Moon*, especially pp. 216, 302.

2. On Rubicam: Stephen R. Fox, *The Mirror Makers: A History of American Advertising and Its Creators* (New York: William Morrow and Company, Inc., 1984), p. 129. On Getchell: quoted in Fox, pp. 167, 164.

3. Even Martin Mayer points this out. "Advertising's contribution here is, on

the whole, to increase diversity," he writes. "Advertising lives by the product difference, real or asserted, by appealing to different tastes in values. . . . If advertising looks
like other advertising, as so much of it does, the fault lies in the limited skill of many
practitioners (and in the fact that advertisers, knowing that their competitors are
smart, insist on ads similar to the competition's ads). The purpose is not to make
anyone 'conform'" (Mayer, *Madison Avenue, U.S.A.*, pp. 318–19).

4. Dobrow, *When Advertising Tried Harder*, p. 12.

5. Rothenberg, *Where the Suckers Moon*, p. 66.

6. In *The Cultural Contradictions of Capitalism*, Daniel Bell argues that a certain
species of cultural and philosophical "antinomianism"—"an antinomian attitude to
moral norms and even to the idea of cultural judgment itself"—has become the central doctrine of postmodernity. Aesthetic modernism's assault on "orthodoxy" has become a commonplace of bourgeois life, he asserts, and transgression has become an
act of routine: "The paradox is that 'heterodoxy' itself has become conformist in liberal circles, and exercises that conformity under the banner of an antinomian flag"
(Bell, *The Cultural Contradictions of Capitalism*, pp. xxii, xxvii).

7. Bob Levenson, *Bill Bernbach's Book* (New York: Villard, 1987), pp. xvi, xvii.
This work is a compilation of Bernbach's aphorisms, writings, and DDB's best-remembered ads.

8. *Bill Bernbach Said . . .* , pamphlet, n.d., n.p, in the library of the DDB-
Needham [Doyle Dane Bernbach], New York; *Advertising Age*, July 3, 1967, p. 8.
Levenson, *Bill Bernbach's Book*, p. ix.

9. Bill Bernbach, "Facts Are Not Enough," pamphlet reprinting a speech given
at the 1980 meeting of the AAAA, p. 9. In the library of DDB-Needham, New York.

10. *Bill Bernbach Said*, n.p.

11. Mayer, *Madison Avenue, U.S.A.*, pp. 67–68.

12. Bob Levenson and Len Sirowitz, interview by Henry Lee, *Madison Avenue*,
June 1969, p. 28.

13. George Lois recalls the significance of the resulting change in the way advertising was produced: "Up to that time, basically, most creative work was written
by writers, who maybe met with clients, but basically took their information from
marketing people, and then they handed what they wanted to do to the art director,
and the art director laid it out. They were called 'layout men.' And it all changed
with Bernbach saying no, putting these two talented people in there with the marketing people, getting all the information, and let them create something mind-
bogglingly fresh and different." George Lois, interviewed by Thomas Frank, May 13,
1992. Jerry Della Femina offers a similar picture of the prerevolutionary creative
process: "To the establishment agencies, an art director is a guy who draws. 'He's our
drawing guy.' So they go in to their drawing guy with a headline that says 'Fights
Headaches Three Ways.' Maybe the copywriter has got a little scribble of how the ad
should look. . . . The copywriter comes in and says, 'Okay, here's what we did. We
want to say 'Fights Headaches Three Ways' and I think we should show a big pill.'
The art director says, 'Terrific.'" See Jerry Della Femina, *From Those Wonderful Folks
Who Gave You Pearl Harbor: Front Line Dispatches from the Advertising War*, edited by
Charles Sopkin (New York: Simon and Schuster, 1970), p. 153.

14. Interview with Phyllis Robinson in Tadahisa Nishio, *Great American Copywriters, Vol. 2* (Tokyo: Seibundo-Shinkosha Publishing Co., 1971), p. 238.

15. Phyllis Robinson, acceptance speech upon being elected to the Copywriters
Hall of Fame, as printed in DDB's house journal, *DDB News*, July 1968, p. 2.

16. As quoted in Mayer, *Madison Avenue, U.S.A.*, p. 67.

17. Charlie Moss, interviewed by Thomas Frank, at Wells, Rich, Greene, New York, June 2, 1992.

18. Victor Navasky, "Advertising Is A Science? An Art? A Business?" *New York Times Magazine*, November 20, 1966, pp. 170, 169.

19. Charlie Moss, June 2, 1992, interview with author.

20. Rothenberg refers to one of these, an ad done by Wieden & Kennedy and featuring Lou Reed, "art that explicated, through irony, camp, iconic reference or self-reference, the commercial itself and the consumer culture of which it was a part" (*Where the Suckers Moon*, p. 211). Twitchell calls these "The jig is up" advertising, and notes their prevalence in appealing to "Generation X." See Twitchell, *Adcult USA* (New York: Columbia University Press, 1996), pp. 238–42.

21. Rothenberg, *Where the Suckers Moon*, p. 66.

22. Advertisement for the 1959 Dodge, *Life*, October 20, 1958.

23. Advertisement for the 1958 Edsel, *Life*, April 14, 1958; Advertisement for the 1961 Buick, *Life*, March 17, 1961.

24. These were features discussed in advertising for, respectively, the 1958 Chevrolet, the 1958 Pontiac, and the 1959 Dodge. "Quadra-Power Roadability" was apparently a suspension system. "Finger-tip TorqueFlite" referred to the 1959 Dodge's push-button transmission controls. See *Life*, February 3, 1958; January 13, 1958; October 20, 1958.

25. 1955 Cadillac and 1963 Chevrolet commercials in collections of Museum of Television & Radio (MT&R), New York.

26. Advertisement for the 1959 Chevrolet, *Life*, October 20, 1958.

27. Herbert Marcuse, *One Dimensional Man* (Boston: Beacon Press, 1964), p. 226.

28. In 1959, art director Wallace W. Elton noted that, "Every car artist had his own pet system for 'stretching' cars," involving "wide-angle lenses and print manipulation" in order to "keep pace in the trend toward exaggeration." See *Advertising Directions*, edited by Edward M. Gottschall and Arthur Hawkins (New York: Art Directions Book Company, 1959), p. 90.

29. Navasky, "Advertising Is a Science?" p. 169; Dobrow on buzzwords and photo-retouching, *When Advertising Tried Harder*, p. 9.

30. Della Femina, *From Those Wonderful Folks Who Gave You Pearl Harbor*, p. 27.

31. Volkswagen advertisements, *Life*, November 5, 1965; June 9, 1961; November 2, 1962; October 8, 1965; February 5, 1965.

32. Lowrey: 1965 *Annual*. Utica: 1963 *Annual*. Benson & Hedges: WRG agency reel. Listerine: JWT collection, Duke University library.

33. Volkswagen advertisements, *Life*, February 10, 1961; November 10, 1961; July 15, 1966.

34. Volkswagen advertisements, *Life*, April 17, 1964; September 16, 1966; February 4, 1966. This last ad contained this immortal line: "When you drive the latest fad to a party, and find 2 more fads there ahead of you, it catches you off your avant-garde."

35. Volkswagen ads, reproduced in 1964, 1963 *Annuals*.

36. Volkswagen advertisement, 1965 *Annual*.

37. Volkswagen commercial, Museum of Television & Radio (MT&R).

38. Volkswagen commercial, 1969, MT&R. Print ad from 1960 reproduced in Dobrow, *When Advertising Tried Harder*, p. 85.

39. George Lois with Bill Pitts, *George, Be Careful: A Greek Florist's Kid in the Roughhouse World of Advertising* (New York: Saturday Review Press, 1972), p. 57. The irony that the creative revolution originated in the collaboration of a largely Jewish

notes

agency and a German company manufacturing the Nazi car has since become a standard part of advertising lore. See Robert Glatzer, *The New Advertising* (New York: Citadel Press, 1970), p. 19; Rothenberg, *Where the Suckers Moon,* pp. 63-64; Charles Goodrum and Helen Dalrymple, *Advertising in America* (New York: Harry N. Abrams, 1990), p. 244.

40. Larry Dobrow writes that the Volkswagen campaign is "considered by most experts to be the best in the history of advertising" (Dobrow, *When Advertising Tried Harder,* p. 9). In *Advertising in America: The First 200 Years,* Charles Goodrum and Helen Dalrymple write that "the innovative Doyle Dane Bernbach campaign had a major part" in Volkswagen's expanding export business. Furthermore, "people stopped at the ads and read every word and were able to recall the illustration and the point months after the publication . . ." ([New York: Harry N. Abrams, 1990] p. 244).

41. Advertisement for Parker pens, *Life,* November 10, 1961.

42. Advertisement for El Al airline, *Life,* January 20, 1967.

43. Ad for American Tourister luggage, *Life,* December 6, 1968.

44. Commercial for American Tourister, MT&R. Here, as in the Volkswagen commercial mocking the game show, one can discern a certain ugly undercurrent of contempt for consumerism's suckers.

45. Advertisement for Chivas Regal, reprinted in the 1964 *Art Directors' Annual,* n.p.

46. Advertisements for Calvert Whiskey, *Life,* June 19, 1964; September 9, 1966.

47. Advertisements for Calvert Whiskey, *Life,* October 7, 1966; December 18, 1964.

48. This ad reproduced in *Madison Avenue,* September, 1966.

49. Advertisement for Avis, reproduced in 1965 *Annual.* The Avis campaign was one of DDB's most spectacular successes. In 1967, *Editor & Publisher* quoted Winston Morrow, president of Avis, as saying: "Since 1963, when DDB launched us on the We Try Harder road 'because we're only No. 2,' the results of this campaign have been the best that ever happened to Avis and indeed to the whole rent-a-car industry."

"Trying harder, via the now famous DDB theme," the magazine continued, "has seen Avis business climb from $20 million to $100 million in a four-year period. And as more people slammed Avis doors, the ad budget—split roughly between print and electronic media—grew accordingly from $1.2 million to $6 million" (Tony Brenna, "A Cause for Client—Agency Contentment," *Editor & Publisher,* December 9, 1967, p. 18).

50. Commercials for Campbell's Pork and Beans, n.d. [1965], MT&R; Burlington socks, 1966, MT&R.

51. Alka-Seltzer television commercial, 1970, MT&R. This commercial is discussed in almost every book on the advertising of the 1960s. Nonetheless, it was not a successful ad in the most tangible of ways for DDB: soon after it appeared, DDB lost the Alka-Seltzer account (although the reasons for this are, of course, hotly disputed).

52. Commercial for Johnson for President, 1964, DDB reel, MT&R.

chapter four

1. Reebok commercial quoted in Jean-Marie Dru, *Disruption: Overturning Conventions and Shaking Up the Marketplace* (New York: John Wiley & Sons, 1996), p. 104. The commercial was made by the ultra-creative Chiat/Day firm, and the language quoted here seems to intentionally echo certain of Bill Bernbach's famous sayings.

early 1970s, in which Nice 'n' Easy hair-coloring is sold with the slogan: "It lets me be me."

2. Specifically advertising writer Robert Glatzer (quoted in Jerry Mander, *Four Arguments for the Elimination of Television*, excerpted in *The Book of Gossage: A Compilation* [Chicago: The Copy Workshop, 1995], p. 301).

3. Howard Gossage, *Is There Any Hope for Advertising?*, reprinted in *The Book of Gossage*, pp. 5, 7, 35. The article for Harper's was entitled "The Golden Twig" and was included as Chapter 4 in *Is There Any Hope*.

4. Gossage, *The Book of Gossage*, pp. 17, 39, 38.

5. In *Is There Any Hope for Advertising?* Gossage claims that both campaigns were great successes. The peculiar mail-in coupons that accompanied the Irish Whiskey effort generated unusually large responses, even when nothing was being given away (pp. 177–78). The pink air campaign is legendary, and Gossage stresses that it was designed the way it was because Fina was more interested in prestige and public awareness than sales per se (p. 56).

6. Charles Sopkin, "What a Tough Young Kid with Fegataccio . . . ," *New York Times Magazine*, January 26, 1969, p. 32.

7. Della Femina, *From Those Wonderful Folks Who Gave You Pearl Harbor*, pp. 13, 14–15.

8. Ibid., p. 66; chapter 4, passim; p. 68. When Della Femina takes a job at the (small, creative) Daniel & Charles agency, "I found that the whole place was filled with young guys who suddenly discovered that somebody was going to pay them a lot of money for the rest of their lives for doing this thing called advertising, and all of us got caught up in the insanity of it and went crazy. A whole group of people slowly went out of their skulls."

9. Ibid., p. 35.

10. Ibid., p. 252.

11. George Lois, interview with author, May 13, 1992.

12. George Lois with Bill Pitts, *What's the Big Idea? How to Win with Outrageous Ideas* (New York: Doubleday, 1991), p. 272.

13. Lois, *What's the Big Idea?*, pp. 12–13, 46.

14. Henry Lee, "Lois Holland Callaway Inc.'s George Lois," *Madison Avenue*, March 1970, p. 22.

15. Paul Leinberger and Bruce Tucker, *The New Individualists: The Generation after the Organization Man* (New York: HarperCollins, 1991), see chapter 2.

16. George Lois, *The Art of Advertising* (New York: Harry N. Abrams, Inc., 1977), passim.

17. George Lois with Bill Pitts, *George, Be Careful*, pp. 46, 38–39.

18. Ibid., p. 85.

19. Ibid., p. 78.

20. Ibid., pp. 76, 121, 80, 78, 77.

21. George Lois, letter to the editor of *Madison Avenue*, March, 1965, p. 13. Ad agencies making public stock offerings seems to have been one of the less auspicious upshots of the rage for professionalization that accompanied the Revolution. It later backfired badly.

22. Lois, *George, Be Careful*, p. 161.

23. Henry Lee, "George Lois," *Madison Avenue*, March 1970, p. 20. Italics in original.

notes

24. "The Three Musketeers," *Madison Avenue*, January, 1968, p. 13.

25. Clarence Newman, "3 Admen, 1 Room Equal $30 Million," *Newsday*, June 11, 1968, pp. 11A, 13A.

26. George Lois, interview with author, May 13, 1992.

27. Lois, *What's the Big Idea?*, p. 78.

28. Ibid., pp. 79, 4, 145. Italics in original.

29. Ibid., p. 50. There is a paragraph break between these two sentences; they are in a list of Lois's adages.

30. Newman, "3 Admen, 1 Room Equal $30 Million."

31. *Newsday*, June 11, 1968, p. 11A.

32. Both ads are in the collection of the Museum of Television & Radio (MT&R), New York.

33. Lois, *George, Be Careful*, pp. 170, 172.

34. "Shut Up, Whites": 1964 *Annual*. "Who Says": Lois, *George, Be Careful*, p. 83. Anecdote: ibid., pp. 81, 82. Italics in original.

chapter five

1. "How To Do It Different" was the title of a speech given by Bill Bernbach in 1956 (Mayer, *Madison Avenue, U.S.A.*, p. 66). Epigraph is from *Bill Bernbach Said . . .* , n.p.

2. *Madison Avenue*, January, 1970, pp. 33, 35.

3. Della Femina, *From Those Wonderful Folks Who Gave You Pearl Harbor*, p. 29.

4. George Lois, interview with the author, May 13, 1992.

5. *Madison Avenue*, October, 1965, p. 46. The presidents of AWANY at the time were Lon Hill and Martin Solow of Solow/Wexton. Italics in original.

6. *Advertising Age*, February 14, 1966, pp. 3, 40. See also *New York Times*, February 9, 1966, p. 51.

7. Kevin Goldman, *Conflicting Accounts: The Creation and Crash of the Saatchi and Saatchi Advertising Empire* (New York: Simon and Schuster, 1997), p. 85.

8. Dave Cleary, a vice president at Young & Rubicam, quoted in Hanley Norins, *The Compleat Copywriter* (New York: McGraw-Hill, 1966), p. 14.

9. Advertisement for Geer, DuBois in *The New Yorker*, January 21, 1967.

10. Nicholas Samstag, "You Can't Make a Good Advertisement Out of Statistics," *Madison Avenue*, January 1966, pp. 27, 62. This is a selection from Samstag's book *Bamboozled: How Business is Bamboozled by the Ad-Boys* (New York: J. H. Heineman, 1966). Italics in original.

11. Sherman E. Rogers, "Impatience Is the Virtue," *Printers' Ink*, April 8, 1966, p. 72.

12. Hanley Norins, "Must 'Science' Be a Dirty Word in the Creative Department?" *Madison Avenue*, December 1966, p. 35, 34. It's unclear, but I think the second quotation is from someone by the name of Rudolph Flesch.

13. Chester Posey, "Today's Ads Must Search for the Unexpected," *Advertising Age*, December 6, 1965, pp. 101–5.

14. Bev (R. Beverley) Corbin, "Conform with the Non-conformists," Creative Forum Paper #9, November, 1966, J. Walter Thompson Company. In JWT archives, Duke University. Reprinted in *Madison Avenue*, January 1967, p. 10.

15. Quoted in Victor Navasky, "Advertising Is a Science? An Art? A Business?" *New York Times Magazine*, November 20, 1966, p. 172.

16. Rothenberg, *Where the Suckers Moon*, p. 441n.

17. *Advertising Age*, May 17, 1971, p. 63.

18. "Chat with an ad-man head," *Marketing/Communications*, January 1968,
p. 65.

19. One such was the Ad Age columnist Harry McMahan, who wrote unhappily in 1968 that "Very positively, the agency business is in transition from the 'Marketing' and 'Research' banners of the '50s to the gold-tasseled 'Creative' banner of the '70s. Major clients have let it be known to Madison Ave. by their account shifts, agency to agency. The rise of Wells, Rich, Greene to $100,000,000 in billing in the last two years has confirmed the ugly truth to even the old line slide rule boys." Quoted in Harry McMahan, *Ad Age*, October 14, 1968. From WRG library, New York City.

20. Martin Mayer, "The Big Invisible Sell," *Saturday Evening Post*, March 13, 1965, p. 25.

21. *Newsweek*, August 18, 1969, p. 62.

22. All quotes from "Leber Katz Paccione," *Madison Avenue*, December 1965, pp. 39, 40, 39. LKP specialized in racy double-entendres that appealed to partisans of the Sexual Revolution, then still in its *Playboy* phase. Their campaign for Revlon's Intimate perfume featured a headline that read, "What makes a shy girl get Intimate?," and their ads for a brand of brassiere asked "Undress a chic woman and what do you see?"

23. All quotes from "Delehanty, Kurnit & Geller," *Madison Avenue*, January, 1966, pp. 48–53, 61.

24. All quotes from "Solow/Wexton," *Madison Avenue*, April, 1966, pp. 50, 47.

25. Dust jacket, Lois, *George, Be Careful* (1972).

26. Ibid., p. 86.

27. Georg Olden, "Conference Report," in Art Directors' Club of New York, *45th Annual of Advertising and Editorial Art and Design* (New York: Comet Press, 1966), n.p.

28. Carl Ally, quoted in Victor Navasky, "Advertising Is A Science? An Art? A Business?" *New York Times Magazine*, November 20, 1966, p. 170.

29. *Madison Avenue*, March, 1970, pp. 14, 40.

30. Della Femina, *From Those Wonderful Folks Who Gave You Pearl Harbor*, p. 152.

31. Ibid., p. 153.

32. Robert Glatzer, *The New Advertising* (New York: The Citadel Press, 1970), p. 139. This is a little overstated. Fairfax Cone was renowned for creativity, and Glatzer goes on to praise FCB's famous campaigns for Clairol and Contac.

33. All quotes from "What's Up with Jack Tinker and Partners?" *Madison Avenue*, August, 1965, pp. 14, 17, 18, 51; and "What's with Jack Tinker and Partners?" *Madison Avenue*, January, 1967, p. 25. Two articles with almost identical titles.

34. *Madison Avenue*, September, 1966, pp. 29, 32.

35. "A Creative Evolution at Benton & Bowles," *Madison Avenue*, October 1966, pp. 35, 38, 37; "New Creative Wave at Benton & Bowles," *Madison Avenue*, January 1970, pp. 15, 18.

36. Jerry Fields, "Is Immaturity Incurable in Youth?" *Madison Avenue*, July 1966, p. 25.

37. Jerry Della Femina, "The Big Cold Agency," *Marketing/Communications*, October 1967, p. 61. Della Femina heaps much scorn on Ted Bates in his 1970 memoirs. Della Femina and Sopkin, p. 102.

38. Interview with Shepard Kurnit by Henry Lee, *Madison Avenue*, April 1969, p. 22.

notes

39. Bob Fearon, "Punt, Ron," *Madison Avenue*, November 1969, pp. 40, 39. Rosenfeld himself opined in 1969 that "Many of them [the admen he worked with at JWT] were using their intelligence and creativity to keep their jobs, instead of using it to do their jobs. Any originality on their parts threatened the 'system.'" Ron Rosenfeld quoted in *Advertising News of New York* (ANNY), October 24, 1969, p. 11.

chapter six

1. Cadwell and Davis of the Cadwell Davis Company, in *Madison Avenue*, May 1968, p. 20.

2. The exact date of this merging is little-discussed in industry histories. Stephen Fox, who characterizes the advertising industry as a cultural laggard rather than a cultural instigator, refers to the change but gets his dates strangely wrong. He erroneously puts the "Summer of Love" in 1965 (the term usually refers to the summer of 1967) and then asserts that Mary Wells's "Love Power" slogan only came into use in 1968, thereby establishing a lag time of three years. But, in fact, Wells had already made "love" into one of the pillars of her advertising theory by May 1967, at the very beginning of the "Summer of Love." (See *Advertising Age*, May 29, 1967, "Present Product with Love: Wells; Don't Overdo Presentation: Frank to WSAAA"). Fox, *The Mirror Makers*, p. 271.

3. Bill Pitts in George Lois, *The Art of Advertising*, n.p.

4. *The Book of Gossage*, pp. 13, 14.

5. Richard Lorber and Ernest Fladell, *The Gap* (New York: McGraw-Hill, 1968), pp. 16, 25, 6. Excerpts from *The Gap* were printed as a cover story by none other than *Life* magazine, May 17, 1968.

6. As quoted in *Madison Avenue*, June 1967, p. 22. Italics in original. See also the scathing editorial in the *Wall Street Journal*, August 15, 1966, p. 8.

7. Merle Steir, "The Now People," *Madison Avenue*, June 1967, p. 24. Steir was a partner in a firm called "Youth Concepts," which specialized in the hip market and was the subject of the *Fortune* article quoted below.

8. Leo Burnett, "Advertising and the Critical Generation," *Madison Avenue*, June 1967, p. 28. In particular, Burnett singled out "their refusal to come limply into line . . . their insistence on a reexamination of what someone has called 'received values' . . . their sharp-eyed scrutiny of 'hand-me-down' beliefs, 'hand-me-down' ways of doing things." Ellipses in original.

9. Hanley Norins, "Join the Revolution—Get Ad readers into the Act," *Advertising Age*, December 1, 1969, p. 86.

10. E. B. Weiss, "Youth Junks the 'Junk Culture,'" *Advertising Age*, September 7, 1970, p. 35.

11. Leo Bogart, "Youth Market Isn't All That Different," *Advertising Age*, April 12, 1971, p. 37.

12. Both statistics vary from place to place. The source at hand is *Madison Avenue* magazine, which gives the proportion of the youth population to the population as a whole as half of the people being under the age of twenty-five already in 1967 (June 1967, p. 21). On other occasions, the statistic is given as half under twenty-eight or under thirty; sometimes it has not yet happened but will by 1970 or 1975. The $13 billion figure is cited in an article that appeared in *Esquire* in 1965; the article goes with more than half of the population being under the age of twenty-five by the end of 1965 and also gives $25 billion as an equally correct figure, if one counts the youth market as spanning the ages of thirteen to twenty-two rather than fifteen to nineteen. See Grace and Fred M. Hechinger, "In the Time It Takes You to Read

These Lines the American Teen-ager Will Have Spent $2,378.22," *Esquire*, July
1965, p. 65.

Some more precise figures are provided by Sam B. Vitt of the media department of Ted Bates, who defined the youth market as being between the ages of ten and twenty-four, making up "51 million people, or about 26 percent of the U.S. population. We shall also assume this age bracket to represent directly and/or indirectly from 12 to 100 billion dollars" (Sam B. Vitt, "Media and the Youth Market," *Madison Avenue*, June, 1967, p. 38).

The flexibility gives this seemingly exact marketing premise a certain air of myth, like the announcements of the various figures in the *Woodstock* film that their gathering is the "third largest city in New York," and later the "third largest city in the world." Any way one looks at it, the youth market was massive during the 1960s.

13. *Advertising Age*, January 9, 1967, p. 55.

14. Merle Steir, "The Now People," *Madison Avenue*, June 1967, p. 50.

15. Vitt, "Media and the Youth Market"; also Hechingers, "Teen-ager Will Have Spent $2,378.22," p. 65.

16. "The New Creativity," Creative Forum Paper #22, January, 1968, reprinted from *Ad Daily*. In JWT archives, Duke University.

17. "Advertising's Creative Explosion," *Newsweek*, August 18, 1969, pp. 62–71.

18. Cf. Roland Marchand, *Advertising the American Dream: Making Way for Modernity, 1920–1940* (Berkeley: University of California Press, 1985), pp 44–48.

19. In 1968, Philip Dougherty of the *New York Times* observed the startling number of comparatively young people then heading large agencies. The president of N. W. Ayer, he noted with surprise, was planning to retire at the age of forty-seven, and giant Young & Rubicam had just that year appointed 36-year-old Stephen O. Frankfurt president (*New York Times*, September 4, 1968, p. 70).

20. E. B. Weiss, "Is Creative Advertising a Young Business?" *Advertising Age*, September 2, 1968, p. 41.

21. Jerry Fields, "Think Young," *Madison Avenue*, February 1965, pp. 52, 53.

22. E. B. Weiss, "Ad World's Young Potential Rebels Are Copping Out," *Advertising Age*, December 7, 1970, p. 1. It is interesting to note that Maxwell Dane, another of DDB's principals, was number four on Richard Nixon's list of "political enemies" to be harassed, apparently because of the agency's role in the 1964 Johnson campaign. See *Advertising Age*, July 2, 1973, p. 1.

23. *Advertising Age*, January 29, 1968, p. 76.

24. Fox, *The Mirror Makers*, p. 270.

25. *Marketing/Communications*, January 1968, pp. 63–65. M/C was the successor magazine to *Printer's Ink*.

26. Fred Danzig, "Ten Who Make Madison Avenue Move," *Rapport*, n.d. (ca. 1969), pp. 32, 35.

27. Paul Lippman, "Evolution of the Art Director," *Madison Avenue*, February 1967, p. 71.

28. Charlie Moss, interviewed by Thomas Frank at the offices of Wells, Rich, Greene, New York City, June 2, 1992.

29. Danzig, "Ten Who Make Madison Avenue Move," pp. 30, 31, 35.

30. "Besides raw talent, the most precious trait a creative person can have is 'openness'—being open to ideas, to people, to experience, to change. Hanley is one of the most open, least-judgmental people I know. He's the kind of man who discovered the Beatles before his kids. In fact, I remember one of our colleagues saying, 'Can you imagine having Hanley for a father? You'd have nothing to rebel against.'"

notes

Alex Kroll in Hanley Norins, *The Young & Rubicam Traveling Creative Workshop* (Englewood Cliffs, NJ: Prentice-Hall, Inc., 1990), p. xiii.

31. Charlie Moss, interview with author on June 2, 1992.

32. Packard, *Hidden Persuaders*, p. 19 and passim; Dichter's report is quoted in *Advertising Age*, October 16, 1967, p. 34.

33. Carol Callaway Muehl and Thomas D. Murray, "Psychedelic Advice for the Creative Adman," *Madison Avenue*, September 1967, pp. 34, 42, 42. Ellipsis and italics in original.

34. *Advertising Age*, January 19, 1970, p. 42.

35. Case is quoted in *Advertising Age*, January 23, 1967, p. P2; Steir, "The Now People," p. 24.

36. Hanley Norins, "Join the Revolution—Get Ad Readers Into the Act," *Advertising Age*, December 1, 1969, p. 87.

37. *Advertising Age*, March 22, 1971, p. 6.

38. Lee Adler, "Cashing-In on the Cop-Out," *Business Horizons*, February 1970, pp. 26–27.

39. *Advertising Age*, April 29, 1968, p. 64. "The Youthful World of Spade and Archer," *Madison Avenue*, April 1968, pp. 39, 40.

40. Hanley Norins, "Join the Revolution—Get Ad Readers Into the Act," *Advertising Age*, December 1, 1969, pp. 85–86, 87.

41. See, in particular, Hollander and Germain, *Was There a Pepsi Generation Before Pepsi Discovered It?* p. 97.

42. Mary Wells Lawrence, "Baby Boom, Creative Boom," *Advertising Age*, June 18, 1990. WRG library, New York City.

43. Jerry Fields, "Think Young," *Madison Avenue*, February 1965, p. 15.

44. *Madison Avenue*, June 1967, p. 22.

45. *Advertising Age*, September 26, 1966, p. 24.

46. *Merchandising Week*, May 6, 1968, p. 8.

47. "Why Youth Needs a New Definition," *Business Week*, December 12, 1970, pp. 34, 35.

48. *Advertising Age*, October 27, 1969, p. 100.

49. Study quoted in *Advertising Age*, November 7, 1966, p. 2.

50. *Advertising Age*, March 22, 1971, p. 6.

51. Bob Fearon in *Madison Avenue*, May 1968, pp. 55–56. It is not stated who is being quoted, or why. First paragraph entirely in boldface.

52. Steir, "The Now People," p. 24.

53. *Advertising Age*, November 22, 1971, p. 36.

54. *Madison Avenue*, December 1967, p. 16.

55. Don Grant, interview with Mary Wells Lawrence, *Advertising Age*, April 5, 1971, p. 1.

56. Quoted in *Newsweek*, October 3, 1966, p. 82.

57. Mary Wells Lawrence, "Baby Boom, Creative Boom," *Advertising Age*, June 18, 1990.

58. Mary Wells Lawrence interview, *Advertising Age*, April 5, 1971, p. 58.

59. Robert Dietsch, "The Creative Ad Age Is Here," *Fort Worth Press*, December 20, 1967. In WRG library, New York City.

60. Mary Wells, "Profile of the New Advertising Agency," *Newsweek*, July 3, 1967. WRG library, New York City.

61. Quoted in *Advertising Age*, April 17, 1967. WRG Library, New York City.

62. As quoted in Harry McMahan's column, *Advertising Age*, March 25, 1968.
Also in *Advertising Age*, March 11, 1968. In WRG library, New York City.
63. Quoted in Philip Siekman, "On Lovable Madison Avenue with Mary, Dick, and Stew," *Fortune*, August 1966, p. 144.
64. Mary Wells Lawrence, "Baby Boom, Creative Boom," *Advertising Age*, June 18, 1990.
65. "The disadvantages of advertising Benson & Hedges 100s." *Life* magazine, February 16, 1968. The Benson & Hedges campaign was another of the decade's great advertising successes, with a commercial that always makes "best of" lists and an impressive sales record. An early verdict came from a "top Philip Morris" executive: "In all my experience in this business, I have never seen such an immediate sales result from an ad." Quoted in *Newsweek*, October 3, 1966, p. 84.
66. "Driving school," "Try It, You'll Like It," and "Oh, the Disadvantages" are included in a WRG agency reel; the Javelin spot and the Alka-Seltzer 'tummy commercial' are at the Museum of Television & Radio (MT&R), New York.
67. See *Advertising Age*, May 29, 1967, and May 13, 1968. WRG library, New York City.
68. Charlie Moss, interview with author, June 2, 1992.
69. Della Femina, *From Those Wonderful Folks Who Gave You Pearl Harbor*, p. 151.
70. This bizarre gathering, held at the briefly fashionable "Drugstore 13" in Paris, probably merits more discussion. The event was covered in the *New York Times*, January 28, 1969, p. 30; and in the *Philadelphia Evening Bulletin*, January 30, 1969. Both are in the WRG library, New York City.
71. As quoted in *Drug Trade News*, February 24, 1969, p. 25.
72. Ads for Love cosmetics, *Life*, March 7, 1969; April 18, 1969. The university-library copies of *Life* magazine where I read these ads had had every picture of rock stars and other countercultural heroes clipped out. Oddly, many of the Love ads had been similarly edited, curious testimony to their appeal.

chapter seven
1. Advertisements for Campbell's, *Life*, December 6, 1968; S & H Green Stamps, *Life*, September 6, 1968; Raleigh bicycles, *Life*, April 18, 1969; Buick, *Life*, October 10, 1969; Montgomery Ward, *Life*, April 18, August 1, and October 10, 1969.
2. Quoted in *Forbes*, September 15, 1969, p. 88.
3. Advertisement for St. Regis Paper Company, *Forbes*, August 1, 1969.
4. Advertisement for Vaco tools, *Esquire*, May 1969.
5. Ad for Clairol cosmetics, *Ladies Home Journal*, October 1967.
6. Ads for Dash, *Ladies Home Journal*, June and October 1967.
7. Top Job commercial, the Grey Advertising reel, Museum of Television & Radio (MT&R), New York.
8. Advertisements for Gordon's gin, *Life*, November 17, 1967; Heublein cocktails, *Life*, July 12, 1968; Gilbey's gin, *Life*, January 31, 1969; Wolfschmidt Vodka, Life, December 6, 1968; Smirnoff Vodka, *Macleans*, September and November 1970.
9. Ad for Oldsmobile, *Life*, October 13, 1967; ad for Colby's department stores, *Life*, May 10, 1968.
10. Commercial for Barney's Men's Store, MT&R. Variations on the "We Let You Be You" slogan have been used by many different companies, most notably a

campaign for Clairol Nice 'n' Easy hair-coloring in 1971 and a Chiat/Day campaign for Reebok, where it resurfaced in the late 1980s as "Let U.B.U.," thus including a clever Jarry reference and winning the athletic footwear dollars of dadaists everywhere.

11. Ads for Suzuki motorcycles, *Esquire*, May 1969; *Life*, March 10 and April 7, 1972.

12. Bell & Howell ad, *Life*, May 8, 1970; Old Gold ad, *Life*, February 11, 1972; Van Heusen ad, *Esquire*, January 1969.

13. Commercial for Datsun, 1973, MT&R.

14. Ads for Polaroid, *Life*, April 10, 1964; Tappan gas ranges, *Ladies Home Journal*, June 1968.

15. Advertisements for Booth's House of Lords Gin, *Madison Avenue*, September and November 1965, p. 19. These appeared as ads, not the subjects of an article. On the posters, see *Madison Avenue*, October 1966, p. 83.

16. Advertisement for Smirnoff Vodka, *Life*, June 5, 1970.

17. Ad for Nabisco Shredded Wheat, *Life*, June 12, 1964; ad for National Steel, *Life*, April 21, 1967.

18. Ad for Teacher's scotch, *Life*, January 3, 1969; commercial for Heinz Spaghetti Sauce, n.d. [late 1960s], MT&R; commercial for Gillette razor blades, 1968, MT&R. The product's slogan was "The Spoiler."

19. Ads for Fritos Corn Chips, *Life*, May 17, 1968; L & M cigarettes, *Life*, February 14, 1969; Kellogg's Corn Flakes, *Life*, January 8, 1965.

20. Lois commercials, George Lois Presentation Reel, MT&R. Lois revived the "I Want My Maypo" line in the early 1980s for MTV, "I Want My MTV."

21. Foster Grants, see *Life*, May 10, 1968; ad for Scripto pens, *Life*, April 25, 1969; ad for Land Rover reprinted in *The Book of Gossage*, p. 181; commercial for Canada Dry Ginger Ale, 1967, Grey advertising reel, MT&R; ad for the *Wall Street Journal*, in *Life*, November 25, 1966.

22. Ad for House of Stuart scotch, *Life*, February 10, 1967.

23. Ads for Whirlpool, *Life*, November 17, 1967; Westclox, *Life*, March 7, 1969; Kitchen Aid dishwasher, *Life*, November 11, 1966.

24. The strategy seems especially curious given the actual retraction-ads that the FTC began requiring makers of deceptive advertising to produce in the early 1970s. Ads for Renault, *Life*, March 11 and October 7, 1966.

25. Ads for Chiquita banana, *Look*, August 9, 1966; Contac cold remedy, *Life*, November 3, 1967; Philco televisions, *Life*, March 8, 1968; GE dishwashers, *Life*, April 19, 1968; Pontiac, *Life*, June 26 and December 8, 1967.

26. Ads for Fiat, ("One look is better than ten thousands words of brainwashing") *Life*, December 11, 1964; Fidelity insurance, *Life*, December 23, 1966; Sanforized clothes, *Life*, September 29, 1967; Fisher stereo, *Life*, February 10, 1967.

27. Volvo ad, *Life*, January 18, 1963, ellipses in original.

28. Volvo ads, *Life*, October 16, 1964; April 21, 1967; April 10, 1964; February 21, 1964.

29. Volvo commercial, MT&R.

30. Volvo ads, *Life*, September 22, 1967; October 6, 1967; November 18, 1966. 1967 was also the year of the "paper dress," a short-lived fad that must have seemed foolish indeed to Volvo's target consumers.

31. Volvo ads, *Life*, June 12 and November 6, 1964.

32. Television commercial for Volvo, MT&R. The effectiveness and strategy of

the Volvo ads was explained in 1967, when the account was transferred from Carl Ally to Scali, McCabe, Sloves. "Marvin Sloves, agency president, talking about the campaign in an interview," *Advertising Age* reported, "said the Ally strategy was retained because it was a good one and had aided sales" (*Advertising Age*, September 18, 1967, p. 12). In 1970, the magazine reported that "the Swedish car manufacturer has been pushing longevity for several years, obviously with success, because the same theme is being used in the 1970 tv and print campaign" (*Advertising Age*, February 16, 1970, p. 3).

33. Television commercials for Volvo, MT&R.

34. This ad is reproduced in the *46th Annual of Advertising and Editorial Art and Design of the Art Director's Club of New York* (New York: Comet Press, 1967), n.p. As it ran in *Life* magazine (and as it is reproduced here in the gallery) this ad bore a slightly different headline and body copy, substituting "out of style" for "obsolete." Ad for Volvo, *Life*, September 30, 1966.

35. This commercial and the radio ad that follows are in the collections of the Museum of Television & Radio (MT&R), New York. Everyone in advertising is aware that Procter & Gamble are the single largest advertising spender in the nation; the moon's resemblance to its logo could hardly have been coincidence.

36. Ad for Camel cigarettes, *Life*, September 22, 1972.

37. Ads for Lark cigarettes, *Life*, November 5, 1965; Buick, *Life*, September 22, 1967, *Life*, October 10, 1969.

38. Ads for Coronet Brandy, *Life*, April 25, 1969; Day & Night air-conditioners, *Life*, May 9, 1969, Olivetti typewriters, *Life*, April 7, 1972.

39. Robert S. Berman, "You've Come a Long Way, Baby," *Madison Avenue*, February 1969, p. 6.

40. Laurel Cutler, "She's Doing Her Own Thing," *Madison Avenue*, May 1969, p. 29.

41. Advertisement for FDS, *Good Housekeeping*, January 1970. Ellipses and emphasis in original.

42. Advertisement for Massengill, *Good Housekeeping*, June 1970.

43. Advertisements for Pristeen, *Good Housekeeping*, February and June 1970. Pristeen's ads were particularly irksome to the feminist movement, which singled them out for censure in its various confrontations with the industry (*New York Times*, August 26, 1970, p. 44).

44. This advertisement is part of the J. Walter Thompson collection, Duke University.

45. Ibid. These ads ran in *Life* and *Look*, not *Ms*.

46. Virginia Slims television commercial (1968), Museum of Broadcast Communications. An interesting account of the development of this campaign is offered by Robert S. Berman, "You've Come a Long Way, Baby," *Madison Avenue*, February 1969. Needless to say, the campaign (and the brand) were wildly successful, and the slogan and feminist theme are still in use today.

47. See appendix.

48. Ads for Mustang, *Life*, January 15, 1965, p. 47, February 5, 1965, p. 93, March 19, 1965, p. 47; ad for Mercury Comet, *Life* November 5, 1965; ad for Plymouth Fury, *Life*, May 21, 1965; ad for Chevrolet Corvair, *Life*, November 5, 1965. Mustang's ads were particularly noteworthy; they were done by J. Walter Thompson.

49. Oldsmobile commercials in the collections of the Museum of Television & Radio (MT&R), New York.

notes

50. Ibid.

51. Oldsmobile ad, *Life*, October 13, 1967. Oldsmobile television commercial, Museum of Broadcast Communications.

52. This commercial is part of the holdings at the Museum of Television & Radio.

53. Ad for Oldsmobile, *Life*, October 11, 1968. This ad promised "escape" in, of all things, a massive and respectable Olds 98. Ad for Oldsmobile, *Esquire*, March 1969.

54. Oldsmobile ads, *Life*, October 3 and November 7, 1969. In ads today, of course, computers are devices of liberation, not of office slavery.

55. Charles Brower, chairman of the board of BBDO, quoted in Navasky, "Advertising Is a Science?" p. 172.

56. Dodge print ads in *Life*, October 8 and November 5, 1965; Dodge 1967 television commercials in the collections of the Museum of Television & Radio (MT&R), New York; ad for Dodge, *Look*, November 15, 1966. As usual, the agency responsible for the Dodge Rebellion, in this case BBDO (who also invented the Pepsi Generation), claimed the campaign to be extremely successful. "In two different awareness studies the commercials have had the highest ratings of any automobile campaigns. It's the most successful television campaign for automobiles in years" ("The Rebel," *Madison Avenue*, June 1966, pp. 39–41).

57. These Dodge Fever commercials are in the holdings of the Museum of Television & Radio.

58. Ibid.

59. Ibid. This brief vignette of hipster and Southern policeman is also interesting in the way it bridges the various characterizations of the running battle between these two great symbolic foes. It stands somewhere between the dark portrayal of *Easy Rider* and the later, more lightsome pageants of *Smokey and the Bandit*, *Eat My Dust*, *The Dukes of Hazard*, and the various other films and television shows of the 1970s in which the hipster easily twitted the Man.

60. Pontiac television commercials in the holdings of the Museum of Television & Radio. The commercial ends responsibly, showing the robbers driving their Pontiac station wagon into a building marked "Police Garage," from whence a burst of gunfire is heard.

61. Pontiac ad, *Life*, October 11, 1968. Pontiac television commercial, MT&R.

62. GTO television commercial, 1969, MT&R. "The Humbler's" print ads extended the car's menace to nature, Pontiac's usual adversary, announcing, "Hill, lay low" and "Curve, straighten out" (Pontiac ad, *Life*, October 3, 1969).

63. Young people between the ages of thirteen and twenty-two accounted for fully 55 percent of soda sales. As quoted in Sam B. Vitt, "Media and the Youth Market," *Madison Avenue*, June 1967, p. 40.

64. Television commercial for Dr. Pepper, 1970, MT&R.

65. Dr. Pepper commercial, Museum of Broadcast Communications (MBC), Chicago. This commercial dates from the 1970s.

66. Television commercial for Dr. Pepper, n.d. (mid-1970s), MT&R.

67. John Furr of J. Walter Thompson, interviewed by Thomas Frank, July 6, 1993, at his office in Chicago. Mr. Furr is presently Worldwide Director of Training for JWT.

68. 7-Up ads in J. Walter Thompson collection, Duke University library.

69. John Furr interview with author, July 6, 1993.

70. Ibid.

71. 7-Up ads in JWT collection, Duke University library. The Uncola billboards were so popular that the company actually sold reproductions of them.
72. 7-Up television commercials in archives of J. Walter Thompson Company, Chicago.
73. Ibid. Promotional "Unside Down" glasses were sold by 7-Up during the 1970s.
74. The Uncola campaign was very successful. JWT claimed that 7-Up sales increased fully 20 percent after the campaign broke in 1968. From 1968 to 1972, 7-Up sales grew 17.6 percent, faster than either Coke or Pepsi. Percentages obtained from intraoffice memoranda dated ca. 1976 at the J. Walter Thompson Company in Chicago; photocopies in collection of author.

chapter eight

1. Phil Dusenberry, who worked on Pepsi advertising in the 1960s for BBDO, explains: "It's a product that no one really needs. The difference in terms of quality is purely a matter of perception. And creating that perception is difficult. It isn't like you have a distinct product difference. . . . So it's very difficult to stake out a position for any soft drink other than an imagery position, which is what we've done" (Phil Dusenberry, interviewed by Dr. Scott Ellsworth in New York, December 11, 1984). Recording of the interview is in the collection of the Archives Center, National Museum of American History (NMAH).

In 1980, *Advertising Age* estimated that Pepsi had spent some $345 million placing their advertising message since the advent of the Pepsi Generation in 1962. See James P. Forkan, "Pepsi Generation Bridges Two Decades," *Advertising Age*, May 5, 1980, p. 43.

2. Roger Enrico, president of the Pepsi-Cola Bottling Company, wrote in 1986, "We spend [those millions] so carefully—and agonize so much over the creation of these commercials—that it may seem . . . as if Pepsi is a company that creates advertising, and oh, by the way, we make soft drinks too." See Roger Enrico and Jesse Kornbluth, *The Other Guy Blinked: How Pepsi Won the Cola Wars* (New York: Bantam Books, 1986), pp. 15–16.

Bill Backer of McCann-Erickson, Coca-Cola's advertising agency, is quoted in J. C. Louis and Harvey Z. Yazijian's book *The Cola Wars* as declaring, "The product of the Coca-Cola company is not Coca-Cola—that makes itself. The product of the Coca-Cola Company is advertising" (*The Cola Wars* [New York: Everest House, Publishers, 1980], p. 148).

3. The years of the slogan "The Taste that Beats the Others Cold" (1967–69) and the famous "Pepsi Challenge" (1975–83), in which the product's superiority to Coke were the focus have been the only major exceptions to this pattern.

4. James P. Forkan, "Pepsi Generation Bridges Two Decades," *Advertising Age*, May 5, 1980, p. 43.

5. Enrico does this (*The Other Guy Blinked*, p. 86), as does Tom Dillon, president of BBDO, in an interview conducted May 23, 1984, by Dr. Scott Ellsworth. Recording in the Archives Center of the National Museum of American History (NMAH).

6. Allen Rosenshine, interviewed by Dr. Scott Ellsworth, New York, December 10, 1984. Recording in collection of Archives Center, NMAH.

7. Pepsi advertisement, c. 1961–63, in the Archives Center, NMAH. My emphasis.

notes

8. Pepsi advertisement for *Ebony* magazine, c. 1961–63, Archives Center, NMAH.

9. Forkan, "Pepsi Generation Bridges Two Decades," p. 43. Elsewhere he cites these famous statistics: "To confirm its claim that the 'Pepsi Generation' defines an attitude more than an age group, Pepsi execs quote research indicating that 62 percent of men and women aged 13 to 24 identified with the Pepsi generation description—but so did 43 percent of those aged 35 to 49, the youth market of past decades" (p. 43).

10. Rosenshine interviewed by Dr. Scott Ellsworth, New York, December 10, 1984. Recording in collection of Archives Center, NMAH.

11. This awareness is such that the two companies' advertising in fact forms "one integral symbolic network." See Louis and Yazijian, *The Cola Wars*, p. 241.

12. Dillon, interview conducted May 23, 1984, by Dr. Scott Ellsworth. Recording in the Archives Center of the National Museum of American History (NMAH).

13. Louis and Yazijian, *The Cola Wars*, pp. 233–34.

14. Tedlow, *New and Improved*.

15. Enrico and Kornbluth, *The Other Guy Blinked*, p. 16.

16. Transcript of John Bergin interview by Dr. Scott Ellsworth, February 6, 1985. Archives Center, NMAH, n.p.

17. Alan Pottasch, in speech recorded on Pepsi-Cola Co. publicity videotape, "Development of Pepsi Advertising."

18. Ibid.

19. Forkan, "Pepsi Generation Bridges Two Decades," p. 41. Enrico explains the 1983 revival of the Pepsi Generation in this way: "(W)e'd put Pepsi on the leading edge of what was happening. And we'd show that leading edge through the eyes of youth. Not just for teenagers—we'd appeal to everyone, using young people as the vehicle. They're fun; they're exciting; they're innovative" (Enrico and Kornbluth, *The Other Guy Blinked*, p. 86).

20. Tom Anderson, interviewed by Dr. Scott Ellsworth, New York, November 14, 1984. Recording in collections of Archives Center, NMAH.

21. John Bergin, one-time vice president of BBDO (now vice chairman of McCann-Erickson Worldwide), referred to "The Sociables" in 1985 as "a terrifying flop" that "concoct(ed) kind of a caste system . . . ": "Every snob in the country was portrayed in that advertising" (John Bergin, transcript of interview by Dr. Scott Ellsworth, February 6, 1985. Archives Center, NMAH, n.p.).

22. "Think Young" ads in the collection of the Archives Center of the NMAH.

23. "Come Alive!" ads in the collection of the Archives Center of the NMAH.

24. Louis and Yazijian, *The Cola Wars*, p. 235.

25. Quoted in Forkan, "Pepsi Generation Bridges Two Decades," p. 41.

26. Pepsi ads, NMAH.

27. "Rope Swing" and "Surf Football" ads from "Taste That Beats the Others Cold" campaign in the collection of the Archives Center of the NMAH. Others from the Museum of Broadcast Communications, Chicago.

28. This commercial is in the collections of the Museum of Broadcast Communications, Chicago.

29. Transcript of John Bergin interview, NMAH.

30. Ibid.

31. Print ad from the collection of the Archives Center of the NMAH.

32. PepsiCo, *Media Ordering Catalog* for 1970 (n.p., n.d. [1969?]), n.p. In the collection of the Archives Center of the NMAH.

33. "Live/Give" commercials in the collection of the Archives Center of the
NMAH.
34. Transcript of John Bergin interview.

chapter nine

1. René König, A La Mode: On the Social Psychology of Fashion (New York: Seabury Press, 1973), pp. 78, 157–58.
2. "Traditionally Conservative": Leonard Sloane, New York Times, August 29, 1965, p. 14F. "Epatez me again, baby": Irving Howe, "New Styles in 'Leftism,'" reprinted in Selected Writings 1950–1990 (New York: Harcourt Brace Jovanovich, 1990), pp. 205–6.
3. "Male Plumage '68," Newsweek, November 25, 1968, p. 70.
4. "The Guys Go All-out to Get Gawked At," Life, May 13, 1966, p. 81.
5. GQ, September 1971, p. 16.
6. "Sociology of Fashion," Fortune, July 1952, p. 56.
7. As quoted in "Editor's Corner," Men's Wear, September 4, 1959, p. 22. Ellipses in original. Men's Wear is hereafter referred to as "MW."
8. GQ, February 1965, p. 84.
9. Daily News Record, January 14, 1966, pp. 4–5; Henry Roth, president of Louis Roth clothiers, quoted in Daily News Record, January 10, 1966, p. 32. Emphasis in original.
10. Jason McCloskey, "Aquarius Rising," GQ, March 1970, p. 115.
11. "Off the Cuff," GQ, September 1966, p. 13.
12. Ellen Stewart, quoted in MW, February 24, 1967, p. 81. Italics in original.
13. Daily News Record, March 1, 1967, p. 10.
14. MW, August 23, 1968, p. 109.
15. MW, July 12, July 26, 1968. This may have been another Fairchild hype.
16. Cf. MW, April 11, May 9, and July 11, 1969.
17. Cf. MW, February 6 and March 6, 1970.
18. Daily News Record, January 31, 1972, p. 1.
19. MW, June 25, 1971, pp. 59, 72. These are, of course, only the highest-profile items to be discussed in trade magazines: each publication also carried photographs and descriptions of dozens of even less mainstream clothes.
20. Daily News Record, January 10, 1972, p. 6.
21. Sanford Josephson, "Peacock Is Alive and Well and Still Struts Its Stuff," Daily News Record, March 14, 1972, pp. 1, 16.
22. Roland Barthes, The Fashion System, translated by Matthew Ward and Richard Howard (Berkeley, CA: University of California Press, 1990).
23. See especially Fred Davis, Fashion, Culture, and Identity (Chicago: University of Chicago Press, 1992), p. 16; and Alison Lurie, The Language of Clothes (New York: Random House, 1981), p. 11.
24. "Certainly the fashion industry might like us to throw away all our clothes each year and buy a whole new wardrobe," writes Alison Lurie, "but it has never been able to achieve this goal" (Lurie, The Language of Clothes, p. 11). Lurie's example is the "maxiskirt," a flop that was promoted heavily by none other than the Fairchild company during the late 1960s; Fred Davis's is the "midi look," which was promoted during the same period by the same people. See Davis, Fashion, Culture, and Identity, p. 12n.
25. Mod, for example, was so wildly overpromoted, that, as Jason McCloskey later recounted, "In January and February of 1966, Daily News Record played a daily

notes

game of trying to figure out another new way to use the word Mod in the boldest typeface possible in about 75 feature articles" (McCloskey, "Aquarius Rising," p. 114).

26. *New York Times*, February 8, 1970, section 3, p. 17.

27. *New York Times*, August 1, 1965, section 3, p. 1.

28. *New York Times*, January 17, 1966, p. 130. au: p. no. correct?

29. Nora Ephron, "The Man in the Bill Blass Suit," *New York Times*, December 8, 1968, section 6, p. 52.

30. See *New York Times*, April 1, 1968, p. 73.

31. *New York Times*, November 12, 1967, section 3, p. 5.

32. Leonard Sloane, "Clothes Make the Man Spend More This Year," *New York Times*, February 2, 1969, section 3, p. 9.

33. Quinn Meyer, interviewed by Thomas Frank over the telephone, January 24, 1993.

34. Advertisement for J & F Dateline Suits, GQ, February 1965, p. 10. "And even if you don't like them . . . at least you'll know what everyone else will be wearing," the ad maintained.

35. MW, May 13, 1966, p. 93.

36. "No More Seasons," MW, March 6, 1970, p. 106.

37. Leonard Sloane, "Men's Clothing Surge Is Seen by Producers," *New York Times*, August 5, 1972, p. 31.

38. Amy Teplin, "Boutique-ing," MW, August 7, 1970, pp. 82, 83. Emphasis in original.

39. Ibid., p. 82. In June 1970, New York hosted the first "Boutique Show," a convention that brought together hundreds of small shop-owners and the various manufacturers aiming at vanguard consumers. Four years later, *Men's Wear* still remembered this event as a "spectacular . . . success," a "wild scene," "tremendously exciting." The show, which was held annually for years afterwards, was often cited as an important influence on the buying decisions of larger retailers.

40. Leonard Sloane, "Men's Wear Looks to Knits," *New York Times*, January 30, 1972, section 3, p. 3. But even then, it should be noted, manufacturers and retailers were hoping that new fashions would bring them out of the slump.

41. Malcolm C. McMaster, letter to the Financial Editor, *New York Times*, October 25, 1970, section 3, page 14. McMaster's grumblings are similar to the academic "conspiracy theories" of fashion blasted by Davis and Lurie. It is unclear, though, whether McMaster was an academic.

42. Jack Hyde, "Rubin Bros. of Montreal," MW, July 23, 1971, pp. 72–73.

43. Quinn Meyer, interviewed by Thomas Frank over the telephone, January 24, 1993.

44. Hyde, "Rubin Bros. of Montreal," MW. Meyer estimates the standard industry delivery time at six to nine months.

chapter ten

1. Charles Reich, *The Greening of America* (New York: Random House, 1970), pp. 251–52; 255.

2. Todd Gitlin, *The Sixties: Years of Hope, Days of Rage* (New York: Bantam Books, 1987), pp. 345, 346.

3. Ad for Dexter shoes, MW, March 18, 1966, p. 9. This ad, like most that appeared in the trade press, were industry ads aimed mainly at retailers.

4. Ad for Gulf Stream Slacks, MW, March 18, 1966, p. 57.

5. Ad for Big Yank Utility Apparel, MW, March 18, 1966, p. 27.

6. Strangely enough, this Hat Corporation ad is undeniably a product of the Creative Revolution. Its copy contains standard DDB techniques: it not only asks some readers to "stop reading right now" in the first sentence, but it jokes about the "deeply ingrained" preferences of executives ("there's no denying that they're in charge. So it pays to humor them."). It is a remarkable document of a commercial culture in transition. The ad appeared in *Life* magazine, March 17, 1961, and is reproduced in this volume's photo gallery. The sixties were hard on the American hat industry. As a 1970 *Business Week* article on the declining fortunes of the Stetson hat company noted, "men just do not wear hats as much as they used to." In the immediate postwar years, the article pointed out, "Stetson's volume was still 1,200 dozen hats daily. Now production is believed to be about 70 dozen felt and straw hats a day" (*Business Week*, December 19, 1970, p. 40).

7. Stan Gellers, "Fashion" column, MW, December 22, 1967, p. 12. Ellipses and emphasis in original.

8. Ibid.

9. Stan Gellers, "Fashion," MW, June 21, 1968, p. 16.

10. "Clothing Shaped for the 70s," MW, February 6, 1970, p. 124.

11. MW, February 11, 1972, p. 147.

12. MW, June 7, 1968, p. 84.

13. MW, June 21, 1968, p. 33; July 26, 1968, pp. 53–56.

14. GQ, September 1968, pp. 88–89.

15. MW, June 25, 1971, p. 59, Amy Teplin, "To Suit Boutiques," MW, June 25, 1971, p. 72.

16. Advertisements for Monte Cristo suits, GQ, March 1965, p. 39; February 1965, p. 51; April 1965, p. 25; Summer 1966, pp. 46–47.

17. Advertisement from GQ, February 1967, p. 115.

18. Advertisement for Tyson shirts, GQ, March 1968, pp. 20–21.

19. Ad for Lamplighter, MW, March 14, 1969, pp. 98–99.

20. Ads for Resilio and Harbor Master, GQ, March 1969, pp. 39, 45.

21. Ad for Phoenix Clothes, MW, September 19, 1969, p. 3.

22. Ad for Moss shirtmakers, MW, September 19, 1969, p. 77. Ellipsis in original.

23. Ad for Kodel polyester, MW, September 19, 1969, p. 51.

24. Ad for Dacron polyester, MW, March 28, 1969, pp. 40–41.

25. Ad for "The Pipe," GQ, Summer 1970, p. 26.

26. "11th Hour," MW, September 5, 1969, pp. 15–16.

27. The Sero shirt is pictured in GQ, February 1970, p. 33; ad for Interwoven socks, MW, March 18, 1966, inside front cover; ad for "WeatheRogues" overcoats, GQ, March 1968, p. 64.

28. In *Esquire*, George Frazier pointed to the Beatles, from their collarless look of 1964 (their suits had been designed by Pierre Cardin) to the colorful Sgt. Pepper era, as the most influential shapers of "the male appearance" since Beau Brummel. "What the Beatles seem to have accomplished," he wrote, "is a shaking of the stability, of the basic sameness over the decades, of male styles." See "The Peacock Revolution," *Esquire*, October 1968, pp. 207, 209. A 1971 "GQ, Inquiry" entitled "American Discovery" described the mechanism of youth's fashion leadership in more committed and ideological terms: "New design for the Seventies—and beyond—emanates from a decidedly volatile generation to be worn by the men who don't necessarily share its age but its attitudes and life-styles." See "American Discovery," GQ, February 1971, p. 62.

notes

29. Nora Ephron, "The Man in the Bill Blass Suit," *New York Times*, December 8, 1968, section 6, p. 52–192. Emphasis in original.

Quinn Meyer points to the same figure—a middle-aged, self-made man—as the central consumer of the Peacock Revolution. Meyer paraphrases one of his colleagues who "used to say the quintessential clothing customer is not a hip young guy; it's a fifty-year-old man who's got the mortgage paid off, the kids out of college . . . and he went out and bought a Cadillac convertible, and he's out for his last piece of strange. This is the guy who is the clothing customer" (Meyer interview, January 24, 1993).

30. Interview with Richard Ohrbach, *Daily News Record*, January 13, 1966, pp. 4–5.

31. MW, June 9, 1967, pp. 42, 51.

32. "The Toiletries Boom: Think Young To Succeed," MW, November 17, 1967, p. 28.

33. "Now Fashion," MW, February 10, 1967, p. 13. Ellipsis in original.

34. "Traditionals Again Lead the Way," MW, March 14, 1969, p. 42.

35. Kevan Pickens, "Etcetera," MW, June 30, 1967, p. 42.

36. Ad for Stetson Hats, MW, July 28, 1967, p. 3.

37. Ad for Kazoo pants, *Daily News Record*, March 16, 1967, section 2, p. 14.

38. Ad for Petrocelli Sport Coats, GQ, Summer 1968, p. 60.

39. Ad for Jantzen, MW, March 14, 1969, p. 52.

40. Ads for Anvil Brand Slacks, MW, March 14, 1969, pp. 186–87; MW, September 19, 1969, p. 50. The youngster says, "Man, like I dig those spaced out threads to cover my bod and I got to know where they're at." He wears collar-length hair, a scarf, a shirt with extremely long collar points and five buttons on the cuff, bell-bottoms, pointed shoes, and a very wide belt.

41. Ad for Jockey sportswear, GQ, October 1969, pp. 18–19. Here, as with advertising, examples of the industry's infatuation with counterculture can be piled up almost limitlessly.

42. Ad for Male slacks, MW, September 25, 1970, p. 16D.

43. Ad for Lee slacks, MW, February 20, 1970, p. 8.

44. Ad for Hickok belts, MW, June 11, 1971, p. 29.

45. Ad for Tads pants, MW, October 9, 1970, p. 130.

46. Ads for "Expressions" by Campus, MW, October 9, 1970, p. 65; MW, April 3, 1970, p. 66.

47. GQ, February 1970, front cover.

48. GQ, March 1970, front cover.

49. GQ, February 1971, front cover; p. 59; pp. 120–24.

50. GQ, September 1971, p. 141.

51. McCloskey, "Aquarius Rising," GQ, March 1970, p. 107.

52. Ibid., p. 117.

53. Ibid., p. 107.

54. Ibid.

55. John Golden, "The Stoned Seventies: Clothes Are as Turned On as Heads," GQ, October 1970, pp. 36, 38.

56. GQ, September 1970, pp. 82, 95.

57. "Publisher's Point," GQ, September 1970, p. 79.

58. "The Fashion Activist," GQ, September 1970, p. 82.

59. Barry van Lenten, "Aftermath of the Designer Conquest," GQ, October 1970, p. 103.

60. McCloskey, "Aquarius Rising," p. 108.

61. Ibid., p. 109.

62. Golden, "Stoned Fashion," p. 38.

63. John D. Golden, "The Formula for Fashionable Fashion," GQ, Summer 1970, pp. 18–20.

64. Thomas M. Disch, "The Corporate Guerrilla," GQ, March 1971, pp. 92–157.

65. Lurie, The Language of Clothes, photo caption, p. 158.

66. "At Home," GQ, March 1971, n.p.

chapter eleven

1. "A New Era: 'Creativity' Plus Plain Talk," Business Week, February 20, 1971, p. 72. On the prize competitions, see New York Times, January 15, 1971, p. 26.

2. On the FTC (which quarreled particularly with Ted Bates, Rosser Reeves's old agency), see the New York Times, March 30, 1971, p. 55. On the NOW, see May 28, 1972, section 6, p. 12.

3. A Chicago menswear retailer with more than fifty years of experience in the field told me in 1993 that cycles of obsolescence in menswear manufacturing were then running to three years. Before the 1960s, by contrast, new models required five to seven years to be obsoleted by manufacturers.

4. Amy Teplin, "Boutique Show Time: Revving Up Those Fabulous Fifties," Men's Wear, May 21, 1971, p. 107.

5. Nor has the bitterness with which the more practical admen regarded the creatives ever entirely dissipated. The Wall Street Journal for April 8, 1997, carries a front-page story of how an ultracreative, rule-smashing, paradigm-questioning advertising campaign made by Chiat/Day for Nissan won all sorts of awards while Nissan sales plummeted. "More than ever before," the Journal asserts, in a line that it might well have printed in 1968 or 1969, "agencies are scrambling to make ads that create a buzz but have little to do with the products their clients sell" (p. 1).

6. French advertising executive Jean-Marie Dru, one of the most fervid ideologues of the marketplace revolution continues to pay homage to Bernbach and Wells in his recent book Disruption (New York: John Wiley & Sons, 1996), pp. 37. But then, Dru's agency, BDDP, now owns Wells, Rich, Greene. Likewise, Karen Stabiner describes how one of Chiat/Day's executives had worked at DDB during the 1960s "and it was the seminal fact of his professional life, the credit that informed everything he did." See Karen Stabiner, Inventing Desire: Inside Chiat/Day, the Hottest Shop, the Coolest Players, the Big Business of Advertising (New York: Simon & Schuster, 1993), pp. 50, 51.

7. Rochelle Gurstein, The Repeal of Reticence (New York: Hill and Wang, 1996), p. 6.

8. Abbie Hoffman, Steal This Book (New York: Pirate Editions, 1971), p. v.

9. Abbie Hoffman, The Best of Abbie Hoffman (New York: Four Walls Eight Windows, 1989), p. 189.

10. Alice Embree, "Madison Avenue Brainwashing—The Facts," in Sisterhood Is Powerful: An Anthology of Writings from the Women's Liberation Movement, edited by Robin Morgan (New York: Vintage, 1970), p. 201.

11. Stuart Ewen makes a similar argument about the consumerism of the twenties. Consumer culture has served business not only by creating demand to match productive capacities; it has also redirected intensely anticapitalist reform movements down a decidedly nonthreatening path. The emerging consumerism of the 1920s, he writes, "tended to define protest and proletarian unrest in terms of the desire to

consume. . . ." As advertisements "cleaved all basis for discontent from the industrial context and focused that discontent within realms that offered no challenge to corporate hegemony, they created a vision of social amelioration that depended on adherence to the authority of capitalistic enterprise." See Stuart Ewen, *Captains of Consciousness: Advertising and the Social Roots of the Consumer Culture* (New York: McGraw Hill, 1976), pp. 28, 109.

12. Mark Crispin Miller, *Boxed In: The Culture of TV* (Evanston, IL: Northwestern University Press, 1988), pp. 14, 324, 15.

13. Daniel Bell, *The Cultural Contradictions of Capitalism* (New York: Basic Books, 1978), pp. 71–72.

14. *New York Times*, September 16, 1996, p. D9.

15. *Business Week*, December 14, 1992; *Advertising Age*, February 1, 1993, p. 16.

16. *Business Week*, December 14, 1992.

index

account executives, 35; in corporate-style agencies, 78, 100; in Creative Revolution of the sixties, 96–97; as WASPs, 96

Adams, John A., 116, 122

Adler, Lee, 116–17

advertising: advertisements of the sixties, 132–67; advertising industry denounced in, 144; anti-advertising, 55, 68; antithetical cultural poles in, 38–39, 47; as art, 56–57, 93; and business revolution of the sixties, 26; central themes of, in the sixties, 136; conformity mocked in sixties', 136–40; on the counterculture, 27, 108–11, 119–23; counterculture in contemporary, 4–5; the counterculture mistrusting, 108; creativity in, 37, 39, 41–42, 50, 88–103, 227; critique of itself, 9, 41; cultural change caused by and reflected in, 31; Federal Trade Commission actions, 225; and Generation X, 233–34; growth during the sixties, 91; and high culture, 36; hip ads as percentage of all ads, 237–43; hip advertisements before 1965, 133–34; hip as staple of, 32; and hip consumerism, 26–28; the hip despising, 107; mass society

criticized in, 55, 76; National Organization of Women accusations, 225; in the nineties, 53, 227; nonconformity recognized by, 89–90, 94; Vance Packard on, 11, 40–41, 45, 62, 75, 209; primary cultural function of, 49; science as principle of, 39–47; self-reference in, 65, 70; silent majority of youth ignored by, 109; skepticism toward, 63, 226, 234; spokesmen, 71–72, 141–42; subliminals in, 31, 250n. 9; before World War II, 133; worst ads as those of the fifties, 47–50; youth culture mocked in, 148–51. *See also* advertising agencies; Creative Revolution in advertising

Advertising Age (magazine), 44, 96, 120, 124, 225

advertising agencies: boutiques, 97, 198; Della Femina on corporate-style, 78–79; dress at, 42; establishment agencies, 100–103; extra-environmental man, 77; firing practices at, 79; as hip places, 35; hot shops, 97; hottest agencies of eighties and nineties, 28; image in the fifties, 35–38, 48, 53, 54; image in the nineties, 53; profit margins of, 91; small, creative agen-

advertising agencies (*continued*) cies appearing, 91, 97–98; and three-martini lunches, 35, 42; traditional relationship with clients, 58–59, 84; women in, 249n. 1; youth culture as obsession of, 35; youth culture at, 111–15. *See also* account executives; art directors; copywriters; *and agencies by name*

Advertising Writers Association of New York (AWANY), 92

affluent society, the, 10, 76

Affluent Society, The (Galbraith), 11

Agee, James, 21

alcoholic beverages: Booth's House of Lords gin, 138–39; Calvert Whiskey ads by DDB, 70; Chivas Regal, 70; Coronet brandy, 151; Gilbey's gin, 135; Gordon's gin, 135; House of Stuart scotch, 142–43; Irish Whiskey, 77, 255n. 5; as marker of the generation gap, 135; martinis drunk by admen, 35, 42; Smirnoff vodka, 135, 139–40; Teacher's scotch, 140; Wolfschmidt vodka, 135

Alka-Seltzer: DDB spot for, 72, 225, 254n. 51; as Jack Tinker client, 101; WRG ads for, 124, 126–27, 128

Ally, Carl, 83, 97, 99, 144, 227, 263n. 32

American Motors, 127–28

American Tobacco, 37

American Tourister, 69

Anacin, 44

Anderson, Tom, 173

Annuals of Advertising Art, 105

anti-advertising, 55, 68

antinomianism: in advertising agencies of the mid-1960s, 93, 94, 97; in consumerism, 121; in DDB advertising, 56–57; in Lois's advertising, 80; sartorial, 210

antispokesmen, 141–42

Anvil Brand slacks, 216, 270n. 40

appliances: Carrier air-conditioners, 239; Fisher stereos, 144; hip ads as percentage of all ads, 237, 240, 242; Whirlpool, 143

art directors: in assembly-line method, 100; and copywriters at DDB, 57, 58, 252n. 13; in Creative Revolution of the sixties, 96–97; and scientific advertising, 39, 40, 46, 47; young people as, 111–12

Art Directors' Club of New York, 105

Art of Advertising, The (Lois), 81

automobiles: ads for Big Three cars, 61–62, 157; American Motors ads by WRG, 127–28; annual design changes, 61, 62, 64; Buick ads, 61, 66, 151; in consumer society, 61; Datsun commercials with Dali, 138; Dodge ads, 61, 159–61, 264nn. 56, 59; foreign car ads denouncing advertising, 144; hip advertising for, 133, 237, 238, 239, 241; Land Rover ads by Gossage, 142; Mustang ads, 157, 263n. 48; National Steel ads on buying American, 140; Nissan ads by Chiat/Day, 271n. 5; Oldsmobile ads, 61, 137, 157–59; Pontiac ads, 144, 161–63, 264nn. 60, 62; Renault scare-headline ads, 143; sixties advertising for, 156–63; as status symbols, 64–65; tailfins, 11, 61, 62, 67; Volvo ads, 144–48, 262n. 32; youth-oriented image transformation for, 109–10. *See also* Volkswagen

Avis Rent-a-Car, 23, 59, 64, 70–71, 254n. 49

baby boom, 27, 118, 124, 233, 234

Bach, Henry, 188–89

Backer, Bill, 171–72

Baker, Stephen, 112, 120

Balanoff, Clem, 245n. 6

Barnes, Fred, 2

Barney's Men's Store, 137

Barthes, Roland, 193

Bates, Ted. *See* Ted Bates Company

BBDO: Dodge ads, 159–61, 264nn. 56, 59; Pepsi-Cola ads, 170–83; youth study of 1966, 120

BDDP, 271n. 6

beads, 187, 191

Beatles, The: advertising people as fans of, 113; in counterculture development, 8; fashion influence of, 187, 190, 269n. 28; liberal cultural leaders on, 13; and the Pepsi Generation, 177

beatniks, 209, 211
Beats, the: as antecedent of the sixties, 15, 247n. 31; as consumerist, 29; contrarian sentiment in, 5
Beck, Julian, 53
Bell, Daniel, 11–12, 21, 232, 249n. 62, 252n. 6
bell bottoms (flared trousers), 191, 207
Benson & Hedges, 64, 124, 126, 127, 261n. 65
Benton & Bowles, 102
Bergin, John, 172, 179–80, 182–83, 266n. 21
Berman, Marshall, 30
Bernays, Edward L., 40
Bernbach, Bill, 55–60; on advertising as art, 56–57; on agency-client relations, 58–59; as angry young man, 111; anti-advertising invented by, 55; creative team system of, 57, 98; on creativity, 89; as Jewish, 68; nineties admen paying homage to, 227; rules opposed by, 56, 57, 80; technocracy opposed by, 56
Black Panthers, in Forrest Gump, 4
Blass, Bill, 213–14, 226
Bloom, Allan, 1–2, 3
Bogart, Leo, 108–9
bohemia: countercultural change in, 6; the counterculture as distinct from preceding, 8; counterculture as massification of, 29; in Gingrich's account of the counterculture, 3; Mailer's democratization of, 13
Bonnie and Clyde (movie), 16, 161–62
boomers, 27, 118, 124, 233, 234
Booth's House of Lords gin, 138–39
Bork, Robert, 2, 3, 245n. 2
boutique ad agencies, 97, 198
boutique retailing, 198, 199, 268n. 39
Braniff, 124, 138, 141
Bronfman, Samuel, 99
Buick, 61, 66, 151
Burlington Mid-Length Socks, 71–72
Burnett, Leo: on the "Critical Generation," 108, 109, 258n. 8; Virginia Slims campaign, 155–56
Burroughs, William S., 4
business: attire of business men, 188, 221; "corporate revolutionaries,"

5; on the counterculture as hopeful sign, 9; creativity crisis in, 22; finding what it wants in youth culture, 234–35; and hip as irreconcilable, 18; hip used by, 230–33; lifestyle experimentation encouraged by, 123; rebellion used by, 31, 249n. 62; revolution in during the sixties, 25–26, 28; in standard myth of counterculture, 6–7; as supplanting all independent culture, 18. See also advertising; capitalism; fashion

Cadwell, Franchellie, 105
Callaway, James, 84
Calvert Whiskey, 70
Camel cigarettes, 150–51
Campbell-Ewald, 114
Campbell's Pork and Beans, 71
Campus "Expressions" line, 217
Canada Dry, 142
Candler, Asa, 170
capitalism: conformity as required by, 18; the counterculture opposing, 6; and critique of mass society, 232; as dynamic, 19; enthusiasm for nonconformity in the sixties, 90–91; fashion as bulwark of late, 185; and hip as fundamentally opposed to, 17, 18; hip as official capitalist style, 224–35; hip capitalism, 26; information capitalism, 29; materialism of, 11. See also business; mass (society) culture; technocracy
Cardin, Pierre, 189, 269n. 28
Carl Ally, 83, 97, 99, 144, 227, 263n. 32
Carnaby street, 190
cars. See automobiles
Carson, Johnny, 191
Case, Gene, 112, 115
Cassini, Oleg, 191
CBS, 86
Certs, 79–80
chains, 187, 191
Charles, Ray, 173
Chiat, Jay, 53
Chiat/Day: advertising's boundaries expanded by, 97; Nissan ad, 271n. 5; Reebok ads, 137, 254n. 1, 262n. 10; workplace madness at, 53

Chiquita bananas, 144
Chivas Regal, 70
cigarettes: Benson & Hedges, 64, 124, 126, 127, 239, 261n. 65; Camels, 150–51; hip ads as percentage of all ads, 237, 238, 239, 242; Larks, 151; Lucky Strikes, 37, 140, 152; Parliaments, 239; Tareytons, 140; Viceroys, 44; Virginia Slims, 155–56, 239, 263n. 46
Cincinnati, 221
civility, 2
Clairol: DDB campaign for, 137, 255n. 1, 262n. 10; FCB campaigns for, 257n. 32; "Great Beige-In," 134
Closing of the American Mind, The (Bloom), 1–2
Coca-Cola, 169–70; in "Cola Wars," 24, 169; hegemony of, 169; image in Pepsi advertising, 170–73; "It's the Real Thing," 179; Kesey's bus in advertising of, 4; marketing paradigm of, 169, 172; and market segmentation, 24; rock music resisted by, 171–72; sixties advertisement for, 133; as symbol of all things American, 170; "Things Go Better With Coke," 176
"Cola Wars," 168–83; as war of symbols, 24. *See also* Coca-Cola; Pepsi-Cola
Colgate toothpaste, 44, 45
Columbia Records' "But the Man Can't Bust Our Music" ad, 7–8, 134, 246n. 12
Communists, 140–41, 142
Cone, Fairfax, 249n. 3, 257n. 32
Confessions of an Advertising Man (Ogilvy), 45–47
conformity: advertising of the sixties mocking, 136–40; advertising recognizing nonconformity, 89–90, 94; business as deploring, 9, 25; capitalism as requiring, 18; capitalist enthusiasm for nonconformity in the sixties, 90–91; creativity as nonconformist rebellion, 90; creativity crisis in business, 22; GQ reader as nonconformist, 189; groupthink, 49, 59, 60; heterodoxy becoming conformist, 252n. 6; in mass society, 10–13; menswear industry opposing, 209; organization man, 10, 11, 21–22, 38; revolt as negation of, 228; and scientific management, 20–21
conservatives, on the sixties, 2–3
consumer cynicism, 126
consumerism: advertising portraying as a fraud, 136, 151; the automobile in, 61; Bernbach harnessing public mistrust of, 55; competitive pressure as driving, 139; in the counterculture, 29–31, 121–23; DDB's critique of, 68–69; distancing products from, 68; feminist critique of, 230; hedonism of, 230, 232; hip as essentially, 30; Hoffman's countercultural view of, 229–30; as popular will, 151; status quest in, 142; of the twenties, 271n. 11; unrestraint required for, 19, 232; Volkswagen ads as critique of, 65–66; the youth market, 118–23. *See also* hip consumerism
co-optation theory, 7–8; advertisers speaking like the young rather than to them, 121; advertising industry as co-optive, 27, 106; and binary narrative of the counterculture, 16–17; and business revolution of the sixties, 25–26; and GQ magazine's countercultural advocacy, 218; as inadequately developed, 8–9; menswear industry as co-optive, 27, 186; in Pepsi's "Live/Give" ads, 182; and soda advertising, 163; versions of, 246n. 12; Volkswagen ads inverting, 67–68
copywriters: and art directors at DDB, 57, 58, 252n. 13; in assembly-line method, 100; in Creative Revolution of the sixties, 96–97, 116; Reeves on new type of, 115; and scientific advertising, 39, 40, 45, 47; young people as, 111–12
Corbin, R. Beverley, 95
Coronet brandy, 151
"corporate revolutionaries," 5
counterculture, the: advertising distrusted by, 108; advertising industry seizing upon symbols of, 27, 108–11, 119–23; as beginning before 1960,

6; binary narrative of, 14–16; business revolution as parallel to, 25–26; business seeing as a hopeful sign, 9; capitalism opposed by, 6; commercial replica of, 7; conservatives on, 2; consumerism of, 29–31, 121–23; in contemporary commerce, 4–5; GQ magazine as advocate of, 217–22; hip consumerism transforming, 229–30; liberal cultural leaders supporting, 13; as lifestyle revolution, 15; mass culture influence on, 8; mass culture transforming symbols of, 229–30; menswear industry seizing upon symbols of, 27, 215–17; middle-class values of, 29–30; Mod in birth of, 190; New Left distinguished from, 246n. 21; as the "Now Generation," 121; as permanent part of American scene, 30–31; self-image of, 6; as signifier for hip consumerism, 121; standard version of myth of, 5–6; Volkswagen as auto of choice of, 67. See also hippies; youth culture

Creative Revolution in advertising, 88–103; antispokesmen in, 141; and client relations, 98–99; the creative workplace, 95–100; on establishment agencies, 100–103; Gossage in, 75; Lois as symbol of, 80; management theories changed by, 92–95; as market-driven, 90; Newsweek story on, 110–11; Peacock Revolution compared with, 187–88; as preceding the counterculture, 27, 238–39; principle of, 68; style of ads of, 54–55, 105; women's liberation in, 152–56; and the youth culture, 104–30

creative team system, 57, 98

creativity: in advertising industry, 37, 39, 41–42, 50, 88–103, 227; Bernbach on practicality of, 89; crisis of the fifties, 22; marijuana and, 112; in menswear industry, 27, 185–86, 188; as nonconformist rebellion, 90. See also Creative Revolution in advertising

criminals, 142, 162

Crumb, R., 185, 218

cultural liberation, 29, 30

cultural studies, 18–19, 89

Cutler, Laurel, 152–53

Dacron polyester, 212

Daily News Record, 188; Kazoo pants ad, 215; on Mod, 190, 267n. 25; on new classicism, 193; on Palm Beach fashion, 192–93; youth as symbol for, 213, 214

Dali, Salvador, 138, 141

Dalrymple, Helen, 254n. 40

Daly, Joe, 58

Dane, Maxwell, 259n. 22

Daniel & Charles, 112, 138–39, 255n. 8

Dash laundry detergent, 134–35

Datsun, 138

Davis, Fred, 267n. 24

Davis, Hal, 105

DDB. See Doyle Dane Bernbach

declension hypothesis, 5

Delanty, Kurnit & Geller, 98, 102

Della Femina, Jerry, 78–80; on account executives, 96; acquired by Ted Bates Company, 102; on art directors and copywriters, 252n. 13; on the assembly-line method, 100; on corporate-style ad agencies, 78–79; on creative departments, 79, 255n. 8; on DDB's creativity, 90; and rock music, 113; on Ted Bates's Certs commercial, 79–80; on Volkswagen campaign, 63

demographics, 23, 109

Denney, Reuel, 21

Details (magazine), 28, 226

Dexter shoes, 208

Dichter, Ernest, 113–14

Dickstein, Morris, 15

Dietsch, Robert, 125

Diggers, 7

Dillon, Tom, 171, 265n. 5

Disch, Thomas M., 221–22

Dobrow, Larry, 55, 251n. 22, 254n. 40

Dodge, 61, 159–61, 264nn. 56, 59

Doors, The, 8

Dougherty, Philip, 259n. 19

Doyle Dane Bernbach (DDB), 55–73; Alka-Seltzer commercial, 72, 225, 254n. 51; American Tourister ads, 69; art competitions withdrawal, 225; Avis ads, 23, 59, 64, 70–71,

Doyle Dane Bernbach (DDB) (continued) 254n. 49; Burlington Mid-Length Socks ads, 71–72; Calvert Whiskey ads, 70; Campbell's commercial, 71; Chivas Regal ads, 70; Clairol campaign, 137, 255n. 1, 262n. 10; client relations at, 58–59; commenting on previous advertising, 69–70; commercial speech conventions violated by, 59; consumerism critiqued by, 68–69; El Al ads, 69; Gillette razor blade ads, 140–41; and Hat Corporation of America ad, 269n. 6; Johnson presidential campaign ad, 72–73, 259n. 22; leadership of Creative Revolution, 55, 90; management style of, 57; Parker 61 pen ads, 69; product pitchmen lampooned by, 71–72; profit margins during the sixties, 91; Robinson at, 249n. 1; rules as ignored at, 56–57; self-reference in ads of, 70; Volkswagen ads, 55, 59, 60, 62–68, 116, 145, 231, 254n. 40; Wells, Rich, Greene compared with, 124; youth study of 1966, 107

Dr. Pepper, 163–64

Dru, Jean-Marie, 271n. 6

drugs: LSD, 114, 135, 216; marijuana, 107, 112; psychedelics, 114, 178

Dunst, Larry, 112, 113

Dusenberry, Phil, 265n. 1

Dylan, Bob, 8, 94, 113

Easy Rider (movie), 16, 161, 218, 264n. 59

Edwardian coats, 187, 191

Edwards & Hanly, 85–86, 141

Eisenhower, Dwight D., 221

El Al, 69

Electronic Data Systems Corporation, 222

Elton, Wallace W., 253n. 28

Embree, Alice, 230

Engineering of Consent, The (Bernays), 40

Enrico, Roger, 172, 265nn. 2, 5

Ephron, Nora, 213–14

Esalen, 14

Establishment, the: in binary narrative of the sixties, 15; Dodge as anti-establishment, 159; establishment advertising agencies, 100–103; Pepsi-Cola challenging, 169; pseudo-hip products used to buy off the counterculture, 16; 7-Up as anti-establishment, 166–67. See also business

Evans, Evan Llewelyn, 37, 98

Ewen, Stuart, 246n. 12, 271n. 11

extra-environmental man, 77

Fables of Abundance (Lears), 38–39

Farber, David, 246n. 10

fashion, 184–222; apparel trade literature on, 193; as bulwark of late capitalism, 185; and business revolution of the sixties, 26; conspiracy theory of, 31, 194; disparity of two consciousnesses required for, 193; as industry, 193–204; persuading men to accept, 188–89; retro, 227. See also menswear industry; women's wear

Fast Company (magazine), 5

FCB. See Foote, Cone & Belding

FDS, 153

Fearon, Bob, 103, 122, 258n. 39

Federal Trade Commission, 225

feminine hygiene deodorants, 153–54

feminism, 152–56; on consumerism, 230; National Organization of Women on advertising, 225

Fields, Jerry, 102, 111, 119

fifties, the: advertising and menswear industries in, 27; advertising's image in, 35–38, 48, 53, 54; and binary historiography of the sixties, 15; creativity crisis in, 22; gray flannel dullness of, 26, 188; individualism vanishing in, 10; management literature of, 21; menswear in, 27, 185–86, 188; retro fashion from, 227; worst ads as those of, 47–50

Fina gas stations, 77–78, 255n. 5

Fisher, Herb, 126

Fisher stereos, 144

Fiske, John, 17–18

Flacks, Richard, 246n. 21
Fladell, Ernest, 107, 135
flared trousers (bell bottoms), 191, 207
flexible accumulation, 25
Foote, Cone & Belding (FCB): creative campaigns of, 257n. 32; as establishment agency, 100; Polykoff at, 249n. 1; profit margins in sixties, 91
Ford, Whitey, 141
Fordism, 25
Forkan, James, 171, 173, 266nn. 9, 19
Forney, Robert C., 194–95
Forrest Gump (movie), 4, 5
Fortune (magazine), 21, 27, 43, 49–50, 188
Foster Grant, 93, 142
Fox, Stephen, 112, 258n. 2
Frankfurt, Stephen O., 97, 225, 259n. 19
Frankfurt School, 13
Frazier, George, 269n. 28
From Those Wonderful Folks Who Gave You Pearl Harbor (Della Femina), 78
"Fruitopia," 4
Furr, John, 48, 165, 166

Galbraith, John Kenneth, 11, 62
Gap, The (Lorber and Fladell), 107
Geer, DuBois, 93
Gellers, Stan, 209–10
generations, 235
Generation X, 233–34
Gentlemen's Quarterly (magazine). See GQ
George, Be Careful (Lois), 81
Germain, Richard, 25, 248n. 52
Getchell, J. Sterling, 54
Gilbey's gin, 135
Gillette razor blades, 140–41
Gingrich, Newt, 2, 5, 245n. 4, 247n. 21
Gitlin, Todd, 208
Glatzer, Robert, 100, 254n. 39, 257n. 32
Gleason, Ralph, 16, 108, 247n. 32
Golden, John D., 220, 221
Goldman, Al, 102
Goldman, Kevin, 92
Goldstein, Richard, 246n. 12
Goldwater, Barry, 72
Goodby, Jeff, 106
Goodrum, Charles, 254n. 40

Gordon's gin, 135
Gorman, Edward, 120
Gossage, Howard, 75–78; advertising industry attacked by, 76–77; Fina gas station ads, 77–78, 255n. 5; Irish Whiskey ads, 77, 255n. 5; Land Rover ads, 142; nineties admen paying homage to, 227; Sierra Club ads, 76; work as affirmation of lifestyle revolution, 106
GQ (magazine), 189–90; and change, 187; countercultural advocacy of, 217–22; distancing itself from fashion extremes, 226; as dominating its market niche, 226; J & F Suits ad, 197–98; on Mod, 190–91; Monte Cristo suit ads, 211; on style as rebellion, 28; on youth as fashion leaders, 213, 216, 269n. 28
Grateful Dead, white suburban audience of, 8
gray flannel, 26, 38, 42, 54, 188
Great Society, Gingrich on, 2, 245n. 4
Greening of America, The (Reich), 14, 207
Grey agency, 116, 122, 140
groupthink, 49, 59, 60
Gulf Stream slacks, 208
Gurstein, Rochelle, 228

hair, 112
Hair (musical), 16, 149
Halberstam, David, 43
Hancox, Clara, 185
Harbor Master raincoats, 211
Harrington, Michael, 29
Harvey, David, 25, 185, 200
Hat Corporation of America, 209, 211, 269n. 6
Hathaway shirts, 45
hats, 209, 211, 215, 269n. 6
Hayes, Harold, 98–99
Heinz spaghetti sauce, 140
Herald-Tribune (newspaper), 86
Hickok belts, 216
Hidden Persuaders, The (Packard), 40–41, 45, 75, 114
high culture, and advertising, 36
Hilfiger, Tommy, 228

Hill, George Washington, 37
Hinckle, Warren, 30
hip: in advertisements before 1965,
    133–34; advertising agencies as, 35;
    advertising despised by the, 107; ad-
    vertising mocking, 149, 150; in bi-
    nary narrative of the counterculture,
    14–16; and business as irreconcil-
    able, 17, 18; business using, 230–33;
    as commercial style, 32; consumer-
    ism as characteristic of, 30; hip ads
    as percentage of all ads, 237–43;
    Mailer on, 12; and obsolescence,
    148; as official capitalist style, 224–
    35; in Pepsi ads, 177; as widespread
    cultural style, 118
hip capitalism, 26
hip consumerism, 26–32; Adler on the
    "new consumer," 116–17; alienation
    transformed into brand loyalty by,
    231; contradiction of work and con-
    sumption resolved in, 232; the coun-
    terculture as signifier for, 121; coun-
    terculture transformed by, 229–30;
    establishment in advertising, 136; as
    perpetual motion machine, 31, 68;
    in soda advertising, 163; as solution
    to problems of mass society, 68
hippies: Diggers' funeral for, 7; fashion
    influence of, 187; Gossage compared
    with, 106; as middle class, 29–30;
    rage still aroused by, 3
Hipps, Ronald, 200
Ho Chi Minh, 23
Hoffman, Abbie: in Forrest Gump, 4;
    hostility to consumerism, 229–30;
    Steal This Book, 229
Hollander, Stanley C., 25, 248n. 52
Hopkins, Claude, 39–40
House of Stuart, 142–43
Howe, Irving, 121, 186
Hucksters, The (Wakeman), 35, 36–38,
    249n. 3
Hudson, Rock, 35
Human Side of Enterprise, The (Mc-
    Gregor), 22

individualism: advertising encouraging
    a forced, 90; in Camel cigarette ads,
    150–51; GQ reader as individualist,

189; in management literature, 20; as
    vanishing in the fifties, 10
information capitalism, 28
Irish Whiskey Distillers Association,
    77, 255n. 5
Iron Butterfly, 8
Is There Any Hope for Advertising? (Gos-
    sage), 75, 76

Jackson, Michael, 173
Jack Tinker & Partners, 101, 112,
    123
J & F Suits, 197–98
Jantzen, 215–16
Jarry, Alfred, 262n. 10
Jockey sportswear, 216
Johnson, Lyndon, 5, 72–73, 259n. 22
jumpsuits, 214
juvenile delinquents, 162
J. Walter Thompson (JWT): Chicago
    office in the fifties, 48; Listerine ads,
    64; Mustang ads, 263n. 48; "The
    New Creativity" at, 110; noncon-
    formity at, 94–95; Pond's hand lo-
    tion ads, 154–55; profit margins dur-
    ing the sixties, 91; reorganizations of,
    102; Rosenfeld at, 102–3, 258n. 39;
    scientific advertising at, 41, 42–43;
    7-Up ads, 164–67
JWT. See J. Walter Thompson

Kazoo pants, 215
Keats, John, 11, 62, 156
Kennedy, John F., 221
Kenyon & Eckhardt, 42
Kershaw, Andrew, 113
Kesey, Ken, 3, 4, 7
Kessler, Chester, 198
Khrushchev, Nikita, 156, 221
Kleiner, Art, 21, 22, 26, 249n. 55
Knickerbocker, Suzy, 154
Kodel polyester, 212
Koenig, Julian, 67, 82, 83
König, René, 185
Kroll, Alex, 113
Kurnit, Shepard, 102

Ladies' Home Journal (magazine): hip
    ads as percentage of all ads, 237–38,
    240, 241; pseudo-hip ads in, 121

Lamplighter knitwear, 211
Land Rovers, 142
Lark cigarettes, 151
Lasch, Christopher, 121
Lauren, Ralph, 192, 226
Lawrence, Mary Wells. *See* Wells Lawrence, Mary
Leach, William, 19
Lears, Jackson, 12, 19, 38–39, 47, 54, 96, 209
Leary, Timothy, 23
Leber Katz Paccione, 98, 257n. 22
Lee slacks, 216
Leinberger, Paul, 81
leisure suits, 187, 192, 221
Lennon, John, in *Forrest Gump,* 5
Leo Burnett: Burnett on the "Critical Generation," 108, 109, 258n. 8; Virginia Slims campaign, 155–56
Lestoil household cleaner, 142
Levenson, Bob, 57
Lhamon, W. T., 15
LHC (Lois Holland Callaway), 84–86
Life (magazine): Hat Corporation of America ad, 209, 211, 269n. 6; hip ads as percentage of all ads, 237–38, 241, 242, 243; hip advertising in 1965, 133; Love cosmetics ads, 261n. 72; mass society criticized by, 11, 13–14; Mod story, 191; pseudo-hip ads in, 121; uniformity of men's clothing in, 185; Volvo ad, 263n. 34
lifestyle: business encouraging experiment with, 123; as focus of the counterculture, 15; Gossage's work and revolution in, 106; hip styles on Madison Avenue, 111; as not revolution, 229
Liston, Sonny, 141
logocentrism, 42, 89, 164
Lois, George, 80–86; on account executives, 96; advertising procedures criticized by, 80–81; antispokesmen in work of, 141–42; on art directors and copywriters, 252n. 13; Braniff commercials, 138, 141; and clients, 99; on DDB's creativity, 90; Edwards & Hanly campaign, 85–86, 141; on good advertising as like poison gas,

85; with Lois Holland Callaway, 84–86; New York *Herald-Tribune* ads, 86; nineties admen paying homage to, 227; as non-organization man, 82–83; Olivetti ads, 152; with Papert Koenig Lois, 82–84; rules opposed by, 81; on Volkswagen as a Nazi car, 67–68, 253n. 39
Lois Holland Callaway (LHC), 84–86
Lonely Crowd, The (Riesman), 10, 11
Lorber, Richard, 107
Lord & Thomas, 91
Louis, J. C., 171
Love cosmetics, 128–30, 261n. 72
Lover Come Back (movie), 35
LSD, 114, 135, 216
Lucky Strike cigarettes, 37, 140, 152
Lurie, Alison, 222, 267n. 24

McCann-Erickson, 94, 101, 102
McCloskey, Jack, 192
McCloskey, Jason, 190, 218–19, 221, 267n. 25
MacDonald, Dwight, 11, 21
McDonald, Myron, 101
McGregor, Douglas, 22, 25, 57
Mack, Walter, 170
MacLeish, Archibald, 21
McMahan, Harry, 257n. 19
McMaster, Malcolm C., 199–200, 268n. 41
Mad (magazine), 5, 15
Madison Avenue. *See* advertising
Madison Avenue (magazine): on advertising men listening to the young, 122; ceasing publication, 225; on copy changes at Scali, McCabe, Sloves, 99; on creative rebels in advertising, 102, 103; on Creative Revolution in advertising, 93, 96, 102; "Evolution of the Art Director" cartoon, 112; on Lucky Strike campaign, 152; on psychedelics in advertising, 114; on thinking young, 119; on Wells, Rich, Greene's growth, 124
Madison Avenue, U.S.A. (Mayer), 41–42
Madonna, 173, 233
Mailer, Norman, 12–13, 16, 233, 246n. 18, 247nn. 24, 31

mainstream culture: Generation X as alienated from, 234; as tepid and uniform, 5. See also mass (society) culture

Making Sense of the Sixties (documentary), 247n. 27

Male Slacks, 216

management literature, 20–26

managerial ideology, 39

Mander, Jerry, 76

Man in the Gray Flannel Suit, The (Wilson), 38

Marchand, Roland, 133

Marcuse, Herbert, 62

marijuana, 107, 112

market segmentation, 23–24; by Pepsi-Cola, 24–25

mass (society) culture, 9–17; advertising of the sixties as critique of, 55, 76; capitalism dealing with critique of, 232; countercultural symbols transformed by, 229–30; counterculture influenced by, 8; dark images of the sixties, 4; DDB's critique of, 68; each generation as hostile to, 235; generalized revolt against, 118; management version of critique of, 20; Oldsmobile ads depicting, 159; theories of, 11; uniformity of men's clothing in, 185; youth culture as subverting products of, 17–18. See also conformity; consumerism

Massengill Feminine Hygiene Deodorant Spray, 153–54

mass media. See media

materialism, 11

Max, Peter, 134, 166, 218

maxiskirts, 267n. 24

May, Henry, 15

Mayer, Martin, 41–42, 45, 57, 97, 250n. 18, 251n. 3

MC-5, 8, 162

media: cultural rebel in contemporary, 227–28; summer of love promoted by, 7, 27; on women's roles, 230. See also advertising; television

Men's Fashion Association of America, 192

men's toiletries, 212

Men's Wear (magazine): Big Yank revolution ad, 208–9; on breaking the rules, 210–11; Dexter shoes ad, 208; the fifties discovered by, 227; men's toiletries ads, 212; on New York "Boutique Show," 268n. 39; "No More Seasons" survey, 198–99; "The Rebel" as "Man of the Year" of, 209–10; on revolutionary styles, 192; on Rubin Brothers, 200, 201; transformation of, 226; on transsexual fashion, 192; on youth as fashion leaders, 213, 215, 216

menswear industry, 184–222; beads, 187, 191; bell bottoms, 191, 207; Blass, 213–14, 226; boutique retailing in, 198, 199, 268n. 39; business attire, 188, 221; Cardin, 189, 269n. 28; chains, 187, 191; conformity opposed by, 209; counterculture as symbol for, 27, 215–17; creative doldrums in the fifties, 27, 185–86, 188; critique of itself, 9; flared trousers, 191, 207; gray flannel, 26, 38, 42, 54, 188; growth during the sixties, 194–96; hats, 209, 211, 215, 269n. 6; and hip consumerism, 26–28; jumpsuits, 214; Lauren, 192, 226; leisure suits, 187, 192, 221; Mod, 190–91, 197, 198, 267n. 25; Nehru jackets, 187, 191, 197, 210, 219; obsolescence in, 196–200, 201–2, 211, 271n. 3; polarization in, 222; rebellion as expressed in, 207–12; retro, 227; sack suits, 188; scarves, 191, 210; stylistic change accepted in, 194; trade press supporting revolution in, 194; turtlenecks, 214; uniformity of men's clothing, 185–86; world leaders' dress in 1960, 221; youth as a symbol for, 212–17. See also Peacock Revolution; ties

Metzner, Jeff, 112

Meyer, Quinn, 197, 200–203, 270n. 29

Midwest, sixties-hatred in the, 3

Miller, Bernard J., 220–21

Miller, Mark Crispin, 231–32

Miller, Martin R., 120

Mills, C. Wright, 15

minimalism: in Creative Revolution advertising, 54, 105; in DDB ads, 68;

in DDB Volkswagen ads, 62–63; in hip ads, 238; in Volvo ads, 145
Mod, 190–91, 197, 198, 267n. 25
Monkees, The, 8, 177
Monte Cristo suits, 211
Moore, Marianne, 141
Morrow, Winston, 254n. 49
Moss, Charlie, 58–59, 112–13, 128
Moss shirtmakers, 211–12
movies: *Bonnie and Clyde*, 16, 161–62; counterculture in contemporary, 4–5; *Easy Rider*, 16, 161, 218, 264n. 59
Munro, William, 177
music: advertising referring to countercultural, 113; "But the Man Can't Bust Our Music" ad, 7–8, 134, 246n. 12; of the counterculture as affected and phony, 8; counterculture myth in, 4. *See also* rock 'n' roll
Mustang automobile, 157, 263n. 48

Nabisco Shredded Wheat, 140
Nader, Ralph, 156
Napoleonic collar, 191
Nathan, Lawrence M., 196
National Organization of Women, 225
National Steel, 140
Navasky, Victor, 159
Nehru jackets, 187, 191, 197, 210, 219
new classicism, 193
New Left: the counterculture distinguished from, 246n. 21; "revolution" as talisman for, 208; Weatherman, 108
New York Times Magazine, 32
Nicklaus, Jack, 162
Nike, 4, 53, 234
1950s. *See* fifties, the
1960s. *See* sixties, the
1970s, postwar prosperity collapsing in the, 28, 225
1990s. *See* nineties, the
nineties, the: advertising in, 53, 227; economic revolution of, 32; language of business revolution of the sixties in, 28
Nissan, 271n. 5
Nixon, Richard, 217, 259n. 22
nonconformism. *See* conformity

Noonan, Peggy, 2
Norins, Hanley, 94, 108, 113, 116, 117–18, 259n. 30
"Now Generation, The," 121, 123
"Now People, The," 107–8, 115–16
N. W. Ayer, 259n. 19

obsolescence: in automobile styles, 62, 64, 68, 123; and countercultural style, 31; in fashion, 188–89; in men's clothing, 196–200, 201–2, 211, 271n. 3; products distancing themselves from, 143; Volvo ads criticizing, 146, 147, 148; youth as receptive to, 122
Ogilvy, David, 39, 45–47, 50
Ogilvy & Mather, 45–47, 251n. 22
Ohrbach, Richard, 214
Olden, Georg, 99
Oldsmobile, 61, 137, 157–59
Olivetti, 152
Organization Man, The (Whyte), 10, 11, 21–22, 38
outsiders, 161, 166

Paccione, Onofrio, 97–98
Packard, Vance, 11, 40–41, 45, 62, 75, 209
Paley, William, 86
Palm Beach, 192–93
Papert, Fred, 82
Papert Koenig Lois (PKL), 82–84
Parker 61 pens, 69
Partisan Review, 11
Peace Corps, 149–50
peace symbol, in advertising, 4, 218
Peacock Revolution: conventional date for beginning of, 189; Creative Revolution in advertising compared with, 187–88; as defeated, 186–87; end of, 226; garment industry acceptance of, 194; inflated prices in, 203; legacy of, 226–27; *Newsweek* story on, 187; "Peacocks" versus "Penguins," 221–22; as preceding the counterculture, 186; Rubin Brothers in, 201; traditional narrative of, 187; typical consumer of, 213–14, 270n. 29; youth's influence on, 213
Peck, Abe, 8

Pepsi-Cola, 169–70; in "Cola Wars," 24, 169; "Come Alive! You're in the Pepsi Generation," 175–76, 177; "Live/Give" campaign, 179–83; and market segmentation, 24–25; "Now It's Pepsi for Those Who Think Young," 174–75; "The Pepsi Challenge," 226, 265n. 3; the Pepsi Generation, 169, 170–74, 265n. 2, 266nn. 9, 19; psychedelic commercial, 178; "The Sociables," 174, 175, 266n. 21; "The Taste that Beats the Others Cold," 265n. 3, 266n. 27; Woodstock II sponsorship, 5
Perlstein, Rick, 5
Petrocelli sport coats, 215
Phoenix Clothes, 211
Pickens, Kevan, 215
pitchmen. *See* spokesmen
Pitts, Bill, 106
PKL (Papert Koenig Lois), 82–84
Polykoff, Shirley, 249n. 1
Pond's hand lotion, 154–55
Pontiac, 144, 161–63, 264nn. 60, 62
Popcorn, Faith, 225
popular culture, 17–18
Posey, Chester, 94
Pottasch, Alan, 170, 172
Powers, John "Shorty," 158
Presley, Elvis, 5
Pristeen, 154, 263n. 43
Procter & Gamble, 149, 263n. 35
psychedelics, 114, 178

Quant, Mary, 154

Rambo, 4
Reality in Advertising (Reeves), 43–45
rebellion: business use of, 31, 249n. 62; creative rebels in advertising, 74–86, 102, 103; cultural rebel in contemporary media, 227–28; as Dodge advertising theme, 159–61; hip consumers as rebels, 232; menswear expressing, 207–12; outsiders, 161, 166; "The Rebel" as *Men's Wear* "Man of the Year," 209–10. *See also* revolution
Reebok, 75, 137, 254n. 1, 262n. 10
Reeves, Rosser, 43–45; Copywriters

Hall of Fame election, 92; on creative types in advertising, 47, 251n. 26; on difference, 44, 49, 89; repetition as method of, 43, 235; retirement of, 92; on the sixties, 115; on the unique selling proposition (USP), 44, 76, 250n. 17
Reich, Charles A., 14, 121, 207, 229
Renault, 143
rep ties, 32, 96, 193
Resilio ties, 211
Resor, Stanley, 43
retro, 227
revolution: business revolution of the sixties, 25–26, 28; "corporate revolutionaries," 5; generalized revolt against mass society, 118; lifestyle revolution, 15, 229; as most overworked word of the sixties, 208; revolt as negation of conformity, 228. *See also* Creative Revolution in advertising; Peacock Revolution; rebellion
Riesman, David, 10, 13
R. J. Reynolds, 4
Robinson, Phyllis, 57–58, 249n. 1
rock 'n' roll: advertising people listening to, 113; Coca-Cola resisting in ads, 171–72; in 7-Up advertising, 165, 166. *See also* Beatles, The
Rogers, Sherman E., 94
Rosenfeld, Ron, 102–3, 258n. 39
Rosenshine, Allen, 171
Ross, Andrew, 11, 30
Roszak, Theodore, 14, 16, 121
Rothenberg, Randall, 53, 55, 60, 95, 253n. 20
Rubicam, Raymond, 53–54
Rubin, Jerry: on becoming an imposter, 207; Bork compared with, 2; consumer values of, 121; on joys of television, 7
Rubin Brothers Clothiers, Ltd., 200–204
rule-breaking. *See* antinomianism

Saatchi and Saatchi, 92
sack suits, 188
St. Regis Paper Company, 134
Samstag, Nicholas, 93
Sanforized products, 144

Scali, McCabe, Sloves, 97, 99, 137, 145, 263n. 32
scare-headlines, 143–44
scarves, 191, 210
Schlesinger, Sid, 198
Schudson, Michael, 48
Schwartz, Delmore, 29
Scientific Advertising (Hopkins), 39–40
scientific management, 20–21, 39
SDS, in *Forrest Gump*, 4
seventies, the, postwar prosperity collapsing in, 28, 225
7-Up, 164–67; Uncola campaign, 165–67; Wet and Wild campaign, 165
Seymour, Dan, 95
Shampoo (movie), 16
Shorris, Earl, 30
silent majority, 109
sixties, the: advertisements of, 132–67; advertising and menswear industries undergoing revolutions in, 27; advertising's central theme in, 136; advertising's growth during, 91; business revolution during, 25–26, 28; as commercial template for our times, 235; conflicting views of, 1–3; creativity crisis in business, 22; Generation X compared with, 233; as high watermark of postwar prosperity, 6; mass culture images of, 4; menswear industry's growth during, 194–96; ordinary, suburban Americans during, 13; "revolution" as most overworked word of, 208; sartorial gaudiness of, 26; summer of love as media promotion, 7, 27. *See also* counterculture, the; Creative Revolution in advertising; Peacock Revolution
Sloan, Alfred P., Jr., 21, 23, 248n. 41
Sloane, Leonard, 197
Sloves, Marvin, 99, 263n. 32
Smirnoff vodka, 135, 139–40
soaps and detergents: Dash laundry detergent, 134–35; hip ads as percentage of all ads, 237, 240
social ethic, 22, 25
soda: Canada Dry, 142; Dr. Pepper, 163–64; image as essential to, 170, 265n. 1; 7-Up, 164–67. *See also* Coca-Cola; Pepsi-Cola

soft drinks. *See* soda
Solow, Martin, 98
Sopkin, Charles, 78
Spade and Archer, 117
Spillane, Mickey, 141
Spindler, Amy, 228
Spock, Dr. Benjamin, 3
spokesmen: antispokesmen, 141–42; lampooned by DDB, 71–72
Stabiner, Karen, 271n. 6
Starbucks, 4
status, 142
Steal This Book (Hoffman), 229
Steir, Merle: on "Now People," 107–8, 115–16, 122–23; on youth as always winning, 116, 235; Youth Concepts, 109, 117, 258n. 7
Stern, Jane and Michael, 246n. 10
Stetson hats, 215, 269n. 6
suburbs: advertising people as suburbanites, 42; and casual dress, 188; in mass society, 10, 11; suburban Americans' enthusiasm for the counterculture, 13
summer of love, media promotion of, 7, 27
Susman, Warren, 19, 232, 248n. 37
Suzuki motorbikes, 137–38

Tads pants, 216
tailfins, 11, 61, 62, 67
Tareyton cigarettes, 140
Taylor, Frederick Winslow, 20–21, 39
Teacher's scotch, 140
technocracy: and advertising of the fifties, 47; Bernbach as opposing, 56; business revolution opposing, 26; corporate culture as, 18; counterculture as opposed to, 14, 16–17; establishment advertising agencies as technocratic, 100; management critique of, 20; uniformity of men's clothing in, 185
Ted Bates Company: Certs commercial, 79–80; Della Femina acquired by, 102; and Federal Trade Commission, 271n. 2; medical testimony in ads of, 250n. 18; under Reeves, 43–45; Reeves's retirement from, 92; Saatchi and Saatchi acquire, 92

Tedlow, Richard S., 23, 24, 169, 172, 248n. 51
television: Alka-Seltzer commercial, 72, 225, 254n. 51; counterculture in contemporary, 4–5; New York *Herald-Tribune* commercials, 86; Pepsi-Cola's "Come Alive!" campaign, 175; preemptive irony in, 231; Rubin influenced by, 7; Virginia Slims commercials, 155–56; Volkswagen commercials, 66; Volvo commercials, 146, 147
Teplin, Amy, 198–99, 210–11
Texas, 222
Theory X, 22, 23, 35, 39, 57, 101
Theory Y, 22, 23, 57, 97, 106
"Think Young" slogan, 121, 171, 174–75
Thom McAn shoes, 247n. 32
Thompson, J. Walter. *See* J. Walter Thompson
Thoreau, Henry David, 212
three-martini lunches, 35, 42
ties: narrow ties, 191; rep ties, 32, 96, 193; Resilio ties, 211; soda compared with, 170; wide ties, 192
Tinker, Jack, 101
Tinker & Partners, 101, 112, 123
toiletries for men, 212
Top Job kitchen cleaner, 135
Townsend, Robert, 23
Tucker, Bruce, 81
Turner, Robert, 196
turtlenecks, 214
"21" (restaurant), 35, 42
Twitchell, James B., 60, 250n. 9, 253n. 20
Tyson Shirt Company, 211

Uncola. *See* 7-Up
"unique selling proposition" (USP), 44, 76, 250nn. 15, 16
Up the Organization (Townsend), 23
USP ("unique selling proposition"), 44, 76, 250nn. 15, 16

vaginal deodorants, 153–54
Van Heusen, 138
Viceroy cigarettes, 44
Vietnam, as cultural archetype, 4

Virginia Slims, 155–56, 263n. 46
Vitt, Sam B., 259n. 12
Volkswagen: as counterculture's auto of choice, 67; DDB ads for, 55, 59, 60, 62–68, 116, 145, 231, 254n. 40; Nazi associations of, 67–68; Volvo ads compared with, 145
Volvo, 144–48, 262n. 32

Wakeman, Frederic, 35, 36–38, 91, 249n. 3
Warhol, Andy, 138, 141
We Are Everywhere (Rubin), 2
Weatherman, 108
Weiss, E. B., 108, 111, 123
Wells Lawrence, Mary: on consumer cynicism, 126; on creative work, 101; on dress at WRG, 113; on Love cosmetics, 130; "love power" slogan of, 128, 258n. 2; nineties admen paying homage to, 227; on sleek advertising agencies, 125–26; on thinking young, 119; on violating advertising convention, 126–27; as woman in advertising, 249n. 1; on WRG as "the agency of today," 124; on youth and creativity, 124–25
Wells, Rich, Greene (WRG), 123–30; advertising convention violated by, 126–27; Alka-Seltzer ads, 124, 126–27, 128; American Motors ads, 127–28; BDDP ownership of, 271n. 6; Benson & Hedges ads, 64, 124, 126, 127, 261n. 65; Braniff ads, 124; as countercultural outpost, 125; Doyle Dane Bernbach compared with, 124; growth of, 97, 234, 257n. 19; as hippest agency in America, 124; Love cosmetics, 128–30, 261n. 72; Moss at, 58; profit margins during the sixties, 91; Wells at, 249n. 1; youth culture attire at, 112–13
Whalen, Jack, 246n. 21
Wheatena, 141–42
Whirlpool, 143
"White Negro, The" (Mailer), 12–13, 246n. 18
Whyte, William H., Jr.: on advertising, 49–50; on organization man, 10, 13, 21–22, 38

Wieden, Dan, 53, 97
Wieden & Kennedy, 53, 97, 253n. 20
Wilson, Sloan, 38
Wired (magazine), 5
Wolfe, Tom, 7
Wolfschmidt vodka, 135
women: in advertising, 249n. 1; feminine hygiene deodorants, 153–54; Virginia Slims cigarettes for, 155–56, 263n. 46. *See also* feminism; women's wear
women's liberation. *See* feminism
women's wear: dollar volume compared with that of men's wear, 197; fashion taken for granted in, 194; maxiskirt, 267n. 24; style changes in, 185
Wonder Bread, 45
Woodruff, Robert, 170
Woodstock II, 5–6
work ethic, 12, 232
WRG. *See* Wells, Rich, Greene

Xerox, 141

Yazijian, Harvey Z., 171
Young & Rubicam: art competitions withdrawal, 225; Dr. Pepper ads, 163–64; handbook for copywriters, 92; Peace Corps ads, 149–50; reorga-

nization of, 97, 259n. 19; "Resist the Usual" slogan, 54
"young thinking," 120, 171, 174–75
Youth Concepts, 109, 117, 258n. 7
youth culture: at advertising agencies, 111–15; advertising agencies as obsessed with, 35; advertising and menswear industries reacting to, 27; advertising mocking, 148–51; business finding what it wants in, 234–35; clothing for expressing rebellion, 207–12; and the Creative Revolution in advertising, 104–30; discretionary spending of young people, 109, 258n. 12; mainstream culture opposed by, 5; mass culture as subverted by, 17–18; menswear industry taking as a symbol, 212–17; Oldsmobile ads turning to, 158; the Pepsi Generation as, 170–74, 176–83; in Pepsi's market segmentation, 24–25; purity of intent of, 14–15; as reaction to postwar cultural environment, 6; as solution to ills of mass society, 13–14; youth as always winning, 116, 235; youth as an attitude, 118–19, 214; youth as desirable to marketers, 248n. 52; as youth market, 118–23. *See also* counterculture, the; hippies